Historic American Buildings Survey
Virginia Catalog

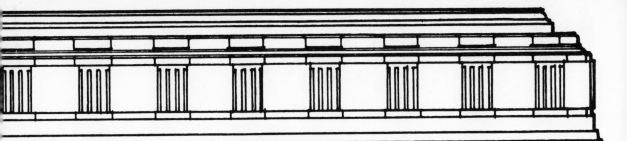

Historic American Buildings Survey

National Park Service, Department of the Interior

Virginia Catalog

A List of Measured Drawings, Photographs, and Written Documentation in the Survey

Compiled by
THE VIRGINIA HISTORIC LANDMARKS COMMISSION

THE HISTORIC AMERICAN BUILDINGS SURVEY

Published for the Historic American Buildings Survey
by the University Press of Virginia   Charlottesville

Historic American Buildings Survey
Office of Archeology and Historic Preservation
National Park Service
Department of the Interior
Washington, D.C.

First published 1976

Library of Congress Cataloging in Publication Data

Historic American Buildings Survey.

    Historic American Buildings Survey: Virginia catalog.

    1. Architecture—Virginia—Catalogs. 2. Virginia—Historic
houses, etc. I. Virginia. Historic Landmarks Commission.
II. Title: Virginia catalog. NA730.V8H5 1974 917.55
74-7402 ISBN 0-8139-0518-4

Printed in the United States of America

Contents

The Virginia Historic
Landmarks Commission

The Virginia Historic Landmarks Commission has as its primary objective the recognition and protection of all structures in the Commonwealth which are of significance. The first step in the fulfillment of this formidable mandate is of course to survey and identify the basic resources that may be of significance. Consequently in June 1967 the newly commissioned agency began its survey of historic buildings and sites within the Commonwealth. Added impetus to this initial thrust was given by the fact that James W. Moody, then Executive Director of the Commission, and James C. Massey, then Chief of the Historic American Buildings Survey (HABS), had agreed that the two agencies would join forces on a cooperative venture which would be undertaken by the staffs of both agencies. The result of this venture is the HABS Virginia Catalog. It was a fortuitous happening that HABS, which had accumulated a wealth of material on buildings in the Commonwealth since its last published *Catalog Supplement* of 1959, determined the need for a revised and updated catalog at the same time the Commission began its work.

During the course of the survey, the Commission staff members took new and more extensive photographs of the previously inventoried properties and marked the exact location of each structure or site on the United States Geological Survey maps which form the Commission's permanent map collection. In its work, the Commission staff also identified many more structures and sites of significance than were in the HABS collection. At present the Commission's files include information for more than 10,000 properties in every county and city in the Commonwealth. The present HABS catalog contains brief entries of approximately 3,800 properties, 190 of which were added to the original HABS list during this survey. While this joint Virginia Historic Landmarks Commission–Historic American Buildings Survey project was one of the first efforts of the fledgling Commission, it is only one of its far-flung activities.

The broad mandate of the Commission, to recognize and protect sites and structures of significance, has many other facets. To mention but a few, the Commission staff offers technical assistance in the fields of preservation, archeology, and architectural history; aids other state, local, and national agencies in their approaches to preservation, such as working closely with the Virginia Department of Highways to insure that preservation is considered in the face of highway development; assists communities in historic district zoning; and receives Open-Space Easements to protect historic properties from inappropriate development by future owners.

The Virginia Historic Landmarks staff was pleased to cooperate with the Office of Archeology and Historic Preservation in preparing this catalog and seeks to enhance and expand the Virginia HABS records in the Library of Congress by cosponsoring student summer recording programs from time to time. The Commission welcomes inquiries on this and other aspects of its several programs. Letters should be addressed to The Virginia Historic Landmarks Commission, 221 Governor Street, Morsons' Row, Richmond, Virginia 23219.

The Historic American Buildings Survey

The Historic American Buildings Survey (HABS) is a long-range program to assemble a permanent national collection of measured drawings, photographs, and written data pertaining to historic American architecture. HABS was initiated in 1933 under a Civil Works appropriation. Its dual purpose was to produce accurate records of significant American Buildings and to provide employment for architects and draftsmen during the economic crisis of the Great Depression. In July 1934 the Survey was made a continuing program under the National Park Service in the United States Department of the Interior. Then, in 1935, a tripartite agreement was signed, by which the National Park Service was to administer the program in close cooperation with the American Institute of Architects and the Library of Congress. This agreement, with some subsequent modifications, remains the operating structure of HABS. The National Park Service, through its Office of Archeology and Historic Preservation, administers the program and is responsible for qualitative standards, organization of projects, and selection of subjects for recording. The Library of Congress is the depository for the records, which are serviced by the staff of the Prints and Photographs Division. The American Institute of Architects provides professional counsel through its national membership.

The Survey intends to provide a thorough and accurate picture of the builder's art throughout the United States by including as many construction types, use types, and styles as possible. Structures represented in the Survey span the period from both prehistoric and colonial times to the early twentieth century and include examples from all fifty states, the District of Columbia, Puerto Rico, and the Virgin Islands. The collection now includes records on approximately 16,000 buildings, represented by about 31,000 drawings, 47,000 photographs, and 23,500 pages of written data.

Those who are interested in consulting the records of the Survey may either visit the Division of Prints and Photographs, Library of Congress, or refer to the catalogs that have been published by the Survey. A comprehensive, geographically arranged *Catalog* was published in 1941; a *Supplement* appeared in 1959. More recently, because of the extensiveness of HABS holdings, new catalogs are being published by states and areas. To date, state catalogs have appeared for New Hampshire (1963), Massachusetts (1965), Wisconsin (1965), Chicago and nearby Illinois Areas (1966), Michigan (1967), the District of Columbia (1968), and Utah (1969). Catalogs for Maine, New Jersey, Philadelphia, South Carolina, Indiana, Ohio, Rhode Island, and Puerto Rico are in progress. Most of these publications can be consulted in major university or public libraries.

Further questions regarding the consultation of records and ordering of reproductions may be addressed to the Division of Prints and Photographs, Library of Congress, Washington, D.C. 20450. Questions regarding HABS recording and publishing programs may be addressed to The Historic American Buildings Survey, National Park Service, Department of the Interior, Washington, D.C. 20240.

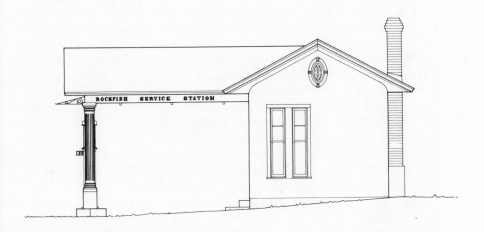

Introduction

The *HABS Virginia Catalog* lists records on more than 3,800 structures, representing the total number of buildings which the Survey has recorded in the Commonwealth. The book is divided into two sections: the catalog proper, which contains over 900 entries, and the inventory, in which approximately 2,900 structures are listed. Buildings listed in the catalog, as a rule, are more completely recorded and documented than those in the inventory. The purpose of this catalog is to present concise descriptions of structures and the HABS records of each, sufficiently informative to prospective users for them to find data they desire and to order duplicates from the Library of Congress. Structures are alphabetically arranged according to (a) city or vicinity and (b) the name of the structure. This arrangement is found in both the catalog and the inventory. County locations are also noted. The number in parentheses following the county name is used for filing purposes at the Library of Congress. Each catalog entry also contains a precise locational description; for properties in rural areas, a nearby natural feature is listed in addition to the nearest highway intersections in order to facilitate locating properties on maps. Names of natural features are generally taken from maps issued by the United States Geological Survey. The location is followed by a succinct architectural description, noting the most significant features, and a brief historical statement if warranted. A "bibliography" of the materials that comprise the HABS records on the structure concludes the entry. The "bibliography" gives the number and types of measured drawings, photographs, and data pages and notes whether the structure is also recorded with an inventory form. Dates following the records refer to the year in which the records on the structure were made. Buildings listed in the inventory have been recorded on a single page, standard 8″ x 10½″ sheet, which provides identification of the structure, concise written historical and/or architectural data, a small photograph, a location diagram, and source references.

The HABS Inventory (HABSI) Form was developed in 1953 by the National Trust for Historic Preservation in cooperation with the National Park Service and the American Institute of Architects to facilitate the recording of large numbers of historic buildings and to identify those structures that were of sufficient importance to warrant a more extensive coverage. In 1962 the inventory form became an integral part of the Survey, and over the several years in which the inventory was conducted, many buildings in Virginia were listed. However, with the passage of the Historic Preservation Act of 1966, the task of gathering a basic inventory of the country's historic resources became the responsibility of The National Register of Historic Places. Subsequently, the HABSI program was eliminated as an integral part of the HABS recording efforts.

Because the information contained on a typical HABSI form is necessarily abbreviated, no attempt is made herein to describe buildings that have been inventoried. Rather, they are listed solely by name and address. The HABSI forms for Virginia have been transmitted to the Library of Congress, where they may be consulted, or where reproductions may be ordered.

As far as possible the entries in this catalog reflect the latest historical research. Entries from the National 1941 *Catalog* and the 1959 *Supplement* have been updated and expanded to provide more useful information; they reflect more clearly the nature and extent of the HABS records and the architectural and historical significance of the structure. In many cases it has been possible to correct dates for buildings or note them precisely and fully. In some cases more historically accurate names have been assigned, with cross references under formerly used names where necessary. Care has been taken to avoid making or repeating errors, but if the reader detects any, HABS will greatly appreciate receiving notification.

Each building or site listed in the catalog has been visited to ascertain its present condition. In general, staff members of The Virginia Historic Landmarks Commission examined sites in the western, central, and southern portions of the state, as well as the Eastern Shore. W. Brown Morton, architect, HABS, visited properties in the northern counties, and the Northern Neck. Mr. Morton also served as coordinator for the efforts of both the Landmarks Commission and HABS. Caroline Reynolds Heath and S. Allen Chambers of the HABS Staff were responsible for the final compilation and editing of the manuscript, under the supervision of John C. Poppeliers, Chief, HABS.

The following abbreviations and symbols have been used in all of the recent Historic American Buildings Survey catalogs:

VA-100 Historic American Buildings Survey number. All structures recorded by the Survey are assigned an HABS number. These numbers have no historical significance, but serve only to facilitate processing. These numbers should be used when inquiring about a structure or ordering a reproduction.

"Sheets" Indicates the number of sheets of measured drawings available for study and reproduction. Sheets are generally a standard size, 15 1/2" x 20" inside border lines. The number of sheets in the set and the kinds of drawings (plans, elevations, sections, details) are listed. Prints of measured drawings are made at actual size. size.

"Photos" ("ext. photos" and "int. photos") HABS negatives are normally 5" x 7" occasionally other sizes, especially 4" x 5" or 8" x 10".

"Data Pages" It is HABS policy to give the physical history of the structure along with a technical architectural description. Original data pages are typewritten and may be duplicated.

"HABSI" HABS Inventory forms. HABSI forms are duplicated at actual size (8" x 10½").

n.d. The date is not ascertainable.

NHL The building has been declared a National Historic Landmark.

NR The building has been entered on the National Register of Historic Places.

(1), (2), etc. after County names HABS material is filed at the Library of Congress according to county locations. These numbers assist in locating material at the Library.

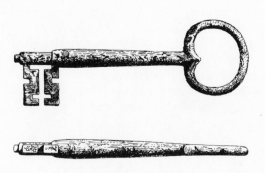

Historic American Buildings Survey

Virginia Catalog

Virginia Catalog

Debtors' Prison (Jailor's House) (VA-623), E side of State Rte. 764, NE corner of intersection with U.S. Rte. 13. Brick, 30' (three-bay front) x 18', one story, gable roof, one exterior end chimney, one interior end chimney; two-room plan. Built late 18th C.; altered; renovated. 4 ext. photos (1960); 2 data pages (1960); HABSI (1958).

Drummond House (VA-692), SE side of Back St., .2 mi. SW of intersection with U.S. Rte. 13. Brick, rectangular (four-bay front), two-and-a-half stories, gable roof with dormers, two exterior end chimneys; rectangular plan; two-story gable-end wing connected to main block by one-story hyphen. Built early 19th C.; later frame addition on rear. 2 ext. photos (1940); HABSI (1958).

Episcopal Rectory (VA-622), NW side of Back St., NE corner of intersection with State Rte. 605. Brick, rectangular (five-bay front), two stories, gable roof, two interior end chimneys, wooden flat arches with keystones; center-hall plan, fine Adam mantel and cornices; two-story kitchen wing connected to main block by one-story hyphen. Built early 19th C. 6 ext. photos (1960), 5 int. photos (1960); 3 data pages (1960, 1961); HABSI (1958).

Fisher-Seymour House (VA-624), SE side of U.S. Rte. 13, .1 mi. E of intersection with State Rte. 605. Frame with clapboarding, rectangular (five-bay front), two stories, gable roof, two interior end chimneys; center-hall plan, fine mantels; one-story gable-roof wing linked to one-story gable-roof kitchen by one-story hyphen. Built early 19th C.; wing built late 18th C. 3 ext. photos (1960), 2 int. photos (1960); 4 data pages (1960, 1962); HABSI (1958).

Ice House (VA-636), SE side of U.S. Rte. 13, .1 mi. E of intersection with State Rte. 605. Brick, circular (17' diameter), partly underground, conical roof with ball finial. Built early 19th C. 1 ext. photo (1960); 1 data page (1960, 1962).

Jailor's House (VA-623), see Debtors' Prison (VA-623), Accomac.

Bowman's Folly, general view from north

Bowman's Folly (VA-625), .2 mi. N of Folly Creek, .4 mi. S of State Rte. 652, 2.5 mi. SE of intersection with U.S. Rte. 13. Frame with clapboarding, brick ends, rectangular (five-bay front), two-and-a-half stories, gable roof with dormers, two interior end chimneys; center-hall plan, fine second-story central Palladian window; side wing. Built early 19th C. 8 ext. photos (1960); 4 data pages (1960); HABSI (1958). NR

Folly, The (VA-626), .1 mi. W of Folly Creek, 1.3 mi. E of State Rte. 605, .4 mi. S of intersection with State Rte. 740. Frame with clapboarding, brick ends, rectangular (three-bay front), one-and-a-half stories, gable roof with dormers, one interior end chimney; irregular plan; two-story gable-roof wing, connecting two-bay kitchen. Built mid 18th C.; wing added early 19th C. 3 ext. photos (1960), 2 int. photos (1960); 4 data pages (1960, 1962); HABSI (1958).

Dove Cote (VA-633), .1 mi. W of Folly Creek, 1.3 mi. E of State Rte. 605, .4 mi. S of intersection with State Rte. 740. Frame, one story, octagonal plan, pyramidal roof with ball finial. Built early 19th C. 1 ext. photo (1960); 1 data page (1960, 1962).

Ice House (VA-632), .1 mi. W of Folly Creek, 1.3 mi. E of State Rte. 605, .4 mi. S of intersection with State Rte. 740. Brick, polygonal (21' diameter), sunk 12'6" in ground, wooden conical roof with ball finial. Built late 18th C. 1 ext. photo (1960); 1 data page (1960, 1962).

Mount Custis (VA-627), .1 mi. S of Parker Creek, .5 mi. N of State Rte. 662, 2.5 mi. E of intersection with U.S. Rte. 13. Frame with clapboarding, U-shaped (three-bay front), two-and-a-half story center section, gable roof with dormers, two interior chimneys; center-hall plan; two-and-a-half story projecting front wings. Built early 18th C.; additions c. 1800, c. 1840; original section renovated. 2 ext. photos (1960), 6 int. photos (1960); 2 data pages (1958); HABSI (1958).

Runnymede (VA-628), .3 mi. NW of Walston Creek, .3 mi. SW of State Rte. 662, 1.7 mi. E of intersection with U.S. Rte. 13. Frame with clapboarding and brick ends, original structure rectangular (one-bay front), one-and-a-half stories, gable roof with dormer, one exterior end chimney; wing: frame, two stories; kitchen and one outbuilding connected to original structure by hyphen. Built late 18th C.; additions early 19th C. 4 ext. photos (1960); 3 data pages (1960, 1961).

5

Mount Custis

Green House (VA-825), see House (VA-825), Nokesville Vicinity.

ALEXANDRIA

Adam Silver Shop (VA-667), 318 King St. Brick, rectangular (two-bay front), three stories, shed roof with parapet, molded brick cornice, wooden lintels, denticulated and bracketed cornice defining projecting store front; two-room plan. Built mid 19th C.; later alterations; demolished 1968. 1 ext. photo (1968); 1 data page (1968).

Alexandria Almshouse (Alexandria Poor House) (VA-134), NW corner E. Monroe Ave. and Jefferson Davis Hwy. (U.S. Rte. 1). Brick (Flemish bond), 80'5" (seven-bay front) x 41'8", two-and-a-half stories with slightly projecting center pavilion, hipped roof with pediment and dormers, four interior chimneys, modified modillion cornice, arched and sidelighted entrance, Palladian window above; longitudinal-hall plan with center access. Built early 19th C.; later additions and alterations; demolished 1952. 8 sheets (1937, including plans, elevations, details).

Alexandria Poor House (VA-134), see Alexandria Almshouse (VA-134), Alexandria.

Appich Buildings (VA-677), 408-14 King St. Brick, rectangular (five-bay front), three stories, shed roof with arched parapet, modified modillion, bracketed, and denticulated cornice, recessed vertical panels, arched windows with molded sills, four units; two-room plan. Built 1866; store front of 408 King St. remained virtually intact while the other three were substantially altered; demolished 1968. 6 ext. photos (1968); 1 data page (1968).

Arch Hall (Lawrence Lewis House) (VA-109), see Lewis, Lawrence, House (VA-109), Lorton Vicinity, Fairfax Co.

Athenaeum (VA-428), see Old Dominion Bank (Free Methodist Church) (VA-428), Alexandria.

Ayres Gun Shop (VA-456), 324 King St. Brick, rectangular (three-bay front), two-and-a-half stories, gable roof, interior chimney. Built late 18th C.; wooden Gothic false front added mid 19th C.; demolished 1958. 2 ext. photos (1958); 1 data page (1958).

Bank of Alexandria (VA-449), 133 N. Fairfax St. Brick (Flemish bond), now stuccoed, rectangular (five-bay front), three-and-a-half stories, flat hipped roof concealed by balustrades, two interior chimneys, ornamental stone cornice, two arched doorways with cast capitals and keystones with eagles, stone columns, platforms, and steps; large banking room with rear hall. Built c. 1805, with early extension; incorporated into composition and development of Green's Mansion House mid 19th C. 3 ext. photos (1958); 1 data page (1958); HABSI (1958).

Bank of Potomac (VA-458), 415 Prince St. Brick (Flemish bond), rectangular (four-bay front), three-and-a-half stories, gable roof with dormers, two interior end chimneys, stone flat arches with keystones, two arched doorways with cast capitals and keystones, stone columns and steps, monumental scale; side-hall plan; rear wing; two-story wing and courtyard with arched brick gateway. Built late 18th C.; major alterations early 20th C. 1 ext. photo (1958); 1 data page (1958); 2 HABSI's (1958, 1959).

Barrett, Kate Waller, House (VA-696), see Dick-Janney House (VA-696), Alexandria.

Bayne-Moore House (VA-453), 811 Prince St. Brick with stucco, rectangular (three-bay front), three stories, low pitched roof, three interior end chimneys, bracketed cornice, monumental scale; side-hall plan, marble mantels, ornamental plasterwork; wing: brick, one story. Built c. 1832. 1 ext. photo (1958); HABSI (1959).

Brown Building (VA-669), 113-15 N. Fairfax St. Brick, rectangular (adjacent two-bay front and three-bay front), two stories, shed roof, wooden lintels; two-room plan and modified side-hall plan. S portion built c. 1875; N portion built c. 1910; demolished 1970. 1 ext. photo (1968); 1 data page (1968).

Brown, Dr. William, House (VA-466), 212 S. Fairfax St. Frame with clapboarding, rectangular (three-bay front), two-and-a-half stories, gable roof with dormers, interior chimney, small entrance porch; side-hall plan, notable interior woodwork, bake oven, boiling kettles, and stone sink; brick ell. Built c. 1775; restored c. 1930. 2 ext. photos (1958), 2 int. photos (1958); 2 data pages (1958); HABSI (1958).

Burson House (VA-933), see Wilson-Hopkins House (Hallowell School) (VA-933), Alexandria.

Bush Hill (Holly Hill School) (VA-507), 1405 Bush Hill Dr. Brick, rectangular (five-bay front), two-and-a-half stories, gable roof with dormers, two interior end chimneys, wooden entrance porch with flat roof and balustrade; center-hall plan; two-story side wing. Built late 18th C.; later addition and alterations. 2 ext. photos (1937).

Carlyle, John, House (VA-101), 123 N. Fairfax St. Historic house museum. Brick with stucco and rusticated stone quoins, 29′9″ (six-bay front) x 38′1″, two-and-a-half stories, hipped roof with dormers, two interior chimneys, slightly projecting center pavilion, wide elliptical doorway, windows framed by masonry architraves, rear terrace on rubble platform with vault beneath; center-hall plan, fully paneled principal room. Built 1752; extensive alterations, undergoing restoration (1974). 8 sheets (1936, including plans, elevations, profiles, details, conjectural restoration); 8 ext. photos (1936, 1937, 1940), 4 int. photos (1936); 1 photocopy, conjectural restoration (n.d.); 3 data pages (1941). NR

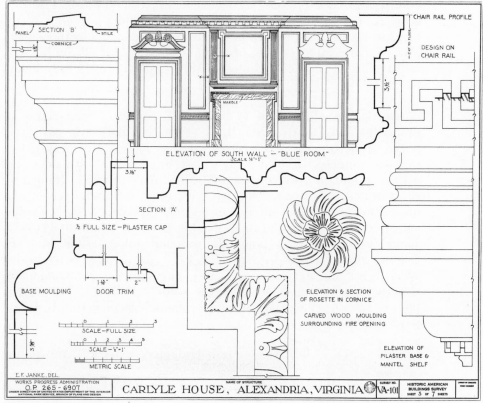

John Carlyle House

Carne School (VA-450), see St. John's Academy (VA-450), Alexandria.

Caton, James R., House (VA-668), 111 S. Fairfax St. Brick, rectangular (two-bay front), two stories, shed roof, pseudo-mansard front of hexagonal slates, two round louvered attic openings, one interior end chimney, pressed brick cornice, prominent use of pressed brick ornament, segmental brick arched lintels over incised wooden frames; side-hall plan. Built c. 1893. 1 ext. photo (1968); 2 data pages (1968).

Chatham, Henry, Houses (VA-680), 106-08 N. Pitt St. Brick, rectangular (six-bay front), two stories, shed roof, bracketed cornice, adjacent bracketed and pilastered entrance doorways sharing common cast-iron stoop; side-hall plans. Built mid 19th C. as a double house; demolished 1968. 1 ext. photo (1968); 2 data pages (1968).

Chequire, Bernard, House (VA-455), 202 King St. Brick (Flemish bond), approx. 23' (four-bay front) x 43', three-and-a-half stories, gable roof with dormers, two interior end chimneys, modillion cornice, stone flat arches with keystones; shop-residence with side-hall plan, notable interior trim, ornamental plaster; rear ell. Built 1797; restored 1942-47. 1 ext. photo (1958), 3 int. photos (1958); 2 data pages (1958); 2 HABSI's (1958, 1959).

Christ Church (Episcopal) (VA-479), SE corner of intersection of Columbus and Cameron Sts. Brick (Flemish bond) with rusticated Aquia stone quoins, 50'6" (three bays) x 77'6½" (five bays), two tiers of windows, hipped roof, square brick tower with octagonal belfry, modillion cornice, pair of pedimented doorways framed by rusticated Aquia stone, Palladian window in E facade; rectangular one-room plan, notable interior furnishings including wineglass pulpit and sounding board (relocated), hand lettered tablets. Built 1767-73, James Wren, architect; James Parsons and John Carlyle, builders; galleries along back and sides added 1785; majority of pews divided 1817; tower and steeple built 1818. 13 sheets (1958, including plans, elevations, sections, details); 34 ext. photos (1936, 1958), 16 int. photos (1936, 1958); 1 photocopy, prototype plan (n.d.); 4 data pages (1958). NR

City Hotel (VA-100), see Mason's Ordinary (VA-100), Alexandria.

City Tavern (VA-100), see Mason's Ordinary (VA-100), Alexandria.

Coffee House (VA-100), see Mason's Ordinary (VA-100), Alexandria.

Christ Church

Commercial Building (VA-619, Area Survey), 103-07 N. Royal St. Brick, rectangular (five-bay front), two stories, gable roof, brick modillion cornice, wooden lintels; store fronts across entire ground floor. Built early 19th C.; altered late 19th C. and early 20th C.; demolished 1963. 1 ext. photo (1960).

Coryton, Catharine, House (VA-686), 522-24 King St. Brick (Flemish bond), rectangular (three-bay front), three stories, gable roof, two interior end chimneys, molded brick cornice, flat stone arches with keystones, stone arched doorway with reeded pilaster, leaded fanlight intact; side-hall plan. Built c. 1815; ground floor remodeled mid 20th C. 2 ext. photos (1968); 1 data page (1968).

Craddock-Crocker House (VA-229), see DeNeale-Craddock-Crocker House (VA-229), Alexandria.

Craik, Dr., House (VA-583), see Murry-Craik House (VA-583), Alexandria.

Dalton-Herbert House (Wise's Tavern) (VA-934), 201 N. Fairfax St. Brick (Flemish bond), L-shaped (five-bay front), three stories above raised basement, hipped roof, two interior end chimneys and one interior chimney, modillion cornice; modified center-hall plan. Under construction in 1777 (appears to have originated as two buildings); continuing alterations, renovations, and rear addition to accommodate differences in use; Aquia stone doorway with arched pediment, now at basement level, apparently shifted from some earlier position. 1 ext. photo (1936); HABSI (1958).

Dalton, John, House (VA-460), 209 N. Fairfax St. Frame with clapboarding and brick, rectangular (three-bay front), one-and-a-half stories above high basement, gable roof with dormers; center-hall plan, notable closed string stair. Built 1749-50; extensive exterior and interior alterations and additions mid 19th C. and late 19th C., including reconstruction of N bay of original frame house in brick, refacing of street facade with brick, alteration of entrance hall, and demolition of original exterior end chimneys. This is thought to be the earliest extant structure in Alexandria constructed on its original site. 1 ext. photo (1958), 1 int. photo (1958); HABSI (1959).

DeNeale-Craddock-Crocker House (Craddock-Crocker House) (VA-229), 323 S. Fairfax St. Frame with shiplapping, rectangular (three-bay front), two stories above raised basement, gable roof, two interior chimneys, stone entrance platform, double incurving steps, wrought-iron railings with lyre motif, pilastered doorway with transom and side lights; center-hall plan, tiered galleries, ornamental plaster; rear wing. Built early 19th C. 3 ext. photos (1936, 1939); HABSI (1958).

Devaughan, James H., House (VA-679), 516 King St. Brick, rectangular (three-bay front), four stories, gable roof, two interior end chimneys, molded brick cornice, small upper windows, wooden lintels; side-hall plan. Built 1855; ground-floor plan and facade extensively altered for commercial purposes early 20th C. and mid 20th C. 2 ext. photos (1968), 3 int. photos (1968); 2 data pages (1968).

Dick-Janney House (Kate Waller Barrett House) (VA-696), 408 Duke St. Brick (Flemish bond), approx. 24' (three-bay front) x 32', three stories, gable roof, two exterior end chimneys, molded brick modillion cornice; side-hall plan; brick ell. Nucleus built c. 1796; completed as projected early 19th C.; numerous frame additions, altered and enlarged mid 19th C., late 19th C., early 20th C. 1 ext. photo (1958); 10 data pages (1967).

Duffey House (VA-454), 203 S. Fairfax St. Frame with clapboarding over brick nogging, rectangular (four-bay front), two-and-a-half stories, gable roof, interior chimney; side-hall plan; two-story rear wing. Built mid 18th C.; later additions and alterations; vestibule added mid 19th C.; remodeled 1958. 1 ext. photo (1958); 2 data pages (1958); HABSI (1958).

Dulany, Benjamin, House (VA-697), 601 Duke St. Brick (Flemish bond), approx. 32' (three-bay front) x 45', two-and-a-half stories above raised basement, gable roof with dormers, interior end chimney combining two stacks, molded cornice with denticulated course con-

Benjamin Dulany House

Benjamin Dulany House

tinuous across gable end, pedimented doorway with fanlight, stone stoop and steps with wrought-iron balusters; side-hall plan, notable interior trim; long Flounder ell. Built 1783-84; entrance doorway and rear-wing extension added early 19th C. 6 ext. photos (1967), 4 int. photos (1967); 9 data pages (1967); HABSI (1958).

Stable (VA-447), SW corner of Dulany House garden, fronting on Duke St. Brick, rectangular (three-bay front), one story with loft, gable roof, stable door to left, arched vehicular opening to right with louvered opening between. Built 1783-84; altered and enlarged c. 1930. 1 ext. photo (1958); 1 data page (1958).

14

Evans Building (VA-666), 320 King St. Brick, rectangular (two-bay front), two stories, shed roof, parapet, bracketed tin cornice, tall upper windows with ornamented and scrolled tin heads. Built late 19th C.; store front altered mid 20th C.; demolished 1968. 1 ext. photo (1968); 1 data page (1968).

Fairfax-Adam-Hodgson House (VA-230), 207 Prince St. Brick (Flemish bond), rectangular (three-bay front), three-and-a-half stories above raised basement, gable roof with dormers, two exterior end chimneys, modillion cornice, stone arched doorway and rusticated platform, wrought-iron railings; side-hall plan; extensive ell. Nucleus built c. 1760; extensively enlarged late 18th C.; interior retrimmed c. 1800; additions and alterations late 19th C. and early 20th C. 3 ext. photos (1936, 1939).

Fairfax House (VA-211), see Yeaton-Fairfax House (VA-211), Alexandria.

Farmers Bank of Alexandria (VA-937), 200 Prince and 201 S. Lee Sts. Brick (Flemish bond), rectangular (five-bay front), three stories, gambrel roof, interior chimney, modillion wooden cornice continuous across gable end, flat stone arches with keystones. Built late 18th C.; divided into two houses and outstanding woodwork removed early 20th C. 1 ext. photo (1936).

Fawcett House (VA-104), see Murray-Dick-Fawcett House (VA-104), Alexandria.

First National Bank (VA-672), 503-07 King St. Brick and concrete, faced with white marble, one story, gable roof, great central grilled window and door motif suggestive of arch or niche, flanking solid masonry piers support Doric pediment, entablature broken to provide for arched opening and ornamental keystone; banking room lined with white brick, high vaulted ceiling and skylight; two stories in rear. Built 1908-09, Vogt and Morrill, architects; Charles J. Cassidy Co. builders; demolished 1968. 2 ext. photos (1968), 3 int. photos (1968); 3 data pages (1968).

Flounder House (VA-618, Area Survey), 403 S. Fairfax St. Brick, rectangular (two-bay front), two-and-a-half stories, half-gable roof with dormers; two interior chimneys; single-room depth. Built early 19th C.; renovated c. 1959. 1 ext. photo (1959).

Flounder House, 511 Queen St.

Flounder House (VA-600, Area Survey), 511 Queen St. Brick, rectangular (two-bay front), two stories, half-gable roof, two interior end chimneys; two-story porch with balcony; single-room depth. Built early 19th C.; restored. 1 ext. photo (1959).

Flounder House (VA-462), 317 S. St. Asaph St. Brick, rectangular, two-and-a-half stories, half-gable roof with dormers, two interior end chimneys, two-story porch with balcony; single-room depth. Built prior to 1779. An outstanding example of the domestic Flounder type. 1 ext. photo (1958); 1 data page (1958); HABSI (1958).

Flounder Tavern Buildings (VA-621), Gazette (Sharpshin) and Market Square Alleys. Brick (Flemish bond), 55'5½" (original six-bay front plus addition) x 35'1", two stories, gable roof with end parapets (formed by double buildings back-to-back), three interior chimneys, sawtooth brick cornice; irregular plan with two entrances. Nucleus built c. 1800 and doubled shortly afterwards; twice enlarged and substantially altered late 19th C.; major interior alterations early 20th C.; demolished 1965. 6 sheets (1964, including plans, elevations); 4 ext. photos (1959, 1963); 5 data pages (1965).

Flounder Warehouse (VA-474), 207 Ramsay's Alley. Brick, rectangular (one-bay front), three stories, half-gable roof; two-room plan. Built late 18th C.; extensive exterior and interior alterations. 1 ext. photo (1958); 1 data page (1959).

Fortney, Jacob, House (VA-619, Area Survey), 207 N. Royal St. Frame with clapboarding, rectangular (five-bay front), two stories, gable roof, exterior end chimney; side-hall plan. Built late 18th C.; later alterations. 1 ext. photo (1960).

Fowle, William, House (VA-574), 711 Prince St. Brick (Flemish bond), rectangular (five-bay front), three stories, gable roof, front gable (three bays wide), two interior chimneys, entrance portico, elliptical arched doorway with side lights, wrought-iron balcony with Palladian window-door above, stone arches and lintels; center-hall plan, circular stair; two-story rear wing. Built late 18th C.; altered and enlarged early 19th C.; restored 1969. 2 ext. photos (1937); HABSI (1958).

Free Methodist Church (VA-428), see Old Dominion Bank (Athenaeum) (VA-428), Alexandria.

Friendship Fire Company (VA-463), 107 S. Alfred St. Museum. Brick, 20'6" (two-bay front) x 34'8", two stories, flat shed roof, tall louvered bell cupola on square base, molded brick cornice, paired tall windows on second floor with ornamental heads, pedimented double doors for vehicular equipment. Built 1855. 5 sheets (1964, including plans, elevations); 5 ext. photos (1958, 1963); 5 data pages (1958, 1964).

Gadsby's Tavern (VA-100), see Mason's Ordinary (VA-100), Alexandria.

General View (VA-919), 100 block S. Fairfax St. Streetscape from NE, including 105-09 S. Fairfax St., the Stabler-Leadbeater Apothecary Shop, and flanking buildings. Built late 18th C. to mid 20th C. 1 ext. photo (1968).

General View (VA-920), 300 block King St. Streetscape from NE, including 308-20 King St. Built mid 18th C. to mid 20th C. 2 ext. photos (1968).

Friendship Fire Company

18

General View (VA-921), 400 block King St. Streetscape from NW, including 400-30 King St. Built early 19th C. to mid 20th C. 1 ext. photo (1968).

General View (VA-922), 500 block King St. Streetscape from NW, including 500-32 King St. Built early 19th C. to mid 20th C. 1 ext. photo (1968).

General View (VA-923), N. Pitt St. Streetscape from SE, including 104-12 N. Pitt, and a view of the First and Citizens National Bank facilities (new building opened 1967). Built early 19th C. to mid 20th C. 1 ext. photo (1968).

General View (VA-924), 103-13 Prince St. Streetscape from SE, including brick houses, two-and-a-half stories, gable roofs with dormers. Built late 18th C. to early 19th C.; restored. 1 ext. photo (1937).

Gordon, John, House (VA-938), 631 King and 100-09 N. Washington Sts. Brick (Flemish bond), 20'5" (two-bay front) x 87', three-and-a-half stories, gambrel roof with dormers, two interior end chimneys, modillion cornice continuous across gable end, flat arches with keystones, circular window in peak of gable; irregular plan. Built 1797-99; wing added early 19th C.; interior extensively remodeled; exterior restored except for ground floor 1955. 2 ext. photos (1963), 1 int. photo (1963); 5 data pages (1964).

Greene Funeral Home (VA-102), see Jockey Club (VA-102), Alexandria.

Gregory, William, Building (VA-674), 400-02 King St. Brick (Flemish bond), rectangular (four-bay x four-bay), three stories, hipped roof, two interior chimneys, brick cornice, flat brick arches with keystones; double-unit plan; one-story rear addition. Built 1829; ground floor altered late 19th C. and early 20th C.; additions c. 1940; demolished 1968. 1 ext. photo (1968); 3 data pages (1968).

Gregory, William, Building (VA-690), 404 King St. Brick (Flemish bond), rectangular (two-bay front), three stories, gable roof, brick cornice, flat stone arches with keystones. Built c. 1841; altered late 19th C. and early 20th C.; demolished 1968. 1 ext. photo (1968).

Gregory, William, House (Old Leadbeater House) (VA-416), 329 N. Washington St. Brick (Flemish bond), rectangular (three-bay front), three stories, gable roof, two interior end chimneys, molded brick

General View, 103-13 Prince St.

cornice, flat brick arches with keystones, stone steps with wrought-iron railings; side-hall plan; two-story ell. Built c. 1821; roof line reputedly raised 1830; interior alterations and side additions c. 1947. 2 ext. photos (1936, 1958), 1 int. photo (1958); 2 data pages (1941, 1959); HABSI (1958).

Hallowell School (VA-694), see Wilson-Hopkins House (Burson House) (VA-694), Alexandria.

Hallowell-Carlin House (VA-617, Area Survey), 215 N. Washington St. Brick, rectangular (five-bay front), three-and-a-half stories, gable roof, four interior end chimneys, roof balustrade, bracketed cornice; center-hall plan. Built 1854; demolished 1965. 1 ext. photo (1960).

Hallowell, James, School for Young Ladies (VA-448), see House (VA-448), Alexandria.

Hampson, Bryan, House (Wales House) (VA-468), 120 S. Fairfax St. Brick (Flemish bond), rectangular (three-bay front), gable roof with dormers, two interior end chimneys, molded brick cornice, gauged flat arches; side-hall plan, notable interior trim, plaster cornice; two-story ell. Built 1805-15; restored c. 1950. 2 ext. photos (1958), 3 int. photos (1958); 1 data page (1958).

Harper-Buckingham-Berry Building (VA-664), 312 King St. Brick with stucco, rectangular (two-bay front), two stories, shed roof, gabled parapet, raked, bracketed, and denticulated cornice, raked window heads and raked and bracketed lintels above, molded sills

Hallowell-Carlin House

21

with panels, gabled cornice with wood drapery defining projecting store front. Built mid 19th C.; interior remodeled c. 1960; demolished 1968. 2 ext. photos (1968); 2 data pages (1968).

Harper-Vowell House (VA-939), 213 Prince St. Brick (Flemish bond), rectangular (three-bay front), three-and-a-half stories, gable roof with dormers, interior end chimney, modillion and fret cornice; side-hall plan, notable interior trim. Built c. 1790; vestibule altered late 19th C. 1 ext. photo (1936), 1 int. photo (1937).

Hollinsbury, John, House (VA-600, Area Survey), 525 Queen St. Brick (Flemish bond), rectangular (three-bay front), two-and-a-half stories, gable roof with dormers, interior chimney, denticulated cornice, flat arches with keystones; side-hall plan; rear lean-to. Built early 19th C.; restored mid 20th C. 1 ext. photo (1959).

Holly Hill School (VA-507), see Bush Hill (VA-507), Alexandria.

House (VA-461), 801 Duke St. Brick, rectangular (three-bay front), three stories, gable roof, interior end chimney, wooden lintels, tall windows on first floor with cast-iron grills, pedimented double entrance doors with octagonal panels; side-hall plan. Built mid 19th C.; minor later alterations. 1 ext. photo (1958).

House (James Hallowell School for Young Ladies) (VA-448), 215 N. Fairfax St. Brick (Flemish bond), rectangular (two-bay front), three-and-a-half stories above raised basement, gable roof, two interior end chimneys, modillion cornice, lintels with corner blocks; center-hall plan; one-story entrance wing with roof balustrade. Built early 19th C., abutting 213 N. Fairfax St.; converted for educational purposes with 213 N. Fairfax St. mid 19th C.; condemned 1962; renovated with balustrade constructed and modillion cornice re-used from demolished King St. building 1963; 213 N. Fairfax: brick (Flemish bond), rectangular (three-bay front), three-and-a-half stories above raised basement, gable roof, two interior end chimneys, molded brick cornice, window lintels with cornerblocks; side-hall plan with principal room full width of second floor. Both structures used as James Hallowell's School for Young Ladies and later as St. Mary's Academy. 2 ext. photos (1958).

House (VA-618, Area Survey), 117 S. Fairfax St. Brick (Flemish bond), rectangular (three-bay front), three stories, gable roof, two interior end chimneys, molded brick cornice; side-hall plan; rear ell. Built late 18th C.; entrance vestibule and ground-floor rooms altered mid 19th C.; restored 1968. 1 ext. photo (1959).

House (VA-618, Area Survey), 118 S. Fairfax St. Brick (Flemish bond), rectangular (three-bay front), three stories, gable roof, two interior end chimneys, molded brick cornice, gauged flat arches; side-hall plan; two-story ell. Built early 19th C. 1 ext. photo (1959).

House (VA-618, Area Survey), 405 S. Fairfax St. Brick (Flemish bond), rectangular (two-bay front), two-and-a-half stories, gable roof with dormers, interior end chimney, sawtooth brick cornice, transomed doorway. Built late 19th C.; later alterations; restored. 1 ext. photo (1959).

House (VA-940), 310 N. Lee St. Arch detail, molded impost blocks, brick arch with angel head probably cast stone. Built late 18th C.; demolished c. 1940. 1 ext. photo (1937).

House (VA-465), 106 S. Lee St. Brick (Flemish bond), rectangular (three-bay front), two-and-a-half stories above raised basement, gambrel roof with dormers, two interior end chimneys, wooden lintels with corner blocks; side-hall plan. Built late 18th C. as warehouse-residence; interior altered early 19th C.; extensive interior renovations 1932, 1967. 1 ext. photo (1958).

House (VA-584), 310 S. Lee St. Frame with clapboarding, rectangular (three-bay front), two-and-a-half stories, gable roof with dormers, interior chimney; side-hall plan. Built late 18th C.; false front with bracketed cornice added late 19th C. 1 ext. photo (1936).

John Carlyle House (see p. 9)

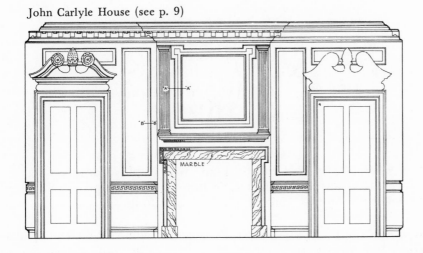

House (VA-620, Area Survey), 403 S. Lee St. Brick, rectangular (three-bay front), two-and-a-half stories above raised basement, gable roof with dormers, interior end chimney, transomed doorway; side-hall plan; two-story rear ell. Built late 18th C. 2 ext. photos (1959).

House (VA-620, Area Survey), 601 S. Lee St. Brick (Flemish bond), rectangular (two-bay front), two-and-a-half stories, gable roof, with dormers, interior end chimney, brick cornice, wooden lintels; three-room plan. Built early 19th C.; later alterations. 1 ext. photo (1959).

House (VA-620, Area Survey), 605 S. Lee St. Brick (Flemish bond), rectangular (three-bay front), two-and-a-half stories, gable roof with dormers, interior end chimney, denticulated cornice, flat arches with keystones; side-hall plan; rear ell. Built late 18th C.; restored mid 20th C. 1 ext. photo (1959).

House (VA-620, Area Survey), 615 S. Lee St. Brick (Flemish bond), rectangular (three-bay front), two-and-a-half stories, gable roof with dormers, interior chimney; side-hall plan; frame, two-story ell; two-story wing with arched entrance door. Built early 19th C.; addition c. 1960. 1 ext. photo (1959).

House (VA-683), 110 N. Pitt St. Frame with clapboarding, rectangular (three-bay front), two stories, gable roof; side-hall plan. Built early 19th C.; altered late 19th C.; demolished 1968. 1 ext. photo (1968).

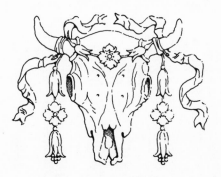

House (VA-683), 112 N. Pitt St. Frame with clapboarding, rectangular (three-bay front), three stories, gable roof; side-hall plan. Built early 19th C.; demolished 1968. 1 ext. photo (1968).

House (VA-446), 214 Queen St. Frame with clapboarding, rectangular (three-bay front), two-and-a-half stories, gable roof with dormers, interior end chimney; side-hall plan, enclosed stair, corner fireplaces; rear ell. Built mid 18th C.; demolished 1960. 1 ext. photo (1958), 1 int. photo (1958); 1 data page (1958); HABSI (1957).

House (VA-600, Area Survey), 308 Queen St. Brick, rectangular (three-bay front), two-and-a-half stories, gable roof with dormers, two exterior end chimneys, molded brick cornice, arched doorway keystone; side-hall plan. Built early 19th C. 3 ext. photos (1959).

House (VA-600, Area Survey), 317 Queen St. Brick, rectangular (three-bay front), three stories, gable roof, interior end chimney, brick modillion cornice, wooden lintels, arched doorway; side-hall plan. Built early 19th C. 1 ext. photo (1959).

House (VA-600, Area Survey), 510 Queen St. Frame with clapboarding, rectangular (two-bay front), two stories, gable roof, common chimney with adjoining unit, transomed doorway; frame and brick ell. Built early 19th C.; restored c. 1960. 3 ext. photos (1959).

House (VA-600, Area Survey), 517 Queen St. Brick, rectangular (three-bay front), three stories above raised basement, gable roof, interior end chimney, sawtooth cornice, wooden lintels; side-hall plan; two-story rear ell. Built mid 19th C. 1 ext. photo (1959).

House (VA-600, Area Survey), 519 Queen St. Frame with clapboarding, rectangular (three-bay front), two stories, gable roof, interior end chimney; side-hall plan; rear ell. Built late 18th C.; doorway altered. 1 ext. photo (1959).

House (VA-600, Area Survey), 523 Queen St. Brick, rectangular (two-bay front), gable roof, exterior rear chimney, sawtooth cornice, segmental arches; two-room plan. Built mid 19th C. 2 ext. photos (1959).

House (VA-619, Area Survey), 109 N. Royal St. Brick, rectangular (three-bay front), two-and-a-half stories, gable roof with dormers, modified modillion cornice, flat arches with fluted keystones, transomed doorway; side-hall plan. Built early 19th C.; later alterations, including ground-floor store front, late 19th C.; demolished 1963. 1 ext. photo (1960).

House (VA-619, Area Survey), 217 N. Royal St. Brick (Flemish bond), rectangular (three-bay front), three stories, shallow gable roof, two interior end chimneys, molded brick cornice; side-hall plan; two-

Jockey Club

story ell. Built late 18th C.; roof line raised and redesigned mid 19th C. 1 ext. photo (1960).

House (VA-293), 219 N. Royal St. Brick (Flemish bond), rectangular (three-bay front), two-and-a-half stories, gable roof with dormers, two interior end chimneys, double sawtooth brick cornice, fanlighted doorway; side-hall plan; two-story ell. Built late 18th C. 1 ext. photo (1936).

House (VA-619, Area Survey), 221 N. Royal St. Brick (Flemish bond), rectangular (three-bay front), two-and-a-half stories, gable roof with dormers, two interior end chimneys, double sawtooth brick cornice, fanlighted doorway, arched areaway; side-hall plan; two-story rear ell. Built late 18th C. 1 ext. photo (1960).

House (VA-619, Area Survey), 112 S. Royal St. Frame with clapboarding, rectangular (three-bay front), two-and-a-half stories, gable roof with dormers, interior end chimney, transomed doorway; side-hall plan; two-story brick ell. Built mid 18th C.; later alterations; remodeled 1967. 1 ext. photo (1960).

House (VA-619, Area Survey), 120 S. Royal St. Brick veneer over frame with clapboarding, rectangular (three-bay front), two stories, gable roof, interior end chimney; side-hall plan; rear ell. Built mid 18th C.; extensive renovations and alterations to facade and plan 1960. 1 ext. photo (1960).

House (VA-619, Area Survey), 122 S. Royal St. Frame with clapboarding, rectangular (three-bay front), two stories, gable roof, interior chimney; side-hall plan; rear ell. Built late 18th C. 1 ext. photo (1960).

House (VA-267), 308 S. Union St. Brick (Flemish bond), rectangular (three-bay front), two-and-a-half stories, gable roof with dormers, interior end chimney, doorway with transom, arched areaway. Built mid 18th C.; ruinous 1936; demolished 1938. 1 ext. photo (1938).

House (VA-617, Area Survey), 209 S. Washington St. Brick (Flemish bond), rectangular (three-bay front), two stories, hipped roof, interior chimney; side-hall plan; rear brick kitchen and frame hyphen. Built early 19th C.; additions late 19th C.; demolished c. 1960. 1 ext. photo (1960).

House (VA-617, Area Survey), 411 S. Washington St. Frame with clapboarding, rectangular (four-bay front), two stories, gable roof,

26

interior chimney, transomed doorway with side lights. Built early 19th C., originally as double unit; later alterations and additions. 1 ext. photo (1960).

Howard House (VA-617, Area Survey), 207 S. Washington St. Brick, rectangular (three-bay front), three stories, gable roof, two interior end chimneys, bracketed cornice; side-hall plan; rear ell. Built mid 19th C.; demolished 1965. 1 ext. photo (1960).

Jacobs-Miner House (VA-673), 113 S. Royal St. Brick, rectangular (two-bay front), three stories, shed roof, interior end chimney, bracketed modillion cornice; side-hall plan. Built 1868; demolished 1968. 1 ext. photo (1968); 1 data page (1968).

Janney, Elisha, House (VA-703), 404 Duke St. Brick (Flemish bond), approx. 30′ (three-bay front) x 35′, three-and-a-half stories, gable roof with dormers, two interior end chimneys, molded brick cornice, gauged arches, monumental scale; side-hall plan, plaster cornices, ceiling medallions; ell: brick with stucco. Completed by 1809; Greek Revival doorway with wrought-iron railings, minor interior restyling, mid 19th C.; rear tiered porches and development of duplex in ell early 20th C.; minor renovations 1960. 4 ext. photos (1967), 2 int. photos (1967); 8 data pages (1967).

Jockey Club

Jockey Club (Greene Funeral Home) (VA-102), 814 Franklin St. Frame with clapboarding under brick veneer, 45′4″ (five-bay front) x 33′5″, two stories, hipped roof, one interior and one exterior end chimney, modified modillion cornice, arched doorway with side lights, porch, oversize windows; center-hall plan, tiered galleries, plaster cornices, Adam marble mantels; rear ell. Built late 18th C.; enclosed with brick, rear galleries filled in, one-story addition 1959. 7 sheets (1937, including plans, elevations, details, sections); 4 ext. photos (1936), 4 int. photos (1936).

Johnston, Ruben, House (VA-618, Area Survey), 213 S. Fairfax St. Brick (Flemish bond), rectangular (three-bay front), two-and-a-half stories, gable roof with dormers, interior end chimney, molded brick cornice; side-hall plan; two-story rear ell. Built early 19th C.; later additions and alterations. 1 ext. photo (1958).

Johnston-Vowell House (VA-451), 224 S. Lee St. Brick (Flemish bond), rectangular (three-bay front), two-and-a-half stories, gable roof with dormers, interior end chimney, Aquia stone flat arches with keystones, fanlighted doorway, side porch with jalousies; side-hall plan; two-story ell. Built late 18th C.; restored. 1 ext. photo (1958); 2 data pages (1958).

Jones Point Lighthouse (VA-641), W bank of Potomac River and N bank of Hunting Creek, S end of S. Lee St., at Woodrow Wilson Bridge. Frame with clapboarding, 38'6" (three-bay front) x 19'1", one-and-a-half stories, gable roof with cast-iron lantern in center, two interior end chimneys, side porch; center-hall plan. Built 1855; active as lighthouse until 1926. One of the oldest inland lighthouses in the United States. Retaining wall for Lighthouse protects initial cornerstone of the District of Columbia. 6 sheets (1967, including plans, elevations, section); 5 ext. photos (1962), 1 int. photo (1962); 7 data pages (1963).

Kennedy Buildings (VA-670), 416-18 King St. Brick, rectangular (originally two-bay fronts), two stories, gable roof, interior chimney for double units, arched areaway. Built mid 19th C.; exterior drastically altered by cornice, window, and store-front changes late 19th C. to mid 20th C.; demolished 1968. 2 ext. photos (1968); 2 data pages (1968).

Korn and Wisemiller Building (VA-704), 202 S. St. Asaph and 502 Prince Sts. Brick (Flemish bond), approx. 38' (four-bay front) x 38', three-and-a-half stories, gable roof with dormers, one interior chimney, modillion cornice, pedimented Doric doorway, fanlighted doorway concealed by millwork frame; side-hall plan. Built 1792; interior radically modified from mid 19th C. to present; enclosed porch addition early 20th C. 3 ext. photos (1967), 1 int. photo (1967); 13 data pages (1967).

Ladd House (VA-212), 320 N. Fairfax St. Arch detail, plain impost block, stone voussoirs with sculptured head. Built late 18th C.; building demolished c. 1940. 1 ext. photo (1937).

Lafayette-Cazenove House (VA-467), see Lawrason, Thomas, House (VA-467), Alexandria.

Lannon's Opera House (VA-675), 500-08 King St. Brick, rectangular (six bays x eight bays), two stories, shed roof with parapet, bracketed cornice with recessed panels between, tall upper windows with segmental arches and molded heads; side-hall plan, stores and shops on ground floor, gallery across rear of auditorium space. Built 1884; altered early and mid 20th C.; pedimented entrance and store fronts virtually intact. 1 ext. photo (1968), 1 int. photo (1968); 3 data pages (1968).

Lawrason, Thomas, House (Lafayette-Cazenove House) (VA-467), 301 S. St. Asaph St. Brick (Flemish bond), rectangular (three-bay front), three stories, gable roof, two interior end chimneys, parapets and balustrades, Aquia stone flat arches with fluted keystones, elliptical arched stone doorway, double fanlights and sidelights; side-hall plan, delicate woodwork, composition ornament and plaster cornices, winding stair; two-story ell. Built c. 1819; minor restorations 1948. 7 int. photos (1958); 2 data pages (1958); HABSI (1958).

Leadbeater Drug Store (VA-948), see Stabler-Leadbeater Drug Corp. (VA-948), Alexandria.

Leadbeater House (VA-457), 414 N. Washington St. Brick, rectangular (three-bay front), two-and-a-half stories, shallow hipped roof, two interior end chimneys, heavy modillion cornice, low frieze windows, Doric entrance portico; center-hall plan. Built early 19th C.; demolished 1960. Used as a Federal hospital during the Civil War. 1 ext. photo (1958); 1 data page (1958); HABSI (1958).

Leadbeater, James, House (VA-641), 213 S. Pitt St. Brick (Flemish bond), rectangular (three-bay front), three stories, gable roof, two interior end chimneys, brick cornice; side-hall plan; two-story ell. Built 1810; later alterations. 4 sheets (1967, including plans, elevations); HABSI (1959).

Leadbeater-Stabler Apothecary Shop (VA-175), see Stabler-Leadbeater Apothecary Shop (VA-175), Alexandria.

Leadbeater House

Lee, Charles, House (VA-617, Area Survey), 407 N. Washington St. Brick, rectangular (three-bay front), three stories, shed roof, one interior chimney, one interior end chimney; side-hall plan, notable interior trim; rear wing: brick, rectangular (four-bay front), two-and-a-half stories, gable roof with dormers, interior end chimney; two-room plan. Portion of main block and rear wing built late 18th C.; main block extensively enlarged in plan and raised from two-and-a-half to three stories late 19th C. 2 ext. photos (1960).

Lee, Edmund J., House (VA-452), 428 N. Washington St. Brick (Flemish bond), rectangular (three-bay front), two-and-a-half stories, gable roof with dormers, interior chimney, modillion cornice continuing across gable end, pedimented doorway, Aquia stone steps,

30

James Leadbeater House

side-hall plan, notable interior trim and hardware; two-story ell. Built 1791; later alterations. 2 ext. photos (1958); 1 data page (1958); HABSI (1958).

Lee, Robert E., House (VA-707), see Potts-Fitzhugh House (VA-707), Alexandria.

Lloyd House (VA-582), see Wise-Hooe-Lloyd House (VA-582), Alexandria.

Lockwood-Cross Building (VA-665), 314 King St. Brick, rectangular (three-bay front), two stories, shed roof, modillion cornice. Built mid 19th C.; extensively altered c. 1960; demolished 1968. 1 ext. photo (1968); 1 data page (1968).

Longden, John, House (VA-689), 111 S. Royal St. Frame with brick veneer, rectangular (two-bay front), two-and-a-half stories, gable roof with dormer, interior end chimney; modified two-room plan. Built early 19th C.; extensive alterations including brick veneer street facade 1956; demolished 1968. 1 ext. photo (1968); 1 data page (1968).

Longden, John, Houses (VA-685), 105-07 S. Royal St. Double house, brick, rectangular (adjacent two-bay fronts), two stories, two interior end chimneys; side-hall plan. Built c. 1787-90; original street facades altered c. 1890; demolished 1968. 1 ext. photo (1968); 2 data pages (1968).

Lyceum (McGuire House) (VA-185), 201 S. Washington St. Brick with stucco, 61'1" (five-bay front) x 45'9", two stories, gable roof with pedimented ends, two interior chimneys, corner antae, intermediate antae on three sides, tetrastyle portico, Greek Doric order, wooden entablature surrounding building; center-hall plan. Built 1840; interior altered 1868-1900; rear addition late 19th C. 10 sheets (1940, including plans, elevations, sections, details); 12 ext. photos (1936, 1940), 5 int. photos (1938); 2 data pages (1937, 1969); HABSI (1958). NR

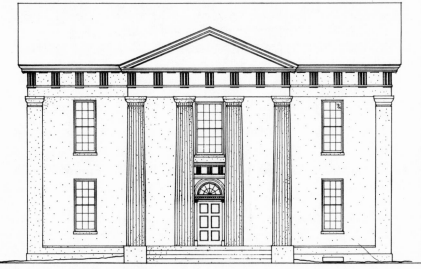

Lyceum

Lynch, Capt., House (VA-476), 708 Wolfe St. Frame with clapboarding, rectangular (three-bay front), two stories, gable roof, interior chimney, transomed entrance; side-hall plan; one-story rear and side wings. Built prior to 1779. 3 ext. photos (1958, including brick smokehouse and dairy); 1 data page (1958); HABSI (1958).

Lynn, Adam, House (VA-676), 518-20 King St. Brick (Flemish bond), rectangular (four-bay front), three stories, gable roof, two interior end chimneys, molded brick cornice, flat stone arches with keystones, stone arched doorway with reeded pilasters, arched areaway;

32

Lyceum

Capt. Lynch House

33

side-hall plan, notable interior trim. Built 1811; minor alterations late 19th C.; store front remodeled mid 20th C. 2 ext. photos (1968), 4 int. photos (1968); 5 data pages (1968).

Lynn, Adam, House (VA-687), 532 King St. Brick, rectangular (three-bay front), three stories, flat roof with parapet, no visible chimneys, bracketed cornice, flat stone arches with keystones. Built c. 1815, originally three-and-a-half stories, gable roof with dormers removed c. 1910, replaced with parapet during extensive renovation and addition to the original structure; ground floor altered for modern commercial purposes mid 20th C. 1 ext. photo (1968); 1 data page (1968).

Lynn, Adam, House (VA-688), 104 S. St. Asaph St. Brick, rectangular (two-bay front), two stories, gable roof, two interior end chimneys; irregular plan; rear ell. Built c. 1815; renovated with tin cornice late 19th C. 1 ext. photo (1968); 1 data page (1968).

McConnell, Alexander, House (VA-459), 201 Duke St. Frame with clapboarding, rectangular (four-bay front), two-and-a-half stories, gable roof, two interior end chimneys; modified center-hall plan; one-and-a-half story wing. Built 1795-97; later additions and alterations; transomed doorway with side lights mid 19th C. 1 ext. photo (1958); 1 data page (1958).

McConnell, Alexander, Tenements (VA-475, Area Survey), 223-25 S. Lee St. Frame with clapboarding, rectangular (two-bay fronts), two-and-a-half stories, gable roof with dormers, double units with common interior chimney. Built late 18th C. 1 ext. photo (1958); 1 data page (1958).

McGuire House (VA-185), see Lyceum (VA-185), Alexandria.

Mason's Ordinary (Coffee House) (with later addition known as Gadsby's Tavern, City Hotel, City Tavern) (VA-100), 128 N. Royal St. Museum. Brick (Flemish bond), 38'1" (five-bay front) x 29', three-and-a-half stories, gable roof with dormers with keystones, two interior end chimneys, modillion cornice with fret, flat arches with vermiculated keystones, stone string course, pedimented and pilastered Doric doorway; center-hall plan, notable mid-Georgian interior. Built 1752 for Charles Mason; Sampson Darnell (?), carpenter-builder. Gadsby's addition: Brick (Flemish bond), rectangular (four-bay front), three-and-a-half stories, gable roof with dormers, three interior end chimneys, modillion cornice, pedimented Doric doorway with en-

Alexander McConnell Tenements

Mason's Ordinary

gaged columns, flat arches with gauged brickwork; modified side-hall plan with stair hall beyond, excellent Georgian woodwork. Built 1792 for John Wise; leased to John Gadsby 1796; alterations and additions late 19th C.; doorway and interior ballroom woodwork acquired by Metropolitan Museum of Art 1917; building restored and ballroom copied and installed 1936-40; original doorway returned 1949. 7 sheets (1936, including plans, elevations, sections, details); 7 ext. photos (1936, 1937), 7 int. photos (1936, n.d.); 1 photocopy (c. 1860's); 4 data pages (1941). NR

Miller, Mordecai, House (VA-618, Area Survey), 109 S. Fairfax St. Brick (Flemish bond), rectangular (three-bay front), three stories, gable roof, two interior end chimneys, brick cornice, wooden lintels with corner blocks beneath; side-hall plan. Built 1828. 2 ext. photos (1959, 1968); 2 data pages (1968).

Miller, Samuel, Building (VA-671), 420 King St. Brick, rectangular (two-bay front), two stories, gable roof with end parapets, flat stone arches with keystones. Built mid 19th C.; altered late 19th and early 20th C.; demolished 1968. 1 ext. photo (1968); 1 data page (1968).

Mason's Ordinary (Coffee House)
complete set of drawings

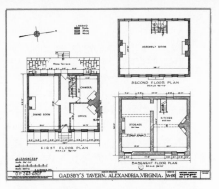

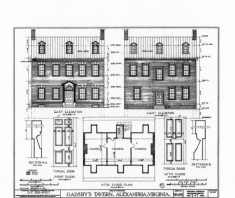

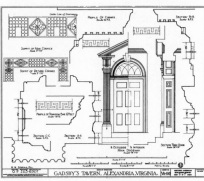

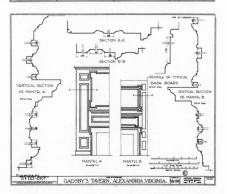

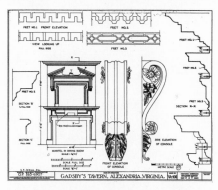

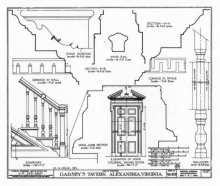

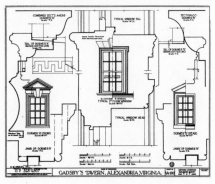

Murray-Dick-Fawcett House (Fawcett House) (VA-104), 517 Prince St. Frame with clapboarding, 32′6″ (five-bay front) x 84′, one-and-a-half stories above basement, gable roof with shuttered dormers, two interior end chimneys, two interior chimneys; side-hall plan, paneled interiors; rear ell housing kitchen, laundry, smokehouse, and necessaries. Built late 18th C.; porch and rear extensions added to create modified L-plan c. 1816. 6 sheets (1936, including plans, elevations, sections); 1 ext. photo (1936), 2 int. photos (1936); HABSI's (1958, 1959).

Murry-Craik House (Craik, Dr., House) (VA-583), 210 Duke St. Brick (Flemish bond), rectangular (three-bay front), three-and-a-half stories, gable roof with dormers, two interior end chimneys, modillion cornice, Aquia stone flat arches with keystones, stone arched doorway, arched areaway passage; side-hall plan, notable interior trim; rear ell. Built 1790; restored 1943. 1 ext. photo (1936); HABSI's (1958, 1959).

Old Dominion Bank (Athenaeum, Free Methodist Church) (VA-428), 201 Prince St. Museum. Brick with stucco, rectangular (three-bay front), one story, gable roof, tetrastyle Greek Doric portico; one-room plan. Built mid 19th C.; interior altered late 19th C.; remodeled as museum 1965. 1 ext. photo (1936).

Old Leadbeater House (VA-416), see Gregory, William, House (VA-416), Alexandria.

Old Presbyterian Meeting House (VA-231), 321 S. Fairfax St. Brick (Flemish bond), approx. 60′ (four-bay front) x 80′, two tiers of windows, gable roof, brick cornice, pediment with round louvered opening, double door opening upon stone platform, outcurving stone steps with iron railings; one-room plan with vestibule, gallery on three sides with two tiers of columns, arched ceiling, pulpit recessed into base of tower. Built 1774-90; gutted by fire 1835; rebuilt 1837; tower added 1843; front extended 1853. 2 ext. photos (1936, 1939), 2 int. photos (1936); HABSI (1958).

Patterson-Fitzgerald Warehouses (Warehouses) (VA-132), 101-05 S. Union St. Brick (Flemish bond), 74′ (nine-bay front) x 44′4″, two-and-a-half stories above rubble basement, gable roof with dormers, two interior chimneys; adjacent one-room sail loft. Built late 18th C. John Patterson, carpenter-builder; alterations and additions mid 20th C. 7 sheets (1937, including plans, elevations, details); 5 ext. photos (1937, 1938), 2 int. photos (1958); 1 data page (1958); HABSI (1958).

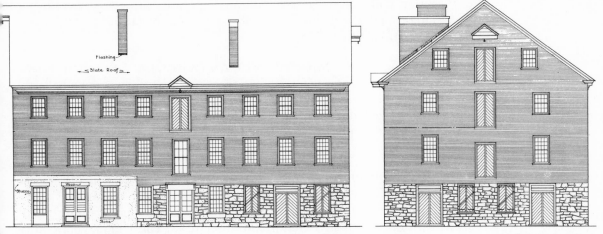

Patterson-Fitzgerald Warehouses   West elevation   South elevation

Plain, George, House (VA-618, Area Survey), 227 S. Fairfax St. Brick, rectangular (three-bay front), three stories, gable roof, interior end chimney, molded brick cornice, wooden lintels, pilastered doorway; side-hall plan; two-story wing. Built 1852. 1 ext. photo (1959).

Potts-Fitzhugh House (Robert E. Lee House) (VA-707), 607 Oronoco St. Historic house museum. Brick (Flemish bond), approx. 55' (five-bay front) x 25', two-and-a-half stories, gable roof with dormers, two interior end chimneys, modillion cornice, slightly projecting pedimented center pavilion, pilastered doorway, dated gutterhead; center-hall plan, notable interior trim, ornamental plaster, patent bake-oven; rear ell. Built 1795; restored 1968. Boyhood home of Robert E. Lee (1811–1816 and 1820–1825). 5 ext. photos (1936, 1967), 7 int. photos (1967); 13 data pages (1967); HABSI (1968).

Pythian Temple (VA-252), 319 Cameron St. Brick, rectangular (three-bay front), three stories, shed roof, bracketed cornice, traceried windows; commercial-loft plan. Built mid 19th C.; first floor converted to store front and interior renovated after fire c. 1936; remodeled 1967. 1 ext. photo (1936).

Ramsay-Atkinson House (VA-464), 113 N. Fairfax St. Brick (Flemish bond), rectangular (three-bay front), three-and-a-half stories, gable roof with dormers, two interior end chimneys, arched and coved cornice, stone flat arches with keystones; side-hall plan, notable interior trim; brick service outbuilding. Built prior to 1785; major alterations. 2 ext. photos (1958), 1 int. photo (1958); 2 data pages (1958); HABSI (1958).

Ramsay, Dennis, House (VA-475, Area Survey), 221 S. Lee St. Frame with clapboarding, rectangular (three-bay front), two-and-a-half stories, gable roof with dormers, interior end chimney, entrance doorway with glazed transom; side-hall plan; two-story, brick rear ell. Built 1760. 4 ext. photos (1936, 1958), 3 int. photos (1936); 1 data page (1958).

Ramsay, William, House (VA-103), 221 King St. Historic house museum. Frame with clapboarding, 39'6" (three-bay front) x 35', one-and-a-half stories above stone and brick basement, gambrel roof with dormers, one exterior and one interior end chimney, one-story entrance porch; irregular plan. Built 1748; possibly moved to present location from another site; extensive later alterations and additions; partially damaged by fire 1942; reconstructed 1955. First home of William Ramsay, a founder of Alexandria and its first and only Lord Mayor. 4 sheets (1936, including plans, elevations, details, sections); 1 ext. photo (1936), 1 int. photo (1936).

Roberdeau, Gen. Daniel, House (VA-469), 418 S. Lee St. Brick (Flemish bond), rectangular (three-bay front), three-and-a-half stories above raised basement, gable roof with dormers, two interior end chimneys, Aquia stone flat arches with keystones, monumental scale; side-hall plan, unusual door pediments; rear wing. Built c. 1790, probably preceded by rear section; altered late 19th C. 1 ext. photo (1958), 2 int. photos (1958); 1 data page (1958); HABSI (1958).

Row Houses (VA-618, Area Survey), 131-37 S. Fairfax St. Brick (Flemish bond), rectangular (two-bay fronts), two-and-a-half stories, gable roofs with dormers; two interior chimneys for four units, brick modillion cornice, transomed doorways. Built 1827-33. 2 ext. photos (1959).

Brass

IRON PADLOCK

Row Houses (VA-618, Area Survey), 207-09 S. Fairfax St. Brick (Flemish bond), rectangular (three-bay fronts), two-and-a-half stories, gable roofs with dormers, four interior end chimneys, deep modillion cornice, Ionic portico for double units; side-hall plans; rear ells. Built early 19th C.; restored. 1 ext. photo (1959).

Row Houses (VA-618, Area Survey), 511-13 S. Fairfax St. Brick (Flemish bond), rectangular (two-bay fronts), two-and-a-half stories, gable roofs with dormers, common chimney for double units, brick sawtooth cornice, stone lintels, transomed doorways. Built early 19th C. 1 ext. photo (1959).

Row Houses (VA-618, Area Survey), 515-17 S. Fairfax St. Brick (Flemish bond), rectangular (two-bay fronts), two-and-a-half stories, gable roofs with dormers, common interior chimney for double units, brick sawtooth cornice, flat brick arches, transomed doorways. Built early 19th C. 1 ext. photo (1959).

Row Houses (VA-600, Area Survey), 301-07 Queen St. Brick, rectangular (three-bay fronts), two stories, gable roofs, four units with two interior chimneys, brick modillion cornice; side-hall plans; two-story rear ells. Built mid 19th C.; later alterations. 3 ext. photos (1959, 1960).

·IRON·PADLOCK·

Row Houses (VA-600, Area Survey), 319-25 Queen St. Brick, rectangular (three-bay fronts), two stories, gable roofs, interior end chimneys, sawtooth cornice, doorways with transoms; four units with side-hall plans; one-and-a-half story ells. Built early 19th C. 4 ext. photos (1959).

Row Houses (VA-600, Area Survey), 513-15 Queen St. Frame with clapboarding (partial shiplapping), rectangular (four-bay front), gable roof, interior chimney; irregular plans (double units); lean-to addition. Built late 18th C.; additions and alterations. 1 ext. photo (1959).

Row Houses (VA-617, Area Survey), 415-17 S. Washington St. Brick rectangular (two-bay fronts), two stories above raised basements, gable roofs, interior end chimneys, wooden lintels. Built early 19th C.; twin units with separate entrances unified with double doors c. 1960. 1 ext. photo (1960).

·IRON·PADLOCK·

St. John's Academy (Carne School) (VA-450), SE corner Duke and S. Columbus Sts. Brick, rectangular (five-bay front), three stories, gable roof; two interior chimneys, bracketed cornice with wide overhang, cupola; modified center-hall plan. Built late 18th C.; greatly altered in Greek Revival style and wing added mid 19th C.; interior alterations late 19th C. and early 20th C. 1 ext. photo (1958); 3 data pages (1959); HABSI (1959).

St. Paul's Episcopal Church (VA-340), 216 S. Pitt St. Brick with stucco, rectangular (five-bay front), two tiers of windows, gable roof, triple arcade of tall pointed arches, stepped parapet returning at

St. Paul's Episcopal Church

corners to give impression of towers, traceried roundels above arcade, triple tiers (upper false) of pointed windows flanking entrance; one-room plan with vestibule, distinctive interior details of clustered columns, interlaced columnettes in gallery. Cornerstone laid 1817, Benjamin H. Latrobe, architect; chancel extended late 19th C.; major additions 1957. Early example of Gothic Revival style in America. 1 ext. photo (1958), 2 int. photos (1958); 2 data pages (1959); HABSI (1959).

St. Paul's Episcopal Church Rectory (VA-708), 417 Duke St. Brick, rectangular (three-bay front), two stories, gable roof, two interior chimneys, wooden lintels with corner blocks; side-hall plan; rear ell. Built early 19th C.; wing added; double doors, wooden steps, and railing installed 1871; steps renewed 1884; entrance restored to elliptical arch with side lights, brick stoop, and wrought-iron railing c. 1930; demolished 1957. 1 ext. photocopy (c. 1900); 2 data pages (1932).

Second Presbyterian Church, Westminster Building (VA-682), NE corner S. St. Asaph and Prince Sts. Brick with limestone trim, rectangular (three bays x eleven bays), two stories present effect of three pavilions, flat roof with parapets (facade parapet with raked blocking, side elevations with mansard sections between pavilions), bracketed cornice, upper windows with semi-circular heads and large windows centered at each second-floor pavilion unit, hooded entrance on facade, projecting one-story bay at first-floor side elevation; center-hall plan with secondary rear entrance. Built 1912. 1 ext. photo (1968); 2 data pages (1968).

Simmonds, Samuel, House (VA-684), 109 S. Royal St. Brick, rectangular (two-bay front), two-and-a-half stories, gable roof with dormer, interior end chimney; modified two-room plan. Built 1787-90; original brick facade covered with brick veneer and ground floor extensively altered c. 1956; demolished 1968. 1 ext. photo (1968); 2 data pages (1968).

Snowden House (VA-944), see Vowell-Snowden-Black House (VA-709), Alexandria.

Stabler-Leadbeater Apothecary Shop (Leadbeater-Stabler Apothecary Shop) (VA-175), 105-07 S. Fairfax St. Pharmaceutical Museum. Brick (Flemish bond), 20′ (three-bay front) x 40′, three-and-a-half

Stabler-Leadbeater Apothecary Shop

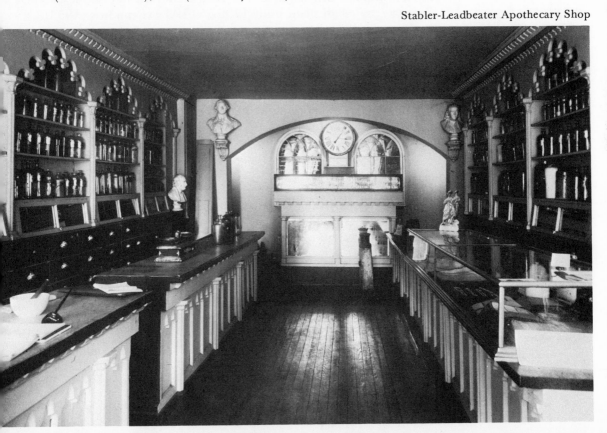

stories, gable roof with dormers, molded brick cornice, upper windows with flat arches and gauged brickwork, bow shop windows; two-room plan, notable interior trim. Built late 18th C.; interiors remodeled mid 19th C.; ground-floor shop fronts reconstructed 1936-39; laboratory building: (interior stripped), similar in general character, but with stone lintels and corner blocks. Built early 19th C.; exterior restored 1939. 2 sheets (1940, shop plan, details, sections); 6 ext. photos (1938, 1940), 5 int. photos (1940); 14 data pages (1934, 1939, 1941); 2 HABSI's (1958, 1959).

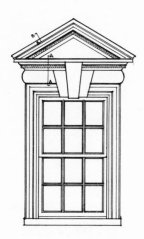

Stabler-Leadbeater Drug Corp. (Leadbeater Drug Store) (VA-948), SW corner King and S. Fairfax Sts. Brick (Flemish bond), rectangular (two bays x five bays), three stories, hipped roof, molded brick cornice. Built early 19th C.; store front added late 19th C.; demolished c. 1940. 1 ext. photo (1936).

Summers-Scott House (VA-600, Area Survey), 312 Queen St. Brick (Flemish bond), rectangular (three-bay front), two-and-a-half stories above raised basement, gable roof with dormers, interior end chimney, modillion and denticulated cornice, flat arches with keystones, arched doorway; side-hall plan. Built 1795-1814. 3 ext. photos (1959).

Swope, Michael, House (VA-292), 210 Prince St. Brick (Flemish bond), rectangular (three-bay front), three-and-a-half stories, gable roof with dormers, interior chimney, modillion and fret cornice, pedimented Doric doorway; side-hall plan, interior trim; two-story ell. Built 1704; main stair removed, minor renovations in ell 1967. 1 ext. photo (1936).

Taylor-Fraser House (VA-678), 109 S. Pitt St. Brick (Flemish bond), rectangular (four-bay front), two-and-a-half stories, gable roof with dormers, two interior end chimneys, sawtooth brick cornice, wooden pedimented doorway, Doric pilasters flanking six-panel door with arched fanlight; side-hall plan, notable interior trim; rear ell. Built early 19th C.; later alterations; entrance doorway added c. 1940. 1 ext. photo (1968), 3 int. photos (1968); 2 data pages (1968).

Thompson, Jonah, Houses (Twin or Married Houses) (VA-251), 211 N. Fairfax St. Brick (Flemish bond), rectangular (five-bay front), three stories, gable roof, two interior end chimneys, denticulated cornice, Aquia stone flat arches with keystones, pair arched doorways with cast capitals and keystones, stone columns, monumental scale; modified side-hall plan, notable woodwork and stair, elaborate plasterwork; rear hyphen and entrance court giving access to adjoining

Palladian unit of two stories with stuccoed facade, basement, gable roof, colonnade above, arcaded gallery below. Built late 18th C.; front-bay addition probably early 19th C.; interior renovations late 19th C. to early 20th C. 5 ext. photos (1936, 1937, 1958), 5 int. photos (1937, 1958); 2 data pages (1958); HABSI (1957).

Twin or Married Houses (VA-251), see Thompson, Jonah, Houses (VA-251), Alexandria.

Van Havre-Daingerfield House (VA-710), 608 Cameron St. Brick (Flemish bond) with stucco ends, approx. 25' (three-bay front) x 34', two-and-a-half stories, gable roof with dormers, two exterior end chimneys, arched over areaway to heavy piers, stone flat arches with keystones, stoop and steps with wrought-iron railings; side-hall plan, plaster cornices, vaulted basement chamber, Franklin stove; ell. Built 1798; vestibule with Greek Revival doorway, minor interior renovation mid 19th C.; alterations and additions to ell early 19th C. and late 19th C.; kitchen fireplace restored 1967. 2 ext. photos (1967), 4 int. photos (1967); 14 data pages (1967).

Vowell-Snowden-Black House (Snowden House) (VA-709), 619 S. Lee St. Brick (Flemish bond), approx. 30' (three-bay) x 40', two-and-a-half stories, gable roof with dormers, two interior end chimneys, arched and coved cornice, flat stone arches with keystones, pedimented doorway with engaged columns, front foundation Aquia stone with stoop, wrought-iron railings; side-hall plan, simple refined trim; brick ell; brick and frame wing with hyphen. Built 1798-1800; hyphen and wing probably mid 19th C.; widow's walk removed late 19th C.; minor renovations early 20th C. 3 ext. photos (1936, 1967), 2 int. photos (1967); 8 data pages (1967); HABSI (1958).

> *Stable* (VA-711), Franklin St., between S. Lee and Fairfax Sts. Brick (Flemish bond), approx. 28'6" (three-bay front with vehicular opening on axis with loft door) x 18', one story with loft, gable roof, ventilators at ends. Built c. 1800; lean-to probably added mid 19th C.; remodeled as double garage and roof repaired 1930's. 2 ext. photos (1967); 5 data pages (1967).

Wales House (VA-468), see Hampson, Bryan, House (VA-468), Alexandria.

Warehouse (VA-133), Strand St., at rear of 105 S. Union St. Brick (Flemish bond), 31'8" (three-bay front) x 50'6", two-and-a-half stories, gable roof with dormers, stone lintels with keystones. Built late

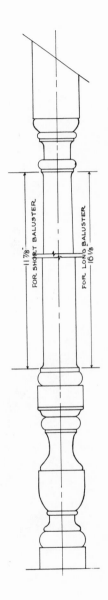

18th C.; demolished c. 1940. 3 sheets (1937, including plans, elevations, details); 2 ext. photos (1937).

Warehouses (VA-132), see Patterson-Fitzgerald Warehouses (VA-132), Alexandria.

Warehouses (VA-621, Area Survey), Tavern Square (Sharpshin Alley), Brick, rectangular (four-bay fronts), three stories, gable and half-gable roofs (latter with two-story lean-to). Built early 19th C.; demolished 1965. 2 ext. photos (1959).

Warfield Building (VA-681), 501 King St. Brick with stone trim, rectangular (three bays x seven bays), three stories, canted corner, flat roof with parapets, cast-iron cornice, half-round upper windows, side entrance to hallway and apartments. Built 1905-06; store front and interior remodeled mid 1950's; demolished 1968. 2 ext. photos (1968), 2 int. photos (1968); 2 data pages (1968).

Washington, George, Reconstructed Town House (VA-597), 508 Cameron St. (Original site). Clapboarding on cinder block, rectangular (three-bay front), one-and-a-half stories above rubble basement, gable roof with dormers, exterior end brick chimney. Built 1960. Replaced the original 1769 building, which was demolished c. 1855. 1 photocopy, early drawing (c. 1855); 14 data pages (1961).

Wilson, James, House (VA-618, Area Survey), 124 S. Fairfax St. Brick (Flemish bond), rectangular (three-bay front), three stories, gable roof, two interior end chimneys, sawtooth brick cornice, flat arches with gauged brickwork, transomed doorway (vestibule late 19th C.); side-hall plan; two-story ell. Built late 18th C. 1 ext. photo (1959); HABSI (1959).

Wilson-Hopkins House (Hallowell School, Burson House) (VA-933), 609 Oronoco St. Brick (Flemish bond), approx. 55' (five-bay front) x 25', two-and-a-half stories, gable roof with dormers, two interior end chimneys, modillion cornice, slightly projecting pedimented center pavilion, pilastered doorway; center-hall plan, notable interior trim, ornamental plaster; rear ell. Built 1795; porch additions and alterations early 20th C. 1 ext. photo (1936); HABSI (1958).

Wise-Hooe-Lloyd House (Lloyd House) (VA-582), 220 N. Washington St. Brick (Flemish bond), 48'2" (five-bay front) x 40'2", two-and-a-half stories, gable roof with dormers, four interior end chimneys, modillion and denticulated cornice continuous across gable ends, flat

Wise-Hooe-Lloyd House

arches with fluted keystones, Doric pedimented doorway, balusters in cellar windows; center-hall plan, plaster cornices, architraves exhibit crossettes and corner blocks. Built 1793-96; additions and major interior alterations c. 1940; renovated 1960. 16 sheets (1959, including plans, elevations, sections, details); 20 ext. photos (1936, 1959), 14 int. photos (1936, 1959); 6 data pages (1959); HABSI (1958).

Wise's Tavern (VA-934), see Dalton-Herbert House (VA-934), Alexandria.

Yeaton-Fairfax House (Fairfax House) (VA-211), 607 Cameron St. Brick (Flemish bond), rectangular (three-bay front), three stories, gable roof, two interior end chimneys, modillion cornice, tall recessed plastered arch containing upper-hall windows, entrance doorway set in recessed vestibule, elliptical fanlight and sidelights, engaged columns, double incurving stone steps and wrought-iron railings, Palladian windows flank entrance; center-hall plan, delicate woodwork, composition ornament and ornamental plaster, winding stair

Wise-Hooe-Lloyd House

48

with niches; two-story rear ell. Built c. 1816, William Yeaton, architect-builder; minor alterations; restorations with additions 1966. 4 ext. photos (1936, 1939), 8 int. photos (1939); 1 data page (1940); HABSI (1958).

AMELIA VICINITY   Amelia County (3)

Hindle House (VA-269), see Woodlands (VA-269), Amelia Vicinity.

Woodlands (Hindle House) (VA-269), .2 mi. W of Nibbs Creek, W side of State Rte. 656, .4 mi. NE of intersection with State Rte. 624. Frame with clapboarding, rectangular (five-bay front), two stories, gable roof, pedimented gable-end front, two interior chimneys; four-room plan, paneled dining room. Built late 18th C. 2 sheets (1940, including sections, details); 1 data page (1941); HABSI (1959).

Yeaton-Fairfax House

Woodlands

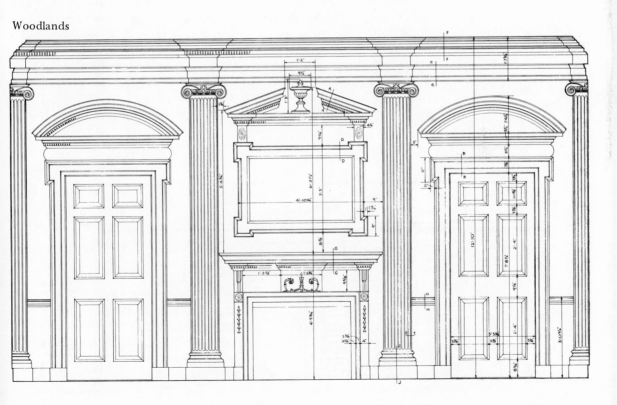

ANNANDALE

Ossian Hall (VA-598), 5001 Regina Dr. Site. Frame with clapboarding, 45′ (five-bay front) x 26′, two-and-a-half stories, gable roof with dormers, two exterior end chimneys, two-story verandah with square columns; center-hall plan. Built late 18th C.; later additions and alterations; burned 1959. 11 sheets (1961, including plans, elevations, sections, details); 8 ext. photos (1936, 1959), 3 int. photos (1936); HABSI (1958).

ANNANDALE VICINITY

Ravensworth (VA-105), 5200 Port Royal Rd. Site. Frame with clapboarding, five-part composition, central block: rectangular (five-bay front), two stories, gable roof with pedimented cross gable over central bay, four interior end chimneys; center-hall plan; flanking two-story wings terminated by pedimented pavilions. Built early 19th C.; burned 1926; coach house and stable: brick, stone foundations, 105′ (six-bay front) x 50′, two stories, gable roof, cornice continued on gable end to form pediment, four-bay arcade on S elevation supported by square brick piers and flanked by blind arches, former carriage entrance at W gable end framed by wooden lintel supported by two brick engaged Doric columns; rectangular plan. Built early 19th C.; demolished 1960. 4 sheets (1936, including plans, elevations, section); 5 ext. photos (1936, 1937), 4 ext. photos, outbuildings and grounds (1936, 1937), 3 int. photos (1936); 3 ext. photocopies (c. 1900), 1 int. photocopy (c. 1900); HABSI (1958).

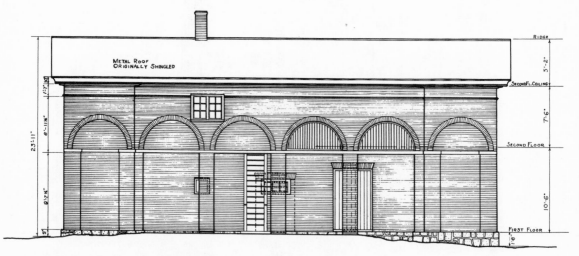

Ravensworth Coach House and Stable

Green Spring Farm (Moss House) (VA-277), 4601 Green Spring Rd. Brick, rectangular (three-bay front), two-and-a-half stories, gable roof with dormers, two interior end chimneys, center-hall plan; flanking one-and-a-half story, brick wings. Built c. 1760; extensive additions and alterations c. 1840, 1942. 2 ext. photos (1936); HABSI's (1958, 1969).

Moss House (VA-277), see Green Spring Farm (VA-277), Annandale Vicinity.

APPOMATTOX VICINITY   Appomattox County (6)

Appomattox Courthouse (VA-716), Appomattox Court House National Historical Park. Museum. Brick, rectangular (three-bay front), two stories, hipped roof, four interior end chimneys, pedimented wooden entrance porch at first-floor level approached by long flight stone and brick steps; three-room plan. Built 1846; burned 1892; reconstructed 1964. 1 ext. photo (1964); 2 ext. photocopies (1865, c. 1890). NR

Clover Hill Tavern (Patteson House) (VA-216), Appomattox Court House National Historical Park. Brick, rectangular (four-bay front), two stories, gable roof, two exterior end chimneys; two-room plan; rear lean-to; two-story brick guest house with projecting gable roof; two-story brick kitchen-guest house. Built early 19th C.; restored, lean-to removed; guest house projecting roof now shelters two-level porch on two sides. 2 ext. photos (1939); HABSI (1957).

Jail (VA-436), Appomattox Court House National Historical Park. Museum. Brick, rectangular (three-bay front), three stories, gable roof, two interior end chimneys; center-hall plan. Built c. 1870; replaced earlier jail probably destroyed mid 1860's. 1 ext. photo (1939); HABSI (1957).

Legrand House (VA-715), .6 mi. S of Plain Branch Run, SE side of State Rte. 631, .5 mi. NE of intersection with State Rte. 634. Frame with clapboarding, rectangular (one-bay front), one story, gable roof, one exterior stone chimney; one-room plan; rear lean-to and side-porch; two-story frame wing built in front of one-story house and connected to it by one-story hyphen. Built early 19th C.; wing added c. 1860; ruinous. 1 ext. photo (1960); HABSI (1957).

Appomattox Courthouse

Clover Hill Tavern

McDearmon-Tibbs House (VA-714), .3 mi. S of N branch of Appomattox River, .7 mi. NE of State Rte. 24, 1.1 mi. NE of intersection with State Rte. 656. Frame with clapboarding, L-shaped (three-bay front), two stories, hipped roof, three exterior end chimneys, one-story wooden porch across S and W fronts; center-hall plan. Built mid 19th C.; later alterations and additions; ruinous. 2 ext. photos (1960); HABSI (1957).

McLean House (VA-240), see Raine-McLean House (VA-240), Appomattox Vicinity.

Old Store (VA-435), Appomattox Court House National Historical Park. Frame with clapboarding, rectangular (three-bay front), two stories, gable roof, two interior end chimneys; side wing. Built mid 19th C.; destroyed. 1 ext. photo (1939).

Patteson House (VA-216), see Clover Hill Tavern (VA-216), Appomattox Vicinity.

Plunkett-Meeks Store and House (VA-432), Appomattox Court House National Historical Park. Museum. Frame with clapboarding, rectangular (two-bay front), two stories, gable roof, central chimney, side lean-to; one-story frame law office outbuilding, exterior end chimney. Built c. 1850; altered with additions; store and house restored, lean-to removed, porch and entrance added on E, door added on S, outside stair to second floor added on N. 2 ext. photos (1939, 1940); HABSI (1957).

Raine-McLean House (McLean House) (VA-240), Appomattox Court House National Historical Park. House museum. Brick, 50'2" (three-bay front) x 22', two stories, gable roof, two interior end chimneys, full-length one-story porch; center-hall plan. Built 1848; dismantled 1893; reconstructed 1948-49. Scene of surrender of Gen. Robert E. Lee to Lt. Gen. Ulysses S. Grant, April 9, 1865. 8 sheets (1940, including plot plan, plans, elevations, details); 2 ext. photocopies (n.d.); 18 data pages (n.d., including specifications for moving and rebuilding structure); HABSI (1957). NR

Sears, J., House (VA-713), .2 mi. S of Plain Branch Run, .4 mi. N of State Rte. 631, .2 mi. W of intersection with State Rte. 634. Frame with clapboarding, rectangular (three-bay front), two stories, gable roof, one exterior end chimney, one-story wooden porches; side-hall plan. Built mid 19th C.; later additions and alterations; ruinous. 1 ext. photo (1960).

Plunkett-Meeks Store and House

Raine-McLean House

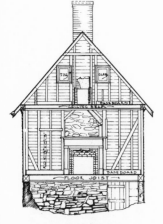

Maria Wright House

Wright, Maria, House (VA-947), Appomattox Court House National Historical Park. Frame with clapboarding, 40' (three-bay front) x 17'11", one story, gable roof, two stone exterior end chimneys, one-story entrance porch; center-hall plan; rear ell. Built c. 1823; alteration and additions c. 1890; interior stripped 1942; renovated. 7 sheets (1959, including plans, elevations, sections, details); HABSI (1957).

54

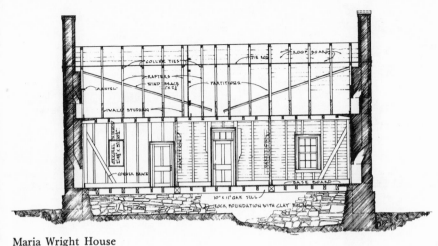

Maria Wright House

ARLINGTON
Arlington County (7)

Arlington House (Custis-Lee Mansion) (VA-443), Arlington National Cemetery. Brick with stucco, central section: rectangular (five-bay front), two stories, gable roof, four interior end chimneys, monumental hexastyle, dipteral Greek Doric portico, stucco of E elevation coursed to resemble stone blocks, walls and columns painted to resemble marble; center-hall plan, imaginative use of interior arches, arcades, and recessed niches; flanking wings: rectangular (three-bay each), one story above raised basement, hipped roof, one interior chimney N wing, one interior end chimney S wing, arched double-hung windows in arched recessed bays; S wing dining room has large scale arched recess in N wall; two dependencies: brick with stucco, rectangular (three-bay front), one story, flanking W entrance court. Flanking wings of main house built 1802-04; center section with portico completed 1817; main drawing room completed 1855; estate confiscated by Federal government 1864; sold to Federal government 1883; partially restored 1929, 1955 to present. Arlington House was built by George Washington Parke Custis, George Washington's adopted grandson. Custis' only daughter, Mary, married Robert E. Lee at Arlington House 1831. The Lees lived there until 1861. 18 sheets (1940, including plans, elevations, sections, details of main house and kitchen). NR

Custis-Lee Mansion (VA-443), see Arlington House (VA-443), Arlington Co.

55

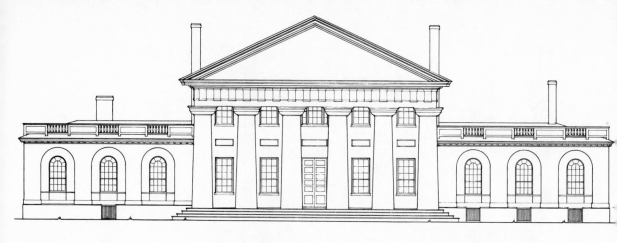

Arlington House

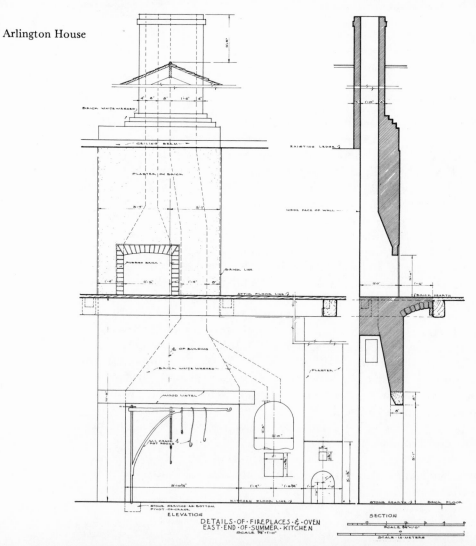

ELEVATION

SECTION

DETAILS·OF·FIREPLACES·&·OVEN
EAST·END·OF·SUMMER·KITCHEN
SCALE ¾"·1'·0"

Church Quarter (VA-751), .6 mi. W of Little River, NE side of State Rte. 738, .8 mi. NW of intersection with State Rte. 688. Log, rectangular (three-bay front), one story, gable roof, two exterior end chimneys; rear ell. Built early 19th C.; addition. 1 ext. photo (1936).

Fork Church (VA-409), .8 mi. W of Little River, NE side of State Rte. 738, opposite intersection with State Rte. 685. Brick (Flemish bond, English bond below water table), rectangular (one-bay front), gable roof, gable-end front, four-bay nave with segmental arch windows, modillion cornice. Built c. 1735; exterior end chimney added in rear. 3 ext. photos (1932, 1936), 1 int. photo (1932); 1 data page (1941); HABSI (1957).   NR

Rocky Mills (Fairfield) (VA-146), see Fairfield (Rocky Mills) (VA-146), Richmond Vicinity, Henrico Co.

Scotchtown (VA-117), .4 mi. S of Newfound River, .2 mi. NW of State Rte. 685, 1.2 mi. NE of intersection with State Rte. 671. House museum. Frame with clapboarding, 84'11" (nine-bay front) x 35'1½", one story, gable roof with jerkinheads, four interior chimneys; center-hall plan; side lean-to. Built c. 1735; restored 1953, lean-to removed, four chimneys removed, and two original interior chimneys restored on ridge line, interior plan altered, ice house reconstructed, office and caretaker's house built partially on old foundations. Home of Patrick Henry 1771-77. 11 sheets (1936, including plans, elevations, details); 8 ext. photos (1934, 1936), 4 int. photos (1936); 5 data pages (1936); HABSI (1957).   NR; NHL

Mt. Wharton (VA-551), 1.4 mi. E of N tributary of Assawaman Creek, .8 mi. SE of State Rte. 679, .6 mi. SW of intersection with State Rte. 781. Frame with brick ends, rectangular (five-bay front), one-and-a-half stories, gable roof with dormers, two interior end chimneys; irregular plan; side wing. Built late 18th C. 2 ext. photos (1940).

Cherry Grove Servants' Quarters (VA-762), .4 mi. NE of N tributary of Acquinton Creek, .4 mi. S of State Rte. 30, .5 mi. SE of intersection with State Rte. 600. Brick, rectangular (two-bay front), one story, gable roof, one exterior end chimney, frame gable ends above eaves. Built mid 18th C.; demolished. 1 ext. photo (1936).

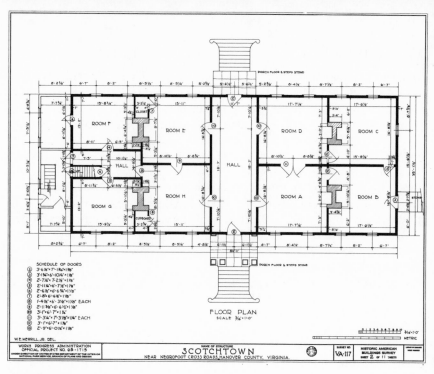

Scotchtown

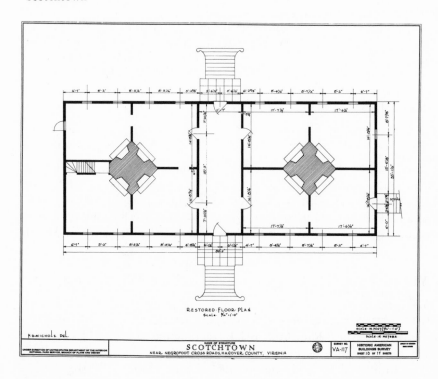

Moeser House (VA-154), .5 mi. N of N tributary of Acquinton Creek, .1 mi. S of State Rte. 30, .2 mi. SE of intersection with State Rte. 600. Log with clapboarding, 21' (two-bay front) x 18'10", one story below two-level attic, gable roof with splayed eaves, basement door has diagonal exterior sheathing. Built early 19th C.; demolished. 6 sheets (1939, including plans, elevations, details); 9 ext. photos (1937, 1938, 1940, n.d.), 1 int. photo (1939); 3 data pages (1941).

Rumford Academy (VA-258), .9 mi. N of Acquinton Creek, .1 mi. E of State Rte. 600, .2 mi. NE of intersection with State Rte. 30. Brick, T-shaped (five-bay front), two stories, gable roof, exterior end chimneys. Built late 18th C.; demolished. 2 data pages (1939).

BACON'S CASTLE VICINITY   Surry County (91)

Bacon's Castle (VA-75), 1.2 mi. SW of Castle Mill Run, .1 mi. N of State Rte. 617, .5 mi. NE of intersection with State Rte. 10. Brick (English bond), 46'1½" (five-bay front) x 25'8", two stories, gable roof with curvilinear ends, two exterior end chimney units each consisting of three stacks set diagonally to each other, S two-story closed porch with N two-story stair tower; brick, two-story additions to the E. Built mid 17th C.; alterations and additions 19th C. Seized and fortified in Bacon's Rebellion, 1676-77. 22 sheets (1940, including plot plan, plans, elevations, sections, details); 14 ext. photos (1937, 1940, including two photos of quarters), 15 int. photos (1937, 1940); 5 data pages (1937, 1940). NHL

BARHAMSVILLE   New Kent County (64)

Union Level (VA-442), .3 mi. W of Richardson Swamp, .2 mi. NE of State Rte. 633, .3 mi. NE of intersection with State Rte. 168. Frame with clapboarding, rectangular (three-bay front), one-and-a-half stories, gable roof with dormers, two exterior end chimneys with pent closet, rear porch; rear ell. Built mid 18th C.; later additions. 2 ext. photos (c. 1934); 1 data page (n.d.).

BARHAMSVILLE VICINITY   New Kent County (64)

Smokehouse (VA-541), .7 mi. W of Davis Pond, .3 mi. NW of State Rte. 30, .8 mi. NE of intersection with State Rte. 633. Frame with clapboarding, approx. square, one story, peaked roof with finial. Built mid 18th C.; ruinous. 1 ext. photo (n.d.).

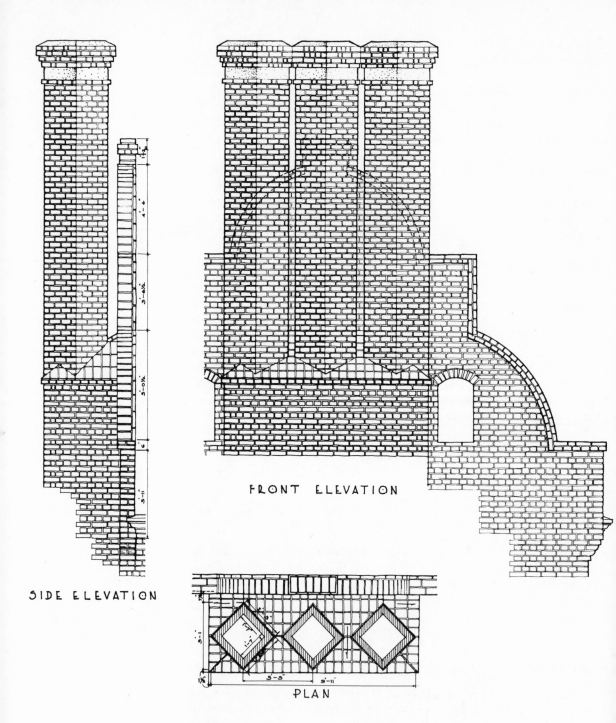

SIDE ELEVATION

FRONT ELEVATION

PLAN

Bacon's Castle

60

Bacon's Castle

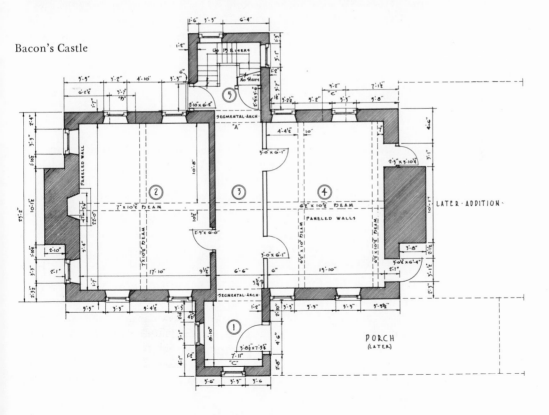

Dewberry (VA-752), .2 mi. SE of Little River, 1 mi. N of State Rte. 684, 1 mi. E of intersection with State Rte. 601. Brick, rectangular (three-bay front), two-and-a-half stories above raised basement, hipped roof with dormer, two interior end chimneys, three-part windows, projecting cross-gable pavilion in rear; center-hall plan, flanking two-story one-bay wings with hipped roofs, connected to central block by hyphens. Built early 19th C.; later additions; dormer removed. 2 ext. photos (1936), 1 int. photo (1936).

Edgewood (VA-749), .95 mi. N of Newfound River, .4 mi. E of State Rte. 671, 1.6 mi. N of intersection with State Rte. 668. Brick, rectangular (three-bay front), two stories, hipped roof, three interior end chimneys; three-room plan, side stair vestibule; frame side-wing; brick doctor's office. Built late 18th C.; wing added late 19th C. 2 ext. photos (1936), 2 int. photos (1936).

Mount Olivet Baptist Church (VA-750), .6 mi. S of S branch of Newfound River, SW side of State Rte. 671, .8 mi. S of intersection with State Rte. 668. Brick, rectangular (two-bay front), two stories, gable roof, gable-end front with two entrances, three-bay nave. Built 1849; side additions. 1 ext. photo (1936).

BELLAMY VICINITY   Gloucester County (37)

Baytop (VA-744), see Capahosic House (VA-744), Bellamy Vicinity.

Capahosic House (Baytop) (VA-744), .1 mi. E of York River, S side of State Rte. 618, opposite intersection with State Rte. 662. Brick, rectangular (three-bay front), two stories, gable roof with jerkinheads, two interior end chimneys, modillion cornice, brick belt course; center-hall plan. Built early 18th C.; later addition. 2 ext. photos (1937); HABSI (1959).

BENA VICINITY   Gloucester County (37)

Little England (VA-515), SE bank of Sarah Creek at York River, .2 mi. W of W end of State Rte. 672, 1.2 mi. W of intersection with State Rte. 642. Brick (Flemish bond), rectangular (five-bay front), two-and-a-half stories above raised basement, gable roof with dormers, two interior end chimneys, modillion cornice, brick belt course and water table; center-hall plan; one-and-a-half story flanking wings. Built mid 18th C.; wings added mid 20th C. 1 ext. photo (1940); HABSI (1959).

BERRYVILLE VICINITY
Clarke County (22)

Clifton (VA-725), .4 mi. N of State Rte. 610, .4 mi. N of intersection with U.S. Rte. 340. Brick with stucco, rectangular (five-bay front), two stories above raised basement, hipped roof, two interior chimneys, NW front with Palladian window in recessed arched bay over wooden one-story pedimented entrance porch with paired Ionic columns, SE front with two-story tetrastyle pedimented Roman Doric portico; center-hall plan, notable interior trim; stone dependency: two stories, gable roof; stone ice house: circular plan with conical wooden shingle roof. Built early 19th C. 2 ext. photos (1936), 1 ext. photo, outbuilding (1936); HABSI (1958).

BIRDHAVEN VICINITY
Shenandoah County (86)

Barb Water Mill (VA-137), bank of Elks Run, exact location unknown. Working platform of timbers carrying saw, driving machinery, including overshot water wheel 4'6" in width, 17'2" in diameter, located below, little or no protection from weather. Built c. 1790 as vertical action metal saw driven by flutter wheel, first overshot wheel installed 1880; circular saw introduced and second overshot wheel constructed c. 1924. 1 ext. photo (n.d.); 3 data pages (n.d.).

BLACKSTONE
Nottoway County (68)

Anderson House (VA-813), see Schwartz Tavern (VA-813), Blackstone.

Schwartz Tavern (Anderson House) (VA-813), 111 Tavern St. Frame with clapboarding, rectangular (three-bay front), one-and-a-half stories, gable roof with dormers, two exterior end chimneys; W wing: frame, rectangular (two-bay front), one-and-a-half stories, gable roof with dormers; E wing: frame, rectangular (two-bay front), one-and-a-half stories, gable roof with dormers, one interior chimney, one-story hyphen with three-part bow projection on N. Built late 18th C.; dormers and both wings added 19th C. 1 ext. photo (1936).

Brass

IRON PADLOCK

BLOXOM VICINITY
Accomack County (1)

Hinman-Mason House (VA-630), see Mason House (VA-630), Bloxom Vicinity.

Mason House (Hinman-Mason House) (VA-630), N bank of Guilford Creek, .4 mi. NW of State Rte. 658, .1 mi. N of intersection with State Rte. 187. Brick with timber frame, 42′ (three-bay front) x 23′, one-and-a-half stories, gable roof with dormers, two interior end chimneys; center-hall plan; frame two-story rear addition. Built early 18th C.; additions mid 19th C. 6 ext. photos (1940, 1960), 17 int. photos (1940, 1960); 3 data pages (1960, 1962).

BOWLING GREEN   Caroline County (17)

Caroline County Courthouse (VA-718), SE corner of intersection of U.S. Rte. 301 and Courthouse Lane. Brick, rectangular (four-bay front), two stories, gable roof, square wooden belfry, four interior end chimneys, four-bay open arcade on ground floor with semi-circular brick arches with stone keystones, Tuscan entablature, pedimented gable end with semi-circular lunette; one-room temple plan. Built early 19th C.; belfry added. 3 ext. photos (1936); HABSI (1957).

Old Mansion (VA-128), .2 mi. W of State Rte. 2 (U.S. Rte. 301), .4 mi. S of intersection with State Rte. 207. Brick (Flemish bond), 47′ (five-bay front) x 30′, one-and-a-half stories, gambrel roof with jerkin-heads, two interior end chimneys, modillion cornice, molded brick water table, full length one-story entrance porch; center-hall plan, corner fireplaces; rear ell: frame with clapboarding, rectangular (five-bay front), one-and-a-half stories, gambrel roof with dormers, one exterior end chimney, modillion cornice, two-room plan. Brick section built late 17th C.; frame ell built late 18th C.; interior trim partially altered early 19th C.; entrance porch added mid 19th C. 16 sheets (1936, including plans, elevations, sections, details); 4 ext. photos (1936), 4 int. photos (1936); 7 data pages (1936); HABSI (1957). NR

Old Mansion

Mulberry Place (VA-719), .8 mi. W of Tanyard Swamp, .9 mi. S of State Rte. 721, .3 mi. SE of intersection with State Rte. 2 (U.S. Rte. 301). Brick, rectangular (five-bay front), two stories, hipped roof, four interior end chimneys, one-story wooden entrance porch with paired square posts, flat deck and balustrade; center-hall plan; kitchen: brick, rectangular (two-bay front), one story, gable roof, one exterior end chimney, brick sawtooth cornice; one-room plan. Built 1827. 1 ext. photo (1936), 1 ext. photo, kitchen (1936); HABSI (1957).

Oak Ridge (VA-720), .5 mi. SW of Elliot's Pond, .4 mi. E of U.S. Rte. 301, .9 mi. S of intersection with State Rte. 207. Brick (Flemish bond), rectangular (five-bay front), one-and-a-half stories, gable roof with dormers, two interior chimneys, wooden box cornice with diamond pattern frieze, arched entrance transom with wooden swag muntins, fretted architrave and carved and paneled door surround with reeded pilasters supporting fretted entablature, molded brick water table; center-hall plan, notable interior trim and plaster work over mantel. Built c. 1800; minor interior alterations; ruinous. 3 ext. photos (1936), 2 int. photos (1936).

BOYCE   Clarke County (22)

Summerville (VA-180), S bank of Page Run, near NW side U.S. Rte. 340. Frame with clapboarding, rectangular (seven-bay front), two stories, gable roof, pediment over three central bays, two interior end chimneys, low entrance porch of coupled columns with parapet; cross-hall plan. Built early 19th C.; burned 1932; restored. 3 sheets (1940, including foundation plans, restoration drawings); 1 ext. photocopy (n.d.); 1 data page (1941).

BOYCE VICINITY   Clarke County (22)

Annefield (VA-256), .2 mi. W of Chapel Run, .1 mi. N of State Rte. 633, 1.4 mi. W of intersection with U.S. Rte. 340. Stone, rectangular (seven-bay front), two stories, hipped roof with flat deck and balustrade, four interior end chimneys, modillion cornice, two-story wooden tetrastyle Ionic entrance portico with modillion pediment and Chinese fret balcony railing at second-floor level; center-hall plan, center hall with modillion and denticulated Ionic entablature supported by fluted Ionic pilasters, notable interior trim in principal ground-floor rooms. Built 1790, later rear additions. 4 ext. photos (1936); 1 data page (1941); HABSI (1958). NR

Saratoga

Old Chapel (VA-352), N bank of Chapel Run, W side of State Rte. 255, at intersection with U.S. Rte. 340. Stone, rectangular (three-bay front), one story, gable roof, interior chimney; one-room plan. Built late 18th C. 1 ext. photocopy (n.d.); 1 data page (1941); HABSI (1958).

Saratoga (VA-246), S bank of Roseville Run, at confluence of Westbrook Run, .4 mi. SW of State Rte. 723, .4 mi. SE of intersection with U.S. Rte. 340. Stone, rectangular (five-bay front), two-and-a-half stories, gable roof with dormers; two interior end chimneys, modillion cornice, one-story tetrastyle wooden entrance porch with arched window above; center-hall plan; smokehouse: frame with clapboarding, rectangular, pyramidal roof. Built 1781; later additions. 2 ext. photos, outbuildings (1936); 1 ext. photocopy (n.d.); 1 data page (1941); HABSI (1958). NR

BRANDY STATION VICINITY   Culpeper County (24)

Little Fork Church (VA-147), .8 mi. N of Hazel River, NE corner of intersection of State Rtes. 624 and 726. Brick, 83'1" (seven-bay lateral facade) x 36'3", one story, hipped roof, modillion cornice, arched window heads, rubbed brick dressings; one-room plan, notable interior trim including original reredos. Built 1774-76, attributed to John Ariss, architect. 3 sheets (1936, including plans, elevations); HABSI (1958). NR

BREMO BLUFF VICINITY   Fluvanna County (33)

Bremo (VA-302), .3 mi. N of James River, 2.4 mi. W of U.S. Rte. 15, .9 mi. N of intersection with State Rte. 656. Brick, rectangular (five-bay front), one story, hipped roof with deck, balustrade at eaves, four interior chimneys, pedimented Tuscan portico on N front, recessed Tuscan portico on S front, E and W Tuscan entrance porticoes; entrance hall with cross-hall plan; two end pavilions: brick, rectangular (one-bay front), one story above high basement, gable roof with pedimented Tuscan portico, connected to main central block by raised terraces; barn: stone, T-shaped plan, two-story, hipped roof, cupola, pedimented stone Tuscan portico; stone stable, brick lodge, brick gardener's house, stone Doric Temperance Spring, two pisé

Bremo

Bremo, Barn

Bremo, Schoolhouse

servants' quarters. Completed by 1820 from designs by owner-builder John Hartwell Cocke (1780-1866), who was influenced by St. George Tucker, Thomas Jefferson, James Dinsmore and John Neilson, the last of whom drafted the final designs; original flat roof replaced by present design 1836. 9 ext. photos (n.d., 1940), 10 ext. photos, outbuildings (1940), 6 int. photos (1940), 2 int. photos, schoolhouse (1940); 1 photo of Temperance vase (1940); 2 data pages (1940); HABSI (1958). NR

BRENTSVILLE VICINITY   Prince William County (76)

Brent House (VA-553), see The White House (VA-553), Manassas Vicinity, Prince William Co.

Old House (VA-554), see Moor Green (VA-554), Manassas Vicinity, Prince William Co.

BRIDGETOWN VICINITY   Northampton County (66)

Belote (VA-544), see Wester House (West House) (VA-544), Bridgetown Vicinity.

Hungar's Church (VA-542), .1 mi. N of NE tributary of Hungar Creek, S side of State Rte. 619, .2 mi. E of intersection with State Rte. 622. Brick (Flemish bond), rectangular (two-bay front), one story, gable roof, two entrances on gable-end front, arched nave windows and entrances. Built c. 1751; structure repaired 1840; shortened from approx. 92' to 74'8" in 1851; renovated and repaired 1922, 1950, 1955. 2 ext. photos (c. 1934, 1940); HABSI (1958). NR

Vaucluse (VA-437), NW bank of Hungar Creek, S end of State Rte. 619, 1.8 mi. S of intersection with State Rte. 657. Brick with frame fronts, rectangular (eight-bay front), two stories, gable roof, one interior chimney and two interior end chimneys, two pedimented entrance porches; center-hall plan; side wing; kitchen ell; icehouse. W four bays between two original chimneys built late 18th C.; additions early 19th C.; two-story S porch added recently. Home of Abel Parker Upshur who served as Secretary of Navy and Secretary of State. 2 ext. photos (c. 1936, 1940); HABSI (1958). NR

West House (VA-544), see Wester House (Belote) (VA-544), Bridgetown Vicinity.

Wester House (Belote, West House) (VA-544), W bank of Westerhouse Creek, .6 mi. N of State Rte. 619, .4 mi. W of intersection with State Rte. 657. Brick (Flemish bond), rectangular (three-bay front), one story, gable roof, two exterior end chimneys; center-hall plan. Built mid 18th C.; W end rebuilt 19th C.; interior ruinous. 3 sheets (1971, including site plan, plan, elevations); 1 ext. photo, chimney (1940).

Winona (VA-543), N bank of Hungar Creek, .7 mi. S of State Rte. 619, .4 mi. NW of intersection with State Rte. 622. Brick (Flemish bond), rectangular (two-bay front), one-and-a-half stories, gable roof with dormers, one end chimney with three stacks set diagonally to each other; side-hall plan; two one-story frame flanking wings. Built late 17th C.; wing additions; altered and renovated. 8 sheets (1971, including plans, elevations, sections, details); 2 ext. photos (1940); HABSI (1958). NR

Winona

Mountain View (VA-291), 6421 Bull Run Post Office Rd. Two units at right angles, first unit: log and frame with clapboarding, rectangular (three-bay front), one-and-a-half stories, gable roof double pitched in front and extended to cover porch, one interior stone chimney; notable interior trim and original hardware; second unit: stone, rectangular (four-bay front), two stories, gable roof, large exterior stone chimney, two-story porch with balcony on two sides; rooms adjacent in plan, no corridors. Built mid 18th C.; later alterations; ruinous condition 1969. 3 ext. photos (1936); HABSI (1958).

Sudley (VA-427), .3 mi. E of Bull Run on Sudley Rd., 1 mi. W of intersection with State Rte. 621. Frame with clapboarding, rectangular (three-bay front), two stories, hipped roof, projecting second-floor room with pedimented gable roof supported by paired square wooden columns which create front porch; rectangular plan; rear ell. Built early 19th C.; later additions and alterations; demolished. 2 ext. photos (1936).

CABIN POINT   Surry County (91)

Ordinary, The (VA-236), SE corner of intersection of State Rtes. 10 and 613. Frame with clapboarding, rectangular (four-bay front), one-and-a-half stories above high brick basement, gable roof with dormers, two exterior end chimneys; rear lean-to. Built late 18th C. 1 ext. photo (1937); HABSI (1958).

CAPEVILLE VICINITY   Northampton County (66)

Arlington (VA-811), S bank of Old Plantation Creek, .1 mi. N of State Rte. 644, .8 mi. NW of intersection with State Rte. 645. Frame with clapboarding, rectangular (three-bay front), two stories, gable roof, two interior end chimneys; side-hall plan; raised stone tombs with incised inscriptions and swag decoration. Main house built early 19th C. 3 ext. photos, Custis Tombs (1960); HABSI, main house (1958).

CATHARPIN VICINITY   Prince William County (76)

Log Cabin (VA-287), 1 mi. N of Lick Branch, E side of State Rte. 701, .6 mi. N of intersection with State Rte. 234. Log, rectangular (two-bay front), one story, gable roof, one stone exterior end chimney; one-room plan. Built early 19th C.; demolished. 3 ext. photos (1936).

Bowlers (VA-728), W bank of Rappahannock River, N side of State Rte. 684, 2.1 mi. NE of intersection with U.S. Rte. 17. Frame with clapboarding, rectangular (three-bay front), one-and-a-half stories, gable roof with dormers, two exterior end chimneys; center-hall plan; kitchen: frame with clapboarding, rectangular, one story, gable roof, one exterior end chimney. Built early 18th C.; later additions and alterations; kitchen demolished. 3 ext. photos (1936), 1 ext. photo, kitchen (1936), 1 int. photo (1936); HABSI (1958).

Mount Verde (VA-729), see Omnium Hill (VA-729), Center Cross Vicinity.

Omnium Hill (Mount Verde) (VA-729), .8 mi. SW of Rappahannock River, .2 mi. SW of State Rte. 660, .4 mi. SE of intersection with State Rte. 684. Frame with clapboarding, rectangular (four-bay front), two stories, gable roof, two exterior end chimneys; center-hall plan; one-story N wing. Built late 18th C.; altered; additional mid 20th C. 1 ext. photo (1936), 1 int. photo (1936); HABSI (1958).

Jammeson, Malcolm, House (VA-280), see Mount Gilead (VA-280), Centreville.

Mount Gilead (Malcolm Jammeson House) (VA-280), 5634 Mount Gilead Rd. Frame with clapboarding, rectangular (three-bay front), one-and-a-half stories, gable roof with dormers, two exterior stone chimneys, one-story wooden entrance porch; center-hall plan. Built c. 1750; additions and alterations 1936, 1952. 1 ext. photo (1936); HABSI's (1958, 1969).

Meat House (VA-282), exact location unknown. Frame with horizontal planks and chinking, stone foundations, square (one-bay front), one story, pyramidal roof with wooden shingles. Built mid 18th C.; demolished. 1 ext. photo (1936).

Fonthill (VA-330), 1.2 mi. S of Occupacia Creek, .1 mi. N of State Rte. 631, 1.7 mi. SW of intersection with U.S. Rte. 17. Frame with clapboarding, rectangular (five-bay front), two stories, gable roof, two exterior end chimneys, one-story entrance porch with paired supports and lattice railing; center-hall plan; flanking one-story wings. Built early 19th C. 1 ext. photo (1939); 1 data page (1941).

St. Anne's Parish Glebe (VA-232), .1 mi. NW of Farmers Hall Creek, .8 mi. SE of State Rte. 632, 3 mi. E of intersection with State Rte. 633, .4 mi. S of intersection with U.S. Rte. 17. Brick (Flemish bond), rectangular (three-bay front), two stories, gable roof, two interior end chimneys, gauged flat brick arches over windows and doors, raking row of glazed brick headers on gable ends, beveled brick water table; center-hall plan, notable trim on chimney breast of W room. Built mid 18th C.; major portion of interior trim dismantled 1967. 2 ext. photos (1939); 1 data page (1941); HABSI (1958).

CHANCELLORSVILLE   Spotsylvania County (89)

Chancellorsville (VA-77), 1.1 mi. NE of Lewis River, NW corner of intersection of State Rtes. 3 and 610. Brick ruins remain from original structure: rectangular (five-bay front), two stories, steep gable roof, two interior end chimneys, full-length two-level porch; flanking wings: brick, rectangular (three-bay front), two stories, hipped roof, wings projected from plane of central block and flanked central porch. Built 1816; partially destroyed by Confederate gunfire May 3, 1863; rebuilt c. 1870: brick, rectangular (six-bay front), two-and-a-half stories, mansard roof with dormers, E three bays of facade set back with two-level porch; burned 1927; remaining walls blown down 1947. 11 sheets (1935, including plans, elevations, details); 5 ext. photos (n.d., 1934, 1935); 3 data pages (n.d.).

CHANTILLY VICINITY   Fairfax County (30)

Leeton (VA-599), Dulles International Airport Site. Brick, rectangular (three-bay front), two-and-a-half stories, hipped roof with dormers, two exterior end chimneys; side-hall plan. Built early 19th C.; extensive later alterations; demolished 1960. 2 ext. photos (1959); 2 data pages (1961); HABSI (1958).

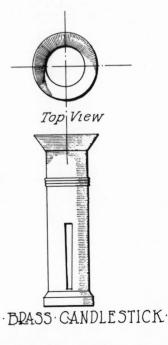

Top View

·BRASS·CANDLESTICK·

Sully Plantation (VA-250), 3601 Sully Rd. Historic house museum. Frame with clapboarding, original section 33′7″ (three-bay front) x 37′8″, two-and-a-half stories, gable roof with dormers, two exterior end chimneys; side-hall plan; one-and-a-half story frame addition; notable outbuildings include stone patent house and smokehouse. Built 1794, attributed to James Wren, Fairfax County builder-architect; later additions 19th C. 17 sheets (1960, including site plan, plans, elevations, details of main house; plan, elevations of patent house; plan, elevation of kitchen-laundry); 16 ext. photos, main house (1936, 1960), 4 ext. photos, patent house (1960), 4 ext. photos, kitchen-laundry (1960), 2 ext. photos, smokehouse (1936, 1960), 1 ext. photo, outbuilding (1960), 16 int. photos, main house (1960), 3 int. photos, kitchen-laundry (1960), 1 ext. photocopy (1890); 7 data pages (1961); HABSI (1958). NR

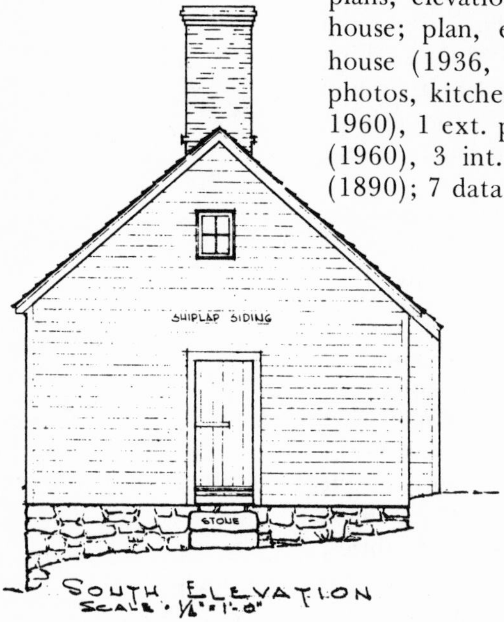

Sully Plantation

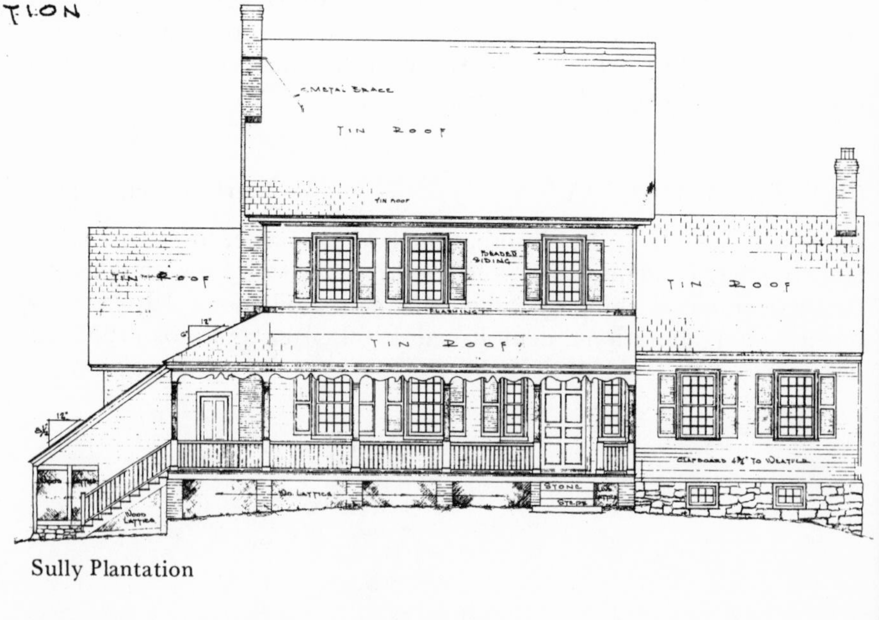

Sully Plantation

Charles City County Courthouse (VA-60), .8 mi. N of Queens Creek, S side of State Rte. 5, .2 mi. W of intersection with State Rte. 155. Brick, T-shaped (three-bay S front), one story, hipped roof, two interior chimneys, segmental arched windows, modillion cornice. Built mid 18th C.; original full-length five-bay arcaded porch sheltered main entrance on N in a structural form similar to courthouses in King William, Hanover, and other counties which it predates; porch bricked-in with windows placed in former openings and entrance moved to S front. 2 ext. photos (1937); 1 data page (1937). NR

Berkeley (VA-363), .3 mi. N of James River, .7 mi. S of State Rte. 633, .3 mi. SE of intersection with State Rte. 5. Brick, rectangular (five-bay front), two-and-a-half stories, gable roof with dormers, two interior chimneys, pedimented gable ends, modillion cornice, two-story three-bay portico combined with front and side one-story porch; center-hall plan. Built c. 1726; altered with additions; porch and portico removed in restoration. Birthplace of Benjamin Harrison, signer of the Declaration of Independence and Governor of Virginia (1781-1784), and of his son, William Henry Harrison (1773-1841), ninth President of the United States. 3 ext. photos (1934, 1935), 2 int. photos (1934, 1935); 1 data page (1941).

Farmington (VA-95), .9 mi. S of Morris Creek, 1.1 mi. E of State Rte. 5, 1.3 mi. SE of intersection with State Rte. 614. Frame with clapboarding, 54'4" (five-bay front) x 35'4", one-and-a-half stories, gable roof with hipped dormers, two exterior end chimneys; center-hall plan; rear lean-to. Built late 18th C.; lean-to added later and recently removed; ruinous. 11 sheets (1935, including plans, elevations, sections, details).

Glebe House (VA-723), .3 mi. SE of Glebe Creek, .2 mi. W of State Rte. 615, 1.6 mi. NE of State Rte. 5. Brick, rectangular (five-bay front), one-and-a-half stories, gable roof with dormers, two exterior end chimneys; center-hall plan; rear one-story hipped-roof structure connected to main block by hyphen. Built mid 18th C.; alterations and additions 19th and 20th C. 2 ext. photos (1937), 1 int. photo (1937); HABSI (1958).

Berkeley

Greenway (VA-23), .3 mi. W of Courthouse Creek, .1 mi. N of State Rte. 5, .6 mi. W of intersection with State Rte. 155. Frame with clapboarding, 56′4¾″ (five-bay front) x 18′3¾″, one-and-a-half stories, gable roof with dormers, two exterior end chimneys; center-hall plan; rear ell. Built late 18th C.; additions. Birthplace and childhood home of President John Tyler. 17 sheets (1934, including plot plan, plans, elevations, sections, details of main house; plan, elevation, details of plantation office); 7 ext. photos (c. 1934, 1935, 1937), 3 ext. photos, outbuildings (c. 1934, 1935), 2 int. photos (1934); 8 data pages (1936); HABSI (1958). NR

House (Indian Field) (VA-376), exact location unknown. Frame with clapboarding, rectangular (three-bay front), two stories, gable roof, one exterior end chimney; side wing: frame with clapboarding, rectangular (two-bay front), one-and-a-half stories, gable roof with dormers, two exterior end chimneys with frame pent closet between; rear ell. Side wing built mid 18th C.; later additions. 1 ext. photo (c. 1934).

Indian Field (VA-376), see House (VA-376), Charles City Vicinity.

Lower Weyanoke (VA-290), see Weyanoke (VA-290), Charles City Vicinity.

Rowe, The (VA-142), E bank of James River, .2 mi. SW of State Rte. 613, .9 mi. SW of intersection with State Rte. 623. Frame with clapboarding, three-part composition; central block: rectangular (three-bay front), two stories, gable roof, one interior chimney, pedimented gable-end front; two flanking wings: rectangular (three-bay front), one-and-a-half stories, gable roof with dormers, one exterior end chimney. Built late 18th C. 2 ext. photos (1937); 1 data page (1940).

Sherwood Forest (VA-722), 1.5 mi. N of James River, .2 mi. S of State Rte. 5, 2 mi. E of intersection with State Rte. 619 (Weyanoke Rd.). Frame with clapboarding, seven-part composition; central block: rectangular (five-bay front), one-and-a-half stories, gable roof with dormers, two exterior end chimneys; center-hall plan; two attached wings: one-and-a-half stories, gable roofs, exterior end chimneys; two

Greenway

Shirley

hyphens connect outer one-story blocks with the attached wings; outbuildings include dairy and smokehouse. Built late 18th C.; additions and alterations 19th C. Home of President John Tyler. 2 ext. photos (1937). NR

Shirley (VA-388), .1 mi. E of James River, .4 mi. SW of State Rte. 608, 1.5 mi. W of intersection with State Rte. 5. Brick, 48′6″ square (five-bay front), two-and-a-half stories, mansard roof with dormers, two interior chimneys, two-level pedimented porticoes on N and S fronts, modillion cornice; four-room plan, extensive interior paneling, suspended stair with scrolled soffit; two brick L-shaped barn dependencies form outer forecourt; frame quarters; brick dove cote, smokehouse, stable, and log shed outbuildings. Dependencies built c. 1740; main house built 1769; porches early 19th C. 3 ext. photos

(c. 1934, 1935), 8 ext. photos, outbuildings (1934, 1937, 1938), 2 int. photos (1937); 3 data pages (1941). NR

Dependencies (VA-364), .1 mi. E of James River, .4 mi. SW of State Rte. 608, 1.5 mi. W of intersection with State Rte. 5. Brick, rectangular (five-bay fronts), two stories, gable roofs with splayed eaves, pedimented gable ends, two interior end chimneys, modillion cornices, segmental arched window design; center-hall plans. Built c. 1740; the two structures form the inner forecourt N of the mansion. 2 ext. photos (1934, 1935).

Westover (VA-402), N bank of James River, at E end of State Rte. 633 extended, 2.4 mi. SE of intersection with State Rte. 5. Brick, rectangular (seven-bay front), two-and-a-half stories, steep hipped roof with dormers, four interior end chimneys, segmental arched windows, Portland stone entrances; modified center-hall plan, exceptional interiors with imported carved mantels and elaborate plaster ceilings; W wing: brick, rectangular (three-bay front), one-and-a-half stories, gable roof with dormers, two interior end chimneys, hyphen connects it to main block; E wing: brick, rectangular (four-bay front), one-and-a-half stories, gambrel roof with dormers, hyphen connects it to main block; two fine wrought-iron entrance gates. Main block built c. 1730 by William Byrd II, but W wing may pre-date it; E wing burned during the Civil War and rebuilt; entire house renovated 1900. 4 ext. photos (1939), 4 int. photos (1939); 1 data page (1940).   NR

Weyanoke (Lower Weyanoke) (VA-290), .5 mi. NW of James River, .1 mi. S of S end of State Rte. 619 (Weyanoke Rd.), 4 mi. S of intersection with State Rte. 5. Frame with clapboarding, rectangular (five-bay front), two-and-a-half stories, hipped roof with dormers, four interior end chimneys, modillion cornice; center-hall plan, Chinese Chippendale stair railing; frame two-story wings with connecting hyphens. Built mid 18th C.; wings added 20th C. 1 ext. photo (1937), 1 int. photo (1937); 2 data pages (n.d.); HABSI (1958).

Westover

University of Virginia (VA-193), S of intersection of University Ave. and Rugby Rd. The Rotunda: brick (Flemish bond), circular, 77′ in diameter (five-bay front), with esplanades extending from either side of N and S fronts, two stories above high basement with attic, domed roof, two-story pedimented Corinthian porticoes on N and S fronts, Corinthian entablature surrounding entire structure at top of second story, cornice surrounding top of attic; one-room plan, domed room encircled by Corinthian colonnade supporting entablature, two galleries behind colonnade. Begun 1823, completed 1826, Thomas Jefferson, architect; original building destroyed by fire 1895, only brick walls survived; structure as it exists today is the result of the rebuilding (1898-1902) by Stanford White, architect; White's departures from Jefferson's original design include the addition of the N portico, the N esplanades, the E and W colonnades, and the present

University of Virginia, Rotunda   University of Virginia, Rotunda

arrangement of interior. Jefferson's interior consisted of two floors rather than one, with center hall and three oval rooms on the first floor, a circular domed library on the second containing a circular composite colonnade. Two-story annex with Corinthian portico added to N front of Rotunda 1853, Robert Mills, architect; destroyed in fire of 1895. Perpendicular to the S front of the Rotunda are four ranges of brick buildings. The two inner ranges each consist of five, two-story pavilions connected by one-story Tuscan colonnades, behind which are individual student rooms. The pavilions vary in design, and each displays one of the three principal orders of Roman architecture. Each was designed to contain a classroom on the first floor, a faculty apartment on the second, and kitchen and service area in the basement. The two outer ranges of buildings each consist of three "Hotels" or dining halls with basement kitchens and service areas. The Hotels are connected by one-story arcades behind which are additional student rooms. Gardens enclosed by serpentine walls are placed between the inner and outer ranges of buildings. Together with the Rotunda, this complex of structures formed the original portion of the University of Virginia as designed by Thomas Jefferson. This "Academical Village" served as the prototype for many institutions of higher learning in the United States. The four ranges of buildings were erected 1817-26. In spite of renovations, alterations, and additions, the basic concept and much of the original fabric survive intact. The Rotunda is currently (1974) undergoing restoration to the Jefferson design. 12 ext. photos, including details of pavilions, ranges, and serpentine walls (1933, 1937). NR; NHL

CHARLOTTESVILLE VICINITY   Albemarle County (2)

Carrsbrook (VA-150), .2 mi. S of South Fork River, .3 mi. NE of State Rte. 631, .4 mi. E of intersection with U.S. Rte. 29. Frame with clapboarding, rectangular (three-bay front), two stories, gable roof, one interior chimney, pedimented gable-end front, pedimented entrance porch; one-room plan with rear hall connecting with wings; two flanking wings: rectangular (one-bay front), one story, gable roof, pedimented gable-end front, connected to central block by hyphens. Built 1791; rear additions, renovated. 4 ext. photos (n.d.), 1 int. photo (n.d.); 1 data page (1939).

Farmington (Farmington Country Club) (VA-253), 1 mi. SE of Ivy Creek, .7 mi. N of U.S. Rte. 250, .9 mi. W of intersection with U.S. Rte. 250-29 Bypass. Brick, rectangular (three-bay front), two stories, gable roof, two interior end chimneys; side-hall plan; two-story octa-

Carrsbrook

gon attached to E side, one two-story room in octagon; hipped roof with deck and pedimented Tuscan portico on E front, two interior end chimneys, modillion cornice, circular second-floor windows; W service wing. Original block built mid 18th C. with main front facing N; E octagonal addition built c. 1802, Thomas Jefferson, architect, at which time E front became main facade; remodeled mid 19th C.; enlargements and extensive W and S additions 1929 after property was acquired by Farmington Country Club in 1927. 1 ext. photo (1938). NR

Farmington Country Club (VA-253), see Farmington (VA-253), Charlottesville Vicinity.

Monticello (VA-241), .6 mi. NE of State Rte. 53, 1.2 mi. E of intersection with State Rte. 20. Historic house museum. Brick (Flemish bond), 110'9" (nine-bay front) x 97'6" with octagonal ended projection in center of W front and recessed portico on E front, octagonal ended projections at each corner connected by enclosed loggias, two stories, deck-on-hip roof with octagonal dome on W front, four interior chimneys, pedimented Doric porticoes on E and W fronts with Doric entablature surrounding entire structure; plan features E entrance hall with drawing room and flanking dining room, bed-

Monticello

rooms, study, and library; richly decorated entablature and mantels in entrance hall, drawing room, master bedroom, and dining room; L-shaped esplanades connected to either side of main block which shelter basement, service, and storage areas, esplanades terminated on N by law office and on S by guest cottage. Monticello is an excellent personal expression and record of the taste and skill of its architect-builder-owner: Thomas Jefferson. Guest cottage built 1769-70; main structure evolved to present appearance 1770-1808, Thomas Jefferson, architect; structural renovations made 1953-54. 8 ext. photos (1937, 1940); 1 data page (1940). NR; NHL

CHATHAM   Pittsylvania County (72)

Pittsylvania County Courthouse (VA-271), .3 mi. W of Tanyard Branch of Cherrystone Creek, E side of intersection of State Rte. 57 and U.S. Rte. 29, .3 mi. N of intersection with State Rte. 832. Brick, rectangular (five-bay front), one story above high basement, gable roof, pedimented Doric portico, square clock tower; center courtroom with row of small rooms and offices on either side. Built 1853, L. A. Shumaker, architect. 2 ext. photos (1940); 1 data page (1941).

CHERITON VICINITY   Northampton County (66)

Eyre Hall (VA-809), .1 mi. N of Eyrehall Creek, 1.2 mi. W of intersection of U.S. Rte. 13 and State Rte. 636, 1.6 mi. N of intersection with State Rte. 680. Frame with clapboarding, rectangular (three-bay front), one-and-a-half stories, gambrel roof with dormers, three interior end chimneys, one interior chimney, wooden pedimented side porches; side-hall plan; long two-story side wing; notable wooden garden fence and brick and picket garden wall; brick overseer's house and orangery ruins; frame with clapboarding dairy and smokehouse; graveyard. Built mid 18th C.; incorporates earlier building; later additions; overseer's house built late 18th C. 6 ext. photos (1960), 4 ext. photos, orangery ruins (1960), 1 ext. photo, graveyard (1960), 2 ext. photos, overseer's house (1960), 1 ext. photo, dairy (1960), 1 ext. photo, smokehouse (1960), 1 ext. photo, brick wall (1960); HABSI (1958). NR

Eyre Hall

Stratton Manor (VA-545), .2 mi. E of Old Plantation Creek, .4 mi. S of State Rte. 642, .3 mi. S of intersection with alternate U.S. Rte. 13. Brick with frame fronts, rectangular (three-bay front), one-and-a-half stories, gable roof with dormers, two exterior end chimneys, full-length front porch; center-hall plan; rear ell. Built early 18th C.; altered with rear ell and porch additions; recent renovations include replacement of porch and addition of aluminum siding. 2 ext. photos (1940); HABSI (1958).

CHESAPEAKE VICINITY

Powers House (VA-228), .8 mi. W of Indian Creek, W side of U.S. Rte. 17, .4 mi. N of intersection with Rte. 614. Brick with frame fronts, rectangular (three-bay front), one-and-a-half stories, gambrel roof with dormers, two exterior end chimneys; frame rear ell. Built mid 18th C.; later addition; altered. 4 ext. photos (1937, 1940).

Ruins of House (VA-249), exact location unknown. Two exterior end chimneys remain from former frame building. Built mid 18th C.; demolished. 1 ext. photo (1937).

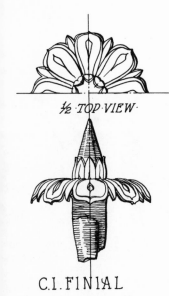

½ TOP VIEW

C.I. FINIAL

CHESCONESSEX VICINITY   Accomack County (1)

Ohio (VA-486), see Wise House (VA-486), Chesconessex Vicinity.

Revil (VA-931), see West House (VA-931), Chesconessex Vicinity.

West House (Revil) (VA-931), S side of Deep Creek, .3 mi. NE of State Rte. 657, .3 mi. SE of intersection with State Rte. 656. Frame with clapboarding and brick ends, approx. 32' (four-bay front) x 20', two stories, gambrel roof with dormers, two exterior end chimneys; two-room plan. Built mid 18th C.; demolished. 3 ext. photos (1940); 1 data page (n.d.).

Wise House (Ohio) (VA-486), SW bank of Deep Creek, .2 mi. NE of State Rte. 656, .1 mi. NE of intersection with State Rte. 657. Frame with clapboarding and brick ends, telescope-type house (ten-bay front), two stories, one-and-a-half stories and one story, gable roof with dormers in center section, two exterior end chimneys, one interior chimney; irregular plan. Earliest part built mid 18th C.; addition early 19th C. 1 ext. photo (1940).

Christ Church (VA-539), .6 mi. S of Rappahannock River, NE side of State Rte. 638, .1 mi. N of intersection with State Rte. 33. Brick (Flemish bond with glazed headers), rectangular (one-bay front), one story, gable roof, semi-circular arched windows; one-room plan, vestibule; wing. Built 1714; considerable rebuilding 1843; renovated in 1900 and 1930's; wing and vestibule additions. 1 ext. photo (c. 1934); HABSI (1959).

Gateposts (VA-800), exact location unknown, possibly .2 mi. ESE of Godwins Millpond, N side of State Rte. 125, at intersection with State Rte. 1032. Wooden, square posts with finials. Built mid 18th C.; demolished. 3 photos (1937).

Quarters, The (VA-199), .2 mi. ESE of Godwins Millpond, N side of State Rte. 125, at intersection with State Rte. 1032. Frame with clapboarding, rectangular (three-bay front), one story above high brick basement, gable roof with overhang, one exterior end chimney. Built early 19th C. 1 ext. photo (1937); HABSI (n.d.).

Pembroke (VA-181), .1 mi. NW of Nansemond River, S side of State Rte. 603, 1.9 mi. SE of intersection with State Rte. 1032. Brick, U-shaped (five-bay front), one-and-a-half stories, gable roof with hipped dormers, four interior end chimneys, porch on land front; center-hall plan. Built early 18th C.; interior burned during War of 1812; renovated and restored 1940, now has gable dormers, interior woodwork replaced, land front porch filled in as cross hall, screen porch added on river front. 5 sheets (1929, including plans, elevations, conjectural restoration); 5 ext. photos (1937, n.d.); 1 data page (1941); HABSI (1958).

House (VA-517), near La Grange Creek, exact location unknown. Frame with clapboarding, rectangular (three-bay front), one-and-a-half stories, gable roof, two interior chimneys, one interior end chimney, rear lean-to. Built early 18th C.; extensive later additions and alterations; ruinous 1940; demolished. 1 ext. photo (1940).

La Grange (VA-516), near La Grange Creek, exact location unknown. Frame with clapboarding, rectangular (three-bay front), one-and-a-half stories, gable roof with dormers, two exterior end chimneys with pent closets; center-hall plan. Built mid 18th C.; demolished. 1 ext. photo (1940).

CLAREMONT VICINITY   Surry County (91)

Brickwork (VA-390), see House (VA-390), Claremont Vicinity.

Claremont Manor Office (VA-430), .2 mi. S of the mouth of Upper Chippokes Creek on the James River, 1.1 mi. NW of State Rte. 613, .1 mi. W of intersection with State Rte. 609. Brick (Flemish bond with glazed headers), rectangular (three-bay front), one-and-a-half stories, gable roof with dormer, one interior corner chimney, modillion cornice. Built early 18th C.; altered. 1 ext. photo (c. 1934).

House (Brickwork) (VA-390), 1 mi. S of Upper Chippokes Creek, E side of State Rte. 10, SE of intersection with State Rte. 613. Frame with clapboarding and brick nogging, rectangular (three-bay front), one-and-a-half stories above brick (English bond), foundation, gable roof with dormers, two exterior end chimneys, some Dutch sized brick (1¾" x 7¼" x 3½") in chimneys, some oversized brick in foundation (3" x 9" x 4¼"). Built early 18th C. 1 ext. photo, foundation wall (c. 1934).

Hotel Cottages

CLARKSVILLE VICINITY   Mecklenburg County (59)

Hotel Cottages (VA-186), .5 mi. W of Buffalo Creek, .1 mi. W of State Rte. 767, .2 mi. N of intersection with U.S. Rte. 58. Frame with clapboarding, line of double unit cottages each being rectangular (four-bay front), one story, gable roof, central chimney. Built early 19th C.; demolished. 1 ext. photo (1940); HABSI (1958).

Prestwould (VA-320), .1 mi. N of Roanoke River, .7 mi. SW of U.S. Rte. 15, .4 mi. NW of intersection with State Rte. 49. Stone ashlar, rectangular (seven-bay front), two stories, hipped roof, two interior stone chimneys, modillion cornice; symmetrical six-room plan, central south stair hall, fine wallpapers. Built c. 1765; front and side porch additions. 3 ext. photos (1939), 1 ext. photo, outbuildings (1940); 1 data page (1941); HABSI (1958). NR

CLEAR BROOK VICINITY   Frederick County (35)

Hopewell Friends Meeting House (VA-693), 2 mi. S of W. Va. line, S side of State Rte. 672, .5 mi. W of intersection with Interstate 81. Random rubble, 63'3" (six-bay front) x 44'3", two stories, gable roof, two interior end chimneys, one interior chimney; one-room plan. Built 1759-61; additions 1788-94. 8 sheets (1972, including plans, elevations, sections, detail); 10 data pages (1972).

CLIFFORD   Amherst County (5)

Brick House (VA-54), 1.7 mi. NE of Buffalo River, E side of State Rte. 151, 1.6 mi. N of intersection with U.S. Rte. 29. Brick, rectangular (seven-bay front), two stories, gable roof, central projecting pedimented portico, four exterior end chimneys, modillion cornice; entrance vestibule with three rooms; rear ell. Built early 19th C.; later additions. 2 ext. photos (1936); 1 data page (n.d.); HABSI (1957).

COLONIAL HEIGHTS   Chesterfield County (21)

Archer's Hill (Oak Hill, Hector's Hill, Dunn's Hill) (VA-135), .2 mi. NW of Appomattox River, W end of Carroll Ave. Frame with clapboarding, H-shaped (seven-bay front), filled into approx. rectangle, one story, hipped roof, two exterior end chimneys, three-part bow ends on S front, four interior chimneys, front and side porches, fine fanlight entrance motif. Built c. 1810. 5 ext. photos (1935), 1 int. photo (1935); 1 data page (1939).

Dunn's Hill (VA-135), see Archer's Hill (Oak Hill, Hector's Hill, Dunn's Hill) (VA-135), Colonial Heights.

Hector's Hill (VA-135), see Archer's Hill (Oak Hill, Hector's Hill, Dunn's Hill) (VA-135), Colonial Heights.

Oak Hill (VA-135), see Archer's Hill (Oak Hill, Hector's Hill, Dunn's Hill) (VA-135), Colonial Heights.

Violet Bank (VA-322), .3 mi. NW of Appomattox River, between Royal Oak and Virginia Aves., N of Jackson Ave., one block E of U.S. Rte. 1. Frame with clapboarding, rectangular (seven-bay front), one story, hipped roof, two exterior end chimneys, two projecting three-part bows at either side of central entrance porch, center-hall plan; rear ell. Built early 19th C.; later additions. 3 ext. photos (1935), 5 int. photos (1935); 1 data page (1941).

CRADDOCKVILLE   Accomack County (1)

Hermitage (VA-483), E bank of Craddock Creek, .6 mi. W of State Rte. 615, .6 mi. SW of intersection with State Rte. 752. Frame with clapboarding and brick ends (Flemish bond with glazed headers), rectangular (five-bay front), one-and-a-half stories, gable roof with dormers; two exterior end chimneys, modillion cornice; center-hall plan, notable original interior woodwork. Built mid 18th C.; restored. 2 ext. photos (1940); 1 data page (n.d.).

CRADDOCKVILLE VICINITY   Accomack County (1)

Hedra Cottage (VA-484), E bank of Scarborough Cut, .3 mi. S of State Rte. 611, .8 mi. SW of intersection with State Rte. 612. Frame with clapboarding, rectangular (three-bay front), two stories, gable roof, two interior end chimneys, side-hall plan; one-and-a-half story wing connected to side of house by one-story hyphen. Built early 18th C. 1 ext. photo (1940); HABSI (1958).

CROAKER VICINITY   James City County (48)

Richardson House (VA-366), 1.2 mi. from Croaker, exact location unknown. Frame with clapboarding, 31'4" (three-bay front) x 26'3", one-and-a-half stories, gable roof with dormers, one brick exterior end chimney; side-hall plan, Chinese Chippendale motif stair railing. Built mid 18th C.; demolished. 7 sheets (1933, including plans, elevations, sections, details); 2 ext. photos (1934, 1935), 2 int. photos (1934); 1 data page (1941).

Cumberland County Courthouse and Clerk's Office (VA-192), .5 mi. W of NW tributary of Little Guinea Creek, NW side of U.S. Rte. 60, opposite intersection with State Rte. 600. Brick, rectangular (five-bay front), one story, gable roof, pedimented Doric portico; large courtroom with two western offices; Clerk's Office: brick, rectangular (three-bay front), one story, gable roof, pedimented Doric entrance porch. Built early 19th C.; rear addition to Clerk's Office. 4 ext. photos (1939); 1 data page (1941); HABSI (1957).

Cumberland County Courthouse and Clerk's Office

CUMBERLAND VICINITY   Cumberland County (25)

Covered Bridge (Trent's Bridge) (VA-13), on Willis River, S corner of intersection of State Rtes. 650 and 622. Frame with batten walls and stone abutments on each bank, interior cross bracing, gable roof, extension of roof as a canopy at both ends of bridge supported by projecting timbers. Built early 19th C. 2 sheets (1934, including plan, elevations, sections); 1 ext. photo (1934), 1 int. photo (1934); 1 data page (1936).

Trent's Bridge (VA-13), see Covered Bridge (VA-13), Cumberland Vicinity.

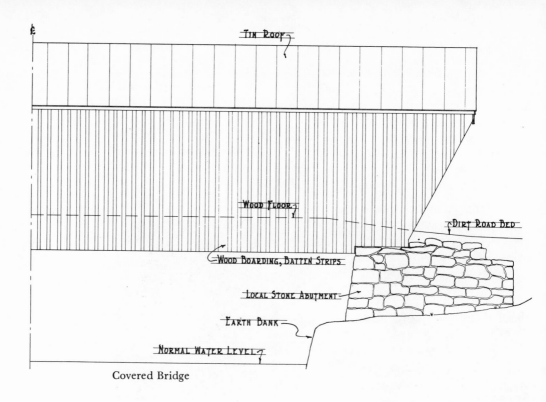

Covered Bridge

DANVILLE VICINITY   Pittsylvania County (72)

Dan's Hill (VA-24), .4 mi. N of Dan River, .6 mi. SW of S end of
State Rte. 1011, .3 mi. S of intersection of U.S. Rte. 58. Brick,
61'8" (five-bay front) x 41', two stories, gable roof, four exterior end
chimneys, two Doric entrance porches; center-hall plan, fine interior
moldings; side lean-to wing; orangery, smokehouses, kitchen, dairy,
privy, and summerhouse outbuildings. Built 1833; later addition. 3
sheets (1934, including plans, elevations, details); 6 ext. photos (1934),
6 int. photos (1934); 2 data pages (1936); HABSI (1958).

DELAPLANE VICINITY   Fauquier County (31)

Oak Hill (VA-5), 1.6 mi. S of Goose Creek, .2 mi. E of U.S. Rte. 17,
.9 mi. S of intersection with State Rte. 713. Frame with clapboarding,
32'3" (five-bay front) x 30'2", one-and-a-half stories, gable roof with
dormers, two exterior end chimneys; modified center-hall plan, notable interior trim. Built late 18th C.; enlarged 1818, by the construction
of an addition adjacent to the frame structure: brick with stucco,

40'2" (three-bay front) x 37'6", two stories, gable roof, two interior end chimneys, pedimented gable entrance facade with modillion cornice and window bays in recessed panels giving effect of being set between engaged pilasters; cross-hall plan, notable interior trim. 34 sheets (1934, including plans, elevations, sections, details); 4 ext. photos (1934), 3 int. photos (1934); 3 data pages (1936); HABSI (1958).

DENDRON VICINITY   Surry County (91)

Crump House (VA-233), see House (VA-233), Dendron Vicinity.

House (Crump House) (VA-233), .5 mi. S of Blackwater River, .1 mi. SE of State Rte. 617, 1 mi. SW of intersection with State Rte. 618. Frame with clapboarding, two units, S unit: rectangular (two-bay front), one story, gable roof, exterior end chimney; one-room plan; rear lean-to with exterior end chimney and rear ell; N unit: rectangular (four-bay front), one-and-a-half stories, gambrel roof with dormers, exterior end chimney; side-hall plan. Built mid 18th C.; altered and enlarged. 1 ext. photo (1938).

DILLWYN VICINITY   Buckingham County (15)

Bellmont (VA-14), .1 mi. S of Hatcher Creek, .5 mi. N of State Rte. 667, .3 mi. NE of intersection with State Rte. 650. Frame with clapboarding, 44' (five-bay front) x 28'5", one-and-a-half stories, gable roof with shed dormers, two interior end chimneys; T-shaped hall with four rooms; side wing. Built mid 18th C.; addition subsequently destroyed. 4 sheets (1934, including plans, elevations, sections, details); 3 ext. photos (1934); 2 data pages (1936).

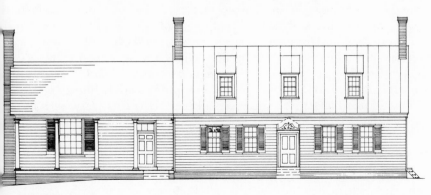

Bellmont

DINWIDDIE   Dinwiddie County (27)

Kingston (VA-384), .8 mi. W of Millrun Branch, .2 mi. W of State Rte. 619, .4 mi. S of intersection with State Rte. 40. Frame with clapboarding, rectangular (five-bay front), two stories, hipped roof, two interior end chimneys, modillion cornice; center-hall plan. Built late 18th C. 2 ext. photos (1936); 1 data page (1941); HABSI (1959).

DINWIDDIE VICINITY   Dinwiddie County (27)

Burnt Quarter (VA-386), .5 mi. NE of Wheelers Pond, .6 mi. S of State Rte. 613, .3 mi. W of intersection with State Rte. 627. Frame with clapboarding, rectangular (three-bay front), two stories, hipped roof, two exterior end chimneys; side-hall plan; rear ell; flanking wings: frame with clapboarding, rectangular (two-bay front), one-and-a-half stories, gable roof with dormers. Built late 18th C.; additions early 19th C. 1 ext. photo (1936); 1 data page (1941); HABSI (1959). NR

Plank House (VA-314), .7 mi. W of Stony Creek, N side of State Rte. 647, .4 mi. W of intersection with State Rte. 656. Planks half-dovetailed at corners, rectangular (two-bay front), one story, gable roof, frame gable ends above eaves, stone and brick exterior end chimney; one-room plan. Built early 19th C. 1 ext. photo (1939); 1 data page (1941); HABSI (1959).

DITCHLEY   Northumberland County (67)

Ditchley (VA-308), S bank of Dividing Creek, N side of State Rte. 607, 1.5 mi. E of intersection with State Rte. 200. Brick (Flemish bond), 57' (five-bay front) x 36', two stories, hipped roof, two interior end chimneys, modillion cornice, brick water table and belt course, rubbed brick dressings, pedimented one-story wooden entrance porches on front and rear elevations; center-hall plan, notable interior trim including stair, dado, denticulated cornice, mantel pieces, and paneled arched alcoves; side wings. Built mid 18th C.; later additions. 5 ext. photos (1929, 1940), 1 ext. photo, smokehouse (1940), 13 int. photos (1940); 2 data pages (1941); HABSI's (1957, 1958).

DUMFRIES   Prince William County (76)

Dumfries House (VA-826), see Williams' Ordinary (Old Hotel) (VA-826), Dumfries.

House (VA-827), N side Main St. (U.S. Rte. 1, S), .3 mi. SW intersection of Jefferson Davis Hwy. (U.S. Rte. 1, N). Frame with clapboarding, rectangular (three-bay front), two stories, gable roof, one interior chimney. Built late 18th C. or early 19th C.; later porch and lean-to additions; demolished. 1 ext. photo (1936).

Merchent House (VA-91), N side Main St. (U.S. Rte. 1, S), .2 mi. SW of intersection of Jefferson Davis Hwy. (U.S. Rte. 1, N). Frame with rusticated wooden siding on front and rear elevations to resemble stone, clapboarding on gable ends, 24'6" (three-bay front) x 16'6", one story above raised stone basement, gable roof, unusual T-shaped brick exterior end chimney with narrow arch between two of the three flues above the level of the roof ridge; side-hall plan. Built mid 18th C.; demolished c. 1940. 14 sheets (1935, including plans, elevations, sections, details, conjectural restoration); 10 ext. photos (1934, 1935, 1936, 1937), 3 int. photos (1936); 4 data pages (c. 1935).

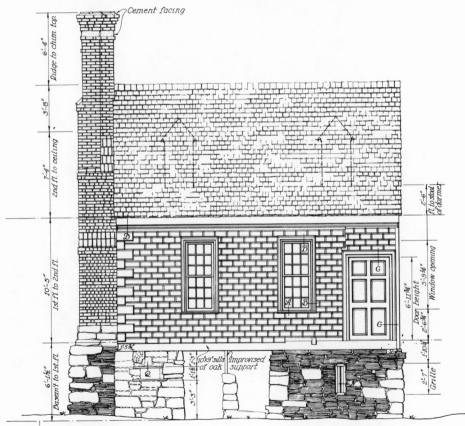

Merchent House

Merchent House

Old Hotel (VA-826), see Williams' Ordinary (Dumfries House) (VA-826), Dumfries.

Tebbs-Mundy House (VA-178), N side Main St. (U.S. Rte. 1, S), .3 mi. SW of intersection of Jefferson Davis Hwy. (U.S. Rte. 1, N). Brick (all header bond E front), rectangular (five-bay front), two stories above raised basement, hipped roof, two interior chimneys, modillion cornice, stone steps leading to pilastered entrance, stone quoins, window and door trim, belt course and foundations; center-hall plan. Built mid 18th C.; demolished 1933. 2 sheets (1932, including plans, elevations); 1 ext. photo (c. 1900); 2 data pages (1941).

Williams' Ordinary (Old Hotel, Dumfries House) (VA-826), N side Main St. (U.S. Rte. 1, S), .2 mi. SE of intersection of Jefferson Davis Hwy. (U.S. Rte. 1, N). Brick (all header bond E front), stone quoins, window lintels and doorway, rectangular (five-bay front), two stories, hipped roof, four interior end chimneys, modillion cornice; four-room plan. Built mid 18th C.; extensive later alterations to interior. 2 ext. photos (1936); HABSI (1959). NR

DUMFRIES VICINITY   Prince William County (76)

Leesylvania (VA-281), between Neabsco and Powells Creeks, .5 mi. S of State Rte. 610 in path of powerline right-of-way, .3 mi. E of intersection with U.S. Rte. 1. Brick and stone foundation and chimney ruins, probably of the 19th C. Fairfax House. Built 1825; burned 1910. 2 ext. photos (1936).

DUNNSVILLE VICINITY   Essex County (29)

Bathurst (VA-129), S bank of Piscataway Creek, .6 mi. N of State Rte. 662, 1.4 mi. N of intersection with State Rte. 611. Frame with clapboarding, T-shaped (three-bay front), one-and-a-half stories, gable roof with jerkinheads and dormers; two exterior end T-shaped chimneys, one interior chimney, covered porch across front; center-hall plan, notable interior trim; square frame, dairy and smokehouse with pyramidal roofs, dairy with brick nogging between studs. Built c. 1700, interiors removed; demolished c. 1937. 10 sheets (1936, including plans, elevations, sections, details), 1 sheet (1936, outbuildings); 4 ext. photos (1936), 2 ext. photos, dairy and smokehouse (1936); 1 photocopy (n.d.); 6 data pages (1936).

Cessford

Ben Lomond (VA-730), 1.3 mi. W of Rappahannock River, .3 mi. NE of U.S. Rte. 17, 1.2 mi. S of intersection of State Rte. 611. Brick, rectangular (four-bay front), two stories above raised basement, hipped roof, four interior end chimneys, one-story wooden Doric entrance porch with flat roof and balustrade; center-hall plan. Built early 19th C.; enlarged mid 19th C.; restored 1954. 1 ext. photo (1936), 1 int. photo (1936); HABSI (1958).

EASTVILLE   Northampton County (66)

Cessford (VA-808), .9 mi. SE of the Gulf, W side of U.S. Rte. 13, .2 mi. S of intersection with State Rte. 631. Brick (Flemish bond), rectangular (five-bay front), two-and-a-half stories, gable roof with pedimented dormers, three interior end chimneys, modillion cornice with dentils, denticulated barge boards, pedimented Tuscan entrance porch; center-hall plan, notable early wallpaper; flanking two-story wing. Built early 19th C.; later addition. 5 ext. photos (1960), 6 int. photos (1960); HABSI (1958).

Courthouse Group (VA-594), 1 mi. E of the Gulf, W side of U.S. Rte. 13, .1 mi. N of intersection with State Rte. 631.

Old Courthouse. Brick (Flemish bond with glazed header rows following rake of roof on rear gable end), rectangular (three-bay front), one-and-a-half stories, gable roof, windows on gable ends above eaves, one exterior end chimney. Built mid 18th C.; new courthouse built 1795, and the old one probably used for a storehouse after that date; moved and renovated 1913, front wall replaced.

Old Clerk's Office. Brick (Flemish bond), rectangular (one-bay front), one story, gable roof, one interior end chimney. Built mid 18th C.; renovated.

Old Debtor's Prison. Brick, rectangular (one-bay front), one story, gable roof. Built early 19th C.

Commercial Building. Brick, rectangular (three-bay front), two stories, gable roof, gable-end front, first-floor store front. Built early 19th C.; altered.

Taylor House (Eastville Inn). Frame with clapboarding, rectangular (eight-bay front), two stories, gable roof, one interior end chimney, full-length one-story front porch; side wing: rear ell. Built late 18th C.; enlarged and altered. 8 ext. photos (1960); 6 data pages (1960); HABSI (1958).

Eastville Inn (VA-594), see Courthouse Group: Taylor House (VA-594), Eastville.

EASTVILLE VICINITY   Northampton County (66)

Caserta (VA-591), S bank of Mattawoman Creek, 1.2 mi. N of State Rte. 630, 1 mi. NW of intersection with U.S. Rte. 13. Frame with clapboarding with brick gable end, rectangular (three-bay front), two stories, gable roof, interior end chimney, roof over side hall raised to accommodate the extension of hall beyond rear wall; side-hall plan; rear ell; kitchen: frame, one-and-a-half stories, gable roof, exterior end chimney, connected to main block by one-and-a-half story five-bay hyphen. Built early 19th C.; later addition. 2 ext. photos (1960), 2 ext. photos, ice house (1960), 1 int. photo, ice house (1960); 3 data pages (1960).   NR

Cherry Grove (VA-592), .1 mi. W of Cherrystone Inlet, .4 mi. SE of State Rte. 634, 2.6 mi. SW of intersection with State Rte. 666. Frame with clapboarding, rectangular (five-bay front), one-and-a-half stories, gambrel roof with dormers, splayed eaves, two interior end chimneys, modillion cornice; center-hall plan, some original paneling; wing. Built mid 18th C.; later addition. 3 ext. photos (1960), 1 int. photo (1960); 3 data pages (1960).

Hollybrook (VA-593), 1 mi. SE of Mattawoman Creek, .1 mi. E of U.S. Rte. 13, .8 mi. NE of intersection with State Rte. 630. Brick with frame front, rectangular (four-bay front), two stories, gable roof, two interior end chimneys, modillion cornice; two-room plan, central entrance vestibule with stair hall behind; rear ell; one-story side kitchen wing connected to main block by colonnade. Built late 18th C.; later additions including entrance vestibule. 5 ext. photos (1960), 6 int. photos (1960); 3 data pages (1960).

Kendall Grove

Kendall Grove

Kendall Grove (VA-807), E bank of Mattawoman Creek, NW end of State Rte. 674, 1.2 mi. NW of intersection with U.S. Rte. 13. Frame with clapboarding, cross-shaped (nine-bay front), two stories, gable roof, three interior end chimneys, advanced central pedimented bays front and rear with semi-circular glazed lunettes in pediments, modillion cornice, one-story flat roofed entrance porches on central bays, four pedimented tetrastyle one-story entrance porches on front and rear of lower two-story wings which flank the principal mass; cross-hall plan, notable interior trim; kitchen: frame with clapboarding, one story, gable roof, two exterior end chimneys, connected to main house by long one-story covered passageway on open-arched brick foundations; three frame service dependencies with pyramidal roofs flank the main house, opposite the kitchen passageway. Built c. 1800. 10 ext. photos, main house (1960), 2 ext. photos, kitchen (1960), 1 ext. photo, passageway (1960), 1 ext. photo, service dependencies (1960), 3 int. photos, main house (1960), 1 int. photo, kitchen (1960), 3 int. photos, passageway (1960).

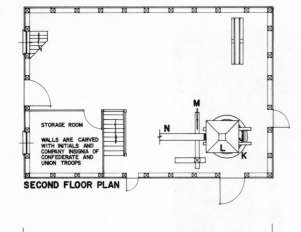

SECOND FLOOR PLAN

STORAGE ROOM

WALLS ARE CARVED WITH INITIALS AND COMPANY INSIGNIA OF CONFEDERATE AND UNION TROOPS

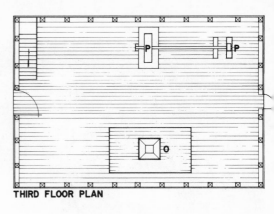

THIRD FLOOR PLAN

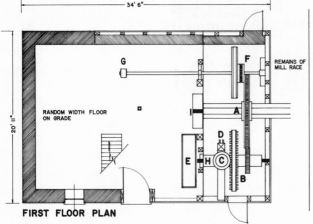

34' 6"

20' 11"

REMAINS OF MILL RACE

RANDOM WIDTH FLOOR ON GRADE

FIRST FLOOR PLAN

Piney Branch Water Mill

NOTES ON MILL MACHINERY
FIRST FLOOR:

A. WHEEL AXLE AND GEAR (ORIGINALLY WITH OVERSHOT WATER WHEEL)
B. GREAT SPUR GEAR AND WHEEL (CLUTCH ARRANGEMENT) WITH WOOD TEETH
C. LANTERN PINION GEAR (WALLOWER) TO TRANSMIT POWER TO STONES
D. BRIDGETREE AND BRAYER, TO ADJUST DISTANCE BETWEEN RUNNER AND BED STONES
E. SIFTER AND MEAL BIN
F. AUXILIARY TAKE-OFF WHEEL TO PULLEYS ABOVE
G. PULLEY (WOOD) WITH LEATHER BELTING
H. SPOUT FROM STONE CASING TO SIFTER
I. IRON GUDGEON SET INTO WOOD AXLE

SECOND FLOOR:

J. PAIR OF MONOLITHIC GRINDSTONES, 54" DIAMETER
K. WOOD STONE CASING, 62" OUTSIDE DIAMETER, TO GATHER GROUND MEAL
L. WOOD GRAIN HOPPER, 48"x48", OFFSET FROM EYE OF RUNNER STONE
M. CRANE WITH IRON TONGS TO LIFT RUNNER STONE FOR DRESSING
N. GRAIN SHUTE FROM UPPER STORAGE AREA

THIRD FLOOR:

O. HOPPER AND SHUTE TO DELIVER GRAIN TO HOPPER BELOW
P. AUXILIARY TAKE-OFF WHEELS

SCALE 1/4"=1'0"

ELLISTON VICINITY   Montgomery County (61)

Fotheringay (VA-348), .5 mi. E of S fork (of Roanoke River), .2 mi. E of U.S. Rte. 11, 1.4 mi. S of intersection with State Rte. 631. Brick, rectangular (five-bay front), two stories, gable roof, hipped eastern end, two exterior end and one interior chimney, two-level portico with pediment; center-hall plan; rear ell. Built late 18th C.; western two bays added. 1 ext. photos (1940), 1 ext. photo, out-building (1940); 1 data page (1941); HABSI (1958). NR

EMMERTON VICINITY   Richmond County (80)

Elmore House (VA-63), S side State Rte. 3, approx. 5 mi. S of War-saw, exact location unknown. Frame with clapboarding, rectangular (three-bay front), one story with attic, gable roof, one large exterior end stone chimney; two-room plan with corner fireplaces. Built mid 18th C.; ruinous 1937; demolished. 1 sheet (1937, including plan, elevations); 6 ext. photos (1934, 1937).

EXMORE VICINITY   Northampton County (66)

Tankard's Rest (VA-806), .4 mi. E of eastern tributary of Nassawadox Creek, .1 mi. S of intersection of State Rtes. 618 and 604, .6 mi. SW of intersection with U.S. Rte. 13. Brick with frame front, rectangular (two-bay front), two stories, gable roof, one interior end chimney; irregular plan; kitchen wing: brick with frame front, one story, gable roof; three one-story outbuildings. Built late 18th C.; destroyed. 5 ext. photos (1940).

FAIRFAX VICINITY   Fairfax County (30)

Hope Park (VA-107), 11807 Popes Head Rd. Frame with clapboarding, original section 32'6" (three-bay front) x 27', one-and-a-half stories, gable roof with dormers, one exterior end chimney; center-hall plan. Built mid 18th C.; outbuildings 18th C.; additions and alterations mid 19th C. 6 sheets (1936, including plan, elevations, details); 5 ext. photos, main house (1936), 2 ext. photos, outbuildings (1936), 2 int. photos, main house (1936); HABSI's (1958, 1969).

Hope Park Mill (VA-741), see Piney Branch Water Mill (Robey's Mill) (VA-741), Fairfax Vicinity.

Innisfail (VA-279), see Stone House (VA-279), Fairfax Vicinity.

Piney Branch Water Mill (Hope Park Mill, Robey's Mill) (VA-741), 1212 Popes Head Rd. Frame with clapboarding and vertical plank siding, rectangular, one story with loft above raised stone basement, gable roof, wooden wheel and millrace. Built early 19th C. 5 sheets (1971, including plans, elevations, sections); 3 ext photos (1936); HABSI's (1958, 1969).

Robey's Mill (VA-741), see Piney Branch Water Mill (Hope Park Mill) (VA-741), Fairfax Vicinity.

Stone House (Innisfail) (VA-279), 11800 Fairfax Station Rd. Stone, rectangular (three-bay front), two-and-a-half stories, gable roof with dormers, two stone interior end chimneys; rectangular plan, rear ell. Built early 19th C.; stone lean-to removed and rear ell added mid 20th C. 1 ext. photo (1936); HABSI (1969).

FALLS CHURCH

Bartlett-Lawton House (Home Hill) (VA-732), 203 Lawton St. Frame with clapboarding, T-shaped (four-bay front), two stories, hipped roof, two interior chimneys, one-story wooden entrance porch on three sides; cross-hall plan; side wing. Built mid 19th C. 2 ext. photos (1967), 5 int. photos (1967); HABSI's (1958, 1967).

Cherry Hill (VA-733), 312 Park Ave. Frame with clapboarding, rectangular (three-bay front), two stories, gable roof, one interior chimney, one exterior end chimney, one-story wooden entrance porch across full width of house; center-hall plan. Built mid 18th C.; extensive later additions and alterations mid 19th C. 3 ext. photos (1967), 8 int. photos (1967); HABSI (1967).

Crossman House (VA-734), 421 N. Washington St. Frame with clapboarding, L-shaped (six-bay front), two stories, gable roof, two interior chimneys, decorated barge boards, one-story entrance porch with scrollwork decoration; center-hall plan. Built mid 19th C.; later alterations. 1 ext. photo (1967).

Dulin House (VA-278), site on Graham Rd. Brick, rectangular (three-bay front), two stories, gable roof, sawtooth brick cornice, two interior chimneys with parapet; side-hall plan; ruins of kitchen, kitchen fireplace, and connecting hyphen. Built early 19th C.; later additions and alterations; demolished. 6 ext. photos (1936).

Falls Church (Episcopal) (VA-288), 115 E. Fairfax St. Brick (Flemish bond), rectangular (five bays x three bays), two stories, hipped roof, modillion cornice, rectilinear windows below, arched windows above, rubbed brick dressings, molded brick water table, brick pediment and pilasters frame W doorway, wooden pediment and pilasters frame S doorway; open plan. Built 1767-69, James Wren, architect and builder; later renovations 1823, 1866, 1905; E end of church substantially altered by connection to parish house 1959. 4 ext. photos (1936), 1 int. photo (1936); 1 int. photocopy (1861-65); HABSI (1958). NR

Home Hill (VA-732), see Bartlett-Lawton House (VA-732), Falls Church.

House (VA-736), 170 E. Broad St. Frame with clapboarding, rectangular (three-bay front), one story, gable roof, one exterior end chimney; modified two-room plan; one-story lean-to; two-story side wing. Built late 18th C.; extensive additions and alterations mid 19th C. and early 20th C.; demolished 1967. 3 ext. photos (1967), 6 int. photos (1967).

House (VA-735), SW corner of intersection of Great Falls and Little Falls Sts. Frame with clapboarding, T-shaped with octagonal corner tower (five-bay front, including tower), two-and-a-half stories, hipped roof with dormer, cross gables, two interior chimneys, projecting bay in center of S front, one-story spindlework porch on two sides. Built late 19th C.; demolished 1967, 1 ext. photo (1967).

Pond-Copeland House (VA-737), 407 E. Columbia St. Frame with asbestos siding, L-shaped (three-bay front), two stories, gable roof, one-story wooden entrance porch with scrollwork decoration; irregular plan. Built late 19th C.; extensive later alterations. 1 ext. photo (1967).

Pope, Loren B., House (VA-638), see Pope-Leighey House (VA-638), Mount Vernon Vicinity, Fairfax Co.

Rollins, George F., House (VA-738), 109 E. Columbia St. Frame with clapboarding and shingles, modified L-shaped (three-bay front), two-and-a-half stories, gable roof with dormers, one interior chimney, one interior end chimney, one-story wooden porch, projecting front bay semi-octagonal first story, semi-circular second story with shingle siding; cross-hall plan. Built late 19th C. 1 ext. photo (1967), 3 int. photos (1967).

FALMOUTH   Stafford County (90)

House (VA-264), 121 Prince St. Frame with clapboarding, rectangular (three-bay front), two stories above raised basement, gable roof, two exterior end chimneys on one end, small entrance porch; side-hall plan. Built late 18th C. or early 19th C.; later additions and alterations. 1 ext. photo (1939).

Union Church, Facade (VA-203), S side of Carter St., 1 block E of intersection with U.S. Rte. 1. Brick, two-bay front, one story, gable roof, rectangular belfry, double entrance doors, semi-circular lights above doors; Latin-cross plan. Built mid 19th C.; only the facade remains following damage to the structure 1948. 2 ext. photos (1939); HABSI (1958).

George F. Rollins House

FALMOUTH VICINITY   Stafford County (90)

Chatham (VA-339), .1 mi. NE of Rappahannock River, .1 mi. NE of
State Rte. 607, .1 mi. NW of intersection with State Rte. 3. Brick,
five-part composition, central block: rectangular (seven-bay front),
two stories, gable roof, two interior end chimneys, modillion cornice;
center-hall plan; flanking symmetrical wings: one story, hipped roofs,
interior chimneys, connected to main house by one-story hyphens.
Built c. 1769; extensive alterations including the removal of pedimented two-story porch from main house and pedimented porches
from connecting hyphens early 20th C. 1 ext. photocopy (c. 1865);
1 data page (1941); HABSI (1957).

FARNHAM   Richmond County (80)

Linden Farm (VA-566), .3 mi. S of headwater tributary of Totusky
Creek, N side of State Rte. 3, .5 mi. NW of intersection with State
Rte. 607. Frame with clapboarding, rectangular (four-bay front),
one-and-a-half stories, gable roof with dormers, two exterior end
chimneys, center-hall plan. Built early 18th C. 1 ext. photo (1934);
HABSI (1958).

North Farnham Episcopal Church (VA-562), .9 mi. E of Bookers Mill Stream, E intersection of State Rtes. 607 and 602. Brick (Flemish bond), cross-shaped (three-bay front), one story, gable roof, one interior end chimney, modillion cornice, arched windows, entrance doorways with molded brick pediments and round gallery windows above; one-room plan with balconies. Built mid 18th C.; vandalized c. 1780; restored c. 1835; burned 1887; partially restored 1924. 1 ext. photo (1934); HABSI (1958).

FISHERSVILLE VICINITY   Augusta County (8)

Tinkling Spring Church (VA-718), S bank of E tributary of Goose Creek, E side of State Rte. 608, .1 mi. S of intersection with State Rte. 631. Brick, 61'10" (four-bay lateral facade) x 44'8", one story, hipped roof, Doric distyle-in-antis entrance, shallow antae projections; one-room plan. Built 1850; altered 1890; later rear additions. 5 sheets (1962, including plot plan, plan, elevations); HABSI (1957).

Poplar Forest

Poplar Forest (VA-303), .2 mi. N of Timber Lake, .9 mi. S of State Rte. 661, .5 mi. S of intersection with U.S. Rte. 460. Brick, octagonal (five-bay front), one-and-a-half stories, two-and-a-half stories in rear due to slope of ground, hipped roof with dormers, four interior end chimneys, two Tuscan porticoes supported by brick arcades; central salon with surrounding rooms; two brick octagonal privies with domical roofs; two brick two-story servants' quarters with gable roofs; brick smokehouse with pyramidal roof; brick kitchen with gable roof. Built 1806 by Thomas Jefferson as his summer retreat; roof and interior trim burned c. 1840 and rebuilt. 9 ext. photos including outbuildings (1940), 3 int. photos (1940); 1 data page (1941); HABSI (1958). NR

Poplar Forest

Old Stone Church (VA-10), 1.1 mi. SE of Mt. Pisgah, W side of U.S. Rte. 11, .2 mi. SW of intersection with State Rte. 616. Random-laid stone, cruciform (five-bay front), one story, gable roof with jerkinheads, spire at crossing, stone arched entrance porch; NE of church is stone, one-story session house. Built c. 1747; originally stone, approx. 40' (two-bay front) x 50', one story, gable roof with jerkinheads; enlarged structure dedicated January 22, 1922. 9 sheets (1934, including plot plan, plans, elevations, sections, details of church and session house); 2 ext. photos (1934); 1 ext. photocopy (n.d.); 3 data pages (1936); HABSI (1957).

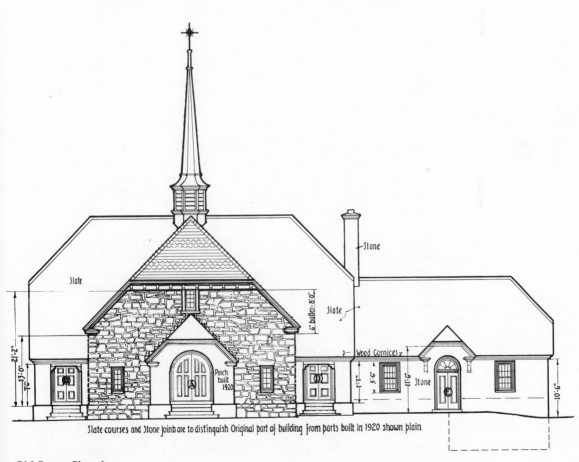

Slate courses and Stone joints are to distinguish Original part of building from parts built in 1920 shown plain

Old Stone Church

109

Brompton (VA-569), Marye's Heights, SE corner of intersection of Sunken Rd. and Hanover St. Brick, temple form (three-bay front), two stories, gable roof, two interior chimneys, pedimented Ionic tetrastyle portico with semi-circular lunette, modillion cornice, center entrance with fanlight and side lights; cross-hall plan; symmetrical one-story flanking wings; frame outbuilding connected to E wing by enclosed passageway. Built 1831; outbuilding mid 19th C.; flat roof of portico changed to pedimented gable late 19th C.; altered mid 20th C. 7 sheets (n.d., including plans, elevations, section); 2 ext. photos (1934), 1 int. photo (1934); HABSI (1957).

Federal Hill, Summer House (VA-4), 510 Hanover St. Frame with horizontal planks and louvers, one story above stone foundation, bell-shaped roof; double louvered doors; octagonal plan. Built late 18th C.; restored. 1 sheet (1934, including plan, elevations, section); 1 ext. photo (1934); 3 data pages (1936).

House (VA-204), 100 Hanover St. Frame with clapboarding, rectangular (three-bay front), one story, gable roof, two exterior end chimneys. Built late 18th C.; later alterations; demolished. 1 ext. photo (1939).

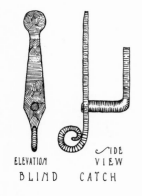

ELEVATION   SIDE VIEW
BLIND CATCH

House (Old Long House) (VA-263), 607 Sophia St. Frame with clapboarding covered with asbestos shingles, rectangular (three-bay front), two stories, gable roof, three exterior end chimneys, front and rear porches; center-hall plan. Built early 19th C.; later addition and alterations. 1 ext. photo (1939).

Houses (VA-206), 307-13 Sophia St. Brick, four units joined by party walls, two of one-and-a-half stories, gable roof with dormers, one interior chimney; two of two stories, gable roof, one interior end chimney. Built early 19th C.; frame lean-to additions; demolished. 2 ext. photos (1939).

Houses (VA-205), 511-19 Sophia St. Brick, five units joined by party walls, rectangular (ten-bay common front), one-and-a-half stories, gable roof with dormers, three interior chimneys. Built late 18th C.; later alterations; demolished. 1 ext. photo (1939).

Houses (VA-207), 710-16 Sophia St. S building: frame with clapboarding, rectangular (two-bay front), two stories, flat roof. Built early 19th C.; demolished. N building: brick, rectangular, one-and-a-

Houses, 307-13 Sophia St.

LANTERN
Rising Sun
Tavern

half stories, gable roof with dormers; one-story rear addition. Built early 19th C.; later alterations and additions; demolished. 1 ext. photo (1939).

Kenmore (VA-305), 1201 Washington Ave. Historic house museum. Brick (Flemish bond), rectangular (five-bay front), two stories, gable roof with jerkinheads, four interior end chimneys, string course and water table, modillion cornice; modified center-hall plan, exceptionally fine interior woodwork and plasterwork ceilings, cornices, and mantel pieces; flanking dependencies. Built 1752 for Col. Fielding Lewis and Betty Washington Lewis, George Washington's sister; restoration begun 1922; original frame dependencies reconstructed in brick. 10 ext. photos, main house (1939, 1940), 1 ext. photo, kitchen (1940), 1 ext. photo, office (1940), 17 int. photos, main house (1939, 1940), 1 int. photo, kitchen (1940); 1 data page (1940); HABSI (1958). NR

Old Long House (VA-263), see House (VA-263), Fredericksburg.

Rising Sun Tavern (VA-1), 1306 Caroline St. Historic house museum. Frame with clapboarding, 46′5″ (five-bay front) x 30′5″, one-and-a-half stories, gable roof with pedimented dormers, two interior end chimneys, pedimented entrance porch; modified center-hall plan, notable interior trim. Built c. 1760; later rear addition; restored 1956.

6 sheets (1934, including plot plan, plans, elevations, details); 4 ext. photos (1934), 5 int. photos (1934); 6 data pages (1936); HABSI (1958). NR

Sentry Box (VA-300), 133 Caroline St. Frame with clapboarding, rectangular (five-bay front), two stories, gable roof, two exterior end chimneys, pedimented entrance porch, modillion cornice; center-hall plan. Built mid 18th C.; later alterations and additions; renovated 1967. 2 ext. photos (1940); HABSI (1957).

Stone Warehouse (VA-262), 915 Sophia St. Museum. Irregular ashlar, rectangular (five-bay front), two stories, gable roof, one-room plan. Built early 18th C.; used as warehouse and as jail; first floor of exterior hidden by landfill for bridge approach; partially restored. 1 ext. photo (1939); HABSI (1957).

Washington, Mary, House (VA-2), 1200 Charles St. Historic house museum. Frame with clapboarding and brick, 101'2" (nine-bay front) x 36'4", one-and-a-half and two stories, gable roof with dormers over one-and-a-half story portions, gable roof over two-story portion, three interior end chimneys, one interior chimney; irregular plan. Built mid 18th C.; extensive later additions and alterations; restored 1929. Purchased in 1772 by George Washington for his mother. 12 sheets (1934, including plot plan, plans, elevations, sections, details of house, plan and elevation of kitchen); 4 ext. photos, house (1934), 1 ext. photo, kitchen (1934), 5 int. photos, house (1934), 1 int. photo, kitchen (1934); 4 data pages (1936); HABSI (1958).

Mary Washington House

EAST (FRONT) ELEVATION

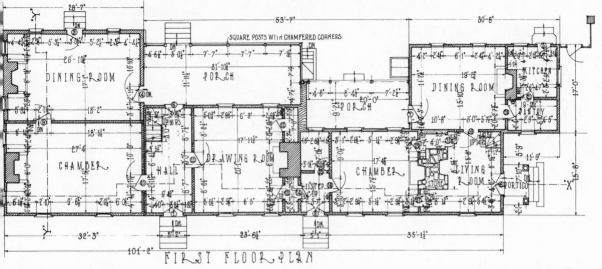

FIRST FLOOR PLAN

Mary Washington House

FREDERICKSBURG VICINITY   Spotsylvania County (89)

Fredericksburg Country Club (VA-570), see Smithfield Hall (VA-570), Fredericksburg Vicinity.

Mannsfield (VA-122), .1 mi. W of Rappahannock River, .4 mi. NE of U.S. Rte. 17, .3 mi. SE of intersection with State Rte. 1303. Ruins remain from original stone ashlar structure, 68'4" (five-bay front) x 47'11¾", two stories, forecourt formed by two dependencies with curving connections, conjectural restoration indicates pedimented central pavilion, modillion cornice, hip-on-hip roof, and quoining. Built mid 18th C.; destroyed in the Fredericksburg campaigns of Civil War, 1862-63; site excavated 1934. 27 sheets (1935, 1940, including archeological remains, plans, elevations, sections, perspective, details, hardware); 36 ext. photos, including photocopies of sketch (n.d., c. 1934, 1935, 1938); 6 photos, artifacts (1935); 12 data pages (n.d., 1935, 1937).

Salem Church (VA-640), 1.4 mi. S of Rappahannock River, S side of State Rte. 3, SE corner of intersection with State Rte. 639, .2 mi. W of intersection with State Rte. 745. Fredericksburg and Spotsylvania County Battlefields Memorial National Military Park. Brick, 42' (three-bay lateral facade) x 38'1", two stories (auditorium with balcony), gable roof, three interior chimneys; one-room plan with balcony. Built 1844, minor alterations 1890, 1929, 1935, 1940, 1953. 10 sheets (1966, including plans, elevations, sections, details).

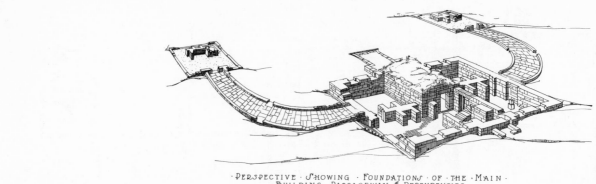

·PERSPECTIVE· SHOWING ·FOUNDATIONS· OF ·THE ·MAIN·
·BUILDING , PASSAGEWAY· & ·DEPENDENCIES·

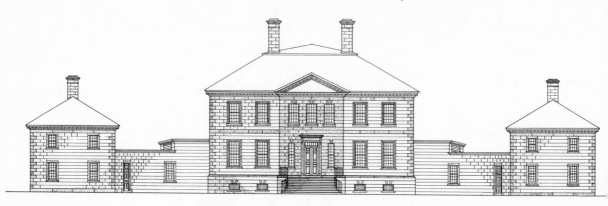

CONJECTURAL RESTORATION - WEST ELEVATION
Mannsfield

Smithfield Hall (Fredericksburg Country Club) (VA-570), .2 mi. SW of Rappahannock River, .4 mi. NE of U.S. Rte. 17, 1.2 mi. SE of intersection with State Rte. 1303. Brick, rectangular (five-bay front), two-and-a-half stories, gable roof with dormers, four interior end chimneys, three-bay two-story pedimented Roman Ionic portico; flanking two-story hipped roof wings. Built 1805; later additions. 2 ext. photos (c. 1934); HABSI (1957).

Steiger House (VA-369), 1.3 mi. S of Rappahannock River, N side of State Rte. 3, .8 mi. SW of intersection with State Rte. 639. Frame with clapboarding, rectangular (three-bay front), one-and-a-half stories, gambrel roof with dormers, exterior end chimney; side wing: brick, rectangular (three-bay front), two stories, gable roof, two interior end chimneys. Built early 19th C.; addition; demolished 1951. 2 ext. photos (c. 1934, 1935), 1 int. photo (c. 1935).

FREDERICKSBURG VICINITY
Stafford County (90)

Ferry Farm, Surveying Office (Washington's Surveying Office) (VA-90), 712 Kings Hwy (State Rte. 3). Museum. Frame with clapboarding, 12'8" (two-bay front) x 13'2", one story, gable roof, one exterior end chimney; one-room plan. Built probably mid 18th C.; restored mid 20th C. Traditionally said to be one of two structures remaining from the original Ferry Farm complex, an early home of George Washington. 7 sheets (1935, including plan, elevations, sections, details); 2 ext. photos (1934); 3 data pages (1936); HABSI (n.d.). NR

Lansdowne, Smokehouse (VA-368), 571 Lansdowne Rd. (State Rte. 638). Frame with clapboarding, square (one-bay front), one story, pyramidal roof, door with wooden hinges; one-room plan. Built early 19th C.; demolished. 2 ext. photos (n.d.), 1 int. photo (n.d.).

Washington's Surveying Office (VA-90), see Ferry Farm, Surveying Office (VA-90), Fredericksburg Vicinity.

· FRAGMENT · OF · ANDIRON ·
No. 14
2 like this

FRONT ROYAL VICINITY
Warren County (94)

Mt. Zion (VA-357), .1 mi. SW of Bordens Marsh Run, NW side of State Rte. 624, opposite intersection with State Rte. 642. Stone, rectangular (five-bay front), two stories, hipped roof, four interior end chimneys, modillion cornice, Palladian window over entrance door; center-hall plan, notable interior trim including triple arch in front hall, elaborately carved mantels and overmantels with dog-ear motif, garlands, masks, and foliated pulvinated frieze; two-story frame side wing; stone outbuildings. Built 1769-71; later additions. 1 ext. photo (1936), 1 ext. photo, stone outbuilding (1936); 1 data page (1941). NR

GAINESVILLE VICINITY
Prince William County (76)

Chinn House (VA-138), W side of Chinn's Branch, .6 mi. W of State Rte. 234, 1.6 mi. SW of intersection with U.S. Rte. 29, Manassas National Battlefield Park. Frame with clapboarding, 52'11" (five-bay front) x 28'7", two stories, gable roof, four exterior end chimneys; center-hall plan. Built late 18th C.; razed to foundation level 1951. The structure was used as a hospital during both battles of Manassas 1861, 1862. 3 sheets (1959, including plot plan, plan, elevations of foundation); 7 ext. photos, house (1936), 7 ext. photos, foundations (1959); 2 data pages (1959).

· FRAGMENT · OF · ANDIRON ·
No. 15
2 like this

115

Mt. Zion

Dogan House (VA-581), .8 mi. N of Young's Branch, NW corner of intersection of U.S. Rte. 29 and State Rte. 622, Manassas National Battlefield Park. Historic house museum. Log and frame, two units connected by passageway, 37'3" (both units) x 13'7", one story, gable roof, one stone interior chimney serving both units; two-room plan. Nucleus built early 19th C.; lean-to addition built late 19th C. and removed 1946; original two units restored 1960. 3 sheets (1959, including plot plans, plans, elevations, details); 26 ext. photos (1936, 1959), 13 int. photos (1959); 3 data pages (1959).

GLEN ALLEN VICINITY   Henrico County (44)

Quarters Cabin (VA-222), .5 mi. E of Big Swamp, .2 mi. W of Gayton Rd., 2.1 mi. S of intersection of U.S. Rte. 250. Frame with clapboarding, rectangular (three-bay front), gable roof, two exterior end chimneys, two front entrances; rear ell. Built mid 18th C.; demolished. 3 ext. photos (1940).

116

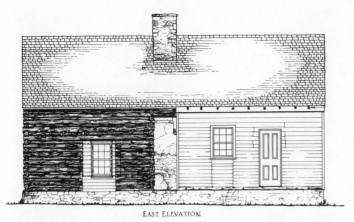

EAST ELEVATION

SOUTH ELEVATION

Dogan House

NORTH ELEVATION

GLOUCESTER   Gloucester County (37)

Botetourt Hotel (VA-513), .5 mi. SW of Beaverdam Swamp, N side of U.S. Rte. 17, opposite intersection with State Rte. 1010. Brick, rectangular (six-bay front), two stories, gable roof, one interior chimney, one interior end chimney, modillion cornice; three-room plan. Built mid 18th C.; altered and enlarged mid 19th C.; restored 1968. 2 ext. photos (1934, 1937); HABSI (1959).

Stable (VA-745), .5 mi. SW of Beaverdam Swamp, N side of U.S. Rte. 17, opposite intersection with State Rte. 1010. Brick, rectangular (one-bay gable front), one story with loft, gable roof possibly with jerkinheads, lateral facade with ventilation slits for stalls. Built mid 18th C.; ruinous 1935; demolished. 3 ext. photos (1935).

Gloucester County Courthouse (VA-511), Court Square. Brick, T-shaped (five-bay front), one story, hipped roof, two interior end chimneys, one exterior end chimney, modillion cornice, arched windows, brick water table, pedimented Ionic tetrastyle portico; two-room plan. Built mid 18th C.; portico added and interior altered 1894; interior renovated 1956. 1 ext. photo (1934); HABSI (1959).

Longbridge Ordinary (VA-512), .2 mi. S of Beaverdam Swamp, NE corner of intersection of U.S. Rte. 17 and State Rte. 14. Frame with clapboarding, rectangular (three-bay front), one-and-a-half stories above raised basement, gable roof with dormers, exterior end chimney, covered porch; side-hall plan; lean-to wings. Built mid 18th C.; extensive later additions and alterations. 1 ext. photo (1934); HABSI (1959).

117

Abingdon Glebe (VA-746), 1.8 mi. S of Fox Mill Run, .3 mi. W of U.S. Rte. 17, .6 mi. S of intersection with State Rte. 615. Brick (Flemish bond), T-shaped (five-bay front), one-and-a-half stories, gable roof with dormers, two exterior end chimneys, one interior end chimney, main front is one-and-a-half stories for three of five bays, end bays form one-story hipped roof extensions with common cornice with central bays; center-hall plan. Built mid 18th C.; extensive alterations mid 20th C. 8 ext. photos (1934, 1937); HABSI (1959). NR

Belroi (Walter Reed Birthplace) (VA-57), 1 mi. NW of Leigh Pond, NW corner of intersection of State Rtes. 614 and 616. Frame with clapboarding, rectangular (three-bay front), one story, gable roof, two exterior end chimneys; two-room plan. Built early 19th C.; restored 1927. Belroi is the birthplace of Dr. Walter Reed, 1851-1902. 2 ext. photos (1937); 2 data pages (1937); HABSI (1959).

Walter Reed Birthplace (VA-57), see Belroi (VA-57), Gloucester Vicinity.

Ware Church (VA-408), .9 mi. NE of Beaverdam Swamp, SE side of State Rte. 3, 1.1 mi. NE of intersection with U.S. Rte. 17. Brick (Flemish bond), rectangular (five-bay lateral front), one story, gable roof, modillion cornice, arched windows, arched entrance door in gable end with semi-circular gauged and rubbed brick architrave; one-room plan. Built mid 18th C.; roof altered and interior damaged c. 1865; partially restored 1929. 4 ext. photos (1934, 1937), 2 photos, brick churchyard wall (1934); 1 data page (1941); HABSI (1959).

GOOCHLAND   Goochland County (38)

Goochland County Courthouse (VA-224), .2 mi. W of Courthouse Creek, .1 mi. E of State Rte. 6, .8 mi. S of intersection with U.S. Rte. 522. Brick, rectangular (three-bay front), two stories, gable roof, gable-end front, pedimented Tuscan portico, two interior end chimneys; one-room plan; rear ell. Built early 19th C.; later addition. 1 ext. photo (1940); HABSI (1957). NR

Lawyer's Office (VA-225), .3 mi. W of Courthouse Creek, E side of U.S. Rte. 522, .1 mi. S of intersection with State Rte. 631. Frame with clapboarding, rectangular (four-bay front), one-and-a-half stories, gable roof, two exterior end chimneys. Built early 19th C.; demolished. 1 ext. photo (1940).

Ware Church

GRAFTON VICINITY York County (100)

York County Poor Farm, Dairy and House (VA-84), .2 mi. E of Harwoods Mill Reservoir, E side of U.S. Rte. 17, .6 mi. S of intersection with State Rtes. 614 and 173. Dairy: frame with clapboarding, 12′3″ (one-bay front) x 12′3″, one story, pyramidal roof with marked overhang, plastered cove cornice, ventilated fretwork frieze; one-room plan; house: frame with clapboarding, one-and-a-half stories, gable roof with dormer. Built early 19th C.; ruinous. 1 sheet, dairy (1934, including plan, elevations, sections, details); 5 ext. photos, dairy (1934); HABSI, house (1958).

GREAT FALLS VICINITY Fairfax County (30)

Colvin Run Mill (VA-502), 10017 Colvin Run Rd. Brick and stone, rectangular (three-bay front), three stories with loft, gable roof, one interior end chimney; open plan. Built c. 1820; restored, S wall and much of the interior reconstructed 1969. 1 ext. photo (1935); HABSI's (1957, 1969).

Colvin Run Miller's House (VA-742), 10015 Colvin Run Rd. Brick, rectangular (five-bay front), two stories, gable roof, two interior end chimneys; center-hall plan. Built c. 1810; later frame addition; extensive renovation 1968; one-and-a-half story frame addition 1969. 1 ext. photo (1935); HABSI's (1957, 1969).

GREENBUSH VICINITY   Accomack County (1)

Bull-Coard House (VA-493), .1 mi. S of Coards Branch of Drummond Pond, E side of State Rte. 764, .7 mi. S of intersection with State Rte. 659. Frame with brick ends, rectangular (two-bay front), one story, gable roof, one exterior end chimney, irregular plan; one-story side wing. Built mid 18th C.; later addition. 1 ext. photo (1940).

GRETNA VICINITY   Pittsylvania County (72)

Yancy Cabin (VA-270), see Yates Tavern (VA-270), Gretna Vicinity.

Yates Tavern (Yancy Cabin) (VA-270), .5 mi. W of Long Branch, .1 mi. N of U.S. Rte. 29, .8 mi. SW of intersection with State Rte. 676. Frame with clapboarding, rectangular (two-bay front), two stories above stone foundation, gable roof, one stone and brick exterior end chimney, framed overhang at second-floor level; two-room plan with closed stair. Built mid 18th C.; overhang marks original eaves line before second floor was added. 3 ext. photos (1940); 1 data page (1941).

GUILFORD   Accomack County (1)

Clayton, George, House (VA-629), Guilford. Simple, frame house, 17' x 34' (three-bay front), one-and-a-half stories, gable roof; central hall, two-room plan. Built c. 1820; rear wing added c. 1900. 4 ext. photos (1960), 3 int. photos (1960); 3 data pages (1960, 1962).

Mason House (VA-952), Guilford. Brick, rectangular (three-bay front), one-and-a-half stories with dormers, splayed gable roof, two interior end chimneys; center-hall plan. Diaperwork in brick panels on facade. 5 sheets (1971, including plans, elevations, sections, details).

George Clayton House

GUINEA VICINITY   Caroline County (17)

Jackson Shrine, The (John Thornton House) (VA-637), Fredericksburg and Spotsylvania County Battlefields Memorial National Military Park, .5 mi. E of Poni River, .1 mi. NW of State Rte. 606, .1 mi. NE of intersection of Richmond, Fredericksburg and Potomac Railroad crossing. Historic house museum. Frame with clapboarding, 32'4" (two-bay front) x 28'3", one story, gable roof, two exterior end chimneys, open shed-roof entrance porch; four-room plan. Built 1828; restored 1927, 1928. Gen. Stonewall Jackson died here of wounds, May 10, 1863. 9 sheets (1962, including plot plan, plans, elevations, section, details).

Thornton, John, House (VA-637), see Jackson Shrine, The (VA-637), Guinea Vicinity.

121

HALLWOOD VICINITY
Accomack County (1)

Wessel's Root Cellar (VA-953), .3 mi. E of State Rte. 701, .1 mi. N of intersection with State Rte. 692. Brick (Flemish bond), rectangular (one-bay front), one story, gable roof, one interior chimney. Built late 18th C. Unique example of type. 2 sheets (1971, including plans, elevations, section). NR

HAMPTON
Accomack County (1)

Campbellton Smokehouse (VA-480), exact location unknown. Frame with clapboarding, rectangular (one-bay front), one story, pyramidal roof with finial. Built early 19th C. 1 ext. photo (n.d.).

Eagle Point (VA-481), exact location unknown. Brick (Flemish bond), rectangular (three-bay front), one-and-a-half stories, gable roof with dormers, rear saltbox extension, one interior end chimney. Built early 18th C.; side addition; demolished. 1 ext. photo (c. 1934).

Fortress Monroe, Main Sally Port (VA-595), .6 mi. E of Hampton Roads, .1 mi. E of U.S. Rte. 60/258 at Old Point Comfort. Brick, sandstone, rectangular with flanking ramparts and central covered passageway, one story, rusticated facade with pilasters and entablature; two casemates on either side of passageway. Built between 1819 and 1834. Jefferson Davis held prisoner at Fortress Monroe 1865-67. 8 sheets (n.d., including plot plan, plan, elevations, details). NR; NHL

HANOVER
Hanover County (43)

Barksdale Theatre (VA-521), see Tavern (VA-521), Hanover.

Hanover County Courthouse (VA-429), .3 mi. SW of Mechumps Creek, NE side of U.S. Rte. 301, at intersection with State Rte. 1005. Brick, T-shaped (five-bay front), one story, hipped roof, three interior end chimneys, five-bay arcaded porch set under roof, modillion cornice. Built c. 1735. 3 ext. photos (1932, 1934); HABSI (1959). NR

Tavern (Barksdale Theatre) (VA-521), .4 mi. SW of Mechumps Creek, SW side of State Rte. 1002, at intersection with U.S. Rte. 301. Frame with clapboarding, T-shaped (nine-bay front), two stories, gable roof, three exterior end chimneys, two interior chimneys, pent closets on S and E gable ends, porch runs along most of street front; rear lean-to. Built early 18th C.; enlarged. 1 ext. photo (1934).

HARRISONBURG

House (VA-907), 106 N. Liberty St. Stone, rectangular (four-bay front), two stories, gable roof, two interior end chimneys, stone jack arches over windows and door, denticulated cornice and barge board; center-hall plan; two-story brick rear wing. Built late 18th C.; demolished. 2 ext. photos (1938).

HAYMARKET   Prince William County (76)

Cabin (VA-283), see McCormack House (VA-283), Haymarket.

McCormack House (Cabin) (VA-283), E side Fayette St., .1 mi. S of intersection with State Rte. 55. Log and frame with clapboarding, rectangular (three-bay front), one story, gable roof sloping to rear lean-to; one exterior end chimney; two-room plan. Built early 19th C.; later additions; renovated mid 20th C. One of the few buildings to survive the burning of Haymarket, November 5, 1862. 1 ext. photo (1936).

HAYMARKET VICINITY   Prince William County (76)

Beverley's Mill (VA-828), N bank of Broad Run, N side of State Rte. 55 at Thorofare Gap. Fieldstone, rectangular (four-bay front), four stories above raised basement, gable roof, one interior end chimney; open plan. Built mid 19th C.; later alterations; the present structure was rebuilt on the site of a mid-18th C. mill. 1 ext. photo; HABSI (1958).

Evergreen (VA-833), 1.4 mi. N of Catharpin Run, .1 mi. E of State Rte. 630, .5 mi. N of intersection with State Rte. 601. Stone with plastered cement wash, rectangular (five-bay front), two-and-a-half stories above raised basement, gable roof with dormers, two stone interior end chimneys, pedimented one-story entrance porch; center-hall plan; flanking wings. Built early 19th C.; extensive later additions and alterations, including addition of two-story columned portico and flanking wings. 1 ext. photo (1936); HABSI's (1958, 1959).

Hagley (VA-276), 1.4 mi. N of Catharpin Run, S side State Rte. 601, .1 mi. W of intersection with U.S. Rte. 15. Log and frame, four adjacent units, one story, gable roof, two stone exterior end chimneys; one-room plan per unit. Built mid 18th C.; demolished mid 20th C. 5 ext. photos (1936).

La Grange (VA-289), .9 mi. E of High Point Mountain, W side of State Rte. 681, .5 mi. S of intersection with State Rte. 601. Brick (Flemish bond), rectangular (four-bay front), two-and-a-half stories, gable roof with dormers, three exterior end chimneys; center-hall plan; one-and-a-half story brick dependency connected to main house by hyphen. Built late 18th C.; later restoration, alterations, and replacement of vandalized interior trim 1936. 5 ext. photos (1936); HABSI (1959).

Mt. Atlas (VA-831), .6 mi. NE of Catharpin Run, .1 mi. E of State Rte. 731, .4 mi. N of intersection with State Rte. 601. Frame with clapboarding, rectangular (three-bay front), two stories, gable roof, one stone and brick exterior end chimney, one-story porch, modillion cornice; side-hall plan; frame smokehouse with diagonal batten door studded with rose-head nails. Built early 19th C.; extensive later alterations including dormer windows. 2 ext. photos (1936).

Poplar Hill (VA-830), .2 mi. W of Catharpin Run, .5 mi. S of State Rte. 601, .5 mi. W of intersection with State Rte. 731. Frame with clapboarding, rectangular (five-bay front), one-and-a-half stories, gable roof with dormers, two stone interior end chimneys, square columned entrance porch; center-hall plan. Built early 19th C.; burned mid 20th C. 2 ext. photos (1936).

Meadowland (VA-829), see Ruins of House near Beverley's Mill (VA-829), Haymarket Vicinity.

Prospect Hill (VA-832), .5 mi. SW of Bull Run, E side of State Rte. 624, .4 mi. N of intersection with State Rte. 701. Log and stucco, rectangular (five-bay front), one-and-a-half stories, gable roof with dormers, two stone exterior end chimneys; center-hall plan; one-story stone wing joined to main house by frame hyphen. Built late 18th C. or early 19th C.; later alterations; stone wing reconstructed 1967. 3 ext. photos (1936), 2 int. photos (1936).

Retreat, The (VA-285), .3 mi. SW of Chestnut Lick, 1 mi. N of State Rte. 601, 1 mi. NE of intersection with State Rte. 234. Frame with clapboarding, three-part composition: (a) rectangular (three-bay front), two stories, gable roof, one exterior end chimney; side-hall plan, flanked by (b) rectangular (two-bay front), one-and-a-half stories, gable roof with dormers, one exterior end chimney; one-room plan, flanked by (c) rectangular (two-bay front), one story, gable roof, one stone exterior end chimney; one-room plan. Built mid 18th C.; enlarged late 18th C., early 19th C. 5 ext. photos (1936), 1 int. photo (1936); HABSI (1959).

Ruins of House near Beverley's Mill (Meadowland) (VA-829), .1 mi. E of Broad Run, N side of State Rte. 55 at Thorofare Gap. Fieldstone walls. Built mid 18th C.; demolished. 1 ext. photo (1936).

Waverly Mills (VA-284), N bank Catharpin Run, S side of State Rte. 679, .4 mi. W of intersection with U.S. Rte. 15. Log with clapboarding, rectangular (three-bay front), one story, gable roof, two stone exterior end chimneys; two-room plan. Built early 19th C.; wing addition and later alterations; demolished. 1 ext. photo (1936).

HEBRON VICINITY   Dinwiddie County (27)

Harris House (VA-726), see House (VA-726), Hebron Vicinity.

House (Harris House) (VA-726), 1.8 mi. S of Namozine Creek, N side of U.S. Rte. 460, .1 mi. E of intersection with State Rte. 620. Frame with clapboarding, rectangular (three-bay front), one-and-a-half stories, gable roof with shed dormers, exterior end chimney; two-room plan; side wing: frame with clapboarding, rectangular (two-bay front), one-and-a-half stories, gable roof with shed dormer, exterior end chimney. Built early 19th C. 1 ext. photo (1936); HABSI (1959).

HERNDON VICINITY   Fairfax County (30)

Dranesville Tavern (VA-642), 119119 Leesburg Pike (State Rte. 7), 8.6 mi. W of Tyson's Corner. Log and frame with clapboarding, 70'7" (five-bay front) x 27'1", two stories, gable roof, two stone

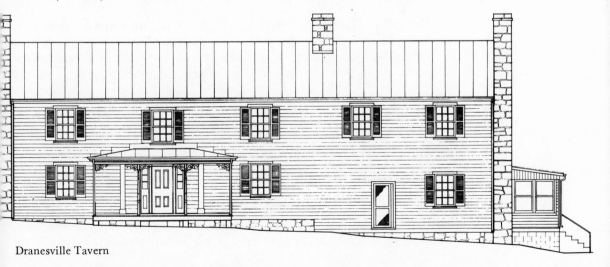

Dranesville Tavern

exterior end chimneys, one stone interior chimney; center-hall plan. Original portion built c. 1830, altered c. 1850, additions 1893, moved 100' S of original location, 1968. 8 sheets (1968, including plans, elevations, sections, details). NR

HICKORY

Old Academy (VA-227), SW corner of intersection of State Rtes. 625 and 170, near Chesapeake. Frame with clapboarding, rectangular (three-bay front), one-and-a-half stories, gambrel roof with dormers, exterior end chimneys, modillion cornice; rear lean-to. Built early 18th C.; demolished. 7 ext. photos (1937, 1939, 1940, n.d.).

HOPEWELL

Appomattox Manor (VA-824), N side of N end of Cedar Lane. Frame with clapboarding, U-shaped (seven-bay front), one-and-a-half stories, gable roof with dormers, three interior chimneys, one exterior end chimney, pedimented pavilion, one-story lattice-work porch; five-room irregular plan; one-story separate kitchen and outbuildings. Kitchen built early 18th C.; main house built 1763; later alterations and extensive additions 1840, 1850, 1913. Title to Appomattox Manor derives in unbroken descent since 1635. 5 ext. photos, main house (1964), 2 ext. photos, kitchen and outbuildings (1964); 4 int. photos, main house (1964); 4 data pages (1959); HABSI (1959). NR

HOPEWELL VICINITY   Prince George County (75)

Flower de Hundred (VA-295), .5 mi. S of James River, E side of State Rte. 639, 2.4 mi. NE of intersection with State Rte. 640. Frame with clapboarding, rectangular (three-bay front), two stories, gable roof, two exterior end chimneys; flanking one-story frame wings with gable roofs; center-hall plan. Built early 19th C.; later additions; demolished c. 1950. 2 ext. photos (1940).

HORNTOWN VICINITY   Accomack County (1)

Chincoteague Farm (VA-489), see Corbin Hall (VA-489), Horntown Vicinity.

Corbin Hall (Chincoteague Farm) (VA-489), .3 mi. W of Chincoteague Bay, 1.2 mi. E of State Rte. 679, .4 mi. NE of intersection with State

Appomattox Manor

Rte. 709. Brick (Flemish bond), rectangular (five-bay front), two stories, gable roof, two interior end chimneys, second-story central Palladian window, center-hall plan, frame, one-story wing. Built late 18th C.; later addition. 3 ext. photos (1940); HABSI (1958).

IRVINGTON VICINITY   Lancaster County (52)

Christ Church (VA-70), .5 mi. N of Ashburn Cove, W side of State Rte. 646, at intersection with State Rte. 709. Brick (Flemish bond), cruciform (three-bay front), one story, steep hipped roof with pronounced bell cast, full entablature main cornice, pulvinated frieze and dentils, molded brick entrance details including pilasters and pediments, high arched windows with molded brick detail and stone impost and keystone, oval windows above entrances; cruciform interior plan, exceptionally fine paneled wooden pews, balcony, pulpit, and reredos. Raised stone tombs of Robert "King" Carter and two of his wives. Built 1732; restored 1967. Christ Church is widely regarded as the finest example of 18th C. Virginia religious architecture. 12 ext. photos (1937, 1939), 2 int. photos (1937), 1 photo, Robert Carter's tomb (1932); HABSI (1958). NR; NHL

Christ Church

IVOR VICINITY   Southampton County (88)

Bailey House (VA-349), see Holmes, Peter, House (House on Blackwater River) (VA-349), Ivor Vicinity.

Binford House (VA-235), .6 mi. W of Blackwater River, .1 mi. NW
of intersection of State Rtes. 621 and 616, 3 mi. N of intersection
with State Rte. 617. Frame with clapboarding, rectangular (three-bay
front), one-and-a-half stories, gable roof with pedimented dormers,
three exterior end chimneys; rear ell. Built mid 18th C.; renovated.
5 ext. photos (1938), 5 int. photos (1938).

Holmes, Peter, House (Bailey House, House on Blackwater River) (VA-349), exact location unknown. Brick (Flemish bond), gable ends with frame fronts, rectangular (five-bay front), one-and-a-half stories, gable roof with dormers, two interior end chimneys. Built mid 18th C. 1 ext. photo (1936), 5 int. photos (1936).

House on Blackwater River (VA-349), see Holmes, Peter, House (Bailey House) (VA-349), Ivor Vicinity.

JAMES STORE VICINITY   Gloucester County (37)

Toddsbury (VA-417), W bank of North River, .3 mi. E of State Rte. 622, 1.1 mi. E of intersection with State Rte. 14. Brick (Flemish bond), L-shaped (six-bay front), one-and-a-half stories, gambrel roof with dormers, three interior end chimneys, modillion cornice, brick water table, projecting two-story pedimented frame entrance porch on E front, tetrastyle Doric columns at ground-floor level supporting two-bay enclosed second story; center-hall plan, notable interior paneling including two fully paneled rooms on ground floor, hall with open string stair, dado, and denticulated cornice; ell. Built mid 17th C., extensive subsequent additions and alterations early 18th C., late 18th C., early 19th C.; restored. 8 ext. photos (1934, 1937); 2 data pages (1941); HABSI (1959). NR

Toddsbury

Ice House (VA-747), W bank of Toddsbury Creek, S side of State Rte. 622, .9 mi. E of intersection with State Rte. 14. Brick, cylindrical (one-bay front), one story, conical roof; one-room plan. Built early 19th C.; partially rebuilt mid 20th C. 1 ext. photo (1933); HABSI (1959).

JAMESTOWN VICINITY James City County (48)

Powhatan (VA-177), S bank of E tributary of Powhatan Creek, .4 mi. W of State Rte. 615, .8 mi. N of intersection with State Rte. 5. Brick (Flemish bond with glazed headers), rectangular (five-bay front), two-and-a-half stories, hipped roof with dormers, two T-shaped interior end chimneys, brick water table and string course, modillion cornice; center-hall plan. Built mid 18th C.; burned Civil War; rebuilt. 1 sheet (1940, including perspective views of restoration); 1 ext. photo (1940); 1 data page (1940). NR

JAMESTOWN ISLAND James City County (48)

Architectural Remains; Project 103, Structure 123 (VA-472). Brick, outside dimensions 10'3" x 15'3", rectangular with entrance steps, brick pavement with floor recess. Probably built early 17th C. 1 sheet (1958, including plan, sections, details).

Architectural Remains; Project 103, Structure 125 (VA-473). Brick, outside dimensions 11'9" x 21'6", rectangular with chimney and shed projections, brick pavement with cistern. Probably built early 17th C. 1 sheet (1958, including plan, sections, details).

Architectural Remains; Project 194, Structure 110 (VA-444), see Architectural Remains; Unit B, Sub-unit 110 (VA-444), Jamestown Island.

Architectural Remains; Project 194, Structure 115 (VA-470). Brick, rectangular with cellar and porch projection at E end, partitions indicating four units. Probably built early 17th C. 3 sheets (1958, including plans, sections, structural details).

Architectural Remains; Project 194, Structure 117 (VA-471). Brick, outside dimensions 18' x 26', inner buttresses, brick pavement and unlined pit, corner porch projection with evidence of charred wood beneath. Probably built early 17th C. 1 sheet (1958, including plan, section).

Architectural Remains; Unit A, Sub-unit 39 (VA-26). Brick foundations and basement paving, outside dimensions 36'4" x 25'4"; rectangular plan. Probably built early 17th C. 10 sheets (1934, including plot plan, plan, sections, details of basement walls, and details of tiles, roof slates, and hardware excavated); 4 ext. photos (1935); 7 data pages (1936).

Architectural Remains; Unit A, Sub-unit 39

Architectural Remains; Unit B, Sub-units 59 and 73 (VA-27). Fieldstone and brick, outside dimensions 52'3" x 16'1", rectangular plan. Probably built early 17th C. 3 sheets (1935, including plot plan, plans, elevations, details of hardware excavated); 3 ext. photos, foundations (1935), 1 photo, hardware (1935); 6 data pages (1935).

Architectural Remains; Unit B, Sub-unit 62 (VA-28). Brick, outside dimensions 48'8" x 21'7", rectangular plan. Probably built early 17th C. 4 sheets (1934, including plans, sections, details of hardware excavated); 3 ext. photos, foundations (1935), 1 photo, hardware (1935); 5 data pages (1935).

Architectural Remains; Unit B, Sub-unit 86 (VA-29). Brick foundations. Probably built early 17th C. 4 sheets (1935, including plan, sections, details of hardware excavated).

Architectural Remains; Unit B, Sub-unit 76 (VA-30). Brick, outside dimensions 33'9" x 118'11", rectangular plan. Probably built early 17th C. 7 sheets (1936, including plan, sections, structural details, details of hardware excavated).

FRAGMENT OF WROUGHT-IRON-SCUTCHEON PROBABLY-FROM-A-DRAWER-OR-A-DOOR-PULL

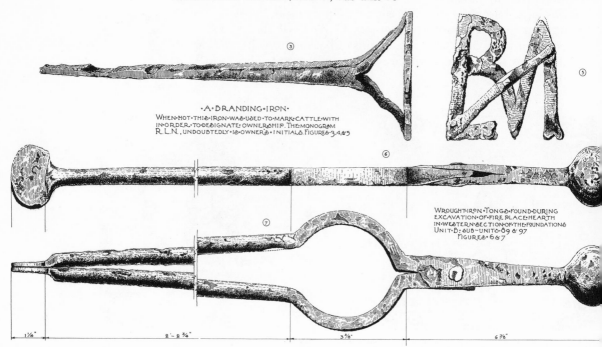

③

·A·BRANDING·IRON·
WHEN·HOT·THIS·IRON·WAS·USED·TO·MARK·CATTLE·WITH
IN·ORDER· TO·DESIGNATE· OWNERSHIP. THE·MONOGRAM
R.L.N., UNDOUBTEDLY·IS·OWNER'S · INITIALS. FIGURES·3,4,&5

⑤

⑥

WROUGHT·IRON·TONGS·FOUND·DURING
EXCAVATION·OF·FIRE·PLACE·HEARTH
IN·WESTERN·SECTION·OF·THE·FOUNDATIONS
UNIT·B: SUB—UNITS·89 & 97
FIGURES· 6 & 7

⑦

1¼"   2'-2¾"   3⅜"   6⅞"

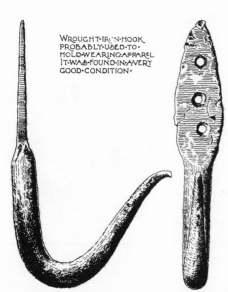

WROUGHT·IRON·HOOK
PROBABLY·USED·TO·
HOLD·WEARING·APPAREL
IT·WAS·FOUND·IN·A·VERY
GOOD·CONDITION·

Architectural Remains; Unit B, Sub-units 89 and 97

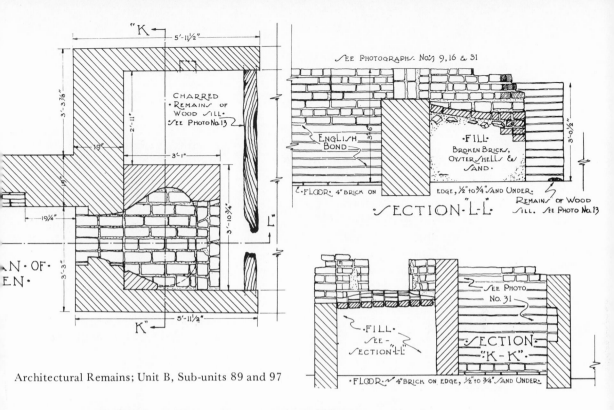

·K· 5'-11½"
CHARRED ·REMAINS· OF WOOD ·SILL· ·SEE PHOTO No.13·

3'-3⅜"
2'-11"
19"
3'-1"
19"
19¼"
3'-3"

·L·

3'-10¾"

·N·OF·
·EN·

5'-11½" **·K·**

SEE PHOTOGRAPH· No's 9,16 & 31

·ENGLISH BOND·

·FILL· BROKEN BRICKS, OYSTER SHELLS & SAND·

3'6"
3'-0½"

·FLOOR· 4"BRICK ON EDGE, ½"to¾"SAND UNDER·

SECTION·L·L·

REMAINS OF WOOD SILL· SEE PHOTO No.13

SEE PHOTO No.31

·FILL· SEE -SECTION·L·L·

·SECTION· ·K-K·

·FLOOR· 4"BRICK ON EDGE, ½"to¾"SAND UNDER·

Architectural Remains; Unit B, Sub-units 89 and 97

Architectural Remains; Unit B, Sub-units 89 and 97 (VA-25). Brick, outside dimensions 63'11" x 43'4", rectangular plan. Probably built early 17th C. 14 sheets (1935, including plans, sections, structural details, details of hardware excavated); 3 ext. photos, foundations (1935), 4 photos, hardware (1935); 7 data pages (n.d.).

Architectural Remains; Unit B, Sub-unit 101 (VA-31). Clay, decorative faience tiles painted in blue monochrome. Probably 17th C. 1 sheet (1935).

Architectural Remains; Unit B, Sub-unit 110 (Architectural Remains; Project 194, Structure 110) (VA-444). Brick, 24'3" x 23', floor paved with tiles; rectangular plan. Probably built early 17th C.; later installation of three fire chambers. 3 sheets (1955, including plan, sections, structural details); 3 ext. photos, foundation (1954).

Architectural Remains; Unit B, Sub-unit 112 (VA-445). Brick, inside dimensions 47'4" x 31'6", cellar across N side. Built early 17th C.; later addition with porch partition; estimated that building burned before 1676. 3 sheets (1955, including plan and sections); 12 ext. photos (1954, 1955).

Mattissippi (Sturgis House) (VA-547), E bank of Chesapeake Bay, 1 mi. W of State Rte. 676, .6 mi. NW of intersection with State Rte. 183. Brick (Flemish bond), 35′7″ (four-bay front) x 20′5″, one story, gable roof, two interior end chimneys; two-room plan, enclosed winder stairs. Built mid 17th C.; ruinous. 8 sheets (1963, including plans, elevations, sections, details); 2 ext. photos (1940).

Sommers House (VA-546), .1 mi. W of Nassawadox Creek, .6 mi. SE of State Rte. 183, .2 mi. SW of intersection with State Rte. 691. Brick (Flemish bond), rectangular (three-bay front), one-and-a-half stories, gable roof with dormers, two interior end chimneys, modillion cornice; side wing. Built mid 18th C.; wing addition removed. 13 sheets (1971, including plans, elevations, sections, details); 2 ext. photos (1940). NR

Sturgis House (VA-547), see Mattissippi (VA-547), Jamesville Vicinity.

Sommers House

JEFFERSONTON VICINITY   Culpeper County (24)

Greenfield (VA-433), .5 mi. N of Bee Branch, .1 mi. SW of State Rte. 621, .6 mi. SE of intersection with State Rtes. 625 and 710. Frame with clapboarding, rectangular (three-bay front), one-and-a-half stories, gable roof with dormers, two exterior end chimneys; center-hall plan; one-story flanking side wings. Built early 19th C.; demolished 1947. 1 ext. photo (c. 1934).

KING GEORGE VICINITY   King George County (50)

Marmion (VA-145), .2 mi. N of Pepper Mill Creek, at W end of State Rte. 649, .8 mi. E of intersection with State Rte. 609. Frame with clapboarding, 53′ (seven-bay front) x 33′, two stories, gable roof with jerkinheads, two notable exterior end chimneys with molded brick detail and glazed headers, modillion cornice, flush corner pilasters on front and rear elevations, small pedimented one-story wooden porch on front elevation, one-story wooden porch with shed roof along full length of rear elevation; center-hall plan, corner fireplaces, outstanding interior paneling, stair with turned balusters; original wooden dependencies include dairy, icehouse, smokehouse, kitchen, and schoolroom-office. Built late 17th C.; greatly altered and enlarged mid 18th C.; painted, paneled drawing room interior removed 1916,

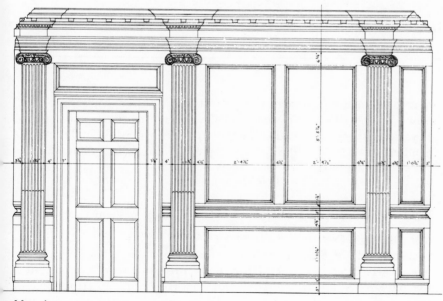

Marmion

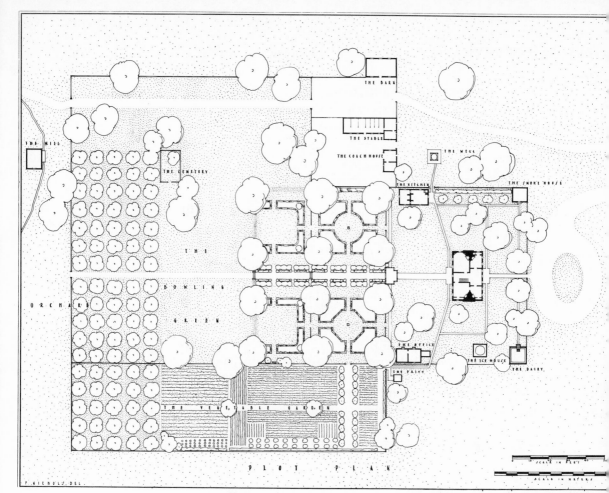

Marmion

re-erected in the American Wing of the Metropolitan Museum of Art, New York, 1924. 25 sheets (1936, including plot plan, plans, elevations, interior elevations, details); 22 ext. photos, including dependencies (1935, 1936), 8 int. photos, including dependencies (1935, 1936); HABSI (1958). NR

KING WILLIAM   King William County (51)

King William County Courthouse (VA-123), .6 mi. E of Acquinton Creek, E side of State Rte. 619, .1 mi. N of intersection with State Rte. 1301. Brick, T-shaped (three-bay front), one story, hipped roof, five-bay arched loggia set under roof on S front, one exterior end and two interior end chimneys, modillion cornice; courtroom with two

136

flanking rooms. Built c. 1735. 7 sheets (1936, including plan, elevations, details); 4 ext. photos (1934, 1936), 1 ext. photo, stable (1936); 4 data pages (1936); HABSI (1958). NR

KING WILLIAM VICINITY   King William County (51)

Acquinton Church (VA-760), .6 mi. S of Acquinton Creek, N side of State Rte. 629, at intersection with State Rte. 618. Brick with stucco, rectangular (one-bay front) with projecting vestibule, one story, gable roof, vertical boarding in gable ends above the eavesline, three-bay nave with lancet windows built into the older arched openings. N wing built c. 1760 as addition to original building 1734; demolished; wing renovated in Gothic Revival style c. 1875; ruinous, roof destroyed. 1 ext. photo (1936); HABSI (1958).

Green Level (VA-759), .6 mi. S of E tributary of Acquinton Creek, .2 mi. N of State Rte. 621, 1.3 mi. W of intersection with State Rte. 633. Brick and frame with clapboarding, rectangular (five-bay front), two-and-a-half stories, gable roof with dormers, two exterior end chimneys, frame second floor over brick first floor; center-hall plan; side wings; brick servants' quarters. Built late 18th C.; original frame part elevated to second-floor level when brick first floor was built mid 19th C. 1 ext. photo (1936), 1 ext. photo, servants' quarters (1936); HABSI (1958).

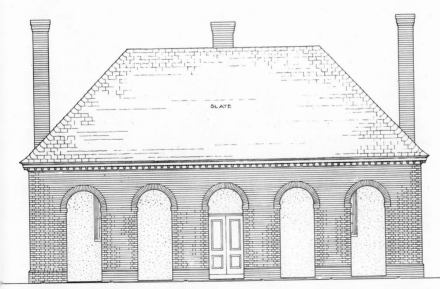

King William County Courthouse

Winterham (VA-761), .2 mi. E of N tributary of Jacks Creek, .2 mi. E of State Rte. 629, .8 mi. S of intersection with State Rte. 618. Brick and frame, rectangular (two-bay front), two-and-a-half stories, gable roof with dormers, one exterior end chimney, frame second floor over brick first floor; two-room plan; side wing: frame with clapboarding, rectangular (one-bay front), one-and-a-half stories, gable roof with dormer. Built early 19th C.; enlarged. 1 ext. photo (1936); HABSI (1958).

LANCASTER   Lancaster County (52)

Clerk's Office (VA-360), S side State Rte. 3. Brick (Flemish bond), rectangular (four-bay front), one story, gable roof, two interior end chimneys, studded wooden diagonal planked shutters; one-room plan. Built mid 18th C.; later alterations. 1 ext. photo (detail, 1938); 1 data page (1940); HABSI's (1957, 1958).

Hughlett House (VA-412), State Rte. 3, exact location unknown. Frame with clapboarding, rectangular (five-bay front), one-and-a-half stories, gable roof with dormers and rear slope in form of lean-to, modillion cornice; center-hall plan. Built late 18th C.; demolished 1940. 6 ext. photos (1930, 1931); 1 data page (1941).

LANESVILLE VICINITY   King William County (51)

Elsing Green (VA-67), .2 mi. N of Pamunkey River, 1.2 mi. SW of State Rte. 632, 1.8 mi. W of intersection with State Rte. 623. Brick, U-shaped (seven-bay front), two stories, hipped roof, four interior chimneys, modillion cornice, molded brick pedimented S entrance; T-shaped hall defines four rooms surrounding it; two flanking brick dependencies, one-and-a-half stories. Built mid 18th C.; burned c. 1800; rebuilt within old walls; renovated; E dependency built mid 18th C., W one built 19th C. 8 ext. photos (n.d., 1936, 1937); 2 data pages (1939); HABSI (1958). NR

LEE MONT VICINITY   Accomack County (1)

Clayton, George, House (VA-629), 1.2 mi. E of Hunting Creek, .2 mi. S of State Rte. 673, .5 mi. W of intersection with State Rte. 658. Frame with clapboarding, rectangular, 34' (three-bay front) x 17', one-and-a-half stories, gable roof with dormers, two brick exterior end chimneys. Built early 19th C.; rear addition c. 1900; demolished. 4 ext. photos (1960), 3 int. photos (1960); 3 data pages (1960, 1962).

Drummond House (VA-487), .1 mi. N of Drummond Ponds, NE side of intersection of State Rtes. 661 and 658, 1.3 mi. S of intersection with State Rte. 669. Frame with clapboarding and brick ends, rectangular (four-bay front), one-and-a half stories, gable roof with dormers, two exterior end chimneys; irregular plan. Built mid 18th C.; later side additions. 2 ext. photos (1940).

Drummond Store (VA-488), E bank of Drummond Ponds, S side of intersection of State Rtes. 658 and 661, 1.3 mi. S of intersection of State Rte. 669. Frame with clapboarding, rectangular (three-bay front), one story, gable roof; flanking wings. Built early 19th C. 1 ext. photo (1940).

LEESBURG   Loudoun County (54)

Commercial Building (Drugstore) (VA-375), 1-5 N. King St. Brick, rectangular (six-bay front, three adjacent units of two bays, five-bay lateral facade), two stories, gable roof, five interior chimneys; shops on ground floor, two-room plan above. Built early 19th C.; later alterations. 1 ext. photo (1934).

Commercial Building (Nichols Law Office) (VA-438), 13 S. King St. Brick, rectangular (two-bay front), two-and-a-half stories, mansard roof, elaborate window with semi-elliptical fanlight on ground floor; commercial floor plan. Built early 19th C.; extensive alterations late 19th C.; street front stripped of detail mid 20th C. 2 ext. photos (1934).

Drugstore (VA-375), see Commercial Building (VA-375), 1-5 N. King St., Leesburg.

Nichols Law Office (VA-438), see Commercial Building (VA-438), 13 S. King St., Leesburg.

Old Bank (VA-378), see Valley Bank (VA-378), 1 N. Church St., Leesburg.

Valley Bank (Old Bank) (VA-378), 1 N. Church St. Brick, rectangular (six-bay front), two-and-a-half stories, gable roof, two interior end chimneys, one interior chimney, shallow central pediment motif with elliptical attic light; irregular plan. Built early 19th C.; extensive later alterations and additions including reconstruction of S front. 1 ext. photo (1937); HABSI (1958).

Log Cabin (VA-536), near Goose Creek. Log, rectangular (three-bay front), one story above raised basement, wood shingle gable roof, two exterior stone chimneys. Built late 18th C.; demolished c. 1937. 1 ext. photo (1933).

Oatlands Historic District (VA-949), E and W sides of U.S. Rte. 15, 6 mi. S of Leesburg. Rural historic district composed of early 19th C. manor house (Oatlands), subsidiary plantation buildings, gardens, and surrounding lands. Also included are the Church of Our Savior and Mountain Gap School, both historically related to the Oatlands property. 2 sheets (1973, including title sheet and site plan).

Oatlands (VA-949A), .9 mi. N of Goose Creek, .5 mi. NE of U.S. Rte. 15, 1 mi. S of intersection with State Rte. 651. Historic House Museum of National Trust for Historic Preservation. Brick with stucco, 107' (nine-bay front) x 64', three stories (central block) and two stories (wings) above raised basement, hipped roof, two interior chimneys, monumental tetrastyle portico; symmetrical plan with two octagonal ended stair towers, Adamesque details. Built

Oatlands

1800-03, attributed to George Carter; portico added 1827; minor interior alterations early 20th C. 13 sheets (1973, including plans, elevations, sections, details), 3 ext. photos (1973), 2 int. photos (1973). NHI.

Bachelor Cottage (VA-949B). Brick and frame with clapboarding, 18′ (one-bay front) x 25′, two stories, gable roof, one interior chimney, two-story porch. 1 sheet (1973, including plans, elevations).

Greenhouse (VA-949C). Brick, glass, and frame with clapboarding, 57′ (four-bay front) x 33′, one story, gable roof, two exterior end chimneys. 1 sheet (1973, including plans, section, elevation).

Studio (VA-949D) and *Servants' Quarters* (VA-949E). Brick, one-and-a-half story units, gable and hipped roofs. 1 sheet (1973, including plans, elevations).

Carter Barn (VA-949F). Brick, rectangular, three stories, gable roof, one-story stone wing, gable roof. 2 sheets (1973, including plans, elevations, detail).

Little Oatlands (VA-949G). Stone, rectangular, one-and-a-half stories, one interior chimney, gable roof; octagonal ended wing, frame with clapboarding, two stories, one interior chimney; later wing added to N of original portion. 2 sheets (1973, including plans, elevations).

Mountain Gap School (VA-949K). W side of U.S. Rte. 15, .2 mi. N of entrance to Oatlands. Frame, 20′ (one-bay front) x 30′, one story, gable roof, one interior chimney; one-room plan. Typical one-room schoolhouse. 1 sheet (1973, including plan, elevations, section).

Noland's Ferry House (VA-538), .1 mi. W of Potomac River, W side of State Rte. 660, .7 mi. N of intersection with State Rte. 662. Brick, rectangular (five-bay front), two stories, gable roof, two interior end chimneys, modillion cornice, belt course and water table, semi-circular fanlight over the entrance door; center-hall plan; two-story flanking wings. Begun late 18th C., left unfinished; extensive additions and alterations executed c. 1968. 1 ext. photo (1930); HABSI (1958).

Cottage, The (VA-537), exact location unknown. Log with stucco, rectangular (five-bay front), one story, gable roof, full-length front porch, three exterior stone and brick end chimneys; rear lean-to. Built mid 18th C.; demolished 1937. 1 ext. photo (1937).

LEXINGTON   Rockbridge County (82)

Alexander, William, House and Store (VA-905), NW corner of Main St. and Washington St. Brick (diaper work), 44'6" (four-bay front) x 34', 3 stories, shallow hipped roof with deep bracketed cornice, four interior corner chimneys, stone ground-floor exterior facing, cast-iron balcony at first-floor level; modified central-hall plan. Built c. 1790 for William Alexander; partially destroyed by fire 1796 and rebuilt; street lowered approx. 10' c. 1850 and stone ground-floor exterior installed; roof replaced mid 19th C. 6 sheets (1970, including plot plan, plans, elevations, sections, details); 4 ext. photos (1969); 9 data pages (1969); HABSI (1957).

House (Pendleton-Coles House) (VA-898), 319 Letcher Ave. Board and batten, 34'3" (three-bay front) x 41'6", two stories, steep gable roof, decorated barge board, two interior chimneys, one-story wooden entrance porch, bay windows, diamond-shaped window panes; irregular plan. Built c. 1850. 3 ext. photos (1968), 4 int. photos (1968); 3 data pages (1969).

Jordan's Point (Stono) (VA-900), N side of intersection of State Rte. 303 and U.S. Rte. 11. Brick (Flemish bond), temple form (three-bay front), two stories, gable roof, two-story pedimented tetrastyle Roman Doric portico with brick columns and pilasters, two exterior end chimneys, one interior end chimney; cross-hall plan; flanking one-story wings; one-and-a-half story rear wing; office outbuilding: brick, square, one story above raised stone basement; round stone icehouse; rectangular stone outbuilding. Main house built 1818, John Jordan, owner-architect; extensive later additions and alterations; icehouse and office built early 19th C.; stone outbuilding built c. 1900. 13 sheets (1970, including plot plan, plans, elevations, sections, details); 6 ext. photos (1968), 3 ext. photos, outbuildings (1968), 4 int. photos (1968); 6 data pages (1969); HABSI (1965).

Lee Chapel (VA-906), Washington and Lee University. Brick, rectangular (three-bay front), one story above raised stone basement, gable roof, advanced belfry-entrance tower with concave elongated pyramidal roof, semi-circular window heads, corbel brick decoration on

Pendleton-Coles House

belfry; one-room plan, gallery and memorial apse; rectangular rear wing. Built 1867, under the direction of Robert E. Lee, president of Washington College; memorial apse and Lee crypt added 1879-83; original wooden frame construction replaced with concrete and steel, interiors renovated and partially restored 1962, 1963. 5 ext. photos (1968), 5 int. photos (1968); 9 data pages (1969); HABSI (1965). NHL

Lee-Jackson House (VA-903), 4 University Place. Brick, temple form (three-bay front), two stories, shallow hipped roof, tetrastyle Roman Doric portico, four interior end chimneys; side-hall plan; flanking one-story wings. Built 1841-42, William Gibson, carpenter, James Alexander, mason. President's house of Washington and Lee University from 1842 to 1869 and the home of Major Thomas (Stonewall) Jackson and his wife Elinor Junkin Jackson 1853-1855, and General and Mrs. R. E. Lee 1865-1868. 2 data pages (1969); HABSI (1965).

Main Street Area Survey (VA-897), Main Street. General views and selected details of building groups along Main Street. 10 ext. photos (1968).

Pendleton-Coles House (VA-898), see House (VA-898), 319 Letcher Ave., Lexington.

Reid-White House

Reid-White House (VA-955), S side of Nelson St. (U.S. Rte. 60), between Myers St. and Lee St. Brick, 40′6″ (three-bay front) x 34′6″, two stories above raised basement, gable roof, four exterior end chimneys. Built early 19th C., wings added later. 8 sheets (1970, including plans, elevations, section, details).

Stono (VA-900), see Jordan's Point (VA-900), Lexington.

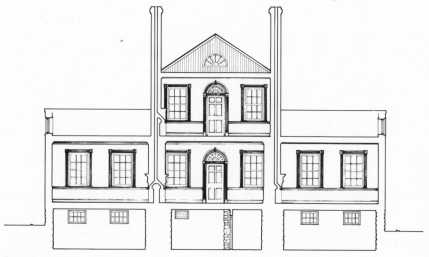

Stono

Virginia Military Institute, Barracks

Valley Railroad Station (VA-904), N side of intersection of McLaughlin and Glasgow Sts. Brick, 142'6" (fifteen-bay front) x 22', one story, steep gable roof, one interior chimney, pressed brick segmental jack arches over openings; interior divided into passenger and freight areas; flanking gable-roof wings. Built 1883 for the Valley Railroad Company of Virginia; acquired by the Chesapeake and Ohio Railroad Co. 1942. 5 ext. photos (1968); 4 data pages (1969).

Virginia Military Institute: Barracks (VA-902), V.M.I. Parade Grounds at end of Letcher Ave. Brick with stucco, quadrangle (thirteen-bay S front), four stories, flat roof, crenellated parapet, octagonal towers flanking S entrance; quadrangular plan with open balconies on interior courtyard. Built 1850-62; burned 1864; rebuilt 1870-73, Alexander Jackson Davis, architect; enlarged 1892, I. E. A. Rose, architect; enlarged 1918-19, B. G. Goodhue, architect; enlarged 1946-48, Carneal and Johnson, architects. 3 ext. photos (1968); 22 data pages (1969); HABSI (1965). NR; NHL

Superintendent's Quarters (VA-901), N side of V.M.I. Parade Grounds. Brick with stucco, irregular (nine-bay front), two stories, flat roof, six concealed interior chimneys; irregular plan; flanked by crenellated octagonal three-story towers. Built 1860-62, Alexander Jackson Davis, architect; dismantled and reconstructed on new site 1914; altered and enlarged 1924, Carneal and Johnson, architects; renovated 1954. 4 ext. photos (1968), 4 int. photos (1968); 4 data pages (1969); HABSI (1965).

Washington and Lee University, Washington Hall

Washington Hall, Washington and Lee University (VA-568), N side of Jefferson St., E of Washington St. Brick, five-part composition, central block: rectangular (three-bay front), three stories, gable roof with cupola, gable-end front with hexastyle pedimented Doric portico, interior end chimneys; terminal blocks: rectangular (three-bay front), three stories, hipped roof with deck, portico with paneled square columns, interior end chimneys; hyphens: rectangular (three-bay front), two stories, gable roof, twin pilaster motif separates bays. Washington Hall built c. 1824; S block built c. 1831; N block and hyphens added 1842. 4 ext. photos (1934, 1968); 1 int. photo (1968); 11 data pages (1969); HABSI (1965).

LEXINGTON VICINITY   Rockbridge County (82)

Covered Bridge (VA-567.) on Maury River, .1 mi. W of intersection of U.S. Rte. 11 and State Rte. 39, at NE line of Lexington city limits. Frame, post supports under bridge platform, two long arched planks anchored on each bank span river to give additional stability, vertical and diagonal framing support gable roof. Built late 19th C.; demolished. 1 ext. photo (n.d.).

146

Stone House

Stone House (VA-899), W bank of Woods Creek, .2 mi. SW of State Rte. 687 (Ross Rd.), at its intersection with Woods Creek. Stone, rectangular (five-bay front), two stories, gable roof, two exterior end chimneys, one interior end chimney, one-story pedimented wooden entrance porch; center-hall plan; one-story side wing connected to main house by hyphen. Built 1797, John Spear, builder; renovated and partially restored 1966. 3 ext. photos (1968), 3 int. photos (1968); 5 data pages (1969); HABSI's (1957, 1965).

Winterview Farm Log Cabin (VA-956), .1 mi. S of interstate 81, 1.5 mi. NE of intersection with U.S. Rte. 11. Log, rectangular (one-bay front), two stories, gable roof with overhang protecting second-floor balcony, one interior chimney; open plan. 5 sheets (1971, including plans, elevations).

LIGHTFOOT VICINITY   James City County (48)

Greenspring (VA-440), .4 mi. W of W tributary of Powhatan Creek, .1 mi. W of State Rte. 614, 1.2 mi. S of intersection with State Rte. 613. Site. Brick, foundations only; rectangular plan with ell. Built mid 17th C.; demolished 1796. 1 sheet (1929, plan); HABSI (1958).

Stone House

Pinewoods (Warburton House) (VA-532), .1 mi. N of NE tributary of Pine Woods Pond, .4 mi. N of State Rte. 613, 1.4 mi. SW of intersection with State Rte. 614. Brick (Flemish bond with glazed headers), rectangular (three-bay front), one-and-a-half stories, gable roof with dormers, two T-shaped interior end chimneys, segmental arched openings, full-length front porch; irregular plan; rear ell. Built late 17th C.; front porch and later additions. 3 ext. photos (1934); HABSI (1958).

Warburton House (VA-532), see Pinewoods (VA-532), Lightfoot Vicinity.

LITWALTON VICINITY   Richmond County (80)

Edge Hill (VA-431), .2 mi. NW of Lancaster Creek, .7 mi. SE of end of State Rte. 605, 1.4 mi. SE of intersection with State Rte. 606. Brick (Flemish bond), rectangular (five-bay front), two stories, hipped roof, two interior end chimneys, modillion cornice, molded brick water table; center-hall plan. Built late 18th C. 3 ext. photos (c. 1930, 1934).

148

Green Hill (VA-419), .5 mi. N of Staunton River, E side of State Rte. 728, .3 mi. SE of intersection with State Rte. 633. Brick, rectangular (five-bay front), two stories, gable roof, two interior end chimneys; center-hall plan; rear: brick, rectangular (three-bay front), one-and-a-half stories, gable roof with dormers, one interior end chimney, brick-columned porch. Built c. 1800; rear ell possibly built earlier. House and subsidiary bldgs. form extremely well-preserved plantation complex. 12 ext. photos (1937, 1960); 1 photocopy, plan of plantation (1960); 6 data sheets (1960); HABSI (1958). NR

Barn (VA-611). Planks, rectangular (one-bay front), one-and-a-half stories, gable roof, "V" timbering at corners, frame above eaves. Built early 19th C. 1 ext. photo (1960); 2 data pages (1960).

Brick Outbuilding (VA-604). Brick, approx. 34' (three-bay front) x 22', one story, gable roof, one exterior end chimney. Built early 19th C. 2 ext. photos (1960); 2 data pages (1960).

Duck House (VA-608). Brick, approx. 10' (one-bay front) x 12', one story, gable roof, wooden gable ends above eaves. Built early 19th C. 1 ext. photo (1960); 2 data pages (1960).

Green Hill

Green Hill

Frame Barn (VA-610). Frame with horizontal boarding partially battened, approx. 14′ square, one-and-a-half stories, gable roof. Built early 19th C. 1 ext. photo (1960); 2 data pages (1960).

Frame Outbuilding (VA-602). Frame with clapboarding, approx. 12′ x 14′, one story, gable roof, shed porch. Built early 19th C.; porch added later. 1 ext. photo (1960); 1 data page (1960).

Gateposts (VA-616). Granite blocks, approx. 10″ x 16″ x 4′, set in dry laid stone fences, grooved to receive gate. Built early 19th C. 1 photo (1960); 1 data page (1960).

Granary (VA-613). Fieldstone, approx. 64′ (two-bay front) x 30′, one-and-a-half stories, gable roof, frame gable end above eaves. Built 1821. 2 ext. photos (1960), 1 int. photo (1960); 3 data pages (1960).

Kitchen (VA-606). Frame with clapboarding, approx. 16′ (two-bay front) x 18′, one story, gable roof, massive stone chimney across E end; one-room plan, three fireplaces. Built early 19th C. 2 ext. photos (1960), 1 int. photo (1960); 3 data pages (1960); HABSI (1958).

Green Hill

Icehouse (VA-603). Fieldstone (dry laid) forms wall of circular pit 15' diameter, covered by frame gable roof with eavesline at ground level. Built early 19th C. 1 ext. photo (1960), 1 int. photo (1960); 1 data page (1960).

Laundry (VA-609). Fieldstone, 14' square, one story, gable roof, stone exterior end chimney, stone enclosure with N side open attached to W end. Built early 19th C. 3 ext. photos (1960), 1 int. photo (1960); 3 data pages (1960).

Mounting Block (Slave Auction Block) (VA-605). Stone, 3' square, 3' high, four stone piers support stone block; a few feet S is stone block, 1'2" x 3' x 10". 2 photos (1960); 1 data page (1960).

Slave Auction Block (VA-605), see Mounting Block (VA-605), Long Island Vicinity.

Slave Quarters (VA-607). Frame with clapboarding, approx. 20' (one-bay front) x 14', one story, gable roof, stone exterior end chimney. Built early 19th C.; exterior part of chimney stack destroyed. 1 ext. photo (1960); 2 data pages (1960).

Stable Ruins (VA-612). Fieldstone, rectangular (three-bay front), walls remain up to window lintel level. Built early 19th C. 1 ext. photo (1960); 1 data page (1960).

Green Hill, Tobacco Barn

Stone Walks and Drives (VA-615). Fieldstone laid in mortar, walks are approx. 6' wide, stone curbing, forms an all-weather link between main building and outbuildings. Built early 19th C. 1 photo (1960); 1 data page (1960).

Tobacco Barn (VA-614). Fieldstone, approx. 50' x 65', two stories, gable roof, roof rake steepens near ridge line on both sides of gable, wooden gable ends above eaves. Built early 19th C. 2 ext. photos (1960), 1 int. photo (1960); 3 data pages (1960).

White Hall (VA-66), 1.6 mi. NE of Staunton River, N side of State Rte. 637, 1 mi. E of intersection with State Rte. 761. Frame with clapboarding, rectangular (five-bay front), one-and-a-half stories, gable roof with dormers, four stone exterior end chimneys; two stone one-story outbuildings. Built late 18th C.; renovated. 3 ext. photos (1936), 1 int. photo (1936); 1 data page (n.d.).

LORETTO VICINITY   Essex County (29)

Brooke's Bank (VA-731), S bank of Rappahannock River, 1.3 mi. N of U.S. Rte. 17, .6 mi. E of intersection with State Rte. 638. Brick

(Flemish bond), rectangular (five-bay front), hipped roof, two interior end chimneys with brick diaper work, modillion cornice, molded brick belt course and water table, one-story wooden Doric entrance porch; center-hall plan, notable interior trim; one-story side wings, brick, one-story kitchen, smokehouse, and privy, frame with clapboarding. Built 1731-34; lateral wings altered and enlarged 1934. 16 sheets (1936, including plans, elevations, details of main house and outbuildings), 15 sheets (1967, adapted from drawings 1933, including plans, elevations, details); HABSI (1958).

Elmwood (VA-323), .5 mi. N of Elmwood Creek, .9 mi. NW of State Rte. 640, .2 mi. W of intersection with U.S. Rte. 17. Brick (Flemish bond), 100' (eleven-bay front) x 33', two-and-a-half stories, hipped roof with dormers; two interior chimneys, modillion cornice, advanced entrance bay with gable and Palladian window above entrance door, gauged belt course, molded brick water table; center-hall plan, notable interior trim including Doric cornice in center hall with triglyphs, metopes, and rosettes; elaborate dado, cornice, overmantels in drawing room and parlor. Built late 18th C.; enlarged late 18th C.; altered 1852; partially restored and renovated 1961-67. 5 ext. photos (1934, 1939), 12 int. photos (1924, 1939); 3 data pages (1941); HABSI (1958). NR

Brooke's Bank

Elmwood

Kinloch

Kinloch (VA-387), 2.7 mi. E of Baylors Pond, .1 mi. N of State Rte. 641, 2.3 mi. E of intersection of U.S. Rte. 17. Brick with stucco, square (five-bay front), three stories above raised basement, shallow hipped roof with deck with balustrade, two interior chimneys, recessed central bay, one-story entrance porch with flat roof, cast-iron balustrade, paired Ionic columns, double flight carved stone entrance steps with cast-iron railing; center-hall plan. Built c. 1840; demolished. 2 ext. photos (1937); 1 data page (1941).

Vauter's Church (VA-410), .1 mi. S of Elmwood Creek, NE side of U.S. Rte. 17, .3 mi. SE of State Rte. 640. Brick (Flemish bond), T-shaped (four-bay lateral front), one story, gable roof, one interior corner chimney modillion cornice, glazed headers above water table, S entrance with square-headed door and triangular brick pediment with gallery windows above, W entrance with arched door and segmental arched brick pediment, windows with arched heads; one-room plan. Built early 18th C.; interior partially destroyed mid 19th C. 1 ext. photo (1932); 1 data page (1941); HABSI (1958).

LORTON VICINITY   Fairfax County (30)

Arch Hall (VA-109), see Lewis, Lawrence, House (VA-109), Lorton Vicinity.

Belmont (Cocke-Washington House) (VA-578), 10913 Belmont Blvd., Belmont Park. Brick, rectangular (three-bay front), one-and-a-half stories, gable roof with dormer, one exterior end chimney; one-room plan with side stair hall. Original house built early 18th C. for Catesby Cocke and purchased by Edward Washington 1742; major portion dismantled 1866; the remaining structure may have been a dependency. 8 ext. photos (1959); 2 data pages (1959); HABSI (1958).

Cocke-Washington House (VA-578), see Belmont (VA-578), Lorton Vicinity.

Colchester Inn (Fairfax Arms Tavern) (VA-413), 10712 Old Colchester Rd. Frame with clapboarding, rectangular (four-bay front), one-and-a-half stories above raised stone basement, gable roof with hipped dormers, two stone and brick exterior end chimneys; irregular plan. Built mid 18th C.; later alterations and renovations. 7 ext. photos (1934, 1937, 1959); 1 data page (1959); HABSI (1958).

Fairfax Arms Tavern (VA-413), see Colchester Inn (VA-413), Lorton Vicinity.

Vauter's Church

Gunston Hall

Gunston Hall

Gunston Hall (VA-141), 10709 Gunston Rd. Historic house museum. Brick (Flemish bond), stone trim, 60'6" (five-bay front) x 40'6", one-and-a-half stories, gable roof with dormers, four interior end chimneys, modillion cornice, wooden pedimented W entrance porch, wooden semi-octagonal Gothic E entrance porch; center-hall plan, notable interior trim including an outstanding Chinese room and a Palladian room. Built 1755-58 for George Mason, author of the Virginia Declaration of Rights; William Buckland, architect-joiner, executed much of the interior work; altered mid 19th C.; partially restored and renovated 1913 by Glenn Brown; further restored 1951-52 under the direction of the National Society of the Colonial Dames of America and the Commonwealth of Virginia. 7 ext. photos (1936, 1938); 6 data pages (1941); HABSI (1969). NR; NHL

House (Metzer House) (VA-580), 10720 Old Colchester Rd. Frame with clapboarding, rectangular (three-bay front), one-and-a-half stories, gable roof with dormers, one interior end chimney; rectangular plan. Built late 18th C.; extensive later alterations. 2 ext. photos (1959); 1 data page (1959).

Lewis, Lawrence, House (Arch Hall) (VA-109), 11701 River Dr. Frame with clapboarding, 50'2" (five-bay front) x 25'3", one-and-a-half stories, gable roof, one exterior end chimney, one interior chimney, entrance doorway with glazed arched transom and sidelights; center-hall plan, large center hall with arched ceiling, notable interior trim. Built late 18th C.; dismantled and moved from 815 Franklin St., Alexandria, 1950; reconstructed with alterations on Belmont Bay, utilizing materials from the original structure 1951; roof raised 18" and dormers added on one side of the gable roof 1951; further alterations included the addition of a two-story wing and increasing the existing one-story wing to one-and-a-half stories 1962. This house was acquired by Lawrence Lewis of Woodlawn Plantation as his town residence in the early 19th C. 11 sheets (1937, including plans, elevations, sections, details); 5 ext. photos (1936, 1959), 5 int. photos (1937); 1 data page (1959); HABSI's (1958, 1969).

Metzer House (VA-580), see House (VA-580), Lorton Vicinity.

Pohick Episcopal Church (VA-190), 9301 Richmond Hwy. Brick (Flemish bond), 66' (five-bay front) x 45'6" (two-bay front), two stories, hipped roof, wooden modillion cornice, rectilinear windows at ground-floor level, arched windows above, sandstone corner quoins, rusticated entrance doorways flanked by Ionic pilasters supporting a cushion frieze and pediment; one-room plan. Built 1769-74, James

Wren and William Weit, architects; Daniel French, builder; William Bernard Sears, finish carpenter and carver; repaired and reroofed 1838; interior vandalized 1860-65; interior refurbished in Gothic Revival style 1874; interior partially restored and interior gallery added 1900-30. 4 ext. photos (1934, 1936, 1938); 3 data pages (1960). NR

LOVINGSTON   Nelson County (63)

Nelson County Courthouse (VA-336), W side of Peebles Mountain, E side of U.S. Rte. 29, .3 mi. N of intersection with State Rte. 56. Brick, rectangular (four-bay front), two stories, gable roof with cupola, gable-end front, five-bay first-floor arcaded porch; courtroom with gallery; rear wings. Built early 19th C.; stucco added; rear wings added 1940. 2 ext. photos (n.d.); 1 data page (1941); HABSI (1957).

LURAY VICINITY   Page County (70)

Fort Egypt (VA-200), .2 mi. N of Shenandoah River, .3 mi. SE of State Rte. 615, 1.8 mi. NE of intersection with U.S. Rte. 340. Log above stone basement, 36' (three-bay front) x 32'2", two stories,

Fort Egypt

hipped roof, one stone interior chimney, fortified stone rooms in basement; four-room plan; notable construction details. Built mid 18th C.; fenestration altered and roof changed from high gable to hipped c. 1840. 11 sheets (1940, including plans, elevations, sections, details, conjectural restoration); 5 ext. photos (1940), 9 int. photos (1940); 3 data pages (1941); HABSI (1958).

Fort Massanutten (VA-341), .4 mi. N of Shenandoah River, .2 mi. S of State Rte. 615, 1 mi. S of intersection with U.S. Rte. 340. Stone with brick gables, rectangular (three-bay front), two stories, gable roof, two brick interior end chimneys, fortified stone rooms in basement; plan unknown, possibly two room. Built mid 18th C.; ruinous 1940; demolished. 3 ext. photos (1940), 1 int. photo (1940); 1 ext. photocopy (n.d.); 1 data page (1941).

Fort Stover (VA-194), .3 mi. E of Shenandoah River, .8 mi. W of State Rte. 660, 1 mi. NW of intersection with U.S. Rte. 340. Stone, 36'5" (three-bay front) x 28', two stories above raised basement, gable roof, two interior end chimneys, stone jack arches over windows, fortified arched stone vaulted room in basement; two-room plan, notable interior construction details. Built c. 1760, Samuel Stover, builder; sash altered late 19th C. 12 sheets (1940, including plans, elevations, sections, details); 4 ext. photos (1940), 1 int. photo (1940); 3 data pages (1941); HABSI (1958).

-NORTH-ELEVATION-

LYNCHBURG

Point of Honor (VA-311), 112 Cabell St. Brick with stucco, irregular shape (nine-bay front), two stories, hipped roof, three exterior end chimneys, center three bays framed by semi-octagonal ended bows; irregular plan, fine Adam-style mantels and doorways; one-story wing. Built 1806; later one-story addition. Stucco removed 1972. 1 int. photo (n.d.); 1 data page (1941); HABSI (1958). NR

LYNCHBURG VICINITY   Campbell County (16)

Johnson, Christopher, Cottage (VA-11), W side of Tomahawk Creek, N side of State Rte. 126, .7 mi. SW of intersection with State Rte. 675. Frame with clapboarding, 32'1" (three-bay front) x 18', one-and-a-half stories above stone foundation, gable roof, two stone exterior end chimneys, front overhang forming porch; two-room plan. Built late 18th C. 3 sheets (1934, including plans, elevations, sections, details); 2 ext. photos (1934); 3 data pages (1936); HABSI (1958).

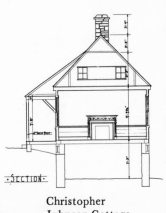

-SECTION-

Christopher
Johnson Cottage

Madison County Courthouse (VA-325), .5 mi. SE of White Oak Run, NW side of U.S. Rte. 29, .3 mi. NE of intersection of State Rte. 231. Brick (Flemish bond), rectangular, temple form (four-bay front), two stories, gable roof with domed octagonal cupola, three interior end chimneys, Tuscan entablature with full Tuscan pediments at either end of building, ground-floor front is four-bay open arcade with brick arches and stone keystones; one-room plan with second-floor gallery. Built 1828, Malcolm F. Crawford, builder; interior ceiling altered and exterior chimneys added. 1 ext. photo (1939); 34 data pages (1941, including 33 pages of photostats of early correspondence concerning construction of the building); HABSI (1958). NR

MADISON VICINITY

Madison County (57)

Hebron Lutheran Church Fence, Gate, and Stile (VA-411), .3 mi. W of White Oak Run, NE side of intersection of State Rtes. 638 and 653, 1 mi. NE of intersection with State Rte. 231. Picket fence with square pickets; gate with double arched picket motif and pierced lower rail; three-step wooden stile. Probably built mid 19th C.; demolished. 1 ext. photo (1937); 1 data page (1941).

MANAKIN

Goochland County (38)

Manakin Village (VA-218), at intersection of State Rtes. 6 and 621. View of the village; near here is the site of the Dover Coal Mines, one of the first coal mining operations in America, which flourished in the mid 18th C. Much of the work force came from Huguenot families who moved to the Manakin area from the original Huguenot settlement south of the James River at Manakin-Town. 1 ext. photo (1940); 4 data pages (1941).

Structure 1 (VA-219), 1 mi. N of James River, W side of State Rte. 621, .2 mi. N of intersection with State Rte. 6. Frame with clapboarding, rectangular (four-bay front), two stories, gable roof, center chimney, entrance at either end of front facade; rear ell. Built early 19th C. 1 ext. photo (1940).

Structure 2 (VA-220), exact location unknown. Frame with clapboarding, rectangular (three-bay front), two stories, gable roof, one interior chimney; irregular plan; one-story side wing. Built early 19th C.; demolished. 1 ext. photo (1940).

Structure 3 (VA-221), 1.2 mi. N of James River, W side of State Rte. 621, .3 mi. N of intersection with State Rte. 6. Frame with clapboarding, rectangular (three-bay front), one-and-a-half stories, gable roof, center chimney, extension of rear roof pitch forms salt-box shape, full-length front porch, enclosed side porch. Built early 19th C.; porch additions. 1 ext. photo (1940).

MANAKIN VICINITY   Goochland County (38)

House (Old House) (VA-315), 1.1 mi. N of James River, W side of State Rte. 621, .3 mi. N of intersection with State Rte. 6. Frame with clapboarding, rectangular (three-bay front), one story, gable roof, center chimney, extension of rear roof pitch forms salt-box shape. Built early 19th C. 1 ext. photo (n.d.).

Old House (VA-315), see House (VA-315), Manakin Vicinity.

Powell's Tavern (VA-748), .9 mi. N of James River, N side of State Rte. 650, .2 mi. E of intersection with State Rte. 647. Two separate buildings. N building: frame, two stories, gable roof, two exterior end chimneys, rear lean-to; central connecting porch. Built late 18th C. S building: brick, two stories, gable roof, two interior end chimneys; rear lean-to. Built early 19th C. Central porch replaced by two-story frame passageway with interior chimney 1957. 1 ext. photo (1940); HABSI (1957).

MANASSAS   Prince William County (76)

Liberia (VA-834), 627 Centreville Rd. Brick, rectangular (five-bay front), two stories, gable roof, two interior end chimneys, sawtooth cornice, two-story Tuscan tetrastyle portico, arched doorway with semi-circular fanlight; modified center-hall plan. Built early 19th C.; later additions. 2 ext. photos (1936), 2 int. photos (1936); HABSI (1959).

Tudor Hall (VA-835), end of Tudor Lane, one block E of intersection with Fairview Ave. Frame with wood siding simulating brick with stone quoining, covered with asbestos siding, rectangular (five-bay front), two stories, gable roof, giant tetrastyle Doric portico, modillion cornice with triglyphs and metopes carried around below modillions; center-hall plan; rear ell. Built late 19th C.; later alterations. 1 ext. photo (1936).

Ben Lomond (VA-836), 1.7 mi. S of Bull Run, .4 mi. E of State Rte. 234, 2.6 mi. SE of intersection with U.S. Rte. 29/211. Stone, rectangular (five-bay front), two stories, gable roof, two interior end chimneys, monumental Tuscan portico extending across W end; center-hall plan; stone outbuildings. Built early 19th C.; later alterations and additions. 2 ext. photos (1936); HABSI (1958).

Stone House

Brent House (VA-553), see White House, The (VA-553), Manassas Vicinity.

Moor Green (Old House) (VA-554), 1 mi. N of Broad Run, .3 mi. W of State Rte. 692, 1 mi. N of intersection with State Rte. 649. Brick (Flemish bond), rectangular (five-bay front), two stories, gable roof, three interior end chimneys, brick cornice; center-hall plan, notable interior trim; rear ell. Built mid 18th C.; later alterations. 2 ext. photos (1937); HABSI (1959).

Old House (VA-554), see Moor Green (VA-554), Manassas Vicinity.

Stone House (VA-144), N side of Youngs Branch, NE corner intersection of U.S. Rte. 29/211 and State Rte. 234, Manassas National Battlefield Park. Historic house museum. Stone, 40' (four-bay front) x 23'7", two stories, gable roof, two stone interior end chimneys; center-hall plan. Built early 19th C. 9 sheets (1959, including plot plan, plans, elevations, details); 8 ext. photos (1936, 1937, 1940, 1959), 21 int. photos (1959); 2 data pages (1959); HABSI (1958).

White House, The (Brent House) (VA-553), .2 mi. S of Broad Run, S side of State Rte. 619, SE corner intersection with State Rte. 678. Brick with cement wash, rectangular (five-bay front), two stories, gable roof, four brick exterior end chimneys with parapets; center-hall plan; wing. Built early 19th C.; later addition. 1 ext. photo (1936); HABSI's (1958, 1959).

MANGOHICK   King William County (51)

Cottage (House) (VA-534), .8 mi. N of Millpond Creek, N side of State Rte. 604, .1 mi. E of intersection with State Rte. 30. Frame with clapboarding, rectangular (two-bay front), one story above high brick basement, gable roof, two exterior end chimneys with pent closet between; rear lean-to. Built early 19th C.; later addition; renovated. 1 ext. photo (1936).

House (VA-534), see Cottage (VA-534), Mangohick.

Mooklar House (VA-764), .7 mi. N of Millpond Creek, NE corner of intersection of State Rtes. 604 and 30. Frame with clapboarding, rectangular (three-bay front), two stories, gable roof, two exterior end chimneys, partially enclosed front porch. Built early 19th C.; demolished; frame kitchen remains. 1 ext. photo (1936).

Hornquarter

MANGOHICK VICINITY   King William County (51)

Hornquarter (VA-149), .6 mi. E of Pamunkey River, .6 mi. N of State Rte. 614, 1 mi. SW of intersection with State Rte. 601. Brick, rectangular (three-bay front), two stories, hipped roof with balustrade deck, four interior end chimneys, two-story pedimented portico, three-part windows, rear five-bay front, sides and rear have rectangular paneled insets on each bay between stories; center-hall plan; two front and two rear one-story brick dependencies. Built mid 19th C. 4 ext. photos (n.d., 1938); 1 data page (1939); HABSI (1958).

Mangohick Baptist Church (VA-763), .6 mi. N of Millpond Creek, N side of State Rte. 638, .2 mi. S of intersection with State Rte. 30. Brick (Flemish bond, English bond below water table), rectangular (one-bay front), one story, gable roof, modillion cornice. Built c. 1730; window sash, interior altered; rear additions. 1 ext. photo (1936); HABSI (1958).

Palestine (VA-765), .3 mi. N of Herring Creek, .4 mi. W of State Rte. 604, .7 mi. N of intersection with State Rte. 628. Frame with clapboarding, rectangular (three-bay front), one-and-a-half stories, gable roof with dormers, one exterior end chimney; frame, one-and-a-half story side wing. Built late 18th C.; later additions; demolished. 2 ext. photos (1936).

164

Retreat (VA-767), .4 mi. E of Malden Creek, .2 mi. NW of State Rte. 604, 2.2 mi. NE of intersection with State Rte. 628. Brick, rectangular (five-bay front), two stories, gable roof, two exterior end chimneys; center-hall plan; brick one-story side wing, entrance porch; frame rear ell. Built early 19th C.; later additions; porch removed. 2 ext. photos (1936), 1 int. photo (1936); HABSI (1958).

Roseville (VA-766), .4 mi. N of Herring Creek, .1 mi. SE of State Rte. 604, 1.1 mi. N of intersection with State Rte. 628. Frame with clapboarding, rectangular (four-bay front), two-and-a-half stories, gable roof with dormers, N exterior end chimney with brick pent closet, S double chimney with brick pent closet between; center-hall plan; frame side wing; frame one-story outbuilding with gable roof and exterior end chimney. Built early 19th C.; later additions; N chimney and pent closet destroyed and replaced by exterior end chimney. 2 ext. photos (1936), 1 int. photo (1936); HABSI (1958).

MANQUIN VICINITY   King William County (51)

Dabney House (VA-244), see Seven Springs (VA-244), Manquin Vicinity.

Fontainebleu (VA-379), .3 mi. E of E tributary of Manquin Creek, .1 mi. N of State Rte. 618, 1.4 mi. E of intersection with State Rte. 661. Frame with clapboarding, rectangular (five-bay front), two-and-a-half stories above raised basement, gable roof with dormers and cupola, four exterior end chimneys. Built mid 19th C.; demolished. 1 ext. photo (1936).

Seven Springs (Dabney House) (VA-244), .2 mi. E of Mehixen Creek, .4 mi. W of State Rte. 604, .1 mi. N of intersection with State Rte. 605. Brick (Flemish bond, English bond below water table), rectangular (three-bay front), one-and-a-half stories, gable roof with jerkinheads and hipped dormers, T-shaped central chimney; entrance hall with three rooms surrounding chimney, two rear rooms have corner fireplaces. Built mid 18th C.; in process of restoration, rear screen porch added. 1 ext. photo (1939); 1 data page (1940); HABSI (1958).

MAPPSVILLE VICINITY   Accomack County (1)

Wharton House (VA-490), .4 mi. W of Assawaman Creek, .3 mi. N of State Rte. 762, .4 mi. SE of intersection with Rte. 679. Brick (Flemish

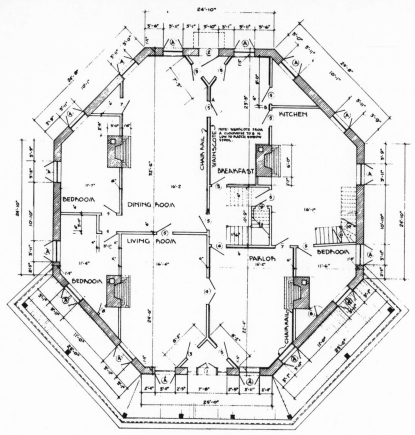

Abijah Thomas House

bond), approx. 46' (five-bay front) x 45', two stories, hipped roof with balustraded deck, two interior chimneys, rectangular panels between first- and second-floor bays; irregular plan, fine carved doorway, plaster ceiling decoration, four signed Philadelphia mantels by R. Wellford; side wing. Built early 19th C. 2 ext. photos (1940); 1 data page (n.d.); HABSI (1958).

MARION VICINITY   Smyth County (87)

Thomas, Abijah, House (VA-639), .25 mi. N of South Fork of Holston River, N side of Thomas Bridge Rd., .5 mi. SE of intersection with Scratch Gravel Rd. Brick, octagonal, 24'10" each side (two-bay side), two stories, octagonal hipped roof, four interior chimneys, one-story porch on three sides; complex interior plan. Built mid 19th C.; abandoned. 13 sheets (1963, including plans, elevations, sections, details).

Abijah Thomas House

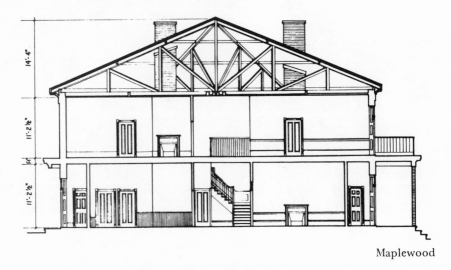

Maplewood

MATTOAX VICINITY   Amelia County (4)

Oaks, The (VA-157), see Oaks, The (VA-157), 307 Stockton Lane, Richmond.

McLEAN VICINITY   Fairfax County (30)

Maplewood (VA-739), 7676 Old Springhouse Rd. Brick, asymmetrical (five-bay front), two-and-a-half stories, mansard roof with dormers, four interior end chimneys, advanced entrance tower with steep mansard roof and paired oval attic windows, bracketed cornice, one-

Maplewood

story bracketed veranda flanking the entrance tower; modified center-hall plan; one-story side wing, unusually large scale. Built c. 1870; exterior altered 1884-1912; interior extensively remodeled 1912-19; demolished 1970. 7 ext. photos (1969); HABSI (1969).

Spring House (VA-740), 7676 Old Springhouse Rd. Stone, rectangular (one-bay front), one story, gable roof, crossed lattice work in gable-end entrance; one-room plan. Built mid 19th C. 2 ext. photos (1969).

MEADOWS OF DAN   Patrick County (71)

Mabry Mill (VA-165), see Mabry Mill (VA-165), Willis Vicinity, Floyd Co.

Maplewood

MECHANICSVILLE VICINITY Hanover County (43)

Dr. Gaines House (VA-335), see Powhite (VA-335), Mechanicsville Vicinity.

Gaines House (VA-78), .2 mi. NE of Sledd's Lake on Fairfield Farm, .2 mi. NW of State Rte. 615, .4 mi. SW of intersection with State Rte. 156. Frame with clapboarding, 26'2½" (three-bay front) x 14'2", one story, gable roof, one interior end chimney, two lean-to closets at either side of chimney end form T-shape; one-room plan with side closets. Built mid 18th C.; enlarged. 3 sheets (1936, including plans, elevations, sections, details); 4 ext. photos (c. 1934, 1935, 1936, n.d.); 1 data page (1941).

Gathwright House (VA-76), N side of N branch of Boatswain Creek, .1 mi. S of State Rte. 156, .4 mi. W of intersection with State Rtes. 619 and 633. Brick and frame, 48'3" (five-bay front) x 18', two stories, gable roof, W interior end chimney, E exterior end chimney, W three bays on first floor are brick; center-hall plan. Built late 18th C.; brick part is original with later frame additions; restored. 13 sheets (1934, 1935, including plans, elevations, details); HABSI (1957).

Pollard House (VA-343), see Williamsville (VA-343), Studley Vicinity.

Powhite (Dr. Gaines House) (VA-335), .3 mi. W of Powhite Creek, 1 mi. SE of State Rte. 615, .4 mi. SW of intersection with State Rte. 156. Frame with clapboarding, rectangular (five-bay front), two stories, gable roof, two interior and one exterior end chimneys, modillion cornice; center-hall plan. Built late 18th C.; demolished. 2 ext. photos (1934).

Rural Plains (VA-753), .4 mi. NE of Totopotomoi Creek, S side of State Rte. 606, .6 mi. W of intersection with State Rte. 643. Brick, rectangular (five-bay front), one-and-a-half stories, gambrel roof with hipped dormers, two interior end chimneys, modillion cornice, two-level entrance porch with enclosed second level; center-hall plan, corner fireplaces. Built early 18th C.; porch additions; interior remodeled mid 19th C. 3 ext. photos (1936); HABSI (1959).

Watt House (VA-477), .2 mi. S of Boatswain Creek, .7 mi. S of State Rte. 156, 1.6 mi. E of intersection with State Rte. 615, at Cold Harbor National Battlefield Park. Frame with clapboarding, 30'6" (three-bay front) x 28', one-and-a-half stories above raised basement, gable roof with dormers, two exterior end chimneys with two frame pent closets; side-hall plan. Built c. 1835; restored 1959. 6 sheets (1956, including plot plan, plans, elevations, sections, details); 4 ext. photos (n.d., 1956); 3 data pages (n.d.).

MERRY POINT VICINITY   Lancaster County (52)

Oak Hill (VA-298), S bank of W branch of Corotoman River, .3 mi. N of State Rte. 604, .3 mi. W of S terminus of Merry Point-Ottoman Wharf Ferry. Frame with clapboarding, rectangular (three-bay front), one-and-a-half stories, gambrel roof with dormers, one exterior end chimney; probably two-room plan. Built c. 1805; demolished. 2 ext. photos (1940); HABSI (1957).

Verville (VA-151), .6 mi. NW of W branch of Corotoman River, W side of State Rte. 611, .3 mi. S of intersection with State Rte. 604. Brick (Flemish bond), rectangular (three-bay front), one-and-a-half stories, gambrel roof with dormers, two interior end chimneys; center-hall plan, notable interior trim; flanking one-story wings. Built c. 1700; later additions; restored. 5 ext. photos (1939, 1940), 2 int. photos (1940); 1 data page (1939); HABSI's (1957, 1958).

Waddel, James, House (VA-297), N bank of W branch of Corotoman River, E side of State Rte. 604, at N terminus of Merry Point–Ottoman Wharf Ferry. Frame with clapboarding, rectangular (three-bay front), one-and-a-half stories, gable roof with dormers, three exterior end chimneys; probably two-room plan; side wing: one-and-a-half story, gambrel roof. Built mid 18th C.; enlarged early 19th C.; ruinous 1940; reconstructed within remaining original chimneys 1956. 2 ext. photos (1940); HABSI (1957).

MIDDLETOWN VICINITY   Frederick County (35)

Belle Grove (VA-259), .2 mi. S of Cedar Creek, E side of State Rte. 727, .5 mi. NW of intersection with U.S. Rte. 11. Historic house museum of National Trust for Historic Preservation. Stone, rectangular (seven-bay front), hipped roof, four interior stone chimneys, one-story pedimented tetrastyle Doric entrance porch, entrance door with arched transom, stone corner quoins; cross-hall plan, notable interior trim including paneled dog-ear motif overmantels and glazed interior doorway transoms; one-story flanking wing above raised basement. Built c. 1794; restored c. 1922. 15 sheets (1972, including plans, elevations, sections, details); 1 ext. photocopy (n.d.), 8 ext. photos (n.d., 1910, 1939, 1964), 6 int. photos (1964); 9 data pages (1940, 1972); HABSI (1958). NR

Old Stone Fort (VA-210), NW bank of Middle Marsh Brook, .6 mi. NW of Chapel Rd., 1.1 mi. N of intersection with U.S. Rte. 11. Stone, rectangular (six-bay front), two stories above raised basement, gable roof, two interior end chimneys, segmental flat stone lintels, nine-over-six window sash with heavy plank frames, three-room plan including long E room the full length of the house. Built mid 18th C. as house with fortified basement room; altered and enlarged early 19th C.; demolished. 3 ext. photos (1938), 2 int. photos (1938); 1 data page (1941).

MILLWOOD   Clarke County (22)

Burwell's Mill (Millwood Mill) (VA-354), S bank of Spout Run, N side of State Rte. 723, .4 mi. SE of intersection with State Rte. 255. Stone, rectangular (two-bay front), gable roof with loft, one interior corner chimney; one-room plan. Built late 18th C. 1 ext. photo (1934), 1 ext. photocopy (n.d.); HABSI (1958). NR

Carter Hall (VA-358), .2 mi. NW of Spout Run, .4 mi. SE of State Rte. 255, .2 mi. NE of intersection with State Rte. 723. Stone, five part composition; central section: rectangular (five-bay front), two stories, hipped roof; hexastyle two-story Ionic portico with parapet,

Burwell's Mill

two interior chimneys, arched fanlight; modified center-hall plan; flanking two-story wings; gable roof terminated by flanking one-story wings, gable roofs; main house flanked by matching dependencies: stone, rectangular (five-bay front), two stories, gable roof, two interior end chimneys. Built 1790-92; altered and enlarged c. 1830, c. 1855, c. 1930. 1 ext. photocopy (n.d.), 1 int. photocopy (n.d.); 1 data page (1941); HABSI (1958).

Millwood Mill (VA-354), see Burwell's Mill (VA-354), Millwood.

MODEST TOWN   Accomack County (1)

Salt Box House (VA-491), .6 mi. W of Northam Creek, E side of State Rte. 679, E corner of intersection with State Rte. 772. Frame with clapboarding and brick (Flemish bond) end, rectangular (three-bay front), one-and-a-half stories, gable roof with dormers, one exterior end chimney; two-room plan; frame, one-story addition. Built mid 18th C.; addition. 3 ext. photos (1940, 1960).

Belmont (VA-296), S side of State Rte. 662, .2 mi. E of intersection with State Rte. 354. Frame with clapboarding, rectangular (five-bay front), gable roof with jerkinheads, dormers, and lean-to slope in rear, two exterior end chimneys; center-hall plan, closed string stair, notable interior trim. Built mid 18th C.; demolished. 2 ext. photos (1940), 4 int. photos (1940).

Saint Mary's Whitechapel (VA-59), 1.1 mi. E of Rappahannock River, NE corner of intersection of State Rtes. 354 and 201. Brick (Flemish bond with glazed headers), 60′ (four-bay front) x 28′, one story, hipped roof, modillion cornice, arched window heads; one-room plan, gallery, cove ceiling. Built c. 1740; extensively altered mid 19th C.; renovated mid 20th C. 5 ext. photos (1937, 1939), 2 int. photos (1937); HABSI's (1957, 1958). NR

Salt Box House

Towles House

Towles House (VA-62), E bank of Rappahannock River, .5 mi. SW of S end of State Rte. 626, 1.4 mi. S of intersection with State Rte. 354. Brick ends and frame with clapboarding on front and rear walls, 39'7½" (four-bay front) x 26'4", one-and-a-half stories, two exterior end chimneys; center-hall plan, notable walnut stair. Built early 18th C.; demolished. 12 sheets (1940, including plot plans, plans, elevations, sections, details); 15 ext. photos (1933, 1937, 1940); 2 ext. photocopies (1893, 1898); 2 data pages (1941).

MOSQUITO CREEK VICINITY   Accomack County (1)

Poplar Grove (Wallop House) (VA-693), exact location unknown. Brick (Flemish bond with glazed headers), rectangular (five-bay front), two stories, gable roof, two interior end chimneys, segmental arched windows; center-hall plan. Built early 18th C.; burned 1944. 3 ext. photos (1940), 1 int. photo (1940); 2 data pages (n.d., 1949).

Wallop House (VA-693), see Poplar Grove (VA-693), Mosquito Creek Vicinity.

MOUNT VERNON   Fairfax County (30)

Mount Vernon (VA-505), Va. shore of Potomac River, .2 mi. S of Mount Vernon Memorial Hwy. at intersection of State Rte. 235.

Mount Vernon

Historic house museum. Frame, beveled-edged wood siding resembling rusticated stonework, 96′ (nine-bay front) x 32′ (not including portico), two-and-a-half stories, hipped roof with octagonal cupola and dormers, two interior chimneys, modillion cornice, monumental two-story portico with eight square pillars extending the width of the E front, modillion cross gable with elliptical lunette on the W front, entrance doorway with architrave frame supporting a frieze and pediment, Palladian window on N front; center-hall plan, notable interior trim, ornamental plaster decoration; frame, one-and-a-half story dependencies connected to main house by quarter circle covered arcades; notable brick and frame outbuildings forming complete plantation complex; notable landscaping and gardens. Probably first built c. 1730 for Augustine Washington, George Washington's father, as a one-and-a-half story dwelling; enlarged to two-and-a-half stories 1758-59; S end extended 1775; N end extended 1776; E portico completed 1777; W cross gable completed 1778; octagonal cupola added 1787; restored by the Mount Vernon Ladies' Association of the Union 1858. Mount Vernon was acquired by George Washington from his half brother's widow in 1754 and was his home until his death in 1799. He is buried on the estate in the tomb erected in 1831. 8 ext. photos, main house (1942, 1969, 1970), 4 ext. photos, outbuildings (1942), 1 ext. photo, tomb (1942); HABSI (1969). NR; NHL

Pope-Leighey House

MOUNT VERNON VICINITY Fairfax County (30)

Pope-Leighey House (VA-638), 9000 Richmond Hwy. Historic house museum of the National Trust for Historic Preservation. Wood and brick, L-shaped, one story, two levels, flat roof, one interior chimney, pierced decorative clerestory window bands, three-layer wooden wall construction consisting of cypress sheathing screwed to both sides of a plywood core; asymmetrical plan of interrelated spaces. Built 1940-41 for Loren B. Pope at 1005 Locust St., Falls Church, Va., Frank Lloyd Wright, architect; sold to Mr. and Mrs. Robert A. Leighey 1946; the National Trust for Historic Preservation and Mrs. Leighey contracted for removal and reconstruction of house at Woodlawn Plantation July 1964; house dismantled autumn 1964; reconstruction completed 1965. This house is an example of Wright's Usonian architecture. 9 sheets (1964, 1973, including plot plan plans, elevations, details); 5 ext. photos before dismantling (April, 1964), 6 ext. photos, after reconstruction (1969), 11 int. photos, before dismantling (April, 1964), 10 int. photos, after reconstruction (1969); 3 data pages (1964); HABSI (1969). NR

Washington's Grist Mill (VA-506), 55414 Mount Vernon Memorial Hwy. Museum. Stone, rectangular (three-bay front), three stories with loft, gable roof, one interior stone corner chimney; open plan. Built mid 18th C., ruinous condition mid 19th C.; reconstructed 1932. 1 ext. photo (1934); HABSI (1969).

Woodlawn Plantation (VA-337), 9000 Richmond Hwy. Historic house museum of the National Trust for Historic Preservation. Brick with stone trim, five part composition, central block: 56' (five-bay front) x 45', two stories, gable roof with jerkinheads and cross gable over central bay, four interior end chimneys, modillion cornice, one-story porch with stucco over brick columns, deck roof with balustrade on E front; center-hall plan, notable interior stair and trim; symmetrical one-and-a-half-story gable-end flanking pavilions connected to the main block by one-and-a-half-story hyphens; separate dairy; smoke-house: brick (Flemish bond) with stone trim, one story, pyramidal roof; one-room plan. Built 1800-05, Dr. William Thornton, architect; flanking wings altered and enlarged early 20th C. Woodlawn was built on part of the Mount Vernon estate for George Washington's adopted granddaughter Eleanor Parke Custis Lewis and her husband, Lawrence Lewis, who was George Washington's nephew. 16 ext. photos (1936, 1939, 1942, 1964), 9 int. photos (1936, 1964); HABSI (1969). NR

Woodlawn Plantation

Brownsville (VA-810), .1 mi. W of Upshur Creek, .6 mi. NE of end of State Rte. 608, 1.2 mi. SE of intersection with State Rte. 600. Brick (Flemish bond), rectangular (three-bay front), two stories, gable roof, one interior end chimney, modillion cornice, pedimented wooden Doric entrance porch; side-hall plan, notable interior trim; one- and one-and-a-half-story frame wings; frame with clapboarding outbuildings. Built early 19th C.; attached frame wing predates main block; later addition. 6 ext. photos (1960), 2 ext. photos, outbuildings (1960), 7 int. photos (1960); HABSI (1958).   NR

Happy Union (VA-805), N bank of Holly Grove Cove, .2 mi. NW of W end of State Rte. 692, 1.4 mi. W of intersection with State Rte. 606. Brick (Flemish bond), rectangular (three-bay front), two stories, gable roof, two interior end chimneys, modillion cornice, entrance door with semi-circular transom in gable end; side-hall plan with three entrance doors; one-story two-bay flanking dependency connected to house by one-story hyphen. Built late 18th C. 4 ext. photos (1960).

Holly Grove (VA-804), S bank of Holly Grove Cove, .8 mi. W of State Rte. 610, .1 mi. S of intersection with State Rte. 606. Brick (Flemish bond), rectangular (four-bay front), two stories, gable roof, two interior end chimneys, modillion cornice; modified side-hall plan; side and rear frame one-story ells. Built 1812; later additions. 3 ext. photos (1960), 3 int. photos (1960).

Woodlands (VA-590), .5 mi. W of Greens Creek, .3 mi. E of State Rte. 600, 2.2 mi. NE of intersection with U.S. Rte. 13. Frame with clapboarding, rectangular (five-bay front), two stories, gable roof, two interior end chimneys, modillion cornice; center-hall plan; one-story frame wing, connecting hyphen; frame outbuildings, including icehouse and dairy. Built late 18th C. 2 ext. photos (1960), 1 ext. photo, dairy (1960), 6 int. photos (1960); 3 data pages (1960).

NAXERA VICINITY   Gloucester County (37)

Land's End (VA-518), N bank of Severn River, .7 mi. S of State Rte. 614, 1.2 mi. S of intersection with State Rte. 629. Brick (Flemish bond), rectangular (three-bay front), one-and-a-half stories above raised basement, gambrel roof with dormers, two interior end chimneys; center-hall plan; rear ell; dairy: frame with clapboarding, one story. Built mid 18th C.; later additions mid 20th C. 4 ext. photos (1940), 1 ext. photo, dairy (1940); 1 data page (1940); HABSI (1959).

NEW CHURCH VICINITY Accomack County (1)

Pitts Neck Farm (VA-492), .3 mi. SE of Pocomoke River, W end of State Rte. 709 at intersection with State Rte. 804, 1 mi. W of intersection with State Rte. 701. Brick (Flemish bond), rectangular (five-bay front), gable roof, two brick interior end chimneys, brick pedimented entrance; center-hall plan; side wing. Built early 18th C. 3 ext. photos (1940).

NEW KENT VICINITY New Kent County (64)

Criss-Cross (VA-126), .5 mi. E of intersection of Pelham Swamp and Rumley Marsh, .3 mi. S of State Rte. 617, .4 mi. SW of intersection with State Rte. 604. Brick and frame with clapboarding, cruciform (three-bay front), W wing: brick with frame gable end above eaves, one story, gable roof; S wing: brick with frame above second-floor windows, two-and-a-half stories, gable roof; E wing: brick with frame above first floor, two stories, gable roof; N wing: frame with clapboarding, two stories, gable roof; two exterior end chimneys, one interior end chimney. Built late 17th C.; originally a T-shaped plan; N wing added later; altered; W wing now: brick, one-and-a-half stories, gable roof with dormers, frame gable end above eaves; S wing: brick, two stories, gable roof, frame gable end above eaves; E wing: brick, one-and-a-half stories, gable roof with dormers, frame gable end above eaves; N wing: brick, one-and-a-half stories, gambrel roof with dormers, frame gable end above eaves. 13 sheets (1936, including plans, elevations, sections, details); 7 ext. photos (1936), 4 int. photos (1936); 4 data pages (1937); HABSI (1958).

NEWPORT NEWS

Jones, Matthew, House (VA-163), S side of intersection of MacAuliffe Ave. and James River Rd. Brick (Flemish bond, English bond below water table), 31'1" (three-bay front) x 21'2", two stories, gable roof, two exterior end chimneys, two-story enclosed front porch; one-story rear lean-to. Built early 18th C.; altered; second story added. 7 sheets (1940, including plans, elevations); 10 ext. photos (c. 1934, 1935, 1940); 1 data page (1941); HABSI (1959). NR

NEWTOWN VICINITY King and Queen County (49)

Drysdale Glebe (VA-398), 1 mi. S of Beverly Run, S side of State Rte. 641, 1.5 mi. W of intersection with State Rte. 625. Brick

Matthew Jones House

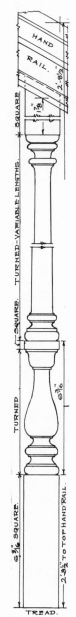

ELEVATION
OF BALUSTER.
ONE HALF F.S.

(Flemish bond with glazed headers), rectangular (three-bay front), one-and-a-half stories, gable roof with dormers, two interior end chimneys; center-hall plan. Built early 18th C.; demolished. 1 ext. photo (1939), 1 int. photo, stair (1939), 1 int. photo, stair (1937, probably of another but similar unidentified stair); 2 data pages (1940, 1941).

Hillsborough (VA-125), N bank of Mattaponi River, .6 mi. SW of State Rte. 633, 1.8 mi. NW of intersection with State Rte. 632. Brick (Flemish bond), gable ends and frame with clapboarding, 52'5" (five-bay front) x 30'4", two stories, hipped roof, four interior end chimneys, modillion cornice, wooden one-story entrance porches; center-hall plan, notable interior trim; side wing; storehouse outbuilding: brick, 32'9" (four-bay front) x 18'8", one story, gable roof; one-room plan. Built c. 1722; extensive alterations and additions including removal of drawing room paneling. 20 sheets, main house (1936, including plans, elevations, sections, details); 2 sheets, storehouse (1936, including plan, elevations, details); 4 ext. photos, main house (1936), 2 ext. photos, storehouse (1936), 7 int. photos, main house (1936); 5 data pages (1936); HABSI (1958).

Jackson Farm Buildings (VA-361), exact location unknown. Three frame barns: two with clapboard siding and gable roof with wooden shingles, one with board and batten vertical siding and standing-seam tin roof; plans unknown. Date of erection unknown. 1 ext. photo (1937).

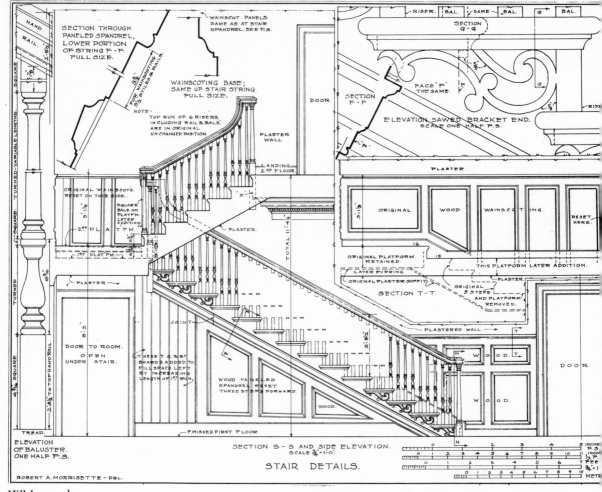

SECTION THROUGH PANELED SPANDREL, LOWER PORTION OF STRING F-F. FULL SIZE.

WAINSCOT PANELS DAME AS AT STAIR SPANDREL. SEE F.S.

WAINSCOTING BASE; SAME UP STAIR STRING. FULL SIZE.

NOTE:— TOP RUN OF 6 RISERS, INCLUDING RAIL & BALS. ARE IN ORIGINAL UNCHANGED POSITION.

SECTION G-G.

SECTION F-F.

FACE "F" THE SAME.

ELEVATION SAWED BRACKET END. SCALE ONE HALF F.S.

PLASTER WALL.

LANDING 2ND FLOOR.

PLASTER.

ORIGINAL WAINSCOT. RESET ON THIS SIDE.

SQUARE BALS. ON PLATF'M. LATER ADDITION.

2ND PLATF'M.

1ST PLATF'M.

PLASTER

DOOR TO ROOM. OPEN UNDER STAIR.

THESE T.G. & B. BOARDS ADDED TO FILL SPACE LEFT BY INCREASING LENGTH OF 1ST RUN.

JOINT.

WOOD PANELED SPANDREL RESET THREE STEPS FORWARD.

WOOD.

FINISHED FIRST FLOOR.

HAND RAIL.

SQUARE

TURNED-VARIABLE LENGTHS.

SQUARE

TURNED

SQUARE

2-½" TO TOP HAND RAIL.

TREAD.

ELEVATION OF BALUSTER. ONE HALF F.S.

ROBERT A. MORRISETTE - DEL.

PLASTER.

ORIGINAL WOOD WAINSCOTING.

RESET HERE.

16

15

ORIGINAL PLATFORM RETAINED.

LATER FURRING.

ORIGINAL PLASTER SOFFIT.

THIS PLATFORM LATER ADDITION.

ORIGINAL 3 STEPS AND PLATFORM REMOVED.

PLASTER.

SECTION T-T.

PLASTERED WALL.

WOOD.

WOOD.

DOOR.

TOTAL 11-4⅞

DOOR.

SECTION S-S AND SIDE ELEVATION.
SCALE ¾"=1'-0"

STAIR DETAILS.

Hillsborough

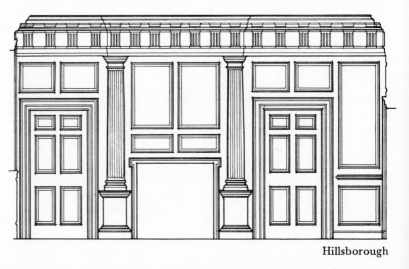

Hillsborough

182

Southworth House (VA-313), exact location unknown. Brick, rectangular (five-bay front), one-and-a-half stories above raised basement, gable roof with shed dormers; center-hall plan. Built late 18th C.; demolished. 1 ext. photo (1938), 1 int. photo, basement stair (1938); 1 data page (1941).

NORFOLK

Purdy-Whittle House (Whittle House) (VA-15), 225 W. Freemason St. Brick, 40'2" (three-bay front) x 40'5", two stories, gable roof, pedimented gable-end front, two brick interior chimneys, modillion cornice, pedimented Tuscan entrance porch, two-level side porch; fine interiors. Built late 18th C.; later addition. 5 sheets (1934, including plans, elevations, sections, details); 1 ext. photo (1934); 2 data pages (1936); HABSI (1958).

Whittle House (VA-15), see Purdy-Whittle House (VA-15), 225 W. Freemason St., Norfolk.

NOKESVILLE VICINITY   Prince William County (76)

Effingham (VA-575), .5 mi. W of Cedar Run, .4 mi. S of State Rte. 646, 1 mi. SE of intersection with State Rte. 611. Frame with clapboarding, rectangular (five-bay front), two stories, gable roof, four exterior end chimneys; center-hall plan; frame and stone outbuildings including blacksmith shop, dairy, and slave quarters. Built mid 18th C.; extensive later alterations and additions including mid 20th C. giant portico across front. 4 ext. photos, main house (1936, 1959), 9 ext. photos, outbuildings (1936), 4 int. photos, main house (1936); 2 data pages (1959).

Fleetwood (VA-275), S side of Slate Run, W side of State Rte. 611, .7 mi. S of intersection with State Rte. 653. Stone, rectangular (four-bay front), two stories, gable roof, three exterior end chimneys, modillion cornice; side-hall plan; flanking one-story wings, log with clapboarding. E wing built late 18th C.; main section and office wing built early 19th C. 4 ext. photos (1936); HABSI (1959).

House (VA-825), .1 mi. W of Cedar Run, N side of State Rte. 646, 1.6 mi. SE of intersection with State Rte. 611. Frame with clapboarding, rectangular (three-bay front), one story, gable roof, two exterior end chimneys; two-room plan; rear ell. Built late 18th C. or early 19th C.; later additions and alterations including dormer windows. 1 ext. photo (1936).

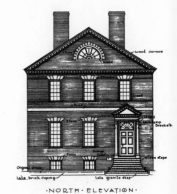

·NORTH·ELEVATION·

Purdy-Whittle House

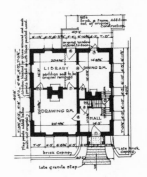

Park Gate (VA-555), .4 mi. N of Slate Run, N side of State Rte. 653, .3 mi. W of intersection with State Rte. 611. Frame with clapboarding, rectangular (three-bay front), one-and-a-half stories, gable roof with dormers, two exterior end chimneys, roof extended to cover porch across front; modified two-room plan. Built mid 18th C.; later lean-to addition and interior alterations. 1 ext. photo (1937); HABSI (1959).

Pilgrim's Rest (VA-837), .2 mi. E of Cedar Run, .2 mi. W of State Rte. 607, opposite intersection with State Rte. 645. Frame with brick nogging and flush siding, rectangular (three-bay front), two stories, gable roof, two exterior end chimneys joined together below the eaves line to form one extra broad chimney; side-hall plan, notable interior trim; side wing. Built late 18th C.; later porch and side-wing additions. 3 ext. photos (1936); HABSI (1959).

NOTTOWAY   Nottoway County (68)

Nottoway County Courthouse (VA-812), .5 mi. E of Crystal Lake, W side of State Rte. 625, .1 mi. S of intersection with U.S. Rte. 460. Brick, rectangular (three-bay front), two stories, gable roof, pedimented Tuscan portico; one-room plan; flanking one-story, one-bay wings with gable roofs. Built c. 1840; later additions. 1 ext. photo (1938); HABSI (1959).

NUTTSVILLE VICINITY   Lancaster County (52)

Belle Isle (VA-64), .1 mi. N of N branch of Deep Creek, at SW end of State Rte. 683, 1 mi. SW of intersection with State Rte. 354. Brick (Flemish bond), three part composition with flanking dependencies, 38'1½" (three-bay front) x 32', two stories, hipped roof, two interior end chimneys, modillion cornice, brick belt course and water table, shallow segmental window lintels; modified asymmetrical plan; flanking one-story, gable roof wings each four bays with interior end chimney; NE dependency: brick, 28'1" (three-bay front) x 19'2½", one story, gable roof with jerkinheads, exterior end chimney; one-room plan. Built mid 18th C.; interiors altered late 18th C.; ground-floor interiors removed c. 1930; ground floor renovated and plan altered c. 1940. Design of house possibly influenced by Robert Morris, *Select Architecture*, London 1750, plate 33. 18 sheets (1940, including plot plan, plans, elevations, interior elevations, details); 13 ext. photos (1937, 1940), 5 ext. photos, dependencies (1934, 1940), 5 int. photos (1940); 1 photocopy plate from Robert Morris (n.d.); 1 data page (1937); HABSI (1957).

Belle Isle

Morattico (VA-73), NE bank of Rappahannock River, at S bank of mouth of Lancaster Creek, .1 mi. W of S end of State Rte. 622, .9 mi. SW of intersection with State Rte. 718. Brick, rectangular (three-bay front), one-and-a-half stories, gable roof with dormers, one interior end chimney; side-hall plan. Built early 18th C.; demolished c. 1925; exceptionally fine interior trim reused in modern structure on site. 1 ext. photocopy (c. 1900); 1 data page (1940).

Oakley (VA-535), .1 mi. N of Little Branch, S side of State Rte. 622, .4 mi. E of intersection with State Rte. 618. Frame with clapboarding, L-shaped (five-bay front), two-story front section, gable roof, one exterior end chimney, one interior chimney; center-hall plan; ell: one-and-a-half story, gable roof with jerkinheads and dormers, one exterior end chimney; outbuilding: frame with clapboarding, rectangular (two-bay front), one story, gable roof, one interior center chimney, two-room plan. Built early 18th C.; extensive later additions and alterations. 2 ext. photos (1930); HABSI (1958).

OCCOQUAN   Prince William County (76)

Mill Ruins and Mill House (VA-576), SW bank of Occoquan Creek, N side of Mill St., at W end. Fieldstone and brick ruins of corner of mill at edge of creek; stone mill house: rectangular (three-bay front), one story, gable roof, one exterior end chimney; one-room plan. Mill built mid 18th C.; ruinous; mill house built late 18th C., reconstructed. 1 ext. photo (1959); 1 data page (1959).

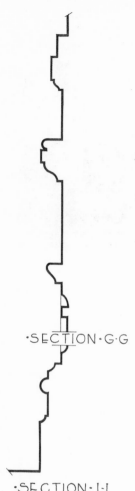

·SECTION·G·G

·SECTION·I·I

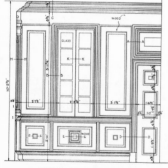

NORTH WALL · ROOM NO.6

Bel Air

Rockledge

Rockledge (VA-577), S bank of Occoquan Creek, S side of Mill St. at W end. Stone, main block 62'9" (six-bay front) x 20'3", two-and-a-half stories, gable roof with pedimented dormers, two interior end chimneys, one interior chimney, modillion cornice; center-hall plan; one-and-a-half story side wing; springhouse. Built mid 18th C., William Buckland, architect; later addition; interior vandalized; ruinous 1970. 11 sheets (1960, including plot plan, plans, elevations, sections, details, main house; plans, elevations, details, springhouse); 20 ext. photos, main house (1959, 1960), 1 ext. photo, springhouse (1959), 12 int. photos (1960); 5 data pages (1959, 1961); HABSI (1959).

OCCOQUAN VICINITY   Prince William County (76)

Bel Air (VA-99), .2 mi. S of Neabsco Creek, .9 mi. W of State Rte. 640, .6 mi. E of intersection with State Rte. 610. Brick (Flemish bond), 50'11" (four-bay front) x 34'9", one-and-a-half stories above raised basement, gable roof with dormers, one exterior end chimney, one interior end chimney; center-hall plan, notable interior trim including removable interior hall partition. Built mid 18th C.; later alterations. 7 sheets (1936, including plan, elevations, details); 6 ext. photos (1936), 2 int. photos (1936); HABSI (1959). NR

186

OLD TOWN NECK   Northampton County (66)

Westover (VA-957), .2 mi. S of Mattawoman Creek, .5 mi. N of State
Rte. 630, .8 mi. W of intersection with U.S. Rte. 1. Brick and frame
with clapboarding, rectangular (five-bay front), one-and-a-half stories,
gambrel roof with dormers, two exterior end chimneys; center-hall
plan, elaborate panelling. Built 18th C. 7 sheets (1971, including
plans, elevations, sections).

ONANCOCK   Accomack County (1)

Kerr Place (VA-494), NE corner of Crockett Ave. and Market St.
Brick, rectangular (seven-bay front), two stories, gable roof with cross
gable, two interior chimneys, two interior end chimneys, central projecting pedimented pavilions on front and rear facades; center-hall
plan, fine Adam-style mantels and woodwork; two-story wing. Built
late 18th C.; later addition. 2 ext. photos (1940); HABSI (1958). NR

Topping House (VA-482), .9 mi. S of Finneys Creek, .8 mi. S of State
Rte. 638, .6 mi. E of intersection with State Rte. 641. Frame with
clapboarding and brick (Flemish bond) end, rectangular (two-bay
front), one-and-a-half stories, gable roof with dormers, two exterior
end chimneys; irregular plan. Built late 18th C.; ruinous. 3 ext.
photos (1940); 1 data page (n.d.).

ORDINARY   Gloucester County (37)

Old House (VA-519), see Sewell's Ordinary (VA-519), Ordinary.

Sewell's Ordinary (VA-519), 1.2 mi. E of Timberneck Creek, W side
of U.S. Rte. 17, opposite intersection with State Rte. 636. Frame
with clapboarding, L-shaped (three-bay front), one-and-a-half stories,
gambrel roof with dormers, two T-shaped exterior end chimneys, one
interior end chimney; center-hall plan; ell. Built mid 18th C.; moved
to present location c. 1960; extensive alterations. 1 ext. photo
(1934); HABSI (1959).

ORDINARY VICINITY   Gloucester County (37)

Belle Farm Site (VA-69), S bank of Vaughans Creek, N side of State
Rte. 656, opposite intersection with State Rte. 641. Landscape and
garden plan of Belle Farm site, house: frame with clapboarding, rectangular (five-bay front), two stories, gable roof, two interior end

chimneys, one exterior end chimney; one-and-a-half story rear ell. Built mid 18th C.; dismantled and moved to Williamsburg. 1 ext. photo, site (1937); 2 data pages (n.d., including garden plan).

OWENS VICINITY   King George County (50)

Saint Paul's Episcopal Church (VA-266), .8 mi. N of Pepper Mill Creek, SE corner of intersection of State Rtes. 206 and 218. Brick (Flemish bond), cruciform (five-bay front), two stories, hipped roof, modillion cornice, arched windows, brick water table; Greek-cross plan. Built mid 18th C.; interior ruinous 1812; converted to school mid 19th C.; partially restored. 1 data page (1940); HABSI (1958).

PAINTER VICINITY   Accomack County (1)

Thunder Castle (Thunder Cottage) (VA-496), .9 mi. W of Machipongo River, .4 mi. S of State Rte. 607, .8 mi. E of intersection with U.S. Rte. 13. Frame with clapboarding and brick ends (Flemish bond with random glazed headers), rectangular (two-bay front), one-and-a-half stories, gambrel roof with dormers, one interior end chimney; side-hall plan. Built early 19th C.; additions. 2 ext. photos (1940).

Thunder Cottage (VA-496), see Thunder Castle (VA-496), Painter Vicinity.

PARIS   Fauquier County (31)

Watts Ashby Tavern (VA-743), SE corner of intersection of State Rtes. 759 and 701. Stone and frame with clapboarding, rectangular (four-bay front), two stories (stone first story, frame second story), gable roof, three exterior stone end chimneys, second story projects beyond first floor on street front to form covered porch below; one-story flanking stone wings. Built mid 18th C.; demolished. 6 ext. photos (1936).

PETERSBURG

Battersea (VA-136), 793 Appomattox St. Brick, covered with stucco, five-part composition, two-story main block, one-story wings and hyphens, pyramidal hipped roof on main block, pedimented gable roofs on wings; notable Chinese trellis stairway. Built c. 1770, attributed to Thomas Jefferson; later alterations. 19 sheets (1940, including plans, elevations, section, details); 32 photos (1935, 1937, 1938).

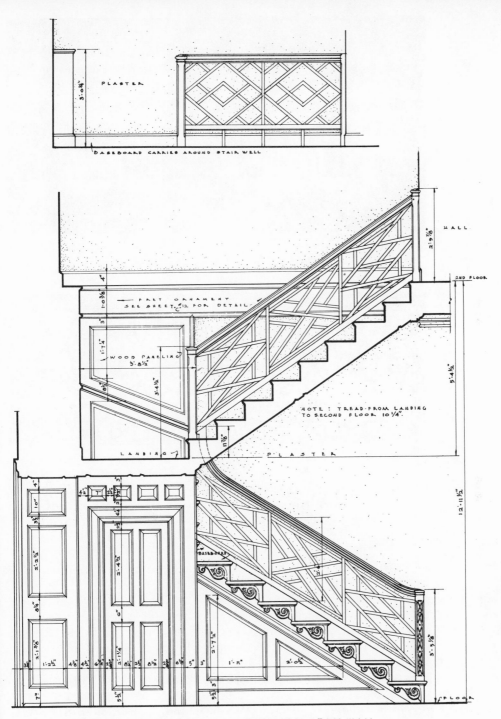

PLASTER

3'-0¼"

BASEBOARD CARRIES AROUND STAIR WELL

HALL

2'-9⅛"

2ND FLOOR

FRET ORNAMENT
SEE SHEET #12 FOR DETAIL

WOOD PANELING
3'-8½"

NOTE : TREAD FROM LANDING
TO SECOND FLOOR 10¼".

5'-4½"

LANDING

PLASTER

12'-11½"

BASEBOARD

3'-5⅜"

FLOOR

SECTION THRU STAIRHALL SHOWING STAIRWAY

Battersea

189

Battersea

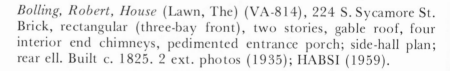

William H. Bowers House

2'-6½"

Bolling, Robert, House (Lawn, The) (VA-814), 224 S. Sycamore St. Brick, rectangular (three-bay front), two stories, gable roof, four interior end chimneys, pedimented entrance porch; side-hall plan; rear ell. Built c. 1825. 2 ext. photos (1935); HABSI (1959).

Bollingbrook (VA-79), on block bounded on S by Franklin St., on N by Henry and Bank Sts., on W by Jefferson St., on E by Madison St. Frame with clapboarding, 48'1" (five-bay front) x 22'1½", one story, gable roof, two interior end chimneys, modillion cornice; side wing: rectangular (three-bay front), one story, gable roof. Built late 18th C.; originally one of two similar buildings, each with two flanking side wings; destroyed. 5 sheets (1935, including plans, elevations, details); 2 ext. photocopies (n.d. 1900); 21 data pages (n.d., 1940).

Bowers, William H., House (VA-68), 254 N. Sycamore St. Brick, 23'7" (three-bay front) x 50', three-and-a-half stories, gable roof with dormers, five interior end chimneys, rectangular insets above first-

190

and second-story windows, oval inserts above third-story windows, iron balconies, first-floor store front; side-hall plan. Built 1828-29; later alterations. 5 sheets (1935, including plan, elevations, details of ironwork); 6 ext. photos (1938, 1969), 3 int. photos (1968); 8 data pages (1939, 1968); HABSI (1959).

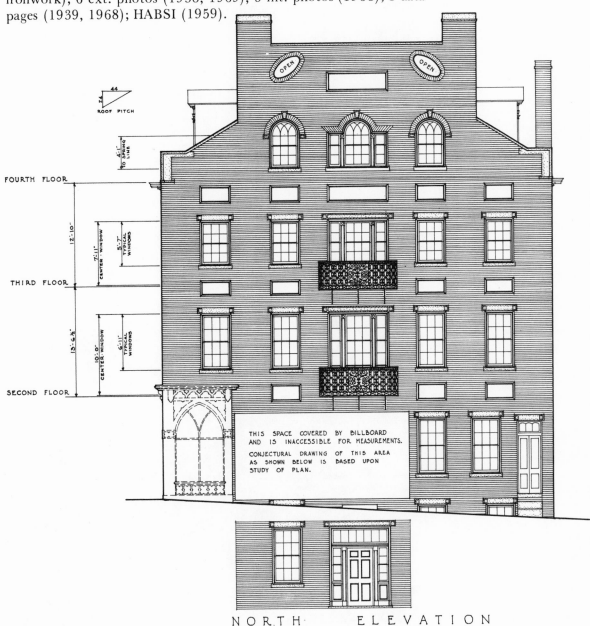

NORTH ELEVATION

William H. Bowers House

Center Hill (VA-815), N of Franklin St., at end of Center Hill Lane. Brick, rectangular (five-bay front), two stories, low hipped roof with cupola, four interior end chimneys, full-length one-story porch; center-hall plan. Built c. 1825; altered with additions c. 1850. 2 ext. photos (c. 1920, 1936); HABSI (1959).

City Hall (VA-659), see Old United States Custom House and Post Office (VA-659), 121-41 N. Union St., Petersburg.

Double House (VA-816), 208-08A Bollingbrook St. Brick, rectangular (four-bay front), three stories, gable roof, two interior end chimneys, arched entrances; side-hall plan. Built early 19th C.; demolished. 1 ext. photo (1935); HABSI (1959).

Dunlop, David, Tobacco Factory (VA-663), 45-127 Old St. Brick, 144' (seventeen-bay front) x 151', four stories, gable roof, one tapered rectangular brick stack, corbeled brick decoration at gable eaves and on cross gable; open plan, wooden interior structural framing. Built 1887-88. 1 ext. photo (1968); 1 ext. photocopy(1894); 6 data pages (1968).

David Dunlop Tobacco Factory

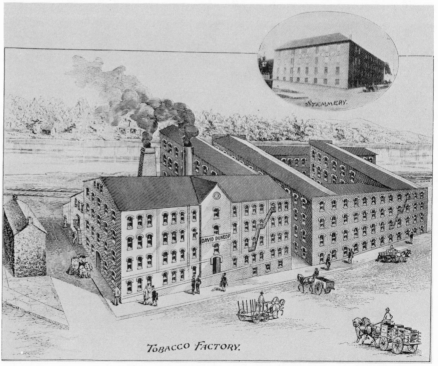

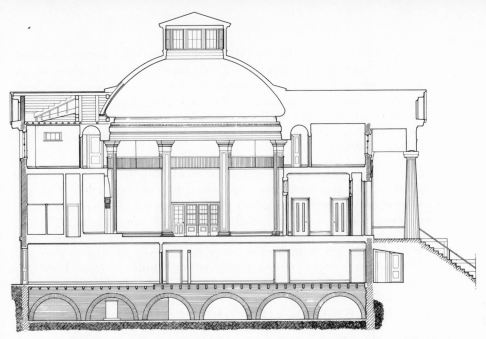

The Exchange

Dunn House (VA-130), 105 S. Sycamore St. Brick, 53′1½″ (five-bay front) x 23′¾″, two stories, hipped roof, interior end chimneys, Tuscan entrance porch; center-hall plan; dairy, smokehouse, and stable outbuildings. Built c. 1833; destroyed. 16 sheets (1936, including plot plan, plans, elevations, sections, details); 2 ext. photos (1936), 5 ext. photos, outbuildings (1936), 6 int. photos (1936); 2 data pages.

Elliott House (VA-662), 269 High St. Frame with clapboarding, rectangular (four-bay front), two-and-a-half stories, mansard roof with dormers, two interior end chimneys, decorative cast-iron roof cresting, three-bay projecting bay window on principal front, elaborate wooden hooded entrance porch with Eastlake decoration and iron cresting; side-hall plan. Built c. 1876; rear addition 1889. 2 ext. photos (1968), 4 int. photos (1968); 5 data pages (1968).

Exchange, The (VA-647), 15-19 W. Bank St. Brick with stucco, 60′4″ (five-bay front) x 79′11″, three stories, hipped roof; dome and ten-sided lantern, monumental tetrastyle Greek Doric portico, one interior end chimney; rectangular plan with central rotunda 39′7″ in diameter with surrounding balcony. Built c. 1840-41, Mr. Berrien, architect; later interior alterations. 8 sheets (1968, including plot plan, plans, elevations, sections, details); 5 ext. photos (1968), 4 int. photos (1968); 7 data pages (1968); HABSI (1959). NR

The Exchange

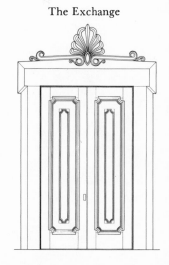

Friend, Nathaniel, Jr., House (VA-651), 27-29 Bollingbrook St. Brick (Flemish bond front), approx. 48' (six-bay front) x 48', three-and-a-half stories, gable roof with dormers, four interior end chimneys; four-room plan, notable interior trim; rear wing. Built 1816; extensive later alterations to ground-floor shop and interior room arrangements. 3 ext. photos (1968), 1 int. photo (1968); 5 data pages (1968); HABSI (1959).

Gill, Erasmus, House (VA-650), 53 S. Market St. Frame with clapboarding, rectangular (three-bay front), two stories, gable roof, two exterior end chimneys; side-hall plan, notable interior trim; one-story side wing (two-bay front), shallow gable roof; one interior end chimney; notable interior trim including arched niches flanking finely detailed gauge-work mantel and overmantel, fluted pilaster door and window trim carrying paneled entablatures. Built c. 1785-91; interior trim and side wing possibly added c. 1800-10; later additions and alterations. 1 ext. photo (1968), 6 int. photos (1968); 1 ext. photocopy (n.d.); 6 data pages (1968); HABSI (1959).

Gilliam Row Houses (VA-817), 102-04 Grove Ave., see Read's, John B., Row (VA-643), 102-04 W. Old St., Petersburg.

Golden Ball Tavern (VA-818), SE corner of Market St. and Grove Ave. Brick with frame fronts, rectangular (six-bay front), one-and-a-half stories above brick basement, gable roof with dormers, one interior chimney and three interior end chimneys; rear ell continues pitch of roof making saltbox shape. Built mid 18th C.; demolished. 2 ext. photos (1935).

Harrison House (VA-642), see Strachan, Dr. Alexander Glass, House (VA-642), 302 Cross St., Petersburg.

Hinton House (VA-426), 416 High St. Brick, rectangular (five-bay front), two stories, hipped roof, four interior end chimneys, modillion cornice. Built early 19th C.; altered. 2 ext. photos (1940), 4 int. photos (1935).

House in Blandford (VA-819), exact location unknown, site possibly S side of Wills St., between Church and Center Sts. in Blandford Cemetery. Brick, rectangular (four-bay front), one story, gable roof, two interior end chimneys. Built early 19th C.; demolished or possibly moved to unknown site. 1 ext. photo (1936).

Hustings Courthouse (VA-657), Courthouse Ave. and N. Sycamore St. Brick with stucco, temple form, 50' (one-bay front) x 100' (seven-bay lateral facade), two stories, gable roof, hexastyle portico, four

Hustings Courthouse

Tower-of-the-Winds-order columns flanked by square pilaster-anta at each end, octagonal clock tower resembling steeple surmounted by statue of Justice; modified center-hall plan, notable plaster ceiling in courtroom. Built 1838-40, Calvin Pollard, architect; later additions and alterations 1877, 1965. 4 ext. photos (1968), 1 int. photo (1968); 1 ext. photocopy (1865); 10 data pages (1968).

Jackson, John, House (VA-661), 410 High St. Brick with stucco, approx. 60' (five-bay front) x 40', two-and-a-half stories above raised basement, mansard roof with dormers; four interior end chimneys, arched cast-iron window lintels, bracketed cornice, entrance porch; center-hall plan; rear ell. Built 1867; ground-floor balcony removed; interior altered. 4 ext. photos (1968), 1 int. photo (1968); 1 ext. photocopy (1894); 8 data pages (1968).

Lawn, The (VA-814), see Bolling, Robert, House, 224 S. Sycamore St., Petersburg.

May's, David, Row (VA-660), 217-23 High St. Brick, four adjoining units approx. 105' (twelve-bay front, each unit three bays) x 55', three stories above raised basement, flat roof, large scale bracketed cornice, eight interior chimneys, two interior end chimneys, shallow pediments over first- and second-story windows, wooden entrance porches, cast-iron entry well fences; side-hall plan. Built 1859; ruinous 1968. 2 ext. photos (1968), 1 int. photo (1968); 1 photocopy (c. 1870); 8 data pages (1968).

O'Hara, Charles, House (VA-820), 244 N. Market St. Brick, trapezoidal (three-bay front), three stories, gable roof, two interior end chimneys, arched entrance; altered one-room plan; absence of parallel walls or right angles. Built c. 1815; renovated. 1 ext. photo (1936); HABSI (1959).

Old Farmers Market (VA-649), NE corner of intersection of W. Old and Rock Sts. Brick, octagonal, 80' in diameter, 33'10" per side (three bays per side), one story, hipped roof, octagonal louvered cupola, two interior end chimneys at each corner, projecting shed roof, 12', with ornamental cast-iron supporting brackets, open shed 60' x 30' on N side; open plan. Built 1878, B. J. Black, architect; H. W. Williams, builder; altered 1952. 4 sheets (1968, including plot plan, plan, elevations, sections); 4 ext. photos (1968); 8 data pages (1968); HABSI (1959). NR

Old United States Custom House and Post Office (City Hall) (VA-659), 121-41 N. Union St. Brick faced with granite, 46' (three-bay front) x 100' (eight-bay lateral facade), three stories, hipped roof, four interior end chimneys, arcaded window and door openings on first floor, pedimented window lintels at second-floor level; modified center-hall plan, cast-iron interior supports with composite capitals. Built 1856, Ammi B. Young, architect; remodeled 1870; lateral facade extended three bays 1908-10; renovated 1938. 5 ext. photos (1968), 1 int. photo (1968); 30 data pages (1968); HABSI (1959).

Pig Alley Block Study (VA-930), Hurt St., Plum St., and Grove Ave., near Appomattox River. Mid 19th C. village complex of cottages, built for laborers in nearby flour and cotton mills. General views; looking S along Hurt St. toward Plum St., and looking N along Hurt St. toward Grove Ave., are included in this entry. 2 ext. photos (1968).

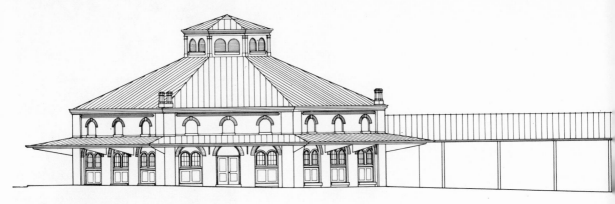

Old Farmers Market

Double House (VA-654), 406-08 Hurt St. Frame with clapboarding, 36' (four-bay front of two units) x 26', one-and-a-half stories, gable roof with dormers, one interior chimney, wooden one-story entrance porch; two-room plan per unit. Built c. 1835; later additions and alterations. 1 ext. photo (1968); 5 data pages (1968).

Double House (VA-645), 411-13 Hurt St. Frame with clapboarding, 36'4" (four-bay front of two units) x 26'3", one-and-a-half stories, gable roof with dormers, one interior chimney, wooden one-story entrance porches; two-room plan per unit. Built c. 1835; later additions and alterations. 7 sheets (1968, including plot plan, plan, elevations, sections); 2 ext. photos (1968); 5 data pages (1968).

Double House (VA-656), 702-04 Plum St. Brick, 40' (four-bay front of two units) x 30', one-and-a-half stories, gable roof with dormers, one interior chimney, wooden one-story entrance porch; two-room plan per unit, corner fireplaces. Built c. 1835; later alterations. 2 ext. photos (1968); 5 data pages (1968).

House and Store (VA-653), 706 Grove Ave. Frame with clapboarding, trapezoidal, approx. 15' (two-bay front) x 60', two stories, gable roof, two exterior end chimneys, gable-end street facade with ground-floor store front; one-room plan; one-story rear wings. Built early 19th C.; ruinous 1968. 5 ext. photos (1968); 4 data pages (1968); HABSI (1969).

Row Houses (VA-655), 703-13 Plum St. Frame with clapboarding covered with asphalt shingles, approx. 100' (ten-bay front of five two-bay units) x 25', one-and-a-half stories, gable roof with dormers, one exterior end chimney, four interior chimneys; two-room plan per unit. Built c. 1835; extensive alterations. 2 ext. photos (1968); 7 data pages (1968).

House and Store

Store (VA-644), 412 Hurt St. Frame with clapboarding, 18'4" (three-bay front) x 36'7", one story, gable roof, one exterior end chimney, heavy stone foundation piers, one-story wooden entrance porch; one-room plan; side and rear wings. Built c. 1835; side and rear additions of one room each early 19th C., mid 20th C. 8 sheets (1968, including plot plan, plan, elevations, sections); 3 ext. photos (1968); 5 data pages (1968).

Pride's Tavern (VA-821), E of 600 N. West St. Brick, L-shaped (three-bay front), one-and-a-half stories, gable roof with dormers, one interior and two interior end chimneys; side lean-to; two brick one-story outbuildings. Built early 19th C.; tavern and one outbuilding demolished; kitchen remains. 2 ext. photos (1936); HABSI (1959).

Read's, John B., Row (Gilliam Row Houses) (VA-643), 102-04 W. Old St. Brick with stone window and door dressings and belt courses, 46'9" (six-bay front, three bays per unit) x 44'3", three stories, gable roof, four interior end chimneys, arched entrance doorways with stone archivolts and keystones, shop fronts on ground floor; side-hall plan on second- and third-floor living quarters. Built 1815-18; later alterations and additions. 9 sheets (1968, including plot plans, plans, elevations, sections, details); 5 ext. photos (1935, 1968), 4 int. photos (1935, 1968); 7 data pages (1968); HABSI (1959).

Pig Alley Block Study, Store

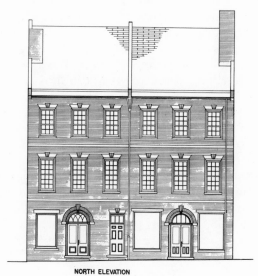

NORTH ELEVATION

John B Read's Row

Albert L. Scott House

Scott, Albert L., House (VA-648), 29 S. Market St. Brick with stucco scored to resemble ashlar, 42'8" (three-bay front) x 45'2" with rear wing 37'1" x 17'3", two stories above raised basement, hipped roof, square bracketed lantern, five interior end chimneys, modillion cornice, main floor windows paired with arched heads, entrance porch with balcony roof, cast-iron entrance gate and piers; center-hall plan, marble mantelpieces. Built 1860-61; remodeled c. 1950. 8 sheets (1968, including plot plan, plans, elevations, sections, details); 4 ext. photos (c. 1950, 1968), 3 int. photos (1968); 6 data pages (1968); HABSI (1959).

Smith's, John H., Row (VA-646), 209-15 High St. Brick, four individual houses forming row, 20'7" (three-bay front single unit) x 34'11", two stories above raised basement, gable roof, two interior end chimneys per unit, rectangular recessed panels between first- and second-story windows; side-hall plan; antherion motif cast-iron fence. Built 1837, as row of five units; one unit demolished c. 1950; ruinous 1968. 9 sheets (1968, including plot plan, plans, elevations, sections, details of cast-iron fence); 4 ext. photos (1968, including fence), 4 int. photos (1968); 7 data pages (1968); HABSI (1959).

Spottswood House (VA-822), see Stirling Castle (VA-822), 320 High St., Petersburg.

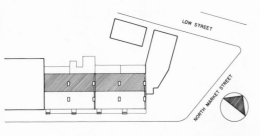

THESE FOUR FINE FEDERAL ROW HOUSES WERE BUILT C. 1837-1838 AND SHOULD BE NOTED ON THE EXTERIOR FOR THE WOODEN DOOR LIGHT AND IRON FENCE REMAINING ON AND ALONG THE SOUTH FACADE OF THE 209 HOUSE. ON THE INTERIOR NOTEWORTHY ARE THE FINE MANTELS AND OTHER WOODWORK. IT SHOULD NOTED THAT THERE WAS ONCE A FIFTH HOUSE OF THIS ROW AT 207 HIGH STREET WHICH WAS DE-STROYED C. 1950.

SITE PLAN

THIS PROJECT WAS JOINTLY SPONSORED BY THE NATIONAL PARK SERVICE, OFFICE OF ARCHEOLOGY AND HISTORIC PRESERVATION, AND THE HISTORIC PETERSBURG FOUNDATION, INC. WITH FINANCIAL ASSISTANCE FROM THE VIRGINIA HISTORIC LANDMARKS COMMISSION. MEASURED AND DRAWN DURING THE SUMMER OF 1968 UNDER THE DIRECTION OF JAMES C. MASSEY, CHIEF OF H.A.B.S., AND BY JOHN M. MCRAE (UNIVERSITY OF FLORIDA), PROJECT SUPERVISOR, RANDALL J. BIALLAS (UNIVERSITY OF ILLINOIS, URBANA), HISTORIAN, AND BY STUDENT ASSISTANT ARCHITECTS MICHAEL HAMILTON (UNIVERSITY OF ARIZONA), THOMAS J. SANFORD (WASHINGTON STATE UNIVERSITY), AND EDWIN S. SMITH, JR. (RHODE ISLAND SCHOOL OF DESIGN) AT THE PETERSBURG NATIONAL BATTLEFIELD.

SOUTH ELEVATION

John H. Smith's Row

Stirling Castle (Spottswood House) (VA-822), 320 High St. Frame with clapboarding, rectangular (five-bay front), two stories, hipped roof, two interior end chimneys, Greek Ionic entrance porch; rear ell. Built late 18th C.; altered; moved from unknown site W of Petersburg early 19th C. 1 ext. photo (1936); HABSI (1959).

Stone House in Blandford (VA-96), SE corner of E. Washington St. and Crater Rd. Stone with clapboarding, 30′5″ (three-bay front) x 30′6½″, one-and-a-half stories, gable roof with dormers, one interior end chimney, stone quoining, frame south wall with clapboarding; side-hall plan. Built c. 1760; demolished. 9 sheets (1935, including plans, elevations, sections, details); 8 ext. photos (1935, 1936); 4 data pages (n.d.).

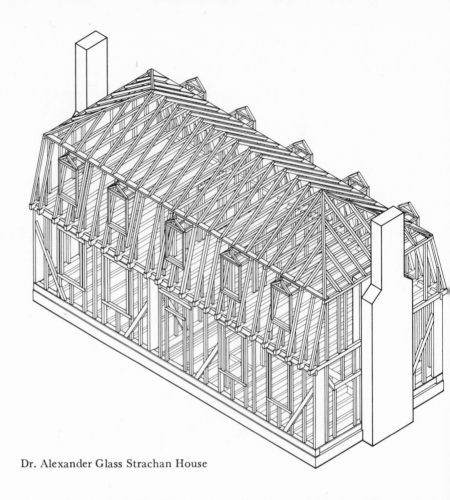

Dr. Alexander Glass Strachan House

Stone Warehouse (VA-823), E side of Market St., between Grove Ave. and the Appomattox River. Random-laid stone, rectangular (six-bay front), two stories, gable roof. Built early 19th C.; altered. 1 ext. photo (1936); HABSI (1959).

Strachan, Dr. Alexander Glass, House (Harrison House) (VA-642), 302 Cross St. Frame with clapboarding, center section 46'4" (five-bay front) x 19'11", one-and-a-half stories, hip on gambrel roof with dormers, two exterior end chimneys; center-hall plan; flanking wings: rectangular (two-bay front), one story, gable roof, N wing is connected to center section by one-bay hyphen. Built mid 18th C.; wings added probably early 19th C.; interior gutted 1968. 7 sheets (1968, including plot plan, plans, elevations, sections, details); 4 ext. photos (1936, 1968), 7 int. photos (1968, including framing details and removed mantels); 6 data pages (1968); HABSI (1959).

Dr. Alexander Glass Strachan House

Tabb Street Presbyterian Church (VA-658), 21 W. Tabb St. Stone and brick with stucco scored to resemble ashlar, temple form, approx. 75' (one-bay front) x 85' (four-bay lateral facade), two stories above raised basement, gable roof, monumental hexastyle Greek Doric portico, cast-iron and granite fence; entrance lobby and auditorium with balcony on three sides, hexastyle modified Corinthian exedra, cast-iron balcony columns; rear ell. Built 1843; addition 1923; octagonal spire on square belfry removed 1938. 2 ext. photos (1968), 3 int. photos (1968); 2 photocopies (1910, 1935); 8 data pages (1968); HABSI (1959).

Washington Street Methodist Church (VA-299), SW corner of Washington and Adams Sts. Brick with stucco, three-part composition, central block: rectangular (five-bay front), two stories above rusticated basement, low hipped roof, two-story three-bay Greek Doric portico; two flanking wings: rectangular (three-bay front), two stories, low hipped roof, two-story Greek Doric porticoes. Built 1842; later additions. 2 ext. photos (1940); HABSI (1959).

PETERSBURG VICINITY   Dinwiddie County (27)

Mayfield (VA-958), .1 mi. N of Cattail Branch, S side of U.S. Rte. 1 (U.S. Rte. 460), .5 mi. E of intersection of Rte. 1 and Rte. 460. Brick, 54' (five-bay front) x 32', one-and-a-half stories over raised basement, clipped gable roof with dormers, two interior end chimneys; center-hall plan, fine interior panelling. Built mid 18th C., moved .5 mi. NW of original location 1969. 10 sheets (1971, including plans, elevations, sections, details). NR

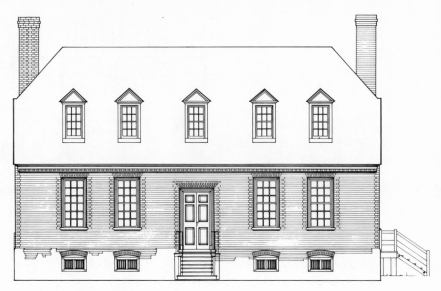

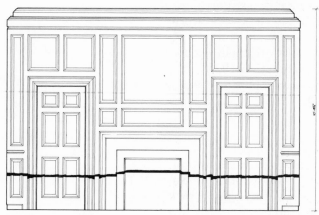

Mayfield

Wales (VA-152), 2 mi. S of Appomattox River, .3 mi. S of U.S. Rte. 460, immediately E of intersection with State Rte. 632. Frame with clapboarding, central unit: approx. 32′ (three-bay front) x 24′, one-and-a-half stories, gable roof with hipped dormers, two exterior end chimneys; modified four-room plan; flanking wings: rectangular (three-bay front), one story, gable roof with hipped end facing central unit, interior end chimney, wings connected to central unit by one-bay hyphens. Built mid 18th C.; later additions. 17 sheets (1935, 1940, including plot plan, plans, elevations, sections, details); 16 ext. photos (1935, 1936, 1940), 10 int. photos (1935, 1940); 2 data pages (1940); HABSI (1959).

Rectory, The (VA-260), E side of State Rte. 1006, adjacent to St. Peter's Episcopal Church. Frame with clapboarding, rectangular (three-bay front), two-and-a-half stories, gable roof with dormers, one interior end chimney; two-room plan, corner fireplaces; side wing: rectangular (three-bay front), two stories, gable roof, one exterior end chimney; side-hall plan. Built mid 18th C.; wing constructed early 19th C. 1 ext. photo (1939); HABSI (1957).

Roy House (VA-721), exact location unknown. Frame with clapboarding, rectangular (three-bay front), one-and-a-half stories, gable roof with dormers, two exterior end chimneys; two-room plan. Built late 18th C.; demolished. 4 ext. photos (n.d.).

Saint Peter's Episcopal Church (VA-261), N side of Water St., between State Rtes. 1002 and 1006. Brick with stucco, rectangular (three-bay front), one story, gable roof, distyle-in-antis entrance bay flanked by lancet windows, pedimented gable end with circular lunette, lancet windows; one-room plan; separate bell tower in churchyard: square with wooden vertical siding, battered base walls, pyramidal roof with scalloped soffitt skirting. Built 1836; bell tower demolished. 1 ext. photo (1939), 1 ext. photo, bell tower (1939); HABSI (1957).

St. Peter's Episcopal Church

Camden (VA-184), S bank of Rappahannock River, .8 mi. N of N end of State Rte. 686, .5 mi. N of intersection of State Rte. 686 and U.S. Rte. 17. Frame with flush siding, T-shaped (three-bay front), two-and-a-half stories, hipped roof with subsidiary crossed gables, three interior end chimneys, one interior chimney, projecting pedimented front pavilion, boldly projecting bracketed eaves, paired and single segmental arched windows, triple round arched windows, one-story roofed front and rear porch flanking semi-circular arcaded conservatory; center-hall plan, offset elliptical staircase, notable marble mantels, plaster cornices, and centerpieces; flanking two-story side wing. Built 1856-69, Nathan G. Starkweather, architect; original square center cupola destroyed c. 1863. 4 ext. photos (1939); 1 data page (1940); HABSI (1957).   NR

Gaymont (VA-306), .5 mi. N of Goldenvale Creek, .5 mi. SE of U.S. Rte. 17, .7 mi. W of intersection with State Rte. 675. Concrete block with stucco, rectangular (five-bay front), two stories, gable roof, two end chimneys, full-length one-story hexastyle front porch; center-hall plan; flanking one-story wings with shallow gable roofs terminated by half-octagons, foundations of octagonal rear wing. Built mid 18th C.; wings and front porch built 1819-20; octagonal rear wing built 1834; half octagon-ends to flanking wings built 1838-39; burned 1959; S wing rebuilt 1960; N wing rebuilt 1962; central block rebuilt in concrete block with stucco to replace original frame construction 1964-65. 17 ext. photos (1939, 1940), 3 int. photos (1940); 1 data page (1940); HABSI (1957).

Belle Grove (VA-274), NE bank of Rappahannock River, .2 mi. W of U.S. Rte. 301, 1.1 mi. S of intersection with State Rtes. 660 and 625. Frame with clapboarding, rectangular (five-bay front), two stories, gable roof, four interior end chimneys, N front with projecting pedimented central pavilions flanked by two-story concave quadrant porticoes at re-entrant angles, modified Corinthian superposed on Doric order, S front with pedimented central portico, Ionic superposed on Doric order; center-hall plan; flanking wings terminated by one-story pedimented pavilions with central arched windows flanked by paired Ionic pilasters. Built early 19th C. 3 ext. photos (1937); 1 data page (1941).

Woodlawn (VA-213), N bank of Rappahannock River, 1.2 mi. S of State Rte. 627, 1.5 mi. E of U.S. Rte. 301. Frame with clapboarding, rectangular (five-bay front), two stories, hipped roof, four interior end chimneys, two-story Doric portico; center-hall plan; W wing added. Built early 19th C.; later additions 1932. 1 ext. photo (1939); 1 data page (1941); HABSI (1958).

POWHATAN   Powhatan County (73)

Tavern (VA-441), .5 mi. E of Fighting Creek, N side of State Rte. 300 at intersection with State Rte. 13. Brick, rectangular (nine-bay front), two-and-a-half stories, gable roof with shed dormers, two interior chimneys, two-level full-length front porch; one-and-a-half story frame side wing; one-story rear ell additions. Built late 18th C.; altered for apartment use. 1 ext. photo (n.d.); HABSI (1958).

POWHATAN VICINITY   Powhatan County (73)

Belnemus (VA-86), .6 mi. N of Sallee Creek, .1 mi. N of U.S. Rte. 60, 1.5 mi. W of intersection with State Rte. 684. Frame with clapboarding, rectangular (three-bay front), two stories, hipped roof with finial, two interior end chimneys; one-room plan; two flanking wings: rectangular (one-bay front), one story, gable roof. Built late 18th C.; altered with later additions in rear. 1 ext. photo (1939), 1 int. photo (n.d.); 1 ext. photocopy (n.d.); 3 data pages (1940); HABSI (1958).

Keswick (VA-164), .8 mi. S of James River, .2 mi. N of State Rte. 711, .6 mi. E of intersection with State Rte. 714. Frame with clapboarding, H-shaped (six-bay E front), two stories, gable roof, four exterior end chimneys; four-room plan. Built early 19th C.; renovated with additions. 3 ext. photos (1936), 2 int. photos (1936).

Outbuildings (VA-85), .8 mi. S of James River, .2 mi. N of State Rte. 711, .6 mi. E of intersection with State Rte. 714. Old house: brick, 38'6" (four-bay front) x 20'8¼", two stories, gable roof, parapet walls on gable ends, two interior end chimneys, corbeled brick cornice, two entrances; the quarters: brick, circular (17'7⁄8" diameter), conical roof, central circular chimney, corbeled cornice; one-room plan with three chimneys in center; one-story brick kitchen; one-story frame smokehouse. Built early 19th C. 11 sheets (1938, 1939, including plans, elevations, sections, details); 9 ext. photos (1936, 1940), 5 int. photos (1936, 1940); 3 data pages (1939, n.d.).

Keswick, Outbuildings

Malvern (VA-338), .9 mi. NW of Bernards Creek, .5 mi. N of State Rte. 711, .6 mi. E of intersection with State Rte. 624. Frame with clapboarding, rectangular (seven-bay front), one-and-a-half stories, gable roof with dormers, four exterior end chimneys with brick pent closets, brick W gable end; center-hall plan, notable paneling. Built late 18th C.; much of fine interior paneling removed 1936-37; renovated. 2 ext. photos (1940), 9 int. photos (1940, n.d.); 1 data page (n.d.); HABSI (1958).

Norwood (VA-148), .6 mi. SW of James River, .1 mi. NE of State Rte. 711, 2 mi. NW of intersection with State Rte. 652. Brick, rectangular (five-bay front), two stories, hipped roof, two interior end chimneys; center-hall plan; flanking wings: rectangular (one-bay front), two stories, hipped roof, interior end chimney. Built late 18th C.; additions· mid 19th C. 2 ext. photos (1936), 2 int. photos (1936); 1 data page (1937).

Woodberry Mill

Woodberry Mill (VA-201), .1 mi. E of Woodberry Pond, .1 mi. W of State Rte. 614, .6 mi. S of intersection with State Rte. 711. Brick, rectangular (three-bay front), two-and-a-half stories above stone foundations, gable roof with two tiers of dormers, segmental arched windows and doors. Built c. 1800; burned. 4 ext. photos (1936).

PRINCE GEORGE VICINITY   Prince George County (75)

Brandon (VA-143), W bank of James River, at E end of State Rte. 611, .3 mi. E of intersection with State Rte. 653. Brick, seven-part composition, central block: rectangular (three-bay front), two stories, hipped roof; one-room plan; two flanking wings: one story, two bays, hipped roof, interior end chimney; one-story hyphens connect central grouping with two terminal pavilions: rectangular (two-bay front), two stories, hipped roof, two interior end chimneys. Built mid 18th C. 1 ext. photo (1935); 2 data pages (1940). NR

Merchants Hope Church (VA-405), .1 mi. W of Walls Run, N side of State Rte. 641, 1 mi. NE of intersection with State Rte. 646. Brick (Flemish bond with English bond below water table), rectangular (one-bay front), gable roof, splayed eaves, gable-end front, rubbed brick arched entrance way, gallery window, four-bay nave, modillion cornice; altered. Probably built mid 17th C. 5 ext. photos (1932), 1 int. photo (1932); 1 data page (1941); HABSI (1958). NR

209

PROVIDENCE FORGE   New Kent County (64)

Dr. Pott's House (VA-912), see Providence Hall (VA-912), Williamsburg.

PROVIDENCE FORGE VICINITY   New Kent County (64)

Cedar Grove (VA-802), .6 mi. SE of Toe Ink Swamp, N side of State Rte. 609, .2 mi. W of intersection with State Rte. 615. Brick, rectangular (three-bay front), two stories, gable roof, one interior end chimney, frame gable ends above eaves, modillion cornice; one-room side-hall plan; two-story frame side wing. Built late 18th C.; altered; later additions. 1 ext. photo (1936), 3 int. photos (1936).

Grist Mill (VA-110), S bank of Old Forge Pond, .1 mi. SW of State Rte. 608, .2 mi. N of intersection with U.S. Rte. 60. Frame with clapboarding, 48'2" (three-bay front) x 32'3", two stories over brick (Flemish bond) foundations on both sides of stream, scroll-cut boards at first-floor joist level. Built mid 18th C.; demolished 1938. 9 sheets (1937, including plans, elevations, sections, details); 12 ext. photos (1937, n.d.), 5 int. photos (1937); 2 data pages (n.d.).

PUNGOTEAGUE   Accomack County (1)

St. George's Church (VA-497), 1 mi. E of Nandua Creek, NW side of State Rte. 178, .3 mi. NE of intersection with State Rte. 180. Brick (Flemish bond front), rectangular (one-bay front), one story, gable roof with belfry, pedimented gable-end front; originally cruciform plan. Built early 18th C.; ruinous after Civil War; rebuilt without transepts 1885. 1 ext. photo (1940); HABSI (1958).

PUNGOTEAGUE VICINITY   Accomack County (1)

Melrose (VA-631), see Shepherds Plain (VA-631), Pungoteague Vicinity.

Shepherds Plain (Melrose) (VA-631), SE bank of Nandua Creek, 1.2 mi. NW of State Rte. 178, 1.3 mi. SW of intersection with State Rte. 180. Frame with clapboarding and brick (Flemish bond) ends, approx. 53' (five-bay front) x 34', two stories, gable roof, two interior end chimneys, modillion cornice, brick quoins, brick rustication around first-floor end windows; center-hall plan, fine interior paneling. Built mid 18th C. 4 ext. photos (1960), 4 int. photos (1960); 2 data pages (1960, 1962).

Grist Mill

QUINBY VICINITY

Accomack County (1)

Warwick (VA-495), .2 mi. W of Upshur Bay, .1 mi. E of State Rte. 605, 1 mi. SW of intersection with State Rte. 182. Brick (Flemish bond), rectangular (six-bay front), one-and-a-half stories, gable roof with dormers, two interior end chimneys; center-hall plan; one-and-a-half story wing. Built early 18th C.; addition; renovated. 1 ext. photo (1934), 2 int. photos (1934); HABSI (1958).

QUINTON VICINITY

New Kent County (64)

Dr. Lucas House (VA-121), 1.1 mi. E of Chickahominy River, .1 mi. N of State Rte. 33, .2 mi. SW of intersection with State Rte. 613. Frame with clapboarding, 45'4" (three-bay front) x 18'1", two stories, gable roof, one exterior end chimney; center-hall plan. Built early 18th C.; W two-bay part is original with E one-bay part added; ruinous, only chimney and foundations remain. 8 sheets (1935, including plans, elevations, sections, details, interior perspective).

Dr. Lucas House

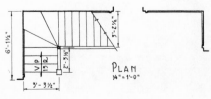

PLAN
¼"=1'-0"

ELEVATION FROM LIVING ROOM

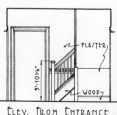

ELEV. FROM ENTRANCE

RICHMOND

Adams, Dr. John, Double House (VA-865), 2501-03 E. Grace St. Brick, rectangular (four-bay front), two-and-a-half stories, gable roof with dormers, two interior chimneys, plastered flat arches over windows; two separate two-room plans; rear ell. Built 1809-10; originally half of four-unit row; exterior restored except for the small rear ell and the retention of the two post-Civil War entrance porches. 1 ext. photo (1936); HABSI (1957).

Allen-Ellett House (Ellett House) (VA-850), 2702 E. Grace St. Brick, rectangular (three-bay front), two-and-a-half stories, gable roof with dormers, two interior end chimneys, Tuscan porch with pediment; side-hall plan. Built 1829. 1 ext. photo (1936); HABSI (1957).

Allen, William C., Double House (VA-869), 4-6 E. Main St. Brick, rectangular (six-bay front), two-and-a-half stories, gable roof with dormers, two interior chimneys, two modified Corinthian entrance porches; side-hall plan. Built 1836; W unit restored 1946; E unit altered by projecting store front. 1 ext. photo (1936); HABSI(1957).

Allison-Moore-Crump Building (VA-896), 1309 E. Main St. Brick with iron store front, rectangular (four-bay front), four stories, low shed roof, parapet walls, Corinthian pilasters on store front supporting cornice, arched windows with metal hood molds above. Built mid 19th C. 3 ext. photos (1969); 4 data pages (1969).

Ampthill (VA-159), 211 Ampthill Rd. Brick, rectangular (five-bay front), two stories, hip-on-hip roof, two interior chimneys, modillion cornice; center-hall plan, fine interior paneling; flanking wings: rectangular (three-bay front), one story, hipped roof, one interior end chimney, connected to main block by hyphens. Built c. 1732; enlarged c. 1750; dismantled and moved from original site .8 mi. W of James River, .4 mi. E of U.S. Rte. 1, .4 mi. S of Richmond city limits in Chesterfield Co.; reconstructed at present location 1929; wings placed closer to central block than before; hyphens added; hipped dormers added later. 1 sheet (1941, plan only); 1 ext. photo (1940), 10 int. photos (1940); 2 data pages (1940).

Barret, William, House (VA-425), 15 S. Fifth St. Brick with stucco, rectangular (three-bay front), two stories, hipped roof, four interior end chimneys, three-piece first-floor windows, Greek Ionic entrance porch, rear two-level verandah; center-hall plan. Built 1844; restored. 2 ext. photos (1936, 1940); HABSI (1957).

Bell Tower (VA-116), Capitol Square. Brick, 25'6" (one-bay front) x 25'7", three stories, ballustrade deck and cupola. Built 1824. 1 sheet (1936, including plans and elevations); 1 ext. photo (1936); 1 ext. photocopy (1886); 5 data pages (1936, n.d.); HABSI (1957). NR

Belvin House (VA-111), see William, William C., House (VA-111), Richmond.

Bott, Miles, House (VA-119), 216 Cowardin Ave. Frame with clapboarding, 47'11" (five-bay front) x 36'3", one-and-a-half stories, gable roof with dormers, two free-standing double chimneys with pent closet at each end; center-hall plan. Built c. 1800; demolished 1941. 12 sheets (1936, including plans, elevations, details); 3 ext. photos (1936), 1 int. photo (1936); 3 data pages (1936).

Bowser, Rosa D., School (VA-862), see Dill, Addolph, House (VA-862), Richmond.

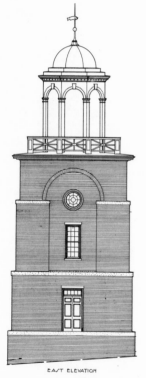

EAST ELEVATION

Bell Tower

Branch-Glasgow House (Glasgow, Ellen, House) (VA-857), 1 W. Main St. Historic house museum. Brick with stucco, rectangular (three-bay front), two stories, hipped roof, interior chimneys, Greek Doric entrance porch; center-hall plan. Built 1841. Home of novelist Ellen Glasgow from 1887 until her death in 1945. 1 ext. photo (1936); HABSI (1957). NR; NHL

Bransford-Cecil House (Bransford, Frederick-Cecil, House) (VA-161), 1005 Clay St. Historic house museum. Brick, rectangular (three-bay front), two stories, hipped roof, four interior end chimneys, Greek Doric entrance porch, two-level rear verandah; one-room plan, fine marble mantels. Built 1840; moved 1953-54 from 13 N. Fifth St.; interior plan and exterior brickwork altered. 5 ext. photos (1939, 1940), 4 int. photos (1940); HABSI (1957).

Bransford, Frederick-Cecil House (VA-161), see Bransford-Cecil House (VA-161), Richmond.

Brockenbrough, Dr. John, House (White House of the Confederacy) (VA-861), 1201 E. Clay St. Historic house museum. Brick with stucco, rectangular (five-bay front), three stories, low hipped roof with cupola, garden front has two-story Doric portico, heavy modillion cornice; modified center-hall plan. Built 1816-18, attributed to Robert Mills, architect; third-floor addition and interior alterations 1850's. Residence of Jefferson Davis during the Civil War. 3 ext. photos (1936, n.d.); HABSI (1957). NR; NHL

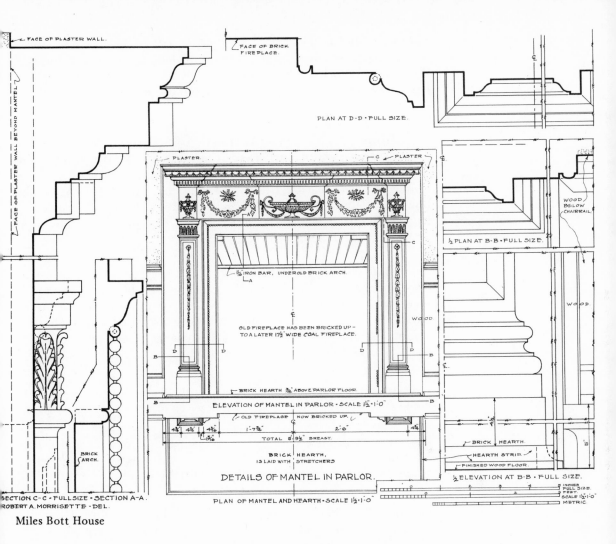

ROBERT A. MORRISETTE · DEL.

Miles Bott House

Building (VA-420), NE corner of Third and E. Main Sts. Brick with stucco, rectangular (seven-bay front), three stories, hipped roof, interior chimneys, central pedimented pavilion; first-floor store front. Built late 19th C.; demolished. 1 ext. photo (1940).

Call, Daniel, House (VA-866), 217 W. Grace St. Frame with clapboarding, rectangular (five-bay front), two stories, gable roof, two interior end chimneys, full-length one-story porch; side wings; rear ell. Built before 1796; moved from SE corner of Ninth and Broad Sts. 1849; dismantled and rebuilt 1936; additions; full-length porch replaced by present entrance porch. 1 ext. photo (1936); HABSI (1957).

Cameron, Alexander, House (VA-876), 519 E. Franklin St. Brick, rectangular (three-bay front), three-and-a-half stories, gable roof with dormer, interior end chimneys; each bay has rectangular inset panels between stories. Built mid 19th C.; demolished 1938. 1 ext. photo (1936).

Carter-Crozet House (Crozet House) (VA-420), 100 E. Main St. Brick, rectangular (six-bay front), two stories, gable roof, two interior end chimneys, two center entrances, heavy cornice, bracketed porch; center-hall plan; rear ell. Built 1814-15; structure divided into double house between 1881 and 1885; renovated 1940; front entrance now has molded brick segmental arch motif. 2 ext. photos (1936), 3 int. photos (1936); HABSI (1957).

Columbian Block (VA-842), 1301-07 E. Cary St. Brick with stucco, trapezoidal (eleven-bay front), three stories, low hipped roof, cupola, sheet-metal cornice, doorway and window trim, iron store fronts on Cary St.; exchange room on third floor uses cast-iron Corinthian columns. Built 1871 as a commodity exchange. 4 ext. photos (1969), 3 int. photos (1969); 6 data pages (1969).

Commercial Building (VA-853), see Donnan-Asher Iron Front Building (VA-853), Richmond.

Cottage (VA-881), 6 Granby St. Frame with clapboarding, rectangular (four-bay front), one story, gable roof; two exterior end chimneys; windows have dado paneling. Built mid 19th C. 1 ext. photo (1936).

Cottage (VA-877), 778 N. Ninth St. Brick, rectangular (three-bay front), one story, gable roof, two interior end chimneys. Built mid 19th C.; demolished. 1 ext. photo (1936).

Crozet House (VA-420), see Carter-Crozet House (VA-420), Richmond.

De Saussure House (VA-114), see Freeman, Samuel, House (VA-114), Richmond.

Dill, Addolph, House (Rosa D. Bowser School) (VA-862), 00 Clay St. Brick, rectangular (three-bay front), two stories, hipped roof, two interior end chimneys, Ionic entrance porch; center-hall plan. Built 1832. 1 ext. photo (1936); HABSI (1957).

Donnan-Asher Iron Front Building

Donnan-Asher Iron Front Building (Commercial Building) (VA-853), 1207-11 E. Main St. Brick with cast-iron front, rectangular (twelve-bay front), four stories, low shed roof, bracketed cornice, arched window openings separated by Corinthian columns. Built c. 1866; center four bays of street front altered. 6 ext. photos (1936, 1969); 7 data pages (1969); HABSI (1957). NR

Double House (VA-875), 311-13 College St. Brick end walls with clapboarding on fronts, two units, S unit: rectangular (three-bay front), one-and-a-half stories, gable roof with dormers, two interior end chimneys, central entrance; N unit: rectangular (three-bay front), one-and-a-half stories, gable roof with dormer, interior end chimney, side entrance. Built early 19th C.; demolished. 2 ext. photos (1936).

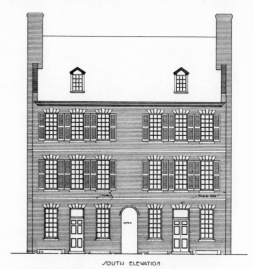

/OUTH ELEVATION

Double House, 212-14 S. First St.

Double House (VA-892), 212-14 S. First St. Brick, rectangular (four-bay front), two-and-a-half stories, gable roof with dormers, central chimney, heavy wooden cornice. Built mid 19th C.; demolished. 1 ext. photo (1936).

Double House (VA-118), 2216-18 E. Main St. Brick, 45′4″ (six-bay front) x 44′4″, three stories, flat roof, stone flat arches with keystones over windows; passageway separates house at first-floor level. Built early 19th C.; gable roof removed early 20th C. 12 sheets (1936, including plans, elevation, details); 2 ext. photos (1936); 2 data pages (1936).

Double House (VA-886), 1200-02 N. Seventeenth St. Brick, rectangular (four-bay front), two stories, gable roof, central chimney. Built early 19th C.; demolished. 1 ext. photo (1936).

Dunlop Mills (VA-925), S side of James River, .1 mi. E of Hull St., at S end of Mayo's Bridge. Brick, two structures form L-shape; W structure: rectangular (five-bay front), five stories, gable roof, parapet end walls, four interior end chimneys, lunettes on gable ends, six-story river front; E structure: rectangular (four-bay front), four stories, gable roof, parapet end walls, gable-end front, four interior end chimneys, lunettes on gable ends, seven-story river front; four-story metal covered frame structure attached to inset of ell on river front. Built 1853; burned and repaired 1865; enlarged; demolished. This mill, with the Gallego and Haxall mills, made Richmond one of the leading flour-producing centers in *ante bellum* America. 2 ext. photos (1936).

Ellett House (VA-850), see Allen-Ellett House (VA-850), Richmond.

Ellett-Todd-Lawrence Building (VA-844), 1019-21 E. Cary St. Brick, rectangular (three-bay front), four stories on north, three stories on south, gable roof, parapet end walls, two interior end chimneys. Built late 19th C. as canal warehouse. 2 ext. photos (1969), 1 int. photo (1969); 4 data pages (1969).

Freeman, Samuel, House (De Saussure House) (VA-114), 316 E. Main St. Brick, 27'5" (three-bay front) x 40'11", two-and-a-half stories above raised basement, gable roof with dormers, two interior end chimneys; bays have inset rectangles between first and second floors; side-hall plan. Built 1838-39, Samuel Freeman, architect; demolished 1940-41. 11 sheets (1936, including plans, elevations, sections, details); 3 ext. photos (1936, 1940); 2 data pages (1936).

Gentry-Stokes-Crew House (VA-873), NW corner of Twenty-eighth and E. Franklin Sts. Brick, rectangular (five-bay front), two stories, hipped roof, cupola, three-bay Doric entrance porch; center-hall plan. Built 1839; second floor and wings added later. 1 ext. photo (1936); HABSI (1957).

Dunlop Mills

George, William O., House (VA-868), 116 S. Third St. Brick, rectangular (three-bay front), two stories, flat roof, two-story portico, flanking two-story wings with projecting three-piece bow windows; modified side-hall plan. Built 1847; altered. 1 ext. photo (1936); HABSI (1957).

Gill House (VA-131), see House (VA-131), Richmond.

Glasgow, Ellen, House (VA-857), see Branch-Glasgow House (VA-857), Richmond.

Gosden House (Tucker House) (VA-852), NW corner of Third and E. Leigh Sts. Brick, rectangular (five-bay front), two-and-a-half stories, gable roof with dormers, two interior end chimneys, modillion cornice. Built early 19th C.; demolished. 1 ext. photo (1936).

Greenhow House (VA-112), 403 E. Grace St. Brick, rectangular (three-bay front), two stories, gable roof, interior end chimney; side-hall plan, refined interior woodwork with Adam influence. Built early 19th C.; demolished 1936. 5 sheets (1936, including plan, elevations, details); 1 ext. photo (n.d.), 8 int. photos (1936); 2 data pages (1937).

Greenhow House

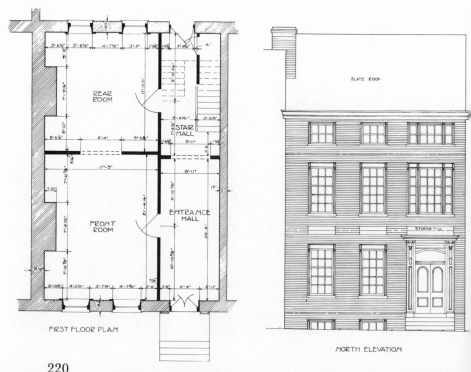

FIRST FLOOR PLAN

NORTH ELEVATION

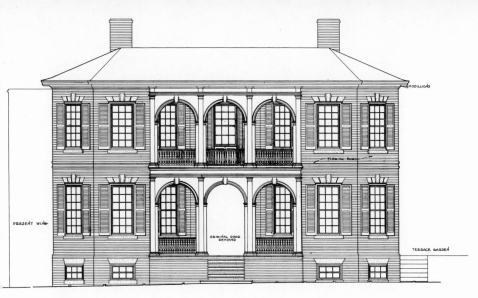

SOUTH EAST ELEVATION

Hancock-Wirt-Caskie House

Hampton-McCurdy House (VA-851), see House (VA-851), Richmond.

Hancock-Palmer-Caskie House (VA-113), see Hancock-Wirt-Caskie House (VA-113), Richmond.

Hancock-Wirt-Caskie House (Hancock-Palmer-Caskie House) (VA-113), 2 N. Fifth St. Brick (Flemish bond, English bond below water table), rectangular (seven-bay front), two stories, hipped roof, three-part bow projection at either side of central entrance and two-level wooden arcaded porch, two interior chimneys, enclosed porch; center-hall plan, fine plaster and wooden door and ceiling ornament; rear ell. Built c. 1809. 12 sheets (1936, including plans, elevations, sections, details); 2 ext. photos (1936), 3 int. photos (1936); 2 data pages (1936); HABSI (1957). NR

Hawes House (VA-115), see Mann-Hawes House (VA-115), Richmond.

Hickock House (VA-855), see Ritter-Hickock House (VA-855), Richmond.

Hobson-Nolting House (Nolting House) (VA-160), 409 E. Main St. Brick, 48′3½″ (three-bay front) x 44′3½″, three stories above raised basement, hipped roof, two brick interior chimneys, three-piece windows, three-story rear portico; center-hall plan, elaborate interior

Hobson-Nolting House

woodwork. Built mid 19th C.; demolished, but some interior columns and moldings are preserved in the Valentine Museum, Richmond. 8 sheets (1940, including plans, elevations); 10 ext. photos (1936, 1940), 11 int. photos (1940); 2 data pages (1940).

House (VA-879), NE corner of Ballard St. and Tobacco Alley. Frame with clapboarding, rectangular (six-bay front), one story, gable roof, interior chimneys; lean-to. Built early 19th C.; demolished. 1 ext. photo (1936).

House (VA-859), 107 E. Cary St. Brick, rectangular (three-bay front), three stories, modified step-gable roof, two interior end chimneys, Greek Ionic entrance porch; center-hall plan. Built mid 19th C.; altered, porch removed and door replaced with window. 1 ext. photo (1936).

House (VA-891), 402 E. Cary St. Brick, rectangular (two-bay front), three stories, flat roof, two interior end chimneys, Roman Doric entrance porch. Built mid 19th C.; demolished. 1 ext. photo (1936).

House (VA-856), see Mann, William, House (VA-856), Richmond.

House (VA-882), 21 W. Clay St. Brick, rectangular (three-bay front), two-and-a-half stories, step gable roof with dormers, two interior end chimneys, Greek Doric entrance porch; side-hall plan. Built mid 19th C. 1 ext. photo (n.d.).

House (VA-887), 706 N. Eighteenth St. Frame with clapboarding, rectangular (four-bay front), two stories, gable roof, two interior end chimneys, canopy porch design with brackets. Built early 19th C.; altered; demolished. 1 ext. photo (1936).

222

House (Hampton-McCurdy House) (VA-851), SW corner of Eighteenth and E. Main Sts. Brick, rectangular (three-bay front), three-and-a-half stories, step-gable roof with dormers, two interior end chimneys; first-floor store front; rear ell. Built 1845; altered and enlarged. 1 ext. photo (1936).

House (VA-888), SE corner of Fifth and E. Leigh Sts. Brick, rectangular (three-bay front), two-and-a-half stories, step-gable roof with dormers, connected interior end chimneys, Greek Doric entrance porch, two-level rear verandah; side-hall plan. Built mid 19th C.; demolished. 2 ext. photos (1936).

House (VA-422), 400 W. Franklin St. Brick with stucco, rectangular (three-bay front), two stories, low hipped roof, heavy bracketed cornice, wooden bracketed full-length porch. Built late 19th C. 1 ext. photo (1940).

House (VA-890), 206 E. Leigh St. Brick, rectangular (three-bay front), two stories, gable roof, two interior end chimneys, entrance porch. Built mid 19th C.; demolished. 1 ext. photo (1936).

House (VA-885), 531 E. Leigh St. Brick, rectangular (three-bay front), two-and-a-half stories, gable roof with dormer, two interior end chimneys, entrance porch; side-hall plan. Built mid 19th C.; demolished. 1 ext. photo (1936).

House (Gill House) (VA-131), 1007 McDonough St. Frame with clapboarding, two stories, gambrel roof with dormers, pedimented entrance porch. Built early 19th C.; demolished. 1 sheet (1936, including plans, elevations, details); 1 ext. photo, porch (1936), 1 int. photo (1936); 3 data pages (1937).

House (VA-864), 2416 E. Main St. Brick (Flemish bond with English bond foundations), rectangular (three-bay front), two-and-a-half stories, gable roof with dormers, two interior end chimneys. Built c. 1800; first-floor entrance and windows altered; demolished. 1 ext. photo (1936).

House (VA-854), 2606 E. Marshall St. Brick, rectangular (three-bay front), two-and-a-half stories, gable roof with dormers, one interior end chimney. Built c. 1810. 1 ext. photo (1936); HABSI (1957).

House (VA-883), SE corner of Seventeenth and Venable Sts. Brick, rectangular (two-bay front), two-and-a-half stories, gable roof, two interior end chimneys, gable-end parapet wall, heavy bracketed cornice. Built early 19th C.; first floor altered by store front; demolished. 1 ext. photo (1936).

House (VA-894), 516 N. Third St. Brick, rectangular (four-bay front), two-and-a-half stories, gable roof with dormers, interior end chimney. Built early 19th C.; demolished. 2 ext. photos (1936).

House (VA-893), 102 S. Third St. Brick, with stucco, rectangular (three-bay front), two stories, hipped roof, cast-iron porch with delicate tracery, heavy cornice; side wing. Built late 19th C.; demolished. 1 ext. photo (1936).

House (VA-880), SW corner of Twenty-second and Venable Sts. Brick, rectangular (five-bay front), one story above raised basement, hipped roof, brick interior end chimneys, entrance porch. Built mid 19th C. 1 ext. photo (1936).

House (VA-884), 9 N. Twenty-third St. Brick, rectangular (three-bay front), two-and-a-half stories, step-gable roof, two interior end chimneys, Tuscan entrance porch; side-hall plan. Built mid 19th C.; demolished. 1 ext. photo (1936).

House (VA-878), SW corner of Venable and Tulip Sts. Brick, rectangular (five-bay front), two-and-a-half stories, gable roof with dormers, central chimney. Built mid 19th C.; altered by store front. 1 ext. photo (1936).

Howard-Palmer House (Palmer House) (VA-867), 211 W. Franklin St. Brick, rectangular (three-bay front), three stories, modified step-gable roof, four interior end chimneys, Roman Doric entrance porch; side-hall plan; rear ell. Built 1852. 1 ext. photo (1936); HABSI (1957).

Jefferson Hotel (VA-840), block bounded by W. Main, N. Jefferson, W. Franklin, and N. Adams Sts. Brick with iron beams, terra cotta and stone decorative trim, symmetrical composition on N front consisting of four-story central block with loggia, flanked by two six-story towers and three-story wings; two clock towers rise behind wings; the S half of hotel has eight-story, U-shaped plan surrounding two-story lobby fronted by a Doric portico; the N end contains the Palm Room, the Marble Hall, and several richly decorated parlors; the S end of the hotel centers around a two-story lobby with a double tier of columns supporting the mezzanine and the cove ceiling. Built 1895, Carrere and Hastings, architects; S two-thirds burned 1901; rebuilt 1905. 9 ext. photos (1969), 15 int. photos (1969); 10 data pages (1969); HABSI (1969). NR

fferson Hotel

Main Street Station

Kent-Valentine House (VA-858), 12 E. Franklin St. Brick, rectangular (five-bay front), three stories, flat roof, interior end chimneys, two-story Ionic portico, heavy bracketed cornice. Built 1845; altered after 1904. 1 ext. photo (1936); HABSI (1957). NR

Lee, General, House (VA-895), see Stewart-Lee House (VA-895), Richmond.

Linden Row (VA-247), 100-14 E. Franklin St. Brick, eight units, each: rectangular (three-bay front), three stories, flat roof, two interior chimneys, Greek Doric entrance porch; side-hall plan. 110-18 built 1847; 100-08 built 1853; 116-18 demolished 1922. 6 ext. photos (1936, 1940); HABSI (1957).

Main Street Station (VA-848), 1520 E. Main St. Brick with stone and terra cotta, rectangular (seven-bay front) with iron train shed projecting from rear, three-and-a-half stories, hipped roof with red tile, six-story clock tower, two levels of dormers, first story and loggia faced in stone. Built 1901, Philadelphia firm of Wilson, Harris and Richard, architects. 9 ext. photos (1969); 6 data pages (1969); HABSI (1969). NR

Malone, James, Row (VA-870), 2301 E. Franklin St. Brick, rectangular (three-bay front), two-and-a-half stories, gable roof with dormer, interior end chimneys; side-hall plan. Built 1827; part of a four-house row including 2303, 2305, and 2307, all of which have been demolished. 1 ext. photo (1936); HABSI (1957).

226

Mann-Hawes House (Hawes House) (VA-115), 506 E. Leigh St. Brick, 46'1" (three-bay front) x 38', two stories, hipped roof, two interior end chimneys; center-hall plan. Built 1816; rear additions. 14 sheets (1936, including plans, elevations, sections, details); 2 ext. photos (1936), 4 int. photos (1936); 2 data pages (1936); HABSI (1957).

Mann, William, House (House, Chamberlayne Ave. and St. Peter St.) (VA-856), SW corner of Chamberlayne Ave. and Jackson St. Frame with clapboarding, rectangular (four-bay front), two stories, gable roof, two interior end chimneys; center-hall plan; E bay; rear ell. Built early 19th C.; later additions; asbestos siding recently added. 1 ext. photo (1936); HABSI (1957).

Marshall, John, House (VA-309), NW corner of Marshall and Ninth Sts. Historic house museum. Brick, two stories, gable roof, two interior chimneys, pedimented gable-end front, modillion cornice; four-room plan, fine woodwork shows Adam influence; rear ell; outbuildings. Built 1790; rear ell added before 1810; the law office, kitchen, and laundry outbuildings have been demolished. 9 ext. photos (1940), 13 int. photos (1940); 1 data page (n.d.); HABSI (1957). NR, NHL

Mason's Hall (VA-21), 1805 E. Franklin St. Frame with clapboarding, 50'10¼" (three-bay front) x 47', two stories, hipped roof with cupola, two interior chimneys, projecting central pedimented pavilion. Built 1785-87. 12 sheets (1934, including plans, elevations, sections, details); 2 ext. photos (1934); 3 data pages (1936); HABSI (1957).

NORTH ELEVATION

Mason's Hall

Monroe, James, Tomb (VA-843), Hollywood Cemetery. Cast-iron cage set on granite base enclosing a simple granite sarcophagus. Erected when Monroe's body was moved from New York 1859; cast in Philadelphia from designs by Richmond architect, Albert Lybrock. 3 ext. photos (1969); 4 data pages (1969). NR, NHL

Morris, John, Cottage (VA-860), 2500 E. Grace St. Frame with clapboarding, rectangular (three-bay front), one-and-a-half stories, gable roof with dormers, interior end chimney; center-hall plan. Built c. 1830. 1 ext. photo (1936); HABSI (1957).

Nolting House (VA-160), see Hobson-Nolting House (VA-160), Richmond.

Oaks, The (VA-157), 307 Stockton Lane, Windsor Farms. Brick, L-shape, four- and five-bay fronts), two stories, gable roof, four interior end chimneys; side-hall plan; flanking one-and-a-half story frame wings. Built mid 18th C.; moved from Amelia Co. to present site early 20th C. 3 ext. photos (1939, 1940), 5 int. photos (1939, 1940); 1 data page (n.d.).

Palmer House (VA-867), see Howard-Palmer House (VA-867), Richmond.

Parsons, Samuel P., House (Virginia Division of Youth Services) (VA-434), 601 Spring St. Brick, rectangular (three-bay front), two-and-a-half stories, gable roof with dormers, two interior end chimneys; side-hall plan, fine front-room mantel; high brick wall curved from shallow entrance shelter out to street; two-story brick rear ells. Built 1818; curved wall demolished. 1 ext. photo (1936); HABSI (1957).

Philip Morris Leaf Storage Warehouse (VA-849), 1717-21 E. Cary St. Brick, rectangular, 88'5" x 93'9", with elevator shaft on W front, five stories, flat roof, exposed brick piers with brick curtain walls, windows with segmental arches. Built early 20th C. 4 ext. photos (1969); 4 data pages.(1969).

Poe Museum (VA-120), see Stone House (VA-120), Richmond.

Pratt's Castle (VA-162), 324 S. Fourth St. Brick with stucco and tin, irregular plan, two stories with stone foundations; corner towers and roof parapet were brick covered with tin forming crenellations. Built 1853-54; demolished. 2 ext. photos (1939, 1940); 1 data page (1940); HABSI (1957).

Pratt's Castle

Quarles, John D., House (VA-871), 1 E. Main St. Brick, rectangular (three-bay front), two-and-a-half stories, gable roof with dormers, two interior end chimneys, Greek Ionic entrance porch; side-hall plan. Built 1839; altered. 1 ext. photo (1936); HABSI (1957).

Ritter-Hickock House (Hickock House) (VA-855), 821 W. Franklin St. Brick, rectangular (three-bay front), two-and-a-half stories, hipped roof with dormers, interior chimneys, pedimented pavilion, heavy entablature, Ionic entrance porch, balustrading on surrounding unsheltered promenade. Built 1855. 1 ext. photo (1936); HABSI (1957).

Rutherfoord-Hobson House (VA-423), 2 W. Franklin St. Brick with stucco, rectangular (three-bay front), two stories, mansard roof with dormers, four interior end chimneys, cast-iron porch with delicate tracery. Built 1842-43; altered and enlarged late 19th C.; demolished 1941. 2 ext. photos (1940).

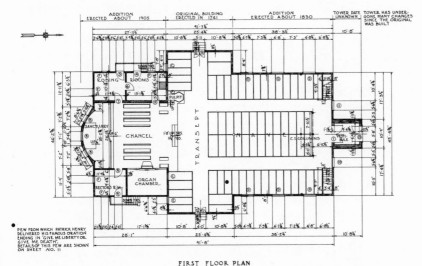

FIRST FLOOR PLAN

St. John's Episcopal Church

St. John's Episcopal Church (VA-22), 2400 block between E. Grace and E. Broad Sts. Frame with clapboarding, cruciform plan, one story, gable roof with belfry. Transept built in 1741; 40' of nave built in 1772; belfry added and nave widened c. 1830; present belfry is third replacement. Oldest public graveyard in Richmond; church was scene of the Virginia Convention, March 23, 1775, where Patrick Henry delivered his "Liberty or Death" speech. 11 sheets (1934, including plans, elevations, sections, details); 6 ext. photos (1934), 1 int. photo (1935); 4 data pages (1936); HABSI (1957). NR

Scott-Clarke House (VA-421), 9 S. Fifth St. Brick, rectangular (three-bay front), two stories, flat roof, four interior end chimneys, three-part first-floor windows, Greek Doric entrance porch; five-room plan. Built 1841; interior plan altered. 2 ext. photos (1940); HABSI (1957).

Smith, John D., House (VA-872), 2617 E. Franklin St. Brick, rectangular (three-bay front), two-and-a-half stories, step-gable roof with dormers, connected interior end chimneys, Greek Doric entrance porch, two-level rear verandah; side-hall plan. Built 1856; restored. 1 ext. photo (1936); HABSI (1957).

Stearns Iron-Front Building (VA-847), 1007-13 E. Main St. Brick with cast-iron front, rectangular (fourteen-bay front), four stories, low shed roof, decorated cornice, arched windows separated by engaged Corinthian columns. Built 1866; ironwork furnished by Hayward, Bartlett of Baltimore. 2 ext. photos (1969); 11 data pages (1969); HABSI (1957). NR

Stewart-Lee House (Lee, General, House) (VA-895), 707 E. Franklin St. Historic house museum. Brick, rectangular (three-bay front), three stories, hipped roof, four interior end chimneys, Greek Doric entrance porch; side-hall plan. Built 1844. 1 ext. photo (1936); HABSI (1957).

Stone House (Poe Museum) (VA-120), 1916 E. Main St. Stone, 32'1", (three-bay front) x 22', one-and-a-half stories, gable roof with three irregularly spaced dormers, two stone and brick interior end chimneys; center-hall plan. Built mid 18th C. Probably the oldest dwelling standing in Richmond. 7 sheets (1936, including plans, elevations, sections, details); 8 ext. photos (1936, 1937, 1939); 4 data pages (1936, 1940); HABSI (1957).

Tomlinson, A. M., House (VA-926), 2427 Venable St. Frame with clapboarding, rectangular (three-bay front), one-and-a-half stories, gable roof with dormers, two interior end chimneys. Built 1840. 1 ext. photo (1940); HABSI (1957).

Tucker Cottage (VA-959), 612 N. Third St. Frame with clapboarding, rectangular (three-bay front), one-and-a-half stories, gambrel roof with dormers. Built c. 1800. One of last remaining gambrel roof cottages in city. 1 sheet (1971, elevations).

Tucker House (VA-852), see Gosden House (VA-852), Richmond.

Turpin-Yarbrough-Pohlig Factory (Yarbrough or Pohlig Factory) (VA-863), SW corner of Twenty-fifth and Franklin Sts. Brick, rectangular (five-bay front), three-and-a-half stories, gable roof with dormers, gable-end front, connected interior end chimneys, parapet wall. Built 1853, John Freeman, architect. 1 ext. photo (1936); HABSI (1957).

Valentine Museum (VA-310), see Wickham-Valentine House (VA-310), Richmond.

Wickham-Valentine House

Virginia Division of Youth Services (VA-434), see Parsons, Samuel P., House (VA-434), Richmond.

Virginia Fire and Marine Insurance Company Building (VA-845), 1015 E. Main St. Brick with cast-iron front, rectangular (four-bay front), four stories, low shed roof, heavily ornamented cornice, recessed first-floor porch with Corinthian columns supporting semicircular arches, upper-story arch windows separated by Corinthian columns. Built c. 1866 to replace structures destroyed in the April 3, 1865, Evacuation Fire. 4 sheets (1970, including elevations, details, section); 3 ext. photos (1969); 5 data pages (1969). NR

White House of the Confederacy (VA-861), see Brockenbrough, Dr. John, House (VA-861), Richmond.

Whitlock Double House (VA-874), 628-30 N. Seventeenth St. Brick, rectangular (six-bay front), two stories, gable roof, central chimney, arched entrances. Built c. 1818; demolished. 1 ext. photo (1936).

Wickham-Valentine House (Valentine Museum) (VA-310), 1015 E. Clay St. Historic house museum. Brick with stucco, rectangular (three-bay front), two stories, hipped roof, two interior chimneys, central pavilion on front facade, three-piece windows, projecting bow in rear, one-story full-length rear porch which follows curve of bow; circular vestibule with spiral stair. Built c. 1812, attributed to Robert Mills, architect; interior altered 1850's. 1 ext. photo (1936), 10 int. photos (1940); 2 data pages (n.d.); HABSI (1957). NR

William, William C., House (Belvin House) (VA-111), 412 N. Eighth St. Brick with stucco, 55'8" (five-bay front) x 44'7", two stories, hipped roof, two interior chimneys, heavy bracketed cornice. Built 1810; burned and roof replaced mid 19th C.; demolished 1936. 5 sheets (1936, including plans, elevations, details); 4 ext. photos (1926, 1936), 4 int. photos (1936); 3 data pages (1936).

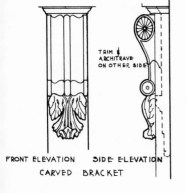

TRIM &
ARCHITRAVE
ON OTHER SIDE

FRONT ELEVATION   SIDE ELEVATION
      CARVED   BRACKET

William C. William House

RESTORED   ELEVATION

Wilton

Wilton (VA-158), N bank of James River, at end of Wilton Rd., .5 mi. S of Cary Street Rd. Historic house museum. Brick, rectangular (five-bay front), two stories, hipped roof, four interior end chimneys, rubbed brick window dressings and quoining, wooden pedimented entrance; center-hall plan, fully paneled rooms. Built c. 1750; dismantled and moved from original site .1 mi. E of James River, 1 mi. W of Wilton Rd., .6 mi. S of Richmond city limits; reconstructed at present location 1935. 13 ext. photos (1933, 1939, 1949), 13 int. photos (1933, 1939); 4 data pages (n.d., 1940).

Wiseham House (VA-889), 804 E. Clay St. Brick with stucco, rectangular (three-bay front), two-and-a-half stories, gable roof with dormers, two interior end chimneys, entrance canopy design with consoles. Built 1823; demolished. 3 ext. photos (1936), 1 int. photo (1936).

Yarbrough or Pohlig Factory (VA-863), see Turpin-Yarbrough-Pohlig Factory (VA-863), Richmond.

RICHMOND VICINITY   Chesterfield County (21)

Ampthill (VA-159), see Ampthill (VA-159), Richmond.

Bellona Arsenal Workshops (VA-139), .1 mi. S of James River, .2 mi. N of State Rte. 673, 2.4 mi. NW of intersection with State Rte. 147. Brick, rectangular (five-bay front), two stories above stone founda-

Bellona Arsenal Workshops

tion, hipped roof, segmental arched windows and entrance; two smaller workshops to N and W: brick, rectangular (three-bay fronts), two stories, hipped roofs, wide segmental arched windows. Arsenal quadrangle completed by U.S. Government 1817; arsenal building on the N matching large and small workshops and officers' quarters on the E and W sides, barracks on the S and powder magazine to the W, outside of the stone walls surrounding the quadrangle; barracks destroyed 1840's; arsenal building, officers' quarters, and one workshop destroyed 1870's; three remaining workshops renovated as a residence and guest house 1942; window sash, chimneys, interior paneling, and porches added to remaining shell of structures. E workshops connected by kitchen hyphen. 10 ext. photos, workshops before renovation (1936); 4 data pages (1937); HABSI (1957). NR

RICHMOND VICINITY   Henrico County (44)

Fairfield (VA-146), see Rocky Mills (VA-146), Richmond Vicinity.

Malvern Hill (VA-89), .2 mi. N of Turkey Island Creek, 1.1 mi. S of State Rte. 156, immediately W of intersection with Carter's Mill Rd. Walls remain from original brick (Flemish and English bonds) structure, 50'10½" (five-bay front) x 20'7", one-and-a-half stories, gable roof with dormers, two interior end chimneys with glazed header diaper pattern, front and rear arched brick porches with gable roofs; two-room plan. Built late 17th C.; altered early 18th C.; burned c. 1905, approx. one bay and end wall remain. 6 sheets (1934, 1935, including plot plan, plan, elevations, sections, including kitchen and icehouse); 3 ext. photos (c. 1934, 1935); 1 ext. photocopy (n.d.); 2 data pages (1941). NR

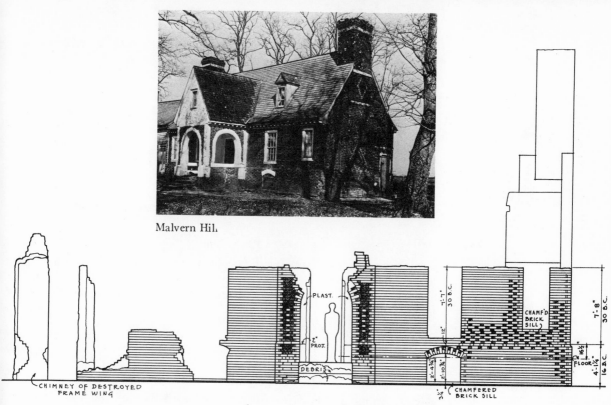

Malvern Hill

CHIMNEY OF DESTROYED
FRAME WING

PLAST.

2"
PROJ.

DEBRIS

7'-7"   30 B.C.

12"

CHAMF'D
BRICK
SILL

2'-4¼"
2'-10¾"

¾"   CHAMFERED
BRICK SILL

16½"

4'-1¼"   16 B.C.

7'-8"   30 B.C.

FLOOR

• S O U T H   E L E V A T I O N •

Rocky Mills (Fairfield) (VA-146), 211 Ross Rd. Brick (Flemish bond), rectangular (five-bay front), two stories above stone foundations, hipped roof, two interior chimneys, stone belt course and quoining, Palladian window centered on N front; central salon-stair hall with hall beyond, two rooms on either side. Built mid 18th C.; dismantled and moved from original site in Hanover Co., rebuilt near Richmond, central pedimented pavilion restored to S front, two bays and stone porch added to S front, brick one-story wing added to E side of structure 1928. 6 sheets (1940, including plans, elevations); 6 ext. photos (1940), 4 int. photos (1940); 6 data pages (1940).

Wilton (VA-158), see Wilton (VA-158), Richmond.

ROANOKE VICINITY   Roanoke County (81)

Garst Fort (VA-359), .2 mi. S of Lock Haven Lake, .3 mi. N of State Rte. 811, 2.2 mi. NE of intersection with State Rte. 116. Planks with clapboarding, rectangular (four-bay front), two stories above stone cellar, gable roof, stone exterior end chimney, planks dovetailed at

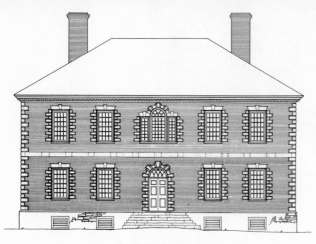

EAST ELEVATION

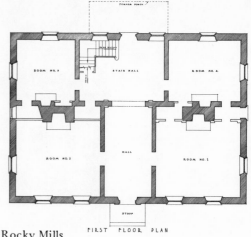

Rocky Mills

FIRST FLOOR PLAN

corners and exposed on front facade up to second-floor window sill level; one-room plan, built over spring for water supply. Built late 18th C.; demolished. 6 ext. photos (1940); 1 data page (1941); HABSI (1957).

SABOT   Goochland County (38)

Saddlebag House (VA-215), .2 mi. E of Dover Creek, S side of State Rte. 6, immediately E of intersection with State Rte. 644. Frame with batten walls, rectangular (three-bay front), one-and-a-half stories, gable roof with dormers, central chimney; structure was rear ell of frame two-story building. Built early 19th C.; two-story building added later; demolished. 1 ext. photo (1940).

SALEM

Moravian House (VA-347), see Williams-Brown House and Store (VA-347), Salem.

Williams-Brown House and Store (Moravian House) (VA-347), 423 E. Main St. Brick, rectangular (three-bay front), two stories, gable roof, two interior end chimneys, recessed two-level verandah on front with two arched side entrances opening on either end of the first-level porch; rear ells. Built mid 19th C.; altered with later additions. 1 ext. photo (1940).

SALEM VICINITY   Roanoke County (81)

Fotheringay (VA-348), see Fotheringay (VA-348), Elliston Vicinity.

Pleasant Point (VA-94), S bank of James River on Timber Neck Creek, N side of State Rte. 637, .5 mi. SE of intersection with State Rte. 31. Brick with frame fronts, rectangular (three-bay front), one-and-a-half stories, gable roof with dormers, two interior end chimneys; glazed brick header pattern parallel to raking on gable ends; center-hall plan; frame kitchen and smokehouse outbuildings. Built mid 18th C.; restored. 1 sheet (1935, detail of paneled cupboard only); 4 ext. photos (1932, 1934); HABSI (1959).

SCOTTSVILLE VICINITY   Albemarle County (2)

Fry House (VA-12), see Viewmont (VA-12), Scottsville Vicinity.

Viewmont (Fry House) (VA-12), .5 mi. W of Hardware River, .4 mi. E of State Rte. 20, 2.3 mi. N of intersection with State Rte. 712. Frame with clapboarding, rectangular (five-bay front), two stories, gable roof, two exterior end chimneys, modillion cornice; rear ell. Built mid 18th C.; burned 1939. 4 sheets (1934, including plans, elevations, details); 3 ext. photos (1934), 2 int. photos (1934); 2 data pages (n.d., 1936).

DETAIL-END BOARD
SCALE 1½"=1'0"

Viewmont

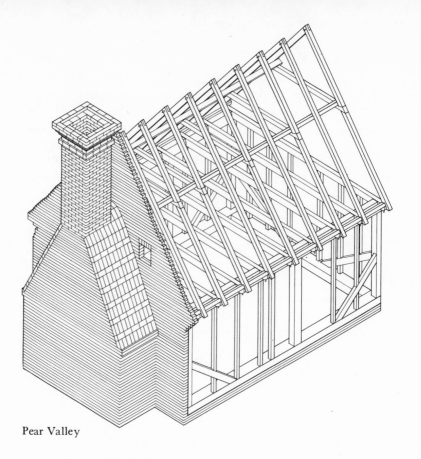

Pear Valley

SEALSTON VICINITY   King George County (50)

Lamb's Creek Episcopal Church (VA-98), .1 mi. W of Lamb's Creek,
NE side of State Rte. 694, .4 mi. N of intersection with State Rte. 3.
Brick (Flemish bond), 80' (seven-bay front) x 34', one story, hipped
roof, modillion cornice, arched windows, molded brick pediments
above entrance doorways, rubbed brick dressings; one-room plan.
Built 1770; interior gutted 1861-65; exterior restored mid 20th C.
3 sheets (1936, including plan, elevation); HABSI (1958).

SHADYSIDE VICINITY   Northampton County (66)

Pear Valley (VA-960), .1 mi. S of State Rte. 628, .5 mi. W of intersection with U.S. Rte. 13. Brick and frame with clapboarding,
rectangular (two-bay front), one story, gable roof, one exterior end
chimney, one-room plan. Built 17th C. Rare example of small
yeoman's cottage. 5 sheets (1971, including site plan, plan, elevations). NR

238

House (Skinquarter) (VA-724), .5 mi. SE of pond at head of Goode Creek, S side of U.S. Rte. 360, .2 mi. W of intersection with State Rte. 603. Frame with clapboarding, rectangular (five-bay front), one-and-a-half stories, gable roof with dormers, two exterior end chimneys; center-hall plan; rear ell. Built early 19th C.; demolished. 1 ext. photo (1936); HABSI (1958).

Skinquarter (VA-724), see House (VA-724), Skinquarter.

Barrett House (VA-140), N side of S. Church St., opposite Cedar St. Brick, rectangular (five-bay front), one-and-a-half stories, gable roof with dormers, frame gable ends above eaves, two interior end chimneys, the E one being T-shaped; center-hall plan. Built mid 18th C.; renovated. 5 ext. photos (n.d., 1936); 1 data page (n.d.); HABSI (1958).

Clerk's Office (Small Office) (VA-754), NE corner of Mason and Main Sts. Brick, rectangular (one-bay front), one story, gable roof, gable-end front, one interior end chimney. Built late 18th C.; renovated. 1 ext. photo (1937); HABSI (1958).

Grove Hotel (VA-301), see Pierce, Thomas, House (VA-301), Smithfield.

Isle of Wight County Courthouse (VA-294), NE corner of Main and Mason Sts. Brick with stucco, rectangular (five-bay front), one-and-a-half stories above high basement, gable roof with dormers, gable-end parapet wall, two interior end chimneys; rear apsidal ell. Built c. 1750; extensively altered; rebuilt 1961, structure now: brick, rectangular (five-bay porch arcade), one story, hipped roof, two interior end chimneys; rear apsidal ell. 3 ext. photos (1937, 1940); HABSI (1958). NR

Masonic Hall (VA-424), near site of present lodge hall at SE corner of Mason and Hill Sts. Brick with stucco, second floor was frame with clapboarding, rectangular (four-bay front), two stories, gable roof, central chimney. Built early 19th C.; demolished. 1 ext. photo (1940).

Pierce, Thomas, House (Grove Hotel) (VA-301), SW corner of Mason and Grace Sts. Brick, rectangular (three-bay front), two-and-a-half stories, gable roof with dormers, two interior end chimneys, pedimented gable end. Built early 19th C.; restored. 3 ext. photos (1937, 1940); HABSI (1958).

Small Office (VA-754), see Clerk's Office (VA-754), Smithfield.

SMITHFIELD VICINITY   Isle of Wight County (47)

St. Luke's Church (VA-20), S side of SW tributary of Jones Creek, .1 mi. E of State Rte. 10, .2 mi. N of intersection with U.S. Rte. 258. Brick (Flemish bond with English bond below grade), 29'4¾" (one-bay front) x 65'7½" with tower, one story, gable roof with step-gable ends; buttressing with plastered splays, some original molded brick mullions remain in lancet windows; tower: rectangular, three stories, peaked roof, arched entrance way with simple detached pediment above. Built late 17th C.; renovated and restored. 10 sheets (1934, including plan, elevations, details); 12 ext. photos (1934, 1937, 1939, 1940), 2 int. photos (1934); 1 ext. photocopy (c. 1890); 2 data pages (1936); HABSI (1958). NR; NHL

SOMERS VICINITY   Lancaster County (52)

Edgehill (VA-930), .8 mi. NE of Deep Creek, .1 mi. E of State Rte. 354, opposite intersection with State Rte. 683. Frame with clapboarding, one-and-a-half stories, gable roof with dormers, two-story side wing. Built early 18th C.; later addition. HABSI (1957).

SOUTH BOSTON VICINITY   Halifax County (42)

Berry Hill (VA-304), .5 mi. N of Dan River, .6 mi. S of State Rte. 659, 1.5 mi. S of intersection with State Rte. 682. Brick with stucco, rectangular (five-bay front), two stories, gable roof, gable-end front with pedimented octastyle Greek Doric portico, four interior end chimneys; modified center-hall plan; office and schoolhouse are temple-form structures which form forecourt. Earlier structures remodeled c. 1839. 9 ext. photos (1940), 4 ext. photos, outbuildings (1940), 4 int. photos (1940); 1 data page (n.d.); HABSI (1958). NR

St. Luke's Church

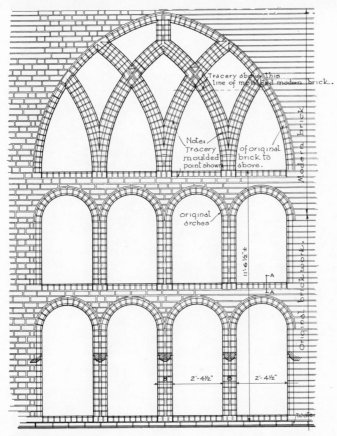

Tracery above this line of modified modern brick.

Note:
Tracery moulded point shown. of original brick to above.

Modern brick

original arches

Original brickwork.

11'-6½"#

A

A

2'-4½"   2'-4½"

water

St. Luke's Church

Berry Hill

Old Tavern (VA-312), 624 Mecklenburg Ave. Frame with clapboarding, rectangular (three-bay front), one story, gable roof, two exterior end chimneys (one of which was stone up to the eaves, the rest being brick). Built mid 18th C.; demolished. 1 ext. photo (n.d.).

Estes Mill (VA-374), S bank of S fork of Thornton River, SW corner of intersection of U.S. Rte. 211 and State Rte. 667. Frame with clapboarding above stone basement, rectangular (three-bay front), one story with lofts above raised basement, gambrel roof, wooden overshot wheel with wooden sluice. Built late 18th C.; wheel removed c. 1940. 4 ext. photos (c. 1934); 1 data page (1941).

Saw Mill (VA-839), NE bank of S fork of Thornton River, SW side of U.S. Rte. 211, 1.9 mi. W of intersection with State Rte. 667. Frame with vertical planking, rectangular (one-bay front), one story, gable roof, wooden saw mill equipment, iron blade for vertical up-and-down cutting; one-room plan. Built early 19th C.; demolished. 1 ext. photo (1936), 2 int. photos (1936).

County Offices (VA-265), see Spotsylvania County Jail (VA-265), Spotsylvania.

Harrison House (VA-392), .7 mi. SW of Ni River, N side of State Rte. 208, .1 mi. NE of intersection with State Rte. 613. Brick end wall and interior end chimney remain from original two-story structure. Built early 19th C.; wall and chimney now demolished. 2 ext. photos (c. 1934, 1935).

Spotsylvania County Jail (County Offices) (VA-265), 1.5 mi. W of Ni River, SE corner of intersection of State Rtes. 208 and 613. Brick, rectangular (two-bay front), two stories, gable roof, central chimney, brick corbeled cornice, walls become thinner at second-floor level. Built early 19th C.; stucco added. 1 ext. photo (1939).

Dabney Farm Outbuildings (VA-391), 1.1 mi. W of Ni River, NW side of State Rte. 208, .1 mi. N of intersection with State Rte. 720.

Smokehouse: brick, rectangular (one-bay front), one story, gable roof; kitchen: frame with batten walls, rectangular (four-bay front), one-and-a-half stories, gable roof with dormers set partially into the front wall, central chimney. Built early 19th C.; altered. 1 ext. photo (1935).

Herndon House (VA-372), .3 mi. N of Po River, .1 mi. SE of State Rte. 612, 1.9 mi. SW of intersection with State Rte. 649. Frame with clapboarding, rectangular (five-bay front), two stories, gable roof, S three bays on both fronts project from facade with the second-floor wall sloped and roofed creating a gambrel roof with dormers, two exterior end chimneys; center-hall plan. Built late 18th C.; altered with later additions. 7 ext. photos (c. 1934, 1935), 1 int. photo (c. 1934).

Todd House (VA-367), exact location unknown. Frame, rectangular (five-bay front), one story, gable roof, one exterior end chimney, two interior chimneys; probably center-hall plan. Built early 19th C. 4 ext. photos (1934, 1935), 1 int. photo (1934).

Todd House

Whig Hill (Wigg Hill) (VA-373), .3 mi. W of Ni River, .2 mi. SE of State Rte. 208, 1 mi. NE of intersection with State Rte. 720. Frame with clapboarding, L-shaped (five-bay front), one-and-a-half stories, gambrel roof with dormers, lower slope of roof is covered with clapboarding, one interior and one interior end chimney; center-hall plan. Built late 18th C.; enlarged. 4 ext. photos (c. 1934, 1935), 1 int. photo (c. 1934); HABSI (1957).

Wigg Hill (VA-373), see Whig Hill (VA-373), Spotsylvania Vicinity.

STAFFORD   Stafford County (90)

Old Stafford County Courthouse Complex (VA-56), SE corner of intersection of U.S. Rte. 1 and State Rte. 630. Complex including: Courthouse: brick, T-shaped (four-bay front), one story, gable roof, two interior end chimneys, cornice forming pediment at gable ends with semi-circular recess simulating a lunette. Built mid 19th C. Clerk's Office: brick, rectangular (three-bay front), one story, gable roof, two interior end chimneys. Built late 18th C. Jail: stone, rectangular (one-bay front), two stories, gable roof, central interior chimney. Built early 19th C. All buildings demolished. 4 ext. photocopies (c. 1900, including Courthouse, Clerk's Office, Jail); 3 data pages (1936).

STAFFORD VICINITY   Stafford County (90)

Aquia Church (VA-415), .8 mi. SW of Aquia Creek, .1 mi. E of U.S. Rte. 1, .1 mi. N of intersection with State Rte. 676. Brick with rusticated stone quoins, cross-shaped (five-bay front), one story with gallery, hipped roof, modillion cornice, three pedimented entrances framed by stone architraves, semi-circular arched window heads at gallery level; one-room Greek-cross plan, gallery on one side, notable interior including three-level pulpit and sounding board, box pews, and reredos. Built 1751; burned; rebuilt 1757; restored. 5 ext. photos, church (1934, 1959), 9 ext. photos, cemetery (1959), 1 int. photo, church (1932); 5 data pages (1941, 1959); HABSI (1958). NR

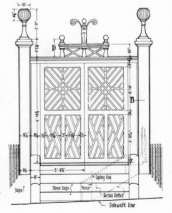

Entrance Gates

STAUNTON

Entrance Gates (VA-7), 120 Church St. Wood, two posts with caps and spherical finials, double leaves with Chinese Chippendale decorative framing. Built late 18th C. 1 sheet (1934, including plan, elevation, details); 2 ext. photos (1934); 2 data pages (1936).

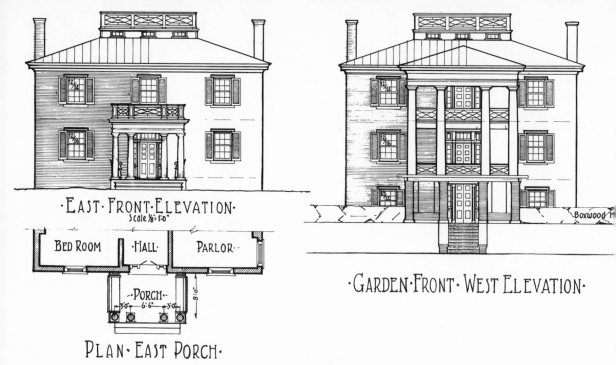

·EAST·FRONT·ELEVATION·
Scale ⅛"=1'-0"

·GARDEN·FRONT·WEST ELEVATION·

Boxwood

BED ROOM	·HALL·	PARLOR·

·PORCH·
3'-0" 6'-6" 3'-0"   8'-0"

PLAN·EAST PORCH·

The Manse

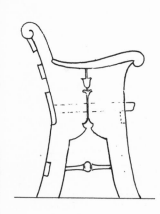

Manse, The (VA-392), SW corner of Frederick and Coalter Sts. House museum. Brick, 44'3" (three-bay front) x 34'3", two stories, hipped roof, four interior end chimneys, E street front had two-level Doric porch with extensions on first-floor level to either side, rear W elevation has two-level porch with two-story Doric columns; center-hall plan. Built c. 1847; altered c. 1897; restored c. 1941; street front now has Greek Doric entrance porch. Birthplace of President Woodrow Wilson, December 28, 1856. 8 sheets (1934, including plot plan, plans, elevations, sections, details); 5 ext. photos (n.d., 1934); 2 data pages (1936). NR

STAUNTON VICINITY   Augusta County (8)

Folly Farms (VA-8), .3 mi. S of Folly Mills Creek, .3 mi. NW of U.S. Rte. 11, .3 mi. SW of intersection with State Rte. 654. Brick (Flemish bond), 50'7" (three-bay front) x 40'4", one story above high basement, hipped roof with deck and balustrade around deck, four interior end chimneys, N and E pedimented tetrastyle Tuscan porticoes, three-part windows, center-hall plan with cross hall; brick, one-and-a-half story side wing; one-story rear ell; brick icehouse with pyramidal roof; brick dairy with gable roof and pedimented portico; brick slave quarters; brick serpentine wall frames garden. Built c. 1818. 10 sheets

(1934, including plot plans, plans, elevations, details, main house and icehouse); 6 ext. photos, including slave quarters, dairy, and icehouse (1934), 1 int. photo (1934); 3 data pages (1936); HABSI (1957).

STRASBURG VICINITY   Shenandoah County (86)

Fort Bowman (Harmony Hall) (VA-909), NW bank of Shenandoah River, at end of Frontage Rd., .6 mi. SE of intersection with U.S. Rte. 11. Stone, rectangular (three-bay front), two stories, gable roof, two interior end chimneys; center-hall plan, notable interior trim including exposed-beam ceiling with beaded beams and joists, fully paneled interior walls, large fireplace with bolection molding surround. Built mid 18th C.; later additions and alterations. 7 sheets (1970, including plans, elevations, sections, details); 1 ext. photo (1938); 2 int. photos (1938); HABSI (1958). NR

Harmony Hall (VA-909), see Fort Bowman (VA-909), Strasburg Vicinity.

Hupp House (VA-908), E bank of Town Run, NW side of U.S. Rte. 11, .2 mi. NE of intersection with State Rte. 55. Stone, approx. 42' (three-bay front) x 25', one story above raised basement, gable roof, stone jack arches above doors and windows; one-room plan. Built mid 18th C.; interior chimney dismantled. 1 ext. photo (1938); HABSI (1958).

Old Tavern No. 1 (VA-35), .7 mi. NW of Shenandoah River, N side of U.S. Rte. 11, .2 mi. E of intersection with Frontage Rd. Stone, rectangular (five-bay front), one story, gable roof, interior stone chimney; log one-story rear wing. Built approx. 1800; demolished. 1 ext. photo (1935).

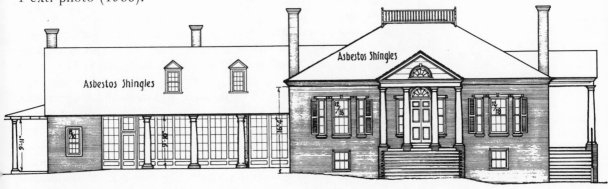

Folly Farms

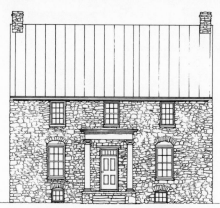

Fort Bowman

Old Tavern No. 2 (VA-35A), .7 mi. NW of Shenandoah River, S side of U.S. Rte. 11, .1 mi. W of intersection with Frontage Rd., approx. location. Stone, rectangular (five-bay front), two stories, gable roof, two stone interior end chimneys, one-story wooden pedimented entrance porch; probably center-hall plan. Built approx. 1800; later alterations and additions; demolished. 1 ext. photo (c. 1934).

STRATFORD   Westmoreland County (97)

Stratford Hall (VA-307), .8 mi. S of Potomac River, .6 mi. NE of State Rte. 214, 1.2 mi. E of intersection with State Rte. 3. Historic house museum. Main house: brick (Flemish bond), H-shaped, 93'6" (nine-bay front) x 62'8", two stories, hipped roof, eight interior chimneys in two clusters of four chimneys with segmental brick arches between the chimneys in each cluster and flat observation deck with turned wooden baluster railings between the chimneys, modillion cornice, ground-floor windows with segmental brick arched lintels set below molded brick water table and forming the base story for the principal second story, windows with rubbed brick jack arches, principal entrance doors to hall on N and S with rubbed brick dressings and molded brick pediments, monumental splayed stone steps to N and S entrance doors, massive brick steps with brick parapet railings to E and W entrance doors; center-hall plan with E and W cross halls, notable interior trim including fully paneled Great Hall, 28'8" x 28'6", with engaged Corinthian pilasters and tray ceiling; SW dependency: brick (Flemish bond), rectangular (four-bay front), one story, gable roof with jerkinheads, one interior chimney; two-room plan; SE dependency (kitchen, laundry): brick (Flemish bond), rectangular (four-bay front), one story, gable roof with jerkinheads, one interior chimney; two-room plan; NW and NE dependencies: brick (Flemish bond), rectangular (three-bay front), one story, hipped

Stratford Hall

roof; one interior end chimney; one-room plan; stable: brick (Flemish bond), rectangular, one story with loft, gable roof. Built c. 1730; extensive interior alterations late 18th C.; exterior alterations early 19th C.; restored 1933-40, Sidney Fiske Kimball, architect for Robert E. Lee Memorial Foundation, Inc.; exterior steps built 1935, 1940. Stratford Hall is an outstanding example of American Georgian architecture. 34 sheets (1969, including plot plan, plans, elevations, sections, details, annotated restoration drawings); 55 ext. photos (1932, 1934, 1938, 1940, 1969), 82 int. photos (1938, 1940, 1969); 2 photocopies (1940); 13 data pages (1940, 1969). NR; NHL

STUDLEY VICINITY   Hanover County (43)

Pollard House (VA-343), see Williamsville (VA-343), Studley Vicinity.

Williamsville (Pollard House) (VA-343), .4 mi. E of Pollard Creek, .4 mi. NW of State Rte. 645, .8 mi. N of intersection with State Rte. 615. Brick, rectangular (five-bay front), two stories, gable roof, three exterior end chimneys; center-hall plan; rear ell. Built c. 1800. 2 ext. photos (1935); 1 data page (1941).

Joiner House

Clerestory House

SUFFOLK VICINITY   Nansemond County (62)

Joiner House (VA-324), exact location unknown. Frame with clap-boarding, rectangular (three-bay front), one-and-a-half stories, gable roof with dormers, two exterior end chimneys, rear porch; side lean-to. Built late 18th C. 4 ext. photos (1938); 1 data page (1941).

SURRY VICINITY   Surry County (91)

Clerestory House (VA-248), .3 mi. W of Green Swamp, .1 mi. E of State Rte. 31, .6 mi. S of intersection with State Rte. 10. Frame with clapboarding, rectangular (three-bay front), one-and-a-half stories, gable roof, full-length clerestory windows on front and rear, two exterior end chimneys; rear ell. Built early 19th C. 1 ext. photo (1938); HABSI (1958).

250

Four Mile Tree Plantation (VA-55), .1 mi. S of James River, .9 mi. N of State Rte. 610, .2 mi. NE of intersection with State Rte. 618. Brick with stucco, rectangular (five-bay front), one-and-a-half stories, hip-on-gambrel roof with dormers, four interior end chimneys, modillion cornice, Ionic porch; center-hall plan; servants' quarters: pisé, one-and-a-half stories. House built late 18th C.; altered; servants' quarters built early 19th C.; demolished. Grounds contain oldest legible tombstone in Virginia (1650). 3 ext. photos, slave quarters (1934), 1 int. photo (1934); 3 ext. photocopies (c. 1900); 1 data page (1940); HABSI (1959). NR

Warren House (VA-397), .6 mi. S of Grays Creek, at end of State Rte. 641, .2 mi. NW of intersection with State Rte. 31, 2 mi. NE of Surry. Brick, rectangular (five-bay front), one-and-a-half stories, gable roof with pedimented dormers, two interior end chimneys, brick segmental arch entrance design; center-hall plan. Originally built c. 1652; rebuilt early 18th C.; restored 1934. 7 ext. photos (1934, 1937, 1939), 1 int. photo (n.d.); 1 data page (1940); HABSI (1958).

Warren House

Windsor Farm (VA-255), see Winsor (VA-255), Sussex Vicinity.

Winsor (Windsor Farm) (VA-255), .4 mi. W of Joseph Swamp, .1 mi. S of State Rte. 602, 4 mi. NE of intersection with State Rte. 35. Frame with clapboarding, rectangular (three-bay front), two stories, gable roof, pedimented gable-end front, one interior and one exterior end chimney, modillion and denticulated cornice; irregular plan; two-story side wing. Built early 19th C.; later addition. 3 ext. photos (1938).

SWEET HALL VICINITY   King William County (51)

House (VA-533), see Seaton House (VA-533), Sweet Hall Vicinity.

St. John's Church (VA-758), 1 mi. SW of Bull Swamp, .1 mi. SW of State Rte. 30, .2 mi. SE of intersection with State Rte. 630. Brick (Flemish bond, English bond below water table), approx. 30'2" (one-bay front) x 50'3", one story, gable roof, molded brick arches on W and N entrances; much original woodwork, N wing. Built 1734; N wing added c. 1760; in process of renovation. 1 ext. photo (1934), 2 int. photos (1938); HABSI (1958).

Seaton House (House) (VA-533), .6 mi. S of Custis Pond, N side of State Rte. 634, .1 mi. W of intersection with State Rte. 625. Frame with clapboarding, rectangular (four-bay front), one-and-a-half stories, gambrel roof with dormers, two exterior end chimneys; center-hall plan. Built early 19th C. 1 ext. photo (c. 1934); HABSI (1958).

Sweet Hall (VA-385), N bank of Pamunkey River, .2 mi. S of State Rte. 634, 1.6 mi. S of intersection with State Rte. 30. Brick (English bond) with partially stuccoed front facade, T-shaped (five-bay front), one-and-a-half stories, gable roof with dormers, two T-shaped interior end chimneys, one exterior end chimney, modillion cornice, side and front porches; rear ell. Built early 18th C.; later additions. 3 ext. photos (n.d., 1937); 1 data page (1941); HABSI (1958).

Waterville (VA-257), see Windsor Shade (VA-257), Sweet Hall Vicinity.

Windsor Shade (Waterville) (VA-257), N bank of Pamunkey River, .4 mi. W of S end of State Rte. 634, 1.7 mi. S of intersection with State Rte. 30. Frame with clapboarding, rectangular (five-bay front), one-and-a-half stories, gambrel roof with hipped dormers, two massive exterior end double chimneys with brick pent closets between, brick (English bond) E gable-end wall up to eavesline; center-hall plan. Built mid 18th C. 1 ext. photo (n.d.); HABSI (1958).

TAPPAHANNOCK   Essex County (29)

Customs House (VA-499), 109 Prince St. Brick with stucco, rectangular (three-bay front), one-and-a-half stories above raised basement, gable roof with pedimented dormers; one interior chimney; side-hall plan. Built mid 18th C. 1 ext. photo (c. 1934); HABSI (1958).

Debtor's Prison (Old Lawyer's Office) (VA-500), 321 Prince St. Brick, rectangular (three-bay front), one story, gable roof, one interior end chimney, wooden box cornice; one-room plan; rear ell. Built mid 18th C.; interior altered and rear ell constructed mid 20th C. 1 ext. photo (c. 1934); HABSI (1968).

Emerson's Ordinary (House) (VA-498), 314 Water Lane. Frame with clapboarding, L-shaped (five-bay front), one-and-a-half stories, gable roof with dormers, one interior chimney, one exterior end chimney; center-hall plan; right-angle wing: frame with clapboarding, one-and-a-half stories, gambrel roof with dormers, one exterior end chimney; center-hall plan. Built in two stages: early 18th C. and mid 18th C. 2 ext. photos (1935); HABSI (1958).

Glebe House (VA-961), Tappahannock. Brick (Flemish bond), rectangular (three-bay front), two stories, gable roof, two interior end chimneys; open plan, elaborate interior woodwork. Built 18th C. 5 sheets (1971, including plans, elevations, sections).

House (VA-498), see Emerson's Ordinary (VA-498), Tappahannock.

Glebe House

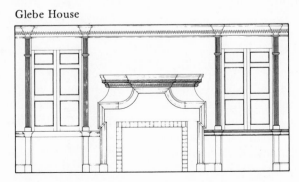

Old Lawyer's Office (VA-500), see Debtor's Prison (VA-500), Tappa-hannock.

Ritchie House (VA-501), 227 Prince St. Brick (Flemish bond), rectangular (six-bay front), one-and-a-half stories, gable roof with dormers; two exterior end T-chimneys, wooden box cornice, brick water table; center-hall plan. Built mid 18th C. in two stages; interior of principal ground-floor rooms removed and rebuilt in the Henry Francis du Pont Winterthur Museum at Winterthur, Del. 4 sheets (1971, including plans, elevations, details); 1 ext. photo (c. 1934); HABSI (1958).

TASLEY VICINITY   Accomack County (1)

Custis House (VA-485), .1 mi. E of Deep Creek, .4 mi. NW of State Rte. 660, 1 mi. NW of intersection with State Rte. 658. Frame with clapboarding, rectangular (four-bay front), one-and-a-half stories, gable roof with dormers, one interior and one exterior end chimney; off-center-hall plan; rear ell. Built late 18th C. 2 ext. photos (1940), 1 int. photo (1940); 1 data page (n.d.).

THE PLAINS VICINITY   Fauquier County (31)

Gordonsdale Cabin (VA-6), 1.9 mi. NW of Broad Run, .1 mi. SW of State Rte. 750, .6 mi. W of intersection with State Rte. 245. Log with stucco, 30'1" (three-bay front) x 20'4", one story, gable roof, three exterior stone chimneys; modified two-room plan; rear lean-to. Built mid 18th C.; later addition. 9 sheets (1934, including plans, elevations, sections, details); 1 ext. photo (1934); 3 data pages (1936); HABSI (1958).

TIDEWATER VICINITY   Richmond County (80)

Indian Banks (VA-74), .1 mi. E of Morattico Creek, W side of State Rte. 606, .8 mi. SW of intersection with State Rte. 673. Brick (Flemish bond), L-shaped (five-bay front), two stories, hipped roof, two interior end chimneys, modillion cornice, brick belt course and water table, scalloped brick jack arch lintel above S entrance door; modified center-hall plan. Built early 18th C. 5 ext. photos (1934, 1937), 2 int. photos (1934, 1937); 1 data page (1937).

Marston House (VA-319), exact location unknown. Frame with clapboarding, two stories, gable roof, exterior end chimney in Flemish
and English bond. Built mid 18th C.; raised from one-and-a-half to
two stories; extensive later additions; demolished. 1 ext. photo,
chimney detail (1938); 1 data page (1941).

TOANO VICINITY   James City County (48)

Hickory Neck Church (VA-214), .6 mi. E of Mill Creek, E side of
U.S. Rte. 60, .8 mi. N of intersection with State Rte. 610. Brick
(Flemish bond above beveled water table and English bond below,
three-course American bond on S end and on S portions of the E and
W walls), rectangular, 36½' (three-bay front) x 28½', one story, gable
roof, modillion cornice, small chimney on S end, porch on S entrance,
vestry on N end; one-room plan. Built 1773-74 as the N transept
addition to 1734 nave and chancel which were destroyed c. 1825;
later additions; interior completely altered. 2 ext. photos (1936,
1940); HABSI (1958).

Martin House (VA-756), N bank of intermittent stream of Mill Creek,
S side of U.S. Rte. 60, .3 mi. W of intersection with State Rtes. 30
and 168-Y. Frame with clapboarding, rectangular (three-bay front),
one-and-a-half stories, gable roof with pedimented dormers, four
exterior end chimneys; center-hall plan. Built late 18th C.; extensive
later additions and alterations; demolished. 1 ext. photo (1936).

Windsor Castle (VA-254), .5 mi. SW of S tributary of Mill Creek, N
side of State Rte. 610, .6 mi. W of intersection with State Rte. 659.
Frame with clapboarding, rectangular (five-bay front), one-and-a-half
stories, gable roof with dormers, four exterior end chimneys; center-
hall plan; side wing; rear ell; log smokehouse. Built mid 18th C.; later
additions and renovations. 2 ext. photos, main house (1936, 1937),
1 ext. photo, smokehouse (1937); 1 data page (1941).

TOWNSEND VICINITY   Northampton County (66)

Fitchett House (VA-548), .2 mi. W of Raccoon Creek, E side of State
Rte. 600, 3.2 mi. S of intersection with State Rte. 645. Brick with
frame fronts, rectangular (three-bay front), two stories, gable roof,
two exterior end chimneys. Built early 19th C.; destroyed; now site
of Cape Charles Air Force Base. 2 ext. photos (1940).

Yeocomico Church (VA-268), .1 mi. SE of Bonum Creek, W side of State Rte. 606, .4 mi. SW of intersection with State Rte. 610. Brick, T-shaped (three-bay entrance front), one story, gable roof, flared eaves, modillion cornice, round window in E gable, paired double-hung sash windows, advanced brick entrance porch with gable roof and flared eaves, triple arched head above porch entrance comprised of two small brick semi-circles surmounted by a third, resembling tracery, massive batten door (6′ x 8′) with a smaller wicket door with its own hinges set into it; T-shaped-open plan. Built 1706; extensive, almost continuous renovations and alterations 1773, c. 1820, 1906, 1928, 1959. 3 ext. photos (1937), 1 ext. photo, wicket door (1937); 1 data page (1941). NR

Castle, The (VA-124), .1 mi. S of Pamunkey River, 1 mi. N of State Rte. 608, 1 mi. E of intersection with State Rte. 606. Brick (Flemish bond), T-shaped (three-bay front), two stories, gable roof, three interior end chimneys, two-story enclosed brick porch; center-hall plan; rear ell. Built c. 1700; originally: one-and-a-half stories, two-story porch; enlarged late 19th C.; rear additions 20th C. 13 sheets (1936, including plans, elevations, sections, details); 2 ext. photos (1936), 4 int. photos (1936); 4 data pages (1936); HABSI (1958).

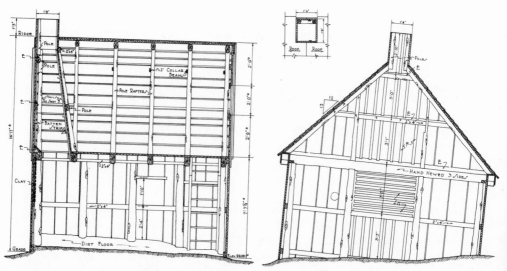

Road View Farm Kitchen

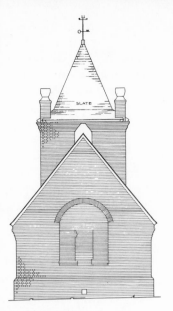
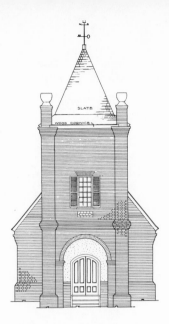

St. Peter's Church

Poplar Grove (VA-801), S side of Pamunkey River, 1.2 mi. N of State Rte. 608, 1 mi. SE of intersection with State Rte. 609. Brick (Flemish bond with glazed headers), rectangular (originally two-bay front), two stories, hipped roof, one brick interior end chimney and one brick exterior end chimney; side-hall plan; two-story brick ell; brick barn, frame office, outbuildings. Built late 18th C.; ell added mid 19th C.; addition early 20th C. 2 ext. photos (1936), 2 ext. photos, outbuildings (1936); HABSI (1958).

Road View Farm Kitchen (VA-97), .6 mi. W of W tributary of St. Peter's Swamp, .1 mi. W of State Rte. 609, .2 mi. N of intersection with State Rte. 606. Frame with vertical boarding, 14'3" (one-bay front) x 14'4½", one story, gable roof, wood and clay chimney. Built early 19th C.; destroyed. 5 sheets (1935, including plans, elevations, sections, details); 2 ext. photos (1935), 3 int. photos (1935, 1936); 3 data pages (1936).

St. Peter's Church (VA-127), .3 mi. S of St. Peter's Swamp, N side of State Rte. 642, .4 mi. NE of intersection with State Rte. 609. Brick (English and Flemish bond), 28'4½" (one-bay front) x 64'4", one story, gable roof, curvilinear gable ends, segmental arched windows, two-story tower with pyramidal roof, open first-floor arches. Built early 18th C.; tower added mid 18th C.; pre-Revolutionary N wing removed mid 19th C. Restored. 9 sheets (1936, including plans, elevations, sections, details); 6 ext. photos (1936); 1 ext. photocopy (c. 1892); 10 data pages (1937); HABSI (1958). NR

Woodland (VA-803), exact location unknown. Frame with clapboarding, rectangular (five-bay front), one-and-a-half stories, gable roof with dormers, two brick (English bond) T-shaped exterior end chimneys; two side lean-to's. Built mid 18th C.; demolished. 1 ext. photo (1936).

UPPERVILLE   Fauquier County (31)

House (VA-478), N side of U.S. Rte. 50, .5 mi. E of intersection with State Rte. 712. Stone with stucco and log, 33'8" (three-bay front) x 25', two stories, gable roof, one interior end chimney, one exterior end chimney; two-room plan; log side wing: 25'5" (three-bay front) x 20', two stories, gable roof; one-room plan. Built late 18th C.; restored. 5 sheets (1953, including plans, elevations).

URBANNA   Middlesex County (60)

Customs House (VA-799), N side of State Rte. 1002, .1 mi. E of intersection with State Rte. 1005. Brick, one-and-a-half stories, gable roof with hipped dormers, modillion cornice. Early 18th C.; renovated. 1 ext. photo (1934); HABSI (1959).

Tobacco Warehouse (VA-589), S side of State Rte. 1002, .1 mi. E of intersection with State Rte. 1005. Brick, rectangular (two-bay front), one story, gable roof, two interior end chimneys, full-length front porch; two-room plan. Built mid 18th C.; restored. 7 ext. photos (1960), 20 int. photos (1960); 6 data pages (1960); HABSI (1959).

URBANNA VICINITY   Middlesex County (60)

Hewick House (VA-540), .7 mi. S of Robinson Creek, .3 mi. N of intersection of State Rtes. 615 and 602, .4 mi. W of intersection with State Rtes. 602 and 1010. Brick, rectangular (five-bay front), two stories, gable roof, two interior end chimneys; center-hall plan; rear ell: brick, T-shaped, one-and-a-half stories, gambrel roof, interior end chimneys. Rear ell built late 17th C.; front block added later; alterations. 2 ext. photos (c. 1935); HABSI (1959).

VARINA VICINITY   Henrico County (44)

Cox House (VA-396), exact location unknown. Frame with clapboarding, rectangular (three-bay front), one-and-a-half stories, gable

258

roof with dormers, one exterior end chimney; rear lean-to; side wing: frame with clapboarding, rectangular (three-bay front), two stories, gable roof, two exterior end chimneys with frame pent closet between; rear lean-to forms saltbox shape. Built late 18th C.; later addition. 5 ext. photos (c. 1934, 1935).

VIENNA VICINITY   Fairfax County (30)

Ash Grove (VA-504), 8900 Ash Grove Lane. Frame with clapboarding, 61'5" (five-bay front) x 20'5", two-and-a-half stories, gable roof with dormers, two interior end chimneys; center-hall plan; rear ell, 29'1" x 17'5". Built late 18th C.; seriously damaged by fire 1960; restored 1961. 15 sheets, main house (1960, including plot plan, plans, elevations, details), 1 sheet, kitchen (1960, including plans, elevations); 13 ext. photos, main house (1930, 1959, 1960), 2 ext. photos, kitchen (1959), 1 ext. photo, smokehouse (1959), 7 int. photos, main house (1960), 5 int. photos, smokehouse (1959); 3 data pages (1961); HABSI's (1958, 1969).

Ash Grove

Brock Farm Quarters

VIRGINIA BEACH

Ackiss, Francis, House (VA-226), exact location unknown. Brick, rectangular (three-bay front), one-and-a-half stories, gambrel roof with shed dormers, two exterior end chimneys. Built late 18th C.; demolished. 2 ext. photos (1940).

Brock Farm Quarters (Brook Farm Quarters) (VA-400), 2.5 mi. E of West Neck Creek, .5 mi. SE of State Rte. 615 (Oceana Blvd.), .9 mi. NE of intersection with State Rte. 632 (London Bridge Rd.). Planks, rectangular, one story above brick (Flemish bond) foundation, gable roof, dovetailed timbering. Built late 18th C.; end chimney destroyed 1937; demolished. 6 ext. photos (1937, 1939); 2 data pages (1941, n.d.).

Brook Farm Quarters (VA-400), see Brock Farm Quarters (VA-400), Virginia Beach.

Cornick, Henry T., House (VA-558), 1.5 mi. SW of Linkhorn Bay, .2 mi. S of intersection of Potters and Colonial Rds., .4 mi. S of intersection with U.S. Rte. 58. Brick with frame fronts, rectangular, two stories, gable roof, two exterior end chimneys; one-story frame rear ell, exterior end chimney. Built c. 1800; demolished. 1 ext. photo (1934).

Eastwood (VA-242), S side of Great Neck Lake, .2 mi. W of Great Neck Rd., .1 mi. S of intersection with First Colonial Rd. Brick (Flemish bond), rectangular (three-bay front), one-and-a-half stories, gable roof with shed dormers, two interior end chimneys (destroyed above roof ridge line); two-room plan. Built mid 18th C.; demolished; bolection molding around one fireplace now in the Henry Francis du Pont Winterthur Museum, Winterthur, Del., as part of the Flock Room woodwork. 2 ext. photos (1934, 1939), 3 int. photos (1938); 1 data page (1940).

Fairfield Plantation Dependency (VA-557), .5 mi. E of E branch of Elizabeth River, .2 mi. W of State Rte. 190, .5 mi. S of intersection with State Rte. 165. Brick with stucco, rectangular (three-bay front), one story, steep gable roof, two interior end chimneys (the N one being T-shaped). Built early 18th C.; later additions and alterations. 1 ext. photo (1935).

Hudgins House (VA-243), E side of Pinetree Branch, S side of U.S. Rte. 58, .1 mi. W of intersection with State Rte. 644. Brick with frame fronts, rectangular (two-bay front), one-and-a-half stories, gable roof with shed dormers, massive E exterior end chimney, W interior end chimney. Built mid 18th C.; demolished. 3 ext. photos (1934, 1939); 1 data page (1940).

Keeling, Adam, House (VA-17), N side of Keeling Drain, SE side of Keeling Rd., opposite intersection with Inlet Rd. Brick (Flemish bond, English bond below water table), 48'3" (five-bay front) x 20'2½", one-and-a-half stories, gable roof with dormers, two interior end chimneys, rows of glazed headers follow roof rake on gable ends, modillion cornice; center-hall plan, fine interior paneling. Built late 17th C.; later additions. 6 sheets (1934, including plans, elevations, details); 5 ext. photos (1934, 1937, 1938), 1 int. photo (1934); 2 data pages (1936); HABSI (1958).

Lovett, Reuben, House (VA-560), .1 mi. S of West Neck Creek, .2 mi. NE of State Rte. 627 (Holland Rd.), .5 mi. N of intersection with State Rte. 149 (Princess Anne Rd.). Frame with clapboarding, rec-

baluster - walnut

Adam Keeling House

261

tangular (five-bay front), one-and-a-half stories, gambrel roof with dormers, two exterior end chimneys; center-hall plan. Built late 18th C.; renovated with rear additions. 1 ext. photo (1934).

Pleasant Hall (VA-238), .1 mi. E of E branch of Elizabeth River, N side of State Rte. 165, .1 mi. W of intersection with State Rte. 646. Brick, rectangular (five-bay front), two stories, gable roof, two interior end chimneys, modillion cornice; center-hall plan; frame rear ell. Built late 18th C.; later addition. 1 ext. photo (1939); 1 data page (1940); HABSI (1958).

Princess Anne County Courthouse (VA-556), .2 mi. E of E branch of Elizabeth River, .1 mi. N of State Rte. 165, .1 mi. W of intersection with State Rte. 646. Brick with stucco, rectangular (five-bay front), two stories, gable roof, one interior end chimney; one-room plan with balcony. Built late 18th C.; ruinous. 1 ext. photo (1934); HABSI (1958).

Salisbury Plains (VA-559), .8 mi. W of Great Neck Creek, S side of State Rte. 1002, .2 mi. E of intersection with State Rte. 635. Brick with frame front, rectangular (three-bay front), one-and-a-half stories, gambrel roof with shed dormers, two interior end chimneys. Built early 18th C.; demolished. 1 ext. photo (1934).

Thoroughgood, Adam, House (VA-209), .1 mi. W of Bayville Creek, at E end of Thoroughgood Lane. Historic house museum. Brick (English bond except for Flemish bond on W front), rectangular (four-bay front), one-and-a-half stories, gable roof with pedimented dormers, one exterior end and one interior end chimney (both being T-shaped), modillion cornice; center-hall plan. Built mid 17th C.; altered 18th C.; restored and opened to public 1957; dormers and cornice removed, both fronts are now three bays with segmental arched, leaded diamond-pane windows. 2 ext. photos (1939); 1 data page (1940); HABSI (1958). NR; NHL

Wishart, James, House (VA-16), .9 mi. NE of Thurston Branch, .1 mi. S of State Rte. 649, .4 mi. E of intersection with State Rte. 652. Brick (English bond), 32'9¼" (three-bay front) x 21'½", one-and-a-half stories, gable roof with connected shed dormers similar to clerestory, two massive T-shaped exterior end chimneys, front porch; two-room plan, closed stair; rear ell. Built late 17th C.; later additions. 3 sheets (1934, including plans, elevations, details); 2 ext. photos (1934), 1 int. photo (1939); 2 data pages (n.d.); HABSI (1958). NR

Adam Thoroughgood House

Woodhouse, Jonathan, House (VA-239), 1.5 mi. E of West Neck Creek, .2 mi. NE of State Rte. 632 (London Bridge Rd.), .7 mi. NW of intersection with State Rte. 615 (Oceana Blvd.). Brick, rectangular (three-bay front), one-and-a-half stories, gambrel roof with shed dormers, two interior end chimneys, rear porch; two-room plan; side-wing. Built mid 18th C.; interior paneling replaced; later additions. 5 ext. photos (1937, 1939); 1 data page (1940); HABSI (1958).

WARDTOWN VICINITY   Northampton County (66)

Fisher House (VA-549), 1 mi. NE of Holly Grove Cove, .2 mi. E of State Rte. 606, .4 mi. S of intersection with State Rte. 607. Frame with clapboarding with one brick end (Flemish bond with glazed headers set in diaper pattern), rectangular (four-bay front), one-and-a-half stories, gable roof with dormers, brick interior end chimneys; irregular plan. Built early 18th C.; demolished 1944. 2 ext. photos (1940).

Locust Grove (VA-550), .1 mi. NW of Nassawadox Creek, 1 mi. S of State Rte. 183, .1 mi. W of intersection with State Rte. 611. Brick with frame fronts, rectangular (five-bay front), one-and-a-half stories, gable roof with dormers, three exterior end chimneys; center-hall plan; rear lean-to forming saltbox. Built early 18th C.; later addition. 2 ext. photos (1940).

Clerk's Office (VA-331), S side U.S. Rte. 360, between State Rtes. T1004 and T1015. Stone with garnetted joints exposed below water table, stone with stucco above water table, rectangular (three-bay front), one story, gable roof, one interior end chimney, central doorway with fluted keystone; one-room plan; rear ell. Built mid 18th C.; altered and enlarged 1935. 2 ext. photos (1938); 1 data page (1941); HABSI (1958).

Lawyer's Office (VA-563), NW corner of intersection of U.S. Rte. 360 and State Rte. 3. Brick, rectangular (three-bay front), two stories, gable roof, one exterior end chimney, wooden box cornice, main entrance on second floor approached by exterior brick stair; one-room plan. Built early 19th C. 1 ext. photo (1934).

Richmond County Courthouse (VA-896), S side of U.S. Rte. 360, between State Rtes. T1004 and T1015. Brick (Flemish bond), rectangular (six-bay front), one story, hipped roof, two interior corner chimneys, modillion cornice, brick water table, arched windows set in recessed arched panels with stone imposts and keystones; one-room plan, advanced brick vestibule. Built mid 18th C.; extensively altered late 19th C.; interior remodeled 1952. 2 ext. photos (1938); HABSI (1958).

Saint John's Episcopal Church (VA-564), N side of U.S. Rte. 360, at NW corner of intersection with State Rte. T1003. Brick (Flemish bond), approx. 54' (four-bay lateral facade) x 34', one story, gable roof, square wooden belfry, recessed porch-vestibule with three-bay arcade supported by brick columns without capitals, arched entrance doors; one-room plan. Built 1837; later rear chancel addition. 2 ext. photos (1934); HABSI (1958).

WARSAW VICINITY   Richmond County (80)

Menokin (VA-156), .2 mi. E of Menokin Bay, .8 mi. W of State Rte. 690, 1.3 mi. NW of intersection with State Rte. 621. Stone, rectangular (three-bay front), two stories, hipped roof with deck, two interior chimneys, corner quoins, double belt course, water table, molded window architrave with rusticated blocks, arched fanlight; four-room plan, notable interior trim including paneled dado and overmantels; stone dependency: rectangular (three-bay front), two stories, gable roof, two interior end chimneys, arched central doorway; two-room plan, notable interior trim including Chinese Chippendale stair rail.

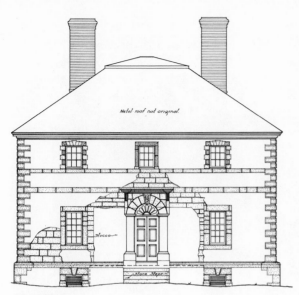

Menokin

Built c. 1769; main house ruinous; dependency demolished. 20 sheets (1940, including plans, elevations, details); 6 ext. photos, main house (1934, 1940), 2 ext. photos, dependency (1940), 5 int. photos, main house (1940), 3 int. photos, dependency (1940); 2 data pages (n.d.); HABSI (1958). NR

Mount Airy (VA-72), .5 mi. S of Mt. Airy Millpond, .3 mi. W of State Rte. 646, .4 mi. N of intersection with U.S. Rte. 360. Stone, five-part composition, main house: rectangular (seven-bay front), two stories, hipped roof, four interior chimneys, advanced three-bay central pedimented pavilions on NE and SW fronts with rusticated cut-stone decoration, NE front with recessed entrance loggia and Doric pilastered piers, SE front with arched rusticated recessed entrance loggia; stone cornice, corner quoins, belt course, water table, and window architrave; center-hall plan; flanking one-story quadrants with shed roofs terminated by dependencies: rectangular (three-bay fronts), two stories, hipped roofs, one interior chimney, corner quoins; SE dependency: four-room plan; NW dependency: three-room plan; entrance court with stone piers and carved stone vases. Built 1758, attributed to John Ariss, architect; interior of main house gutted by fire 1844; rebuilt c. 1845. Mount Airy is the most outstanding 18th C. stone house erected in Virginia. 10 ext. photos, main house (1934, 1937, 1938, 1939), 4 ext. photos, dependencies (1938), 3 ext. photos, entrance court (1938), 1 int. photo (1938); 1 data page (n.d.); HABSI's (1957, 1958). NR; NHL

Mount Airy

Old House (VA-566), see Linden Farm (VA-566), Farnham.

Sabine Hall (VA-155), 1.3 mi. NE of Rappahannock River, .4 mi. S of State Rte. 624, 1.3 mi. S of intersection with U.S. Rte. 360. Brick (Flemish bond), rectangular (seven-bay front), two stories, hipped roof, four interior end chimneys, brick belt course and water table, rusticated stone central bay, stone window lintels with keystones, tetrastyle wooden two-story Doric entrance portico with pediment on NE front; center-hall plan, unusually fine interior trim; flanking wings: one-and-a-half story, gable roof. Built c. 1735; main house connected to kitchen with covered way, porches added, roof lowered 1764; house stuccoed and kitchen demolished 1830-40; W wing added and E wing enlarged 1929. 24 sheets (1940, including plot plan, plan, elevations, details); 14 ext. photos (1934, 1940), 1 ext. photo, gate house (1940); 3 ext. photos, garden (1940), 22 int. photos (1934, 1937, 1940); 5 data pages (1936); HABSI (1958); NR; NHL

266

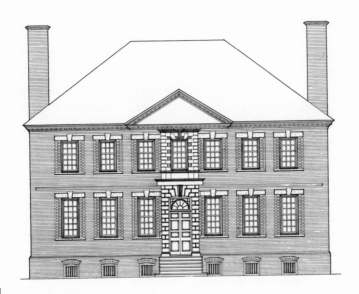

Sabine Hall

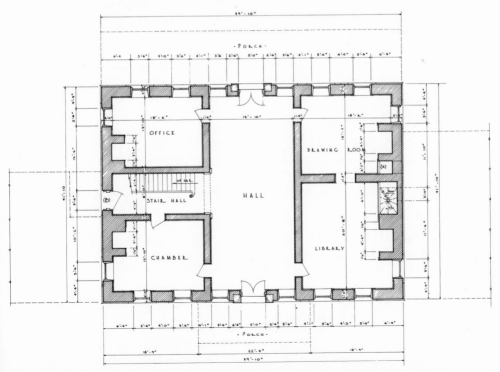

WASHINGTON   Rappahannock County (79)

Lawyer's Offices (VA-561, Area Survey), Court Green. Brick, rectangular (three-bay front), one story, gable roof, two interior end chimneys; two-room plan. Built early 19th C. 1 ext. photo (1934).

Rappahannock County Courthouse (VA-561, Area Survey), Court Green. Brick, rectangular, temple form (three-bay front), two stories, gable roof, square belfry, four interior end chimneys, pedimented gable end with semi-circular lunette, four engaged Doric pilasters; one-room plan. Built early 19th C.; interior remodeled c. 1958. 1 ext. photo (1934); HABSI (1958).

WASHINGTON'S BIRTHPLACE   Westmoreland County (97)

Blenheim (VA-571), .8 mi. S of Bridges Creek, .5 mi. W of State Rte. 204, .8 mi. NE of intersection with State Rte. 3. Brick (Flemish bond), rectangular (three-bay front), two stories, gable roof, two interior end chimneys, segmental window lintels; center-hall plan; side wing: frame with clapboarding, rectangular (two-bay front), two stories, gable roof, one exterior end chimney; one-room plan. Built mid 18th C.; roof altered and wing added early 19th C.; ruinous. 4 sheets (1968, including elevations); 4 ext. photos (c. 1934); HABSI (1958).

George Washington Birthplace National Monument (Wakefield) (VA-393), W bank of Pope's Creek, N end of State Rte. 204, 1.7 mi. N of intersection with State Rte. 3. Historic house museum. Brick, 52' (five-bay front) x 34', one-and-a-half stories, gable roof with dormers, four exterior end chimneys; center-hall plan. Original house built c. 1726, burned 1779; present house erected 1931. Conjectural reconstruction of house in which George Washington was born. Edward W. Donn, Jr., architect for reconstruction. 21 photocopies of working drawings (1930, including plans, elevations, sections, details); 3 ext. photos (1934).

Wakefield (VA-393), see George Washington Birthplace National Monument (VA-393), Washington's Birthplace.

WATERFORD   Loudoun County (54)

Apothecary Shop (VA-777), see Haines-Shuey House (VA-777), Waterford.

Arch House (Miriam Gover House) (VA-380), NE side Main St. Brick, 18' (three-bay front) x 22'3", two-and-a-half stories, gable roof with dormers, interior end chimney, brick archway and covered passage connecting street with rear garden at ground-floor level; two-room plan; rear ell. Built mid 18th C.; altered and enlarged mid 20th C. 1 ext. photo (1937); HABSI (1959).

Atley-Huff House (VA-779), see Hough-Haines House (VA-779), Waterford.

Bank House (Old Bank) (VA-378), SW side Main St. Brick, 37' (five-bay front) x 24', two stories, gable roof, two interior end chimneys, carved wooden cornice with modified triglyphs and metopes, semi-circular fanlight above entrance door; center-hall plan; rear ell. Built late 18th C.; interior plan altered early 19th C. 2 ext. photos (1937); HABSI (1959).

Braden-Rinker House (Charles Moreland House) (VA-768), SW side Main St. Hill. Brick, 22'1" (three-bay front) x 18'2", one story above full stone basement, gable roof, interior end chimney, two-story wooden porch with balcony across full width of street facade; two-room plan. 1 ext. photo (1937); HABSI (1959).

Brick Cottage on Hwy. (VA-776), see Gover-Phillips Cottage (VA-776), Waterford.

Clockmaker's House and Shop (VA-787), see Nettle, W. and Sarah, House (VA-787), Waterford.

Curtis, Lloyd, House (VA-785), see Myer, Mahlon, House (VA-785), Waterford.

Divine, Charles W., House (Loudoun Hotel) (VA-769), NE side Main St. Brick nogging with clapboarding, 38'11" (six-bay front) x 29'2", three stories, gable roof, two interior chimneys, iron balcony across full width of street facade at second story; two-room plan; originally two adjacent houses. Built late 18th C.; later additions and alterations. 2 ext. photos (1937); HABSI (1959).

Dorsey, Edward, House (Middle Huff House) (VA-770), SW side Main St. Hill. Brick, 36'6" (five-bay front) x 20'6", two stories, gable roof, two interior end chimneys, carved wooden cornice with modified triglyph and metope detail; center-hall plan; rear ell. Built 1804. 1 ext. photo (1937); HABSI (1959).

Dutton, John B., House (Steer House) (VA-771), NE corner Second and Mahlon Sts. Frame with clapboarding, 38' (five-bay front) x 25', one-and-a-half stories above raised stone basement, gable roof with dormers, two interior end chimneys; center-hall plan. Built mid 19th C.; altered mid 20th C. 1 ext. photo (1937); HABSI (1959).

Edwards Barn (VA-782), see Hough, William, Barn (VA-782), Waterford.

Edwards House (VA-781), see Hough, William, House (VA-781), Waterford.

Edwards-Hough House (Dr. Edwards House) (VA-772), NW corner intersection of Main St. Hill and Butcher's Row. Brick, 34'2" (five-bay front) x 20'2", two stories, gable roof, two interior end chimneys; originally center-hall plan. Built early 19th C.; extensive alterations and additions mid 20th C. 1 ext. photo (1937).

Fairfax Meeting House (Meeting House) (VA-773), SE corner intersection of State Rtes. 665 and 698. Stone, 70' (seven-bay facade) x 35', two stories, gable roof, two stone interior corner chimneys; original interior plan altered by conversion into residence. Built 1761; reconstructed 1868; altered as residence mid 20th C. 1 ext. photo (1937); HABSI (1959).

French-Atlee House (Sidewell House) (VA-774), NW corner Second and Church Sts. Brick, 26'2" (three-bay front) x 28', two stories, gable roof, interior end chimney; side-hall plan, elliptical arch in entrance hall; one-and-a-half story rear ell. Built early 19th C. 1 ext. photo (1937); HABSI (1959).

General Views: a) View from W. 1 photo (1937); b) View of Main St. 1 photo (1937); c) View up street from Mill. 1 photo (1937); d) View of Bond St. 1 photo (1937); e) View from N. 1 photo (1937).

Gover-Matthews Log House (Log House) (VA-775), NE side Main St., opposite Bank House. Log, 14'5" (one-bay front) x 15'2", two stories, gable roof, interior chimney; one-room plan; frame lean-to side wing. Built late 18th C.; later addition; ruinous. 1 ext. photo (1937).

Gover-James House (VA-382), see Gover, Samuel A., House (VA-382), Waterford.

Gover-Phillips Cottage (Brick Cottage on Hwy.) (VA-776), SW side Main St. Brick, 27'3" (three-bay front) x 16'1", one story, wooden shingle gable roof; one-room plan; rear lean-to. Built early 19th C.; later addition. 1 ext. photo (1937).

Gover, Miriam, House (VA-380), see Arch House (VA-380), Waterford.

Gover, Samuel A., House (Gover-James House) (VA-382), SW side Main St. Log and frame with clapboarding, 33'9" (six-bay front) x 20', two stories, gable roof, brick interior end chimney, stone exterior end chimney; rectangular plan. Built late 18th C.; altered and stone chimney reconstructed mid 20th C. 1 ext. photo (1937).

Haines-Shuey House (Apothecary Shop) (VA-777), NE side Main and Water Sts. Brick, 29'4" (five-bay front) x 22'6", three stories, gable roof, two interior end chimneys, metal supports for balcony across full width of street facade at second-floor level; center-hall plan; rear ell. Built early 19th C.; altered mid 20th C. 1 ext. photo (1937); HABSI (1959).

Haines-Shuey House

Hampier-Robinson House (Nancy Robinson House) (VA-778), NE side Water St., at intersection with Main St. Log, 36' (four-bay front) x 15'11", two stories, gable roof, interior end chimney; two-room plan. Built late 18th C.; enlarged early 19th C.; restored 1959. 1 ext. photo (1937); HABSI (1959).

Hough-Haines House (Atley-Huff House) (VA-779), SW side Main St. Hill. Brick, 26'1" (three-bay front) x 18'1", two stories, gable roof, two interior end chimneys; two-room plan; brick, one-story side wing. Built early 19th C. 1 ext. photo (1937).

Hough, Hector, House (VA-789), see Moore, James, House (VA-789), Waterford.

Hough, John and Samuel, House (Robert Huff House) (VA-780), SW side Main St. Hill. Brick, 34'6" (four-bay front) x 25'4", two stories, gable roof, two interior end chimneys, one exterior end chimney; originally a double house with adjacent three-room plans; rear ell. Built early 19th C.; altered mid 20th C. 1 ext. photo (1937), light-struck negative, print available by special request; HABSI (1959).

Hough, William, Barn (Edwards Barn) (VA-782), W side John Brown's Rdwy. Frame with stone foundations and gable end, rectangular, one story with loft, gable roof. Built late 18th C.; burned 1864; rebuilt. 1 ext. photo (1937).

Hough, William, House (Edwards House) (VA-781), E side John Brown's Rdwy. Brick (Flemish bond), 44'2" (five-bay front) x 28'8", two stories, gable roof, two interior end chimneys, modillion cornice, brick belt course and water table; center-hall plan, notable interior trim including fully paneled wall in principal room with fluted pilasters and dog-ear motif overmantel; kitchen: stone, one story, gable roof, interior end chimney; one-room plan, unusually large fireplace, connected to main house by two-story brick hyphen. Built late 18th C.; alterations, including raising original one-story hyphen to two stories, mid 19th C. 2 ext. photos (1937), 1 int. photo (1937); HABSI (1959).

Huff, Robert, House (VA-780), see Hough, John and Samuel, House (VA-780), Waterford.

Huff, Robert, House (VA-792), see Schooley, Mahlon, House (VA-792), Waterford.

Janney, Mahlon, House (View of Bond St.) (VA-927), N side Bond St., opposite intersection of Leggett St. Stone, 25′11″ (three-bay front) x 20′, two stories above raised basement, gable roof, interior end chimney; one-room plan; rear ell. Stone section built mid 18th C.; brick portion built late 18th C.; both sections originally two separate houses converted into a single residence mid 20th C. 1 ext. photo (1937); HABSI (1959).

Log Cabin (VA-783), SW side Main St., adjacent to Old Mill. Log, 19′6″ (two-bay front) x 14′9″, one story, gable roof, interior end chimney; one-room plan; rear lean-to. Built early 19th C.; moved to present location from outside village c. 1870; later addition. 1 ext. photo (1937).

Log House (VA-775), see Gover-Matthews Log House (VA-775), Waterford.

Loudoun Hotel (VA-769), see Divine, Charles W., House (VA-769) and Talbot's Tavern (VA-929), Waterford.

Mansfield House (VA-795), see Walker-Phillips House (VA-795), Waterford.

Meeting House (VA-773), see Fairfax Meeting House (VA-773), Waterford.

Fairfax Meeting House

Middle Huff House (VA-770), see Dorsey, Edward, House (VA-770), Waterford.

Mock House (VA-793), see Shawen-Schooley House (VA-793), Waterford.

Moore, James, House (Hector Hough House) (VA-789), NE side Main St. Hill. Brick and stone, 26' (three-bay front) x 23'3", two stories, gable roof, two interior end chimneys; two-room plan. Built early 19th C.; later additions and alterations. 1 ext. photo (1937); HABSI (1959).

Moreland, Charles, House (VA-768), see Braden-Rinker House (VA-768), Waterford.

Mount-Silcott House (Shop on Main St.) (VA-381), SW side Main St. Brick, rectangular (three-bay front), one story, gable roof. Built early 19th C.; destroyed 1965. 1 ext. photo (1937).

Myers, Mahlon, House (Lloyd Curtis House) (VA-785), NE side Main St. Hill. Brick, 16'2" (two-bay front) x 25'2", one story, gable roof, interior end chimney; two-room plan; rear ell. Built early 19th C.; altered and enlarged mid 20th C. 1 ext. photo (1937); HABSI (1959).

Nettle, W. and Sarah, House (Clockmaker's House and Shop) (VA-787), W side Second St., between Patrick and Church Sts. Brick, 29' (three-bay front) x 21'2", two stories, gable roof, two interior end chimneys; modified center-hall plan; two-story side wing; rear ell. Built early 19th C.; later additions and alterations. 1 ext. photo (1937); HABSI (1959).

Nettle, William, House (Yellow Brick House) (VA-786), W side Second St., between Church and Main Sts. Brick, 26'6" (three-bay front) x 20'4", two stories, gable roof, two interior end chimneys, wooden denticulated cornice; modified center-hall plan, notable interior trim; one-story rear ell above raised stone basement. Built 1817; later alterations. 1 ext. photo (1937); HABSI (1959).

Old Bank (VA-378), see Bank House (VA-378), Waterford.

Old Mill (VA-788), N bank of Catoctin Creek, at end of Main St. Brick, 36'4" (three-bay front) x 39'1", three-and-a-half stories, gable roof with pulley hoist, interior corner chimney; open plan with heavy

Old Mill

timber posts, metal overshot wheel. Built early 19th C.; converted to exhibition use mid 20th C. 1 ext. photo, detail of working wheel (1937); HABSI (1959).

Patton House (VA-794), see Steer, James M., House (VA-794), Waterford.

Robinson, Nancy, House (VA-778), see Hampier-Robinson House (VA-778), Waterford.

Sappington House (View of Main St. from Bank) (VA-928), SW side Main St. Log with clapboarding, rectangular (three-bay front), two stories, gable roof, interior end chimney; two-room plan. Built early 19th C. 1 ext. photo (1937).

School House (VA-798), see Williams Warehouse (VA-798), Waterford.

Schooley, Elizabeth Hough, House (Nathan Walker House) (VA-789), NW corner Main St. and John Brown's Rdwy. Brick, 47'2" (five-bay front) x 20', two-and-a-half stories, gable roof with dormers, two interior end chimneys; center-hall plan; two-story side wing. Built 1796, dormer windows added 1969. 1 ext. photo (1937); HABSI (1959).

Schooley, Ephraim, House (Stucco House) (VA-790), W side Second St., between Patrick and Mahlon Sts. Stucco over brick, 50'7" (six-bay front) x 22'6", two stories, gable roof, two interior end chimneys; center-hall plan. Originally two adjacent houses; S portion built 1835; N portion built 1850; altered 1959. 2 ext. photos (1937); HABSI (1959).

Schooley, John, House (VA-791), W side Second St., at intersection with Factory St. Brick, 40' (five-bay front) x 18', two-and-a-half stories, gable roof with dormers, two interior end chimneys; modified center-hall plan. Built early 19th C.; additions and alterations mid 20th C. 1 ext. photo (1937); HABSI (1959).

Schooley, Mahlon, House (Robert Huff House) (VA-792), W side Second St., between Mahlon and Patrick Sts. Brick, 30'2" (three-bay front) x 24'6", two stories, gable roof, two interior end chimneys; modified center-hall plan; two-story rear wing. Built 1817; wing added c. 1850; interior altered c. 1900, c. 1930; partially restored 1969. 1 ext. photo (1937); HABSI (1959).

Shawen-Schooley House (Mock House) (VA-793), NE side Main St. Hill. Brick, 61' (seven-bay front) x 24'4", three-part composition, one story, one-and-a-half stories with dormers and two stories, gable roof, three interior end chimneys; modified center-hall plan. Built early 19th C. 2 ext. photos (1937); HABSI (1959).

Shop on Main St. (VA-381), see Mount-Silcott House (VA-381), Waterford.

Sidewell House (VA-774), see French-Atlee House (VA-774), Waterford.

Steer House (VA-771), see Dutton, John B., House (VA-771), Waterford.

Steer, James M., House (Patton House) (VA-794), NE corner Second and Factory Sts. Brick, 46'6" (five-bay front) x 27'3", two stories, gable roof, two interior end chimneys; center-hall plan. S portion built late 18th C.; raised to two stories mid 20th C.; N portion built early 19th C. 2 ext. photos (1937); HABSI (1959).

Stucco House (VA-790), see Schooley, Ephraim, House (VA-790), Waterford.

Talbot's Tavern (Loudoun Hotel) (VA-929), NE side Main St. Stone, 20'4" (three-bay front) x 29'2", three stories, gable roof, interior end chimney; two-room plan; one-and-a-half story side wing. Built late 18th C.; altered and enlarged mid 20th C. 1 ext. photo (1937); HABSI (1959).

View of Bond St. (VA-927), see Janney, Mahlon, House (VA-927), Waterford.

View of Main St. from Bank (VA-928), see Sappington House (VA-928), Waterford.

Walker-Phillips House (Mansfield House) (VA-795), W side Second St., at intersection with Church St. Brick, 23' (three-bay front) x 28'2", two stories, gable roof, interior end chimney; side-hall plan; one-and-a-half-story rear ell. Built early 19th C. 1 ext. photo (1937); HABSI (1959).

Walker, Nathan, House (VA-789), see Schooley, Elizabeth Hough, House (VA-789), Waterford.

Waterford Baptist Church (VA-796), SW corner High and Church Sts. Brick, 39'9" x 59'10" (three-bay lateral facade), one story above raised basement, gable roof, Doric distyle-in-antis entrance vestibule; one-room plan. Built 1853. 1 ext. photo (1937).

Williams, John B., House (VA-797), NE corner Second and Janney Sts. Brick, 28' (three-bay front) x 32', two-and-a-half stories, gable roof with dormers, two interior end chimneys; side-hall plan, notable interior trim; two-story rear ell. Built 1815; addition to rear ell late 19th C.; partially gutted by fire 1968; restored 1969. 1 ext. photo (1937); HABSI (1959).

Williams Warehouse (School House) (VA-798), NE corner Second and Janney Sts. Brick, 26' (two-bay front) x 28'9", one-and-a-half stories, gable roof with dormers; exterior end chimneys; one-room plan. Built 1808; later converted to a school; altered 1937. 1 ext. photo (1937).

Yellow Brick House (VA-786), see Nettle, William, House (VA-786), Waterford.

WAYNESBORO VICINITY   Augusta County (8)

Rockfish Service Station (VA-962), E side of State Rte. 865, 10 mi. N of Waynesboro. One story, rectangular, gable roof, porte-cochere. Example of early 20th C. gasoline station. 6 sheets (1970, including plans, elevations, sections, details).

WEEMS VICINITY   Lancaster County (52)

Corotoman (Spinster's House) (VA-153), N bank of Rappahannock River at mouth of Carter Creek, .2 mi. S of State Rte. 222, at intersection with State Rte. 631. Frame with clapboarding, 62' (three-bay front) x 20'3", one-and-a-half stories, gable roof with dormers, two exterior end chimneys, one interior chimney; modified center-hall plan. Built early 18th C.; demolished. 1 sheet (1940, including plan, elevation); 1 ext. photo (1925); 1 ext. photocopy (c. 1910); 4 data pages (1925, 1929, 1945). NR

WEST POINT VICINITY   King William County (51)

Chelsea (VA-399), W bank of Mattaponi River, 1 mi. NE of State Rte. 634 (Chelsea Rd.), .9 mi. NE of intersection with State Rte. 30. Brick (Flemish bond), rectangular (five-bay front), two stories, hipped roof, two interior end chimneys, entrance porch; three-room plan; rear ell: brick, rectangular (six-bay front), one-and-a-half stories, gambrel roof with dormers, one interior and one exterior end chimney. Built early 18th C.; enlarged; porch now two-story. 2 ext. photos (1934, 1939); 1 data page (1940); HABSI (1958). NR

Chelsea

WHITE MARSH VICINITY   Gloucester County (37)

Abingdon Church (VA-65), .6 mi. E of Piny Swamp, E side of U.S. Rte. 17, .5 mi. S of intersection with State Rte. 614. Brick (Flemish bond), cruciform (five-bay front), one story, gable roof, modillion cornice, rubbed brick corners and window jambs, gauged brick window arches, water table, and door openings, W doorway with arched tympanum and semi-circular paneled transom, N and S doorways

WHITE MARSH   Gloucester County (37)

White Marsh Store (VA-520), White Marsh P.O., U.S. Rte. 17. Frame with clapboarding, rectangular (three-bay front), one-and-a-half stories, wooden shingle gable roof with dormers and rear lean-to slope, two exterior end chimneys. Built late 18th C.; demolished. 3 ext. photos (1934, including plank shutter and door detail).

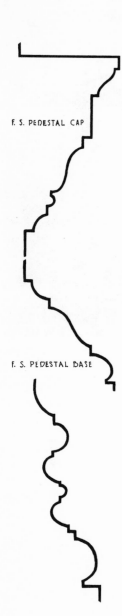

F. S. PEDESTAL CAP

F. S. PEDESTAL BASE

F. S. PILASTER BASE

·E L E V A T I O N · O F · R E R E D O S·

Abingdon Church

with triangular tympanum and without transom; cruciform plan. Built mid 18th C.; altered mid 19th C. 4 sheets (1940, including plans, elevations, details); 5 ext. photos (1937), 5 int. photos (1937, 1939); 2 data pages (1941); HABSI (1959). NR

Rosewell (VA-61), NW bank of Carter Creek, .5 mi. SE of State Rte. 644, .3 mi. S of intersection with State Rte. 632. Brick (Flemish bond), rectangular (five-bay front), three stories, gable roof, molded brick exterior decoration, stone keystones, sills, and chimney caps; highly architectural composition. Built 1726-50; interior stripped c. 1838; burned 1916; extensive ruins remain; 18th C. graves vandalized 1967. 8 ext. photos, main house (1934, 1937, 1939), 3 ext. photos, cemetery (1934, 1937); 1 data page (n.d.); HABSI (1959). NR

WHITE POST VICINITY   Clarke County (22)

Greenway Court Estate Office (VA-332), .1 mi. W of Borden's Marsh Run, .3 mi. W of State Rte. 658, .6 mi. SW of intersection with State

280

Rosewell

Rte. 627. Stone, rectangular (three-bay front), one story, gable roof, one interior end chimney; one-room plan. Built mid 18th C. 4 ext. photos (1936), 2 int. photos (1936, including a photo of interior door possibly from original house now demolished); 1 data page (1941); HABSI (1958). NR; NHL

Powder House (VA-108), .1 mi. W of Borden's Marsh Run, .3 mi. W of State Rte. 658, .6 mi. SW of intersection with State Rte. 627. Log, approx. 12′ (one-bay front) x 12′, one story, conical wood shingle roof; horizontal logs mortised into vertical corner structural members; one-room plan. Built mid 18th C.; moved to new foundations mid 20th C. 4 sheets (1937, including plans, elevations, section); 5 ext. photos (1936), 1 int. photo (1936); 1 data page (1937); HABSI (1958).

Tuleyries, The (VA-353), .8 mi. S of Westbrook Run, .7 mi. NE of State Rte. 628, 1.4 mi. E of intersection with U.S. Rte. 340. Brick with stucco, L-shaped (five-bay front), two stories, hipped roof with flat deck, balustrade, and octagonal domed cupola, two-story pedi-

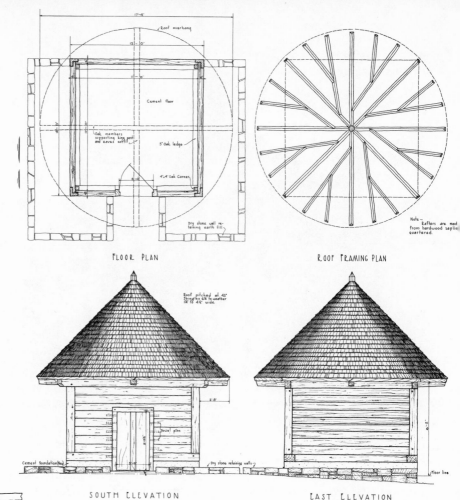

17'-4"

Roof overhang

12'-0"

10'-5"

Cement floor

Oak members supporting king post and eaves soffit

5" Oak ledge

4"x4" Oak Corner

Dry stone wall retaining earth fill

FLOOR PLAN

Note—Rafters are made from hardwood sapling quartered.

ROOF FRAMING PLAN

Roof pitched at 45° Shingles 6½" to weather 18" to 4¾" wide.

2'-8"

Dowel pins

Cement foundation(New)

Dry stone retaining walls

SOUTH ELEVATION

8'-2"

floor line

EAST ELEVATION

2'-8"

8'-2"

Cement floor

SECTION

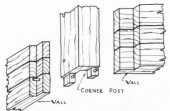

CORNER POST

WALL

WALL

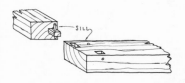

SILL

CORNER CONSTRUCTION

SCALE 1"=1'-0"

Greenway Court Estate Office, Powder House

282

mented tetrastyle Corinthian portico, four interior chimneys; center-hall plan; notable brick outbuildings with stepped gables and arched window and door openings. Built 1828. 1 ext. photocopy (n.d.); 1 data page (1941); HABSI (1958).

WILLIAMSBURG

Barraud, Dr. Philip, House (Mercer House) (VA-234), NW corner of Francis and Botetourt Sts. Frame with clapboarding, approx. 46′ (five-bay front) x 33′, one-and-a-half stories, gable roof with dormers, two interior end chimneys; center-hall plan. Built mid 18th C.; restored 1942. 1 ext. photo (1937).

Blair, Archibald, House (VA-196), N side of Nicholson St. between N. England St. and Palace Green. Frame with clapboarding, rectangular (five-bay front), two stories, gable roof, two interior end chimneys; porch; center-hall plan. Built mid 18th C.; porch added early 19th C.; rear ell removed 20th C.; restored 1930-31. 1 ext. photo (1938); 1 data page (1941).

Blair, John, House (VA-910), N side of Duke of Gloucester St., between Nassau and Henry Sts. Frame with clapboarding, rectangular (seven-bay front), one-and-a-half stories, gable roof with dormers, one exterior end and one interior chimney; modified three-room plan; rear shed. E four bays built early 18th C.; W three bays added late 18th C.; present interior chimney is an expansion of an earlier end chimney; restored. 1 ext. photo (1939), 1 int. photo (1937); 1 data page (1940).

Bland, Richard, House (VA-403), see Bland-Wetherburn House (Wetherburn's Tavern) (VA-403), Williamsburg.

Bland-Wetherburn House (Bland, Richard, House; Wetherburn's Tavern)((VA-403), S side of Duke of Gloucester St., E of Botetourt St. Historic house museum. Frame with clapboarding, rectangular (seven-bay front), one-and-a-half stories, gable roof with jerkinheads and hipped dormers, two interior chimneys, one interior end chimney, modillion cornice. Built early 18th C.; restored. 2 ext. photos (1938, 1939), 2 int. photos (1938, 1939); 1 data page (1940); HABSI (1958).

Bracken-Carter House (VA-523), see Bracken, Rev. John, House (VA-523), Williamsburg.

Bracken, Rev. John, House (VA-523), S side of Francis St., between Queen and Colonial Sts. Frame with clapboarding, rectangular (three-bay front), one-and-a-half stories, gable roof with dormers, two T-shaped exterior end chimneys; center-hall plan; attached rear structure: frame, one story, gable roof, connected by hyphen. Built early 18th C.; restored; rear structure demolished. 1 ext. photo (c. 1934).

Brush-Everard House (Page House) (VA-273), E side of Palace Green, N of Nicholson St. Historic house museum. Frame with clapboarding, rectangular (five-bay front), one-and-a-half stories, gable roof with dormers, two interior end chimneys; modified center-hall plan, interior woodwork probably moved from another structure in 18th C.; rear ell; smokehouse and kitchen outbuildings. Built early 18th C.; altered with additions; restored, second rear ell reconstructed. 6 ext. photos (1937, 1938), 1 int. photo (1937); 2 data pages (1941).

Bruton Parish Church (VA-191), NW corner of Duke of Gloucester St. and Palace Green. Brick, cruciform (three-bay front), one story, gable roof, three-story tower with low spire, arched windows, modillion cornice. Built c. 1714; chancel deepened 1750-52; tower added 1769; restored 1903-07, 1939. 2 ext. photos (1930, 1937). NHL

Camm-Apothecary Shop (VA-316), see Prentis Store (VA-316), Williamsburg.

Capitol (VA-365), E end of Duke of Gloucester St. Historic museum. Brick, H-shaped (nine-bay front), two-and-a-half stories, hipped roof with dormers and central cupola, S projections have apsidal ends with semi-conical roofs, N projections have square ends, central connection has first-floor loggia. Built 1701-05; burned 1747; rebuilt in altered form by 1756; destroyed by 1832; reconstructed 1931-34. 1 ext. photo (1939); 3 data pages (1941).

Chiswell, Col. Charles, House (VA-404), S side of Francis St., E of Botetourt St. Frame with clapboarding, rectangular (four-bay front), one-and-a-half stories, gable roof with dormers, interior chimney; rear ell, side wing. Built early 18th C.; restored with E three bays reconstructed. Structure now: frame with clapboarding, rectangular (seven-bay front), one-and-a-half stories, gable roof with jerkinheads and dormers, two interior chimneys. 2 int. photos (1937); 2 data pages (1941).

Coke-Garrett House (VA-527), N side of Nicholson St., W of Waller St. Four-part composition: W part: frame with clapboarding, approx. 40' (five-bay front) x 18', one-and-a-half stories, gable roof with dormers, exterior end chimney. Built mid 18th C. E office built partially on site of an earlier structure: brick, rectangular (three-bay front), one story, gable roof, gable-end front, pedimented porch. Built between 1810-20. In 1837, the two-and-a-half story, frame with clapboarding structure was built at the E end of the original building, and an 18th C. frame, one-and-a-half story structure was moved from another site and placed between the new building and the older brick office. Restored. 1 ext. photo (1934).

College of William and Mary, The: Brafferton Hall (VA-346), College Yard. Brick, approx. 52' (five-bay front) x 34', two-and-a-half stories, hipped roof with dormers, two interior chimneys; center-hall plan. Built 1723; restored 1931-32. 4 ext. photos (1937, 1938, n.d.); 3 data pages (1941, n.d.).

> *Main Building* (Wren Building) (VA-401), College Yard. Brick, rectangular (thirteen-bay front), two-and-a-half stories, hipped roof with dormers, cupola and central pedimented pavilion; chapel and hall rear ells; W front has arcaded first-floor loggia between the chapel and hall ells. Built 1695-1700; burned 1705; rebuilt by c. 1716; burned and rebuilt 1859; burned 1862; rebuilt 1869; restored 1927-31. Oldest academic building in continuous use in the United States; attributed to Sir Christopher Wren. 1 sheet (n.d., restored first-floor plan only); 4 ext. photos (1937, 1938, 1939); 1 data page (n.d.). NHL

> *President's House* (VA-913), College Yard. Brick, approx. 56' (five-bay front) x 38', two-and-a-half stories, hipped roof with dormers, two interior chimneys; center-hall plan. Building begun 1732, Henry Cary, master builder; interior burned 1781; repairs made 1782-83; restored 1931. 1 ext. photo (1937).

> *Wren Building* (VA-401), see Main Building (VA-401), Williamsburg.

Courthouse (VA-528), Courthouse Green, N side of Duke of Gloucester St., between Queen St. and Palace Green. Historic museum. Brick, T-shaped (five-bay front), one story, hipped roof with octagonal cupola, two interior chimneys, central pedimented portico with Tuscan columns; plan has central courtroom with two-room side wings. Built 1770; interior burned 1911; columns added after fire; restored 1932, columns removed. 1 ext. photo (c. 1929).

De Neufville (Barlow) House (VA-245), see Orr, Captain Hugh, House (VA-245), Williamsburg.

Foundation of Early Church (VA-176), Bruton Parish Churchyard. Brick, 66'2" x 28'5", five buttress bases remain on the S wall foundations, three remain on the N. Completed 1683; demolished 1718. 1 sheet (1938, foundation plan only).

Galt, Annie, House (VA-522), see Nelson-Galt House (VA-522), Williamsburg.

Golden Ball Shop (VA-526), see Hunter, Margaret, Shop (VA-526), Williamsburg.

Governor's Palace (VA-327), N end of Palace Green, N of Duke of Gloucester St. Historic house museum. Brick, rectangular (five-bay front), two-and-a-half stories, steep hipped roof with dormers, ballustraded deck, cupola, two interior chimneys; modified four-room plan, front entrance hall; rear ell; entrance forecourt formed by two brick, one-and-a-half story dependencies. Built 1706-20; altered with additions 1749-51 and 1770-76; burned 1781; reconstructed 1932-33. 4 ext. photos (1938, 1939); 4 data pages (1941).

Greenhow-Repiton Office (VA-406), S side of Duke of Gloucester St., between Nassau St. and Palace Green. Historic museum. Brick, rectangular (three-bay front), one story, gable roof, one exterior end chimney, molded brick water table. Built mid 18th C.; restored 1948, now has dormers. 1 ext. photo (1937); 1 data page (1941).

Hunter, Margaret, Shop (Golden Ball Shop) (VA-526), N side of Duke of Gloucester St., E of Botetourt St. Historic museum. Brick, rectangular (three-bay front), one-and-a-half stories, gable roof with dormers, gable-end front with clapboarding above eaves. Built mid 18th C.; moved and restored. 1 ext. photo (c. 1934).

Jackson, George, House and Store (Lamb, Lucy, House) (VA-524), N side of York St., between Waller and Page Sts. Frame with clapboarding, rectangular (three-bay front), one-and-a-half stories, gable roof with hipped dormers, rear lean-to continues the roof pitch of main structure, exterior end chimney; E wing: frame with clapboarding, rectangular (two-bay front), one-and-a-half stories, gable roof with dormer, exterior end chimney. Built late 18th C.; E wing moved to present location 18th C.; demolished 1933; reconstructed 1953-54, E wing now has three bays. 1 ext. photo (n.d.).

Kerr House (VA-525), see Palmer House (VA-525), Williamsburg.

Lamb, Lucy, House (VA-524), see Jackson, George, House and Store (VA-524), Williamsburg.

Little Christian House (VA-383), see Timson, William, House (VA-383), Williamsburg.

Ludwell-Paradise House (Paradise House) (VA-189), N side of Duke of Gloucester St., between Colonial and Queen Sts. Brick, rectangular (five-bay front), two stories, hipped roof, two interior end chimneys, modillion cornice; center-hall plan; rear lean-to. Built mid 18th C.; restored 1931. 3 ext. photos (1934, 1937, 1938); 1 data page (1941).

McCandlish House (VA-328), see Orrell, John, House (VA-328), Williamsburg.

Magazine, The (Powder Horn) (VA-529), S side of Duke of Gloucester St., between Queen St. and Palace Green. Historic museum. Brick, octagonal, two stories, peaked roof. Built c. 1716; restored 1934-35. 1 ext. photo (c. 1935).

Mercer House (VA-234), see Barraud, Dr. Philip, House (VA-234), Williamsburg.

Moody House (Roper House) (VA-237), S side of Francis St., between Botetourt and Colonial Sts. Frame with clapboarding, rectangular (four-bay front), one-and-a-half stories, gable roof with dormers, two exterior end chimneys; center-hall plan. Built early 18th C.; rear lean-to added; demolished and reconstructed 1939-40. 3 ext. photos (1933, 1937); 2 data pages (1941).

Nelson-Galt House (Galt, Anne, House) (VA-522), N side of Francis St., E of Botetourt St. Frame with clapboarding, rectangular (five-bay front), one-and-a-half stories, gable roof with hipped dormers, two interior end chimneys, E chimney is T-shaped, small end-bay windows light chimney closets; center-hall plan; smaller E structure: frame with clapboarding, rectangular (three-bay front), one-and-a-half stories, gable roof with dormers, T-shaped interior end chimney, connected to main house by hyphen. Built early 18th C.; later additions; restored 1951-52. 1 ext. photo (c. 1935).

Nicolson, Robert, House (VA-188), N side of York St., between Waller and Page Sts. Historic house museum. Frame with clapboard-

Prentis Store

ing, rectangular (five-bay front), one-and-a-half stories, gambrel roof with dormers, two interior end chimneys, modillion cornice; center-hall plan. Built mid 18th C.; W two bays added. 1 ext. photo (1937).

Orr, Captain Hugh, House (De Neufville [Barlow] House) (VA-245), SW corner of Duke of Gloucester and Colonial Sts. Frame with clapboarding, rectangular (four-bay front), one-and-a-half stories, gable roof with dormers, one interior and one exterior end chimney; center-hall plan; rear ell. Built mid 18th C.; restored 1930-31. 1 ext. photo (1939); 1 data page (1940).

Orrell, John, House (McCandlish House) (VA-328), S side of Francis St., between Colonial and Botetourt Sts. Frame with clapboarding, 28′ square (three-bay front), one-and-a-half stories, gambrel roof with dormers, interior end chimney, modillion cornice; modified side-hall plan. Built mid 18th C.; restored 1929-31. 1 ext. photo (1938); 1 data page (1941).

Page House (VA-273), see Brush-Everard House (VA-273), Williamsburg.

Palmer House (Kerr House) (VA-525), S side of E end of Duke of Gloucester St. Brick, rectangular (five-bay front), two-and-a-half stories, gable roof with dormers, two interior end chimneys; center-hall plan. Built mid 18th C.; restored 1951. Structure now: brick, rectangular (three-bay front), two stories, gable roof, interior end chimney; side-hall plan. 1 ext. photo (n.d.).

Paradise House (VA-189), see Ludwell-Paradise House (VA-189), Williamsburg.

Peachy House (VA-197), see Randolph, Peyton, House (VA-197), Williamsburg.

Powder Horn (VA-529), see Magazine, The (VA-529), Williamsburg.

Prentis Store (Camm-Apothecary Shop) (VA-316), NW corner of Duke of Gloucester and Colonial Sts. Historic museum. Brick, rectangular (three-bay front), one-and-a-half stories, gable roof with dormers, pedimented gable-end front with splayed eaves, interior end chimney in rear, store front with central door and large flanking windows. Built mid 18th C.; partially restored. 1 ext. photo (1938); 1 data page (1941).

Providence Hall (Dr. Pott's House) (VA-912), .2 mi. S of Francis St., SE of Williamsburg Inn. Frame with clapboarding, rectangular (five-bay front), one-and-a-half stories, gable roof with dormers, two exterior end double chimneys with brick pent closets between;

smokehouse outbuilding. Built late 18th C.; dismantled and moved from Providence Forge location, .2 mi. SE of Old Forge Pond, now N lane of U.S. Rte. 60, NW side of intersection with State Rte. 608, Providence Forge, New Kent Co.; reconstructed in Williamsburg; smokehouse demolished. 6 ext. photos (1934, 1936, 1937), 3 ext. photos, outbuildings (1934, 1937); HABSI (1958).

Public Gaol (VA-530), N side of Nicholson St., between Waller and Botetourt Sts. Historic museum. Brick, rectangular (three-bay front), one-and-a-half stories, gable roof with dormers, frame gable ends above eaves, two small interior chimneys. Built early 18th C.; restored 1935-36. Building now: brick, L-shaped, one-and-a-half stories, gable roof with jerkinhead at S end and hipped dormers, two exterior end chimneys, one interior chimney, enclosed S yard. 1 ext. photo (1934).

Public Records Office (VA-195), N side of E end of Duke of Gloucester St. Historic museum. Brick, rectangular (five-bay front), one story, hipped roof, two T-shaped interior chimneys, rubbed brick pedimented door ornamentation; three-room plan. Built 1747-48; restored. 1 ext. photo (1937).

Randolph, Peyton, House (Peachy House) (VA-197), NE corner of Nicholson and N. England Sts. Historic house museum. Built in three parts, W part: frame with clapboarding, rectangular (three-bay front), two stories, hipped roof, interior chimney, two-story closed porch on N front. Built c. 1715; restored. E part: frame with clapboarding, rectangular (three-bay front), one-and-a-half stories, gable roof with dormers, interior chimney. Built c. 1724; reconstructed. Middle part added to connect the two buildings: frame with clapboarding, rectangular (four-bay front), two stories, gable roof, interior end chimney. Built mid 18th C.; restored. 1 ext. photo (1938), 5 int. photos (1937, 1938, 1939); 2 data pages (1941). NR; NHL

Randolph-Semple House (VA-911), see Semple House (VA-911), Williamsburg.

Roper House (VA-237), see Moody House (VA-237), Williamsburg.

Semple House (Randolph-Semple House) (VA-911), S side of Francis St., W of Waller St. Frame with clapboarding, rectangular (three-bay front), two stories, gable roof, pedimented gable-end front, two interior end chimneys, Roman Doric entrance porch; three-room plan; flanking one-story, two-bay wings form typical Palladian design. Built late 18th C.; roof of central block burned and replaced c. 1900; restored 1932. 1 ext. photo (1938). NR; NHL

Spencer's Hotel (VA-356), present site of Chowning's Tavern, NW corner of Duke of Gloucester and Queen Sts. Frame with clapboarding, rectangular (six-bay front), two stories, hipped roof with cupola, two-level full-length porch on S and W fronts. Built c. 1840; additions to N and E; demolished c. 1938. 1 ext. photo (1938); 1 data page (1941).

Taliaferro-Cole Shop (VA-531), S side of Duke of Gloucester St. E of Nassau St. Historic museum. Frame with clapboarding, rectangular (four-bay front), two stories, gable roof, two interior end chimneys, gable-end front; lean-to shed added on W. Built before 1782; partially restored; lean-to removed. 1 ext. photo (c. 1934).

Timson, William, House (Little Christian House) (VA-383), NW corner of Prince George and Nassau Sts. Frame with clapboarding, rectangular (three-bay front), one-and-a-half stories, gable roof with dormers, brick interior end chimney. Built early 18th C.; later additions; restored. 1 ext. photo (1938); 1 data page (1941). HABSI (n.d.).

Wetherburn's Tavern (VA-403), see Bland-Wetherburn House (Bland, Richard, House) (VA-403), Williamsburg.

Carter's Grove (VA-351), .2 mi. W of Grices Run, .7 mi. SW of U.S. Rte. 60, .2 mi. SE of intersection with State Rte. 667. Historic house museum. Brick (Flemish bond with belt course and molded water table), rectangular (seven-bay front), two-and-a-half stories, gable roof with hipped dormers, modillion cornice, two interior chimneys, rubbed brick flat arches and quoins, molded brick pedimented entranceways; plan centers on broad, paneled entrance hall with smaller stair hall behind, flanking paneled rooms with imported marble mantel in W parlor; connected side dependencies: brick, rectangular (three-bay fronts), one-and-a-half stories, gable roofs with dormers; hyphens have similar design. Built 1751, David Minitree, builder; roof raised and dormers added 1927-29; dependencies enlarged and connected to house. 2 photos, plantation account book showing payments for house construction (1939); 3 data pages (1941). NR; NHL

Kingsmill Plantation Dependencies (VA-208), .6 mi. S of Kingsmill Pond, 1.5 mi. S of S end of State Rte. 637, 1.8 mi. S of intersection with U.S. Rte. 60. Two dependencies: brick (Flemish bond with glazed headers), rectangular (four-bay front), one story, gable roof, two interior end chimneys, double entrance doorways; two-room plan. Built mid 18th C.; W dependency said to have burned and been rebuilt within the old walls; later frame additions. 2 ext. photos (1938); 2 data pages (1940).

Maine Farm (VA-71), .6 mi. W of Powhatan Creek, .1 mi. E of State Rte. 614, .9 mi. N of intersection with State Rte. 31. Frame with clapboarding, rectangular (five-bay front), one-and-a-half stories, gambrel roof with hipped dormers, two exterior end chimneys, pedimented entrance porch, larger gable dormer over entrance porch. Built late 18th C.; later additions and alterations; demolished c. 1928. 6 ext. photos (1928); 1 data page (n.d.).

Poplar Hall (VA-755), .1 mi. S of Skiffes Creek, .2 mi. N of U.S. Rte. 60, .9 mi. SE of intersection with State Rte. 667. Frame with clapboarding, rectangular (three-bay front), one-and-a-half stories, gambrel roof with dormers, two exterior T-shaped end chimneys; rear ell. Built late 17th C.; later additions and alterations; demolished. 2 ext. photos (1937).

Skiff's Creek House (VA-407), .1 mi. W of Skiffes Creek, 1.6 mi. SE of U.S. Rte. 60, 1.4 mi. SE of intersection with State Rte. 667. Brick, rectangular (three-bay front), one-and-a-half stories, gable roof with dormers, two exterior end chimneys; irregular plan. Built mid 18th C.; enlarged early 19th C.; burned 1964. 3 ext. photos (1934, 1936); 1 data page (1941).

WILLIS VICINITY   Floyd County (32)

Mabry Mill (VA-165), 1 mi. SE of Laurel Fork, E side of Blue Ridge Pkwy., 1 mi. S of intersection with State Rte. 778. Historic museum. Frame with clapboarding and batten walls, rectangular, one story above stone foundations, gable roof; waterwheel; one-story flanking wings lower than central block. Built c. 1900 for use as a saw mill and grist mill; restored. 7 sheets (1940, including plans, elevations, sections, details); 6 ext. photos (1940); 1 data page (1940); HABSI (1958).

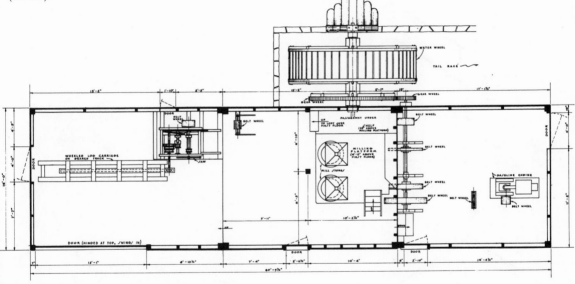

Mabry Mill

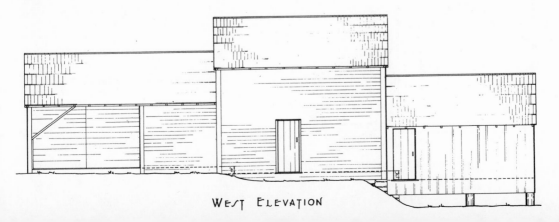

WEST ELEVATION

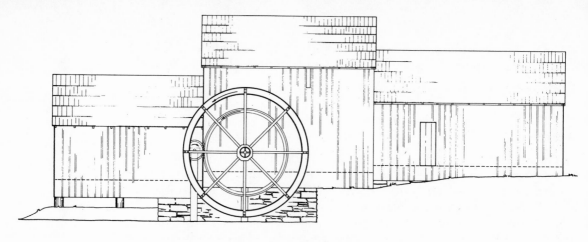

EAST ELEVATION

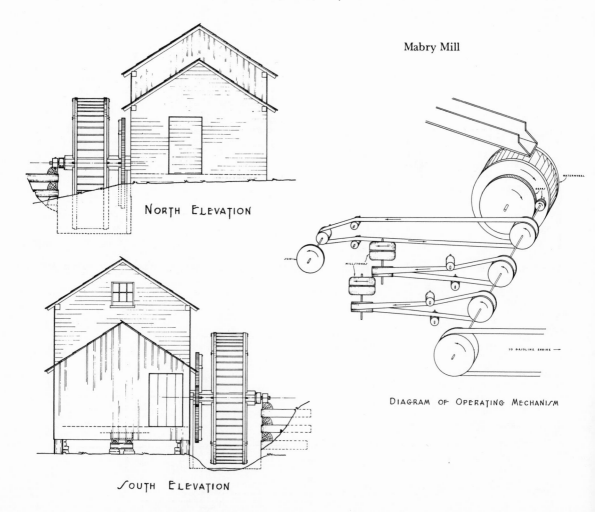

NORTH ELEVATION

Mabry Mill

DIAGRAM OF OPERATING MECHANISM

SOUTH ELEVATION

294

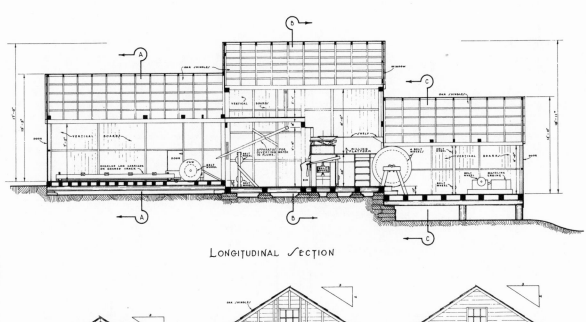

LONGITUDINAL SECTION

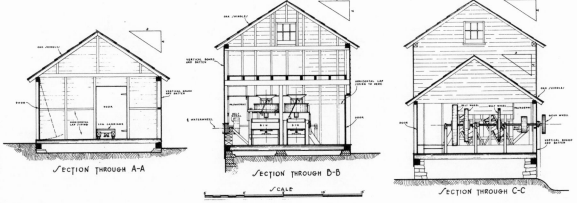

SECTION THROUGH A-A

SECTION THROUGH B-B

SCALE

SECTION THROUGH C-C

Mabry Mill

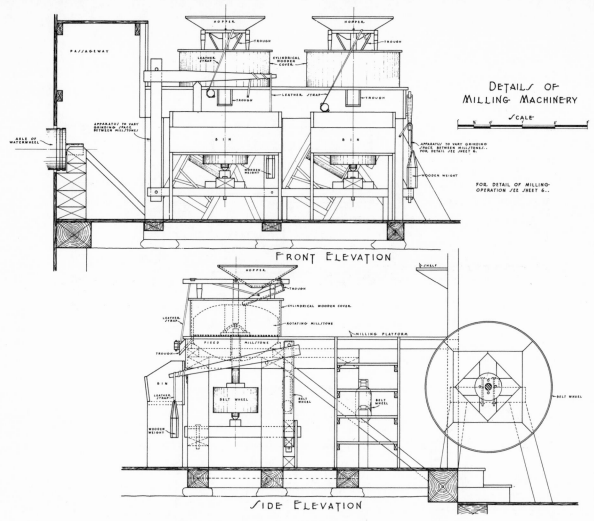

DETAILS OF
MILLING MACHINERY

SCALE

PASSAGEWAY

HOPPER · TROUGH

HOPPER · TROUGH

LEATHER STRAP

CYLINDRICAL WOODEN COVER

TROUGH

LEATHER STRAP

TROUGH

AXLE OF WATERWHEEL

APPARATUS TO VARY GRINDING SPACE BETWEEN MILLSTONES

BIN

BIN

APPARATUS TO VARY GRINDING SPACE BETWEEN MILLSTONES. FOR DETAIL SEE SHEET 6.

WOODEN WEIGHT

WOODEN WEIGHT

FOR DETAIL OF MILLING OPERATION SEE SHEET 6.

FRONT ELEVATION

SHELF

HOPPER
TROUGH

CYLINDRICAL WOODEN COVER

LEATHER STRAP

ROTATING MILLSTONE

MILLING PLATFORM

FIXED MILLSTONE

TROUGH

BIN

LEATHER STRAP

BELT WHEEL

BELT WHEEL

BELT WHEEL

BELT WHEEL

WOODEN WEIGHT

SIDE ELEVATION

Mabry Mill

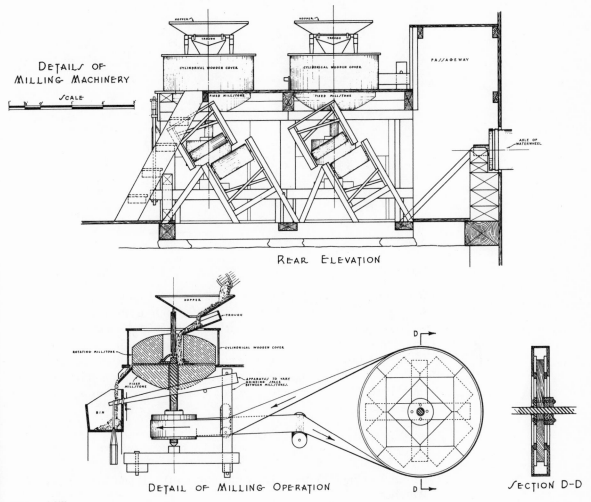

DETAILS OF
MILLING MACHINERY

SCALE

HOPPER

TROUGH

CYLINDRICAL WOODEN COVER

CYLINDRICAL WOODEN COVER

FIXED MILLSTONE

FIXED MILLSTONE

PASSAGEWAY

AXLE OF
WATERWHEEL

REAR ELEVATION

HOPPER

TROUGH

ROTATING MILLSTONE

CYLINDRICAL WOODEN COVER

FIXED
MILLSTONE

APPARATUS TO VARY
GRINDING SPACE
BETWEEN MILLSTONES.

BIN

DETAIL OF MILLING OPERATION

D

D

SECTION D-D

Mabry Mill

297

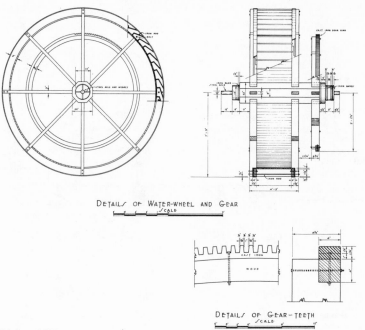

DETAILS OF WATER-WHEEL AND GEAR

DETAILS OF GEAR-TEETH

Mabry Mill

WILSONS VICINITY   Dinwiddie County (27)

Roseberry (VA-727), .9 mi. N of White Oak Creek, .1 mi. N of inter-section of State Rte. 640 and U.S. Rte. 460, .6 mi. E of intersection with State Rte. 724. Frame with clapboarding, rectangular (three-bay front), two stories, gable roof, two exterior end chimneys, full-length one-story porch; one-story side wing; three frame one-story gable roof outbuildings each having one free-standing chimney. Built mid 19th C.; extensively altered; outbuildings demolished. 2 ext. photos (1936).

WINCHESTER

Abram's Delight (VA-692), see Hollingsworth, Isaac, House (VA-692), Winchester.

Amherst Street Area Survey (VA-694), N side of Amherst St. between Washington and Braddock Sts. Mid 19th C. area, containing 5 houses (Robert Long House, 1850; Alexander S. Tidball House, c. 1830; William F. Hottle House, 1880; Dr. William T. McGuire House and office, c. 1880; and Edward McGuire House, c. 1825). 6 sheets (1972, including site plans, plans, elevations, details); 25 data pages (1972).

Durtz, Adam, House (Washington's Headquarters) (VA-696), NE corner S. Braddock St. and W. Cork St. Museum. Rubble stone and log with clapboarding, rectangular (five-bay front), one story, gable roof, one interior chimney; three-room plan. Built c. 1750. 1 photocopy (1899); 11 data pages (1972).

Glen Burnie (VA-698), 801 Amherst St., opposite intersection with Whittier Ave. Brick, rectangular with side and rear wings, two stories, gable roof, two interior end chimneys, one exterior end chimney; center-hall plan. Original portion built c. 1794; altered 19th C.; remodeled 1959. 18 data pages (1972).

Hollingsworth, Isaac, House (Abram's Delight) (VA-692), Rouss Spring Ave. House museum. Random rubble, 38'2" (three-bay front) x 27'4", two stories, gable roof, two interior end chimneys; center-hall plan. Built 1754, two-story gable-end wing. 7 sheets (1972, including plans, elevations, section, details); 11 data pages (1972).

Lawyer's Row (Holliday Office Building) (VA-691), 30-36 Rouss Ave. Brick, 61'3" (ten-bay front) x 36'1", two stories, gable roof, two double interior end chimneys, one double interior chimney, one-story front porch; interior arranged as three offices (first floor), two

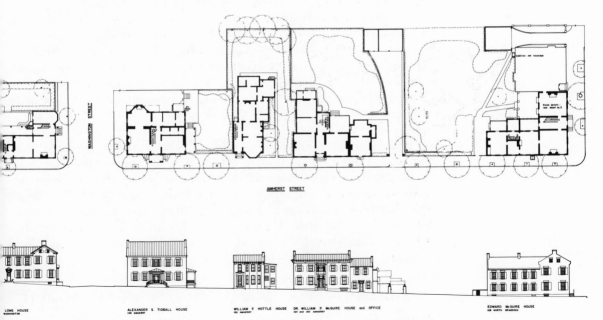

Amherst Street Area Survey

299

offices (second floor). Built 1874. 5 sheets (1972, including plans, elevations, section, details); 10 data pages (1972).

Washington's Headquarters (VA-696), see Durtz, Adam, House (VA-696), Winchester.

WINCHESTER VICINITY   Frederick County (35)

Red Lion Tavern (VA-508), 204-08 S. Loudoun St. Stone, two stories, gable roof; rear ell. Built late 18th C.; later alterations and additions. 1 ext. photo (1935); HABSI (1958).

WOODBRIDGE VICINITY   Prince William County (76)

King's Highway (VA-579), narrow roadway bordered by hedgerows, extending from ferry landing opposite Colchester for several hundred yards to Belmont subdivision. It roughly parallels U.S. Rte. 1 and stands as a ridge across open fields. Built as a colonial post road. 2 photos (1959); 2 data pages (1959); HABSI (1959).

Rippon Lodge (VA-106), .2 mi. NW of Neabsco Creek, .2 mi. NW of State Rte. 638, .8 mi. E of intersection with U.S. Rte. 1. Frame with clapboarding, rectangular (five-bay front), one-and-a-half stories, gable roof with jerkinheads and dormers, two exterior end chimneys, one interior chimney; center-hall plan. Built early 18th C.; extensive later alterations and additions including colonnaded front porch, flanking wings, and rear porch. 9 sheets (1936, including plans, elevations, sections, details); 2 ext. photos (1936), 5 int. photos (1936), 1 int. photo, furnishings (1936), 1 photo, wooden newel post as garden ornament (1936).

Scarlit, Martin, Gravestone (VA-838), W bank of Belmont Bay, between Conrad Point and Deep Hole Point at end of State Rte. 687, 2 mi. SE of intersection with U.S. Rte. 1. Stone, rectangular gravestone with clipped corners, bearing the inscription: "M S 1695. Heare lyes Martin Scarlit Gent." Erected 1695 on gravesite near Marumsco Creek, discarded into Marumsco Creek and gravesite cultivated c. 1900; retrieved and erected at present location approx. 1 mi. E of original site c. 1915. 1 photo (1936).

WOODFORD   Caroline County (17)

Flippo House (Old Sycamore Tavern) (VA-344), Woodford, exact location unknown. Brick nogging with clapboarding, 16'6" (three-

Isaac Hollingsworth House

bay front) x 20'2", one-and-a-half stories, gambrel roof with dormers, one exterior end chimney; one-room plan; shed. Built late 18th C.; demolished. 6 ext. photos (1936); 1 data page (1941).

Old Sycamore Tavern (VA-344), see Flippo House (VA-344), Woodford.

WOODS CROSSROADS VICINITY   Gloucester County (37)

Marlfield (VA-514), .3 mi. N of Poplar Spring Branch, .1 mi. SW of State Rte. 612, 1.4 mi. NW of intersection with State Rte. 613. Brick (Flemish bond), T-shaped (three-bay facade), one-and-a-half stories, gable roof with dormers, two exterior end chimneys, one interior end chimney, modillion cornice; center-hall plan. Built early 18th C.; enlarged; demolished mid 20th C. 3 ext. photos (1934).

Mount Prodigal (VA-510), see Roane House (VA-510), Woods Crossroads Vicinity.

Roane House (Mount Prodigal) (VA-510), 1 mi. E of Poropotank River, .2 mi. SE of U.S. Rte. 17, .4 mi. N of intersection with State Rte. 14. Brick, rectangular (six-bay front), one-and-a-half stories, gable roof with dormers, two interior end chimneys, one-story wooden pedimented entrance porch; center-hall plan; rear ell; dairy and smokehouse: frame with clapboarding, rectangular, one story, pyramidal roofs. Built c. 1700; later additions and alterations. 3 ext. photos (1934), 1 ext. photo, dairy (1935); 1 ext. photo, smokehouse (1935); 1 int. photo (1935); 1 ext. photocopy (n.d.); HABSI (1959).

WORSHAM   Prince Edward County (74)

Jail (VA-552), .8 mi. N of W tributary of Briery Creek, W side of U.S. Rte. 15, SW side of intersection with State Rte. 695. Stone, rectangular (three-bay front), two stories, gable roof, one interior end chimney, brick gable ends above eaves. Built 1823; burned 1845 and rebuilt; burned 1855 and repaired; demolished. 1 ext. photo (c. 1934).

YORKTOWN   York County (100)

Archer House (VA-914), S bank of York River, W side of Water St., Colonial National Historical Park. Frame with clapboarding, rectangular (three-bay front), one-and-a-half stories, gable roof with dormers, one exterior end chimney; center-hall plan. Built mid 18th C.; later alterations c. 1820, 1913; restored. 3 sheets (1958, including plot plan, plans, elevations, sections, details).

Architectural Remains: Bake Oven (VA-915), Commons Lot 117, Water St., Colonial National Historical Park. Brick remains of bake oven. Built early 18th C.; demolished. Site is immediately N of and adjacent to the Archer House. 1 sheet (1960, including plot plan, plan).

Architectural Remains: Structures "L" and "M" (VA-917), Lot 77, Main St., Colonial National Historical Park. Brick foundations of two rectangular structures; structure "L," 36'2" x 18'3"; structure "M," 16'2" x 12'2". Built c. 1706-07; destroyed c. 1755-60. Site is located in the front yard of the Dudley Digges House. 2 sheets (1960, including plot plan, plan, sections).

Ballentine House (Dewsville) (VA-596), S side of Main St., between Comte de Grasse and Nelson Sts. Brick, 39'8" (three-bay front) x 19'4", one-and-a-half stories, gable roof with dormers, one exterior end chimney; two-room plan, notable interior trim. Built c. 1939 from material salvaged from Dewsville, Newton Vicinity, King and Queen Co., which was originally built late 18th C. 3 int. photos (1960, showing salvaged architectural features); 3 data pages (1960).

Customs House (VA-202), W corner of intersection of State Rte. 1004 and Main St. Brick (Flemish bond with glazed headers), rectangular (three-bay front), two stories, hipped roof, interior end chimney, modillion cornice; two-room plan. Built early 18th C.; restored 1929. 3 ext. photos (1934, 1938); HABSI (1959).

Dewsville (VA-596), see Ballentine House (VA-596), Yorktown.

Digges, Dudley, House (West House) (VA-82), NE side of Main St., NW corner of intersection with State Rte. 1002. Frame with clapboarding, rectangular (five-bay front), one-and-a-half stories, gable roof with pedimented dormers, modillion cornice, two interior end chimneys; center-hall plan. Built c. 1760. 18 sheets (1935, including plans, elevations, details); 5 ext. photos (1934, 1937); 1 ext. photocopy (n.d.); 2 data pages (1938).

Foundations (VA-93), SE corner of intersection of Main and Church Sts. in Lot 30, Yorktown. Unexposed. 1 sheet (1935, plan).

Foundations (VA-92), SW corner of intersection of Main and Church Sts. in Lot 31, Yorktown. Unexposed. 1 sheet (1935, plan).

Lightfoot House (Somerwell House) (VA-87), E corner of intersection of State Rte. 1003 and Main St. Brick (Flemish bond with glazed headers), rectangular (three-bay front), one-and-a-half stories, gable

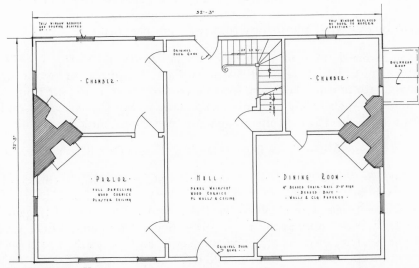

Dudley Digges House

roof with dormers, two exterior end chimneys, rear one-story porch; center-hall plan; rear ell. Built early 18th C.; restored. 3 sheets (1935, including plot plan, plans, elevations); 6 ext. photos (1934, 1937, 1938).

Medical Shop (VA-395), N corner of intersection of State Rte. 1003 and Main St. Colonial National Historical Park. Frame with clapboarding, rectangular (three-bay front), one story, gable roof, one interior end chimney. Built late 18th C.; reconstructed. 1 ext. photo (1939).

Nelson House (VA-58), see York Hall (VA-58), Yorktown.

Sessions-Sheild House (VA-81), S corner of intersection of State Rte. 1005 and Main St. Brick, 49'6" (five-bay front) x 27', one-and-a-half stories, gable roof with jerkinheads and hipped dormers, modillion cornice, two exterior end T-shaped chimneys; center-hall plan; frame rear ell. Built c. 1700. 11 sheets (1933, including plans, elevations, details); 4 ext. photos (1934, 1938); 1 data page (1937); HABSI (1959)

Somerwell House (VA-87), see Lightfoot House (VA-87), Yorktown.

Swan Tavern (VA-83), SW side of Main St., SE side of intersection with State Rte. 1001. Frame with clapboarding, rectangular (five-bay front), one-and-a-half stories, gable roof with jerkinheads and hipped dormers, interior end chimneys. Original structure built early 18th C.; demolished 1862; reconstructed 1934. 10 sheets (1933, including plot plan, archeological remains, plan, elevations, details); 3 ext. photos (1934); 1 photocopy (n.d.); 2 data pages (n.d.).

Two Stone Steps from the Dudley Digges House (VA-916), Lot 77, Main St., Colonial National Historical Park. Fragments of two stone steps with unusual keying as integral part of the stone. Stone is limestone of English origin. Steps made during 18th C.; excavated mid 20th C. 1 sheet (1960, including plans, elevations, molding profiles).

West House (VA-82), see Digges, Dudley, House (VA-82), Yorktown.

Wharf Buildings (VA-371), N side of State Rte. 238, E corner of intersection with George P. Coleman Memorial Toll Bridge. First building: frame with clapboarding, rectangular (five-bay front), gable roof, interior chimney. Built c. 1934. Second building: brick, rectangular (five-bay front), one-and-a-half stories, gable roof, one exterior end chimney. Built c. 1934. 2 ext. photos (1935).

York Hall

York Hall (Nelson House) (VA-58), W corner of intersection of State Rte. 1005 and Main St. Brick, rectangular (five-bay front), two-and-a-half stories, gable roof with hipped dormers, two interior chimneys, pedimented gable ends, modillion cornice, segmental-arched window openings with stone keystones, molded brick water table, brick pedimented entrance motif, stone quoins; center-hall plan. Built mid 18th C.; later alterations. 8 ext. photos (1934, 1937, 1938), 2 int. photos (n.d.); 13 ext. photocopies (c. 1863, 1915), 21 int. photocopies (c. 1915); 4 data pages (1937).

YORKTOWN VICINITY   York County (100)

Kiskiack (VA-183), W bank of S tributary of Lee Pond, 1.6 mi. NW of State Rte. 238, 2.4 mi. NE of intersection with State Rte. 168,

Moore House

Naval Weapons Station. Brick (Flemish bond), rectangular (three-bay front), one-and-a-half stories, gable roof with dormers, two interior T-shaped end chimneys with molded brick caps, brick water table, advanced entrance vestibule; center-hall plan. Built late 17th C.; burned February 24, 1915; renovated 1927; entrance vestibule added 1937. 4 sheets (1940, including plans, elevations). NR

Moore House (VA-80), .1 mi. S of York River, E side of State Rte. 676, .4 mi. SE of intersection with State Rte. 238. Frame with clapboarding, rectangular (five-bay front), one-and-a-half stories, hipped on gable roof with hipped dormers, two exterior end T-shaped chimneys, modillion cornice; center-hall plan. Built mid 18th C.; restored. 16 sheets (1931, including plans, elevations, details, archeological remains); 10 ext. photos (1929, 1934, 1939); 2 ext. photocopies (1864); 1 data page (1940).

YORKTOWN NAVAL WEAPONS
STATION BRANCH VICINITY   York County (100)

Bellfield Cemetery (VA-918), .2 mi. NW of Indian Field Creek, .2 mi. N of intersection of Bellfield and Digges Rds., .4 mi. N of intersection of Digges and Felgates Rds. Marble and brick, table tombs. Erected 18th C.; restored. 1 ext. photo (c. 1900).

Ringfield (VA-318), S bank of King Creek, .2 mi. N of Colonial National Pkwy., 1.8 mi. SE of intersection with State Rte. 641. Brick, rectangular (five-bay front), two-and-a-half stories, gable roof with dormers, two interior T-shaped end chimneys; brick wing. Built 18th C.; altered; demolished c. 1905. 1 ext. photocopy (c. 1900); 3 data pages (1940).

The Inventory

ABINGDON   Washington County (96)

Bank, 225 E. Main St.
Barter Theatre, NW corner of intersection of W. Main St. and Goodman Alley NW.
Bell House, 133 E. Main St.
Campbell House, 220 Main St.
Commercial Building, NW side of U.S. Rte. 11 (Main St.), N side of intersection with State Rte. 75.
Dooley House, 123 Pecan St.
Fields House, 208 W. Main St.
Findlay, Alexander, House, 101 W. Valley St.
Gibson, Andrew, House, 142 E. Main St.
Gibson, James K., House, 281 E. Main St.
Greenway Haven, SW side of Whites Mill Rd., .2 mi. NW of intersection with Honaker St.
House, 114 E. Main St.
House, 123 W. Main St.
House, 304 E. Main St.
House, 239 Valley St. NE.
King, William, House, 108 Court St.
Mont Calm, .2 mi. SW of State Rte. 75, .2 mi. S of intersection with U.S. Rte. 11.
Musser, Daniel, House, 247 Valley Rd. NE.
Oakland, .2 mi. NE of Whites Mill Rd., .2 mi. NW of intersection with Honaker St.
Pitts, Dr., House, 247 E. Main St.
Post Office, SE corner of intersection of W. Main and Cummings Sts. NW.
Preston, Gen. Francis, House (Martha Washington Inn), 150 Main St.
Retirement House (Craig House), 702 Colonial Rd.
Rose House, 133 Main St.
Russell, Andrew, House, 165 E. Main St.
Tavern, 222 E. Main St.
Virginia House, 208 E. Main St.
Washington County Courthouse, SW corner of intersection of Court and E. Main Sts.
White, Col. James, House, 171 E. Main St.

ABINGDON VICINITY   Washington County (96)

Acklin, N side of U.S. Rte. 11, .1 mi. SE of intersection with State Rte. 609.
Altamont, SW side of intersection of State Rte. 609 and U.S. Rte. 11, .1 mi. SE of intersection with State Rte. 702.

Clapp House, E side of State Rte. 794, .2 mi. N of intersection with U.S. Rte. I-81.

Clapp Mill, W side of State Rte. 794, .1 mi. N of intersection with U.S. Rte. I-81.

Cummings House, NE side of U.S. Rte. 19, .8 mi. NW of intersection with State Rte. 766.

Green Hill, W side of State Rte. 75, .1 mi. S of intersection with U.S. Rte. I-81.

Greenway, W corner of intersection of State Rte. 694 and U.S. Rte. 11, .8 mi. NE of intersection with State Rte. 704.

House, SE side of State Rte. 793, .6 mi. SE of intersection with U.S. Rte. I-81.

House, SW side of State Rte. 710, .4 mi. S of intersection with State Rte. 722.

House, E side of State Rte. 611, .4 mi. S of intersection with State Rte. 647.

House, NW side of State Rte. 670, SW side of intersection with State Rte. 794.

Maxwell House, NW side of State Rte. 647, 1.2 mi. SW of intersection with U.S. Rte. I-81.

Meadows, .5 mi. E of State Rte. 75, .6 mi. S of intersection with U.S. Rte. 11.

Panacellie, E side of State Rte. 699, .6 mi. N of intersection with U.S. Rte. 11.

Parson Cummings Manse, NE side of U.S. Rte. 19, .8 mi. NW of intersection with State Rte. 766.

ACCOMAC   Accomack County (1)

Accomack County Courthouse, W side of State Rte. 764, NW side of intersection with U.S. Rte. 13.

Francis Makemie Presbyterian Church, NW side of Back St., .3 mi. SW of intersection with U.S. Rte. 13.

St. James Episcopal Church, E side of State Rte. 605, .1 mi. SE of intersection with U.S. Rte. 13.

St. James Parish House, NW side of Back St., .1 mi. NE of intersection with State Rte. 605.

Seven Gables, NW side of Back St., .2 mi. SW of intersection with U.S. Rte. 13.

ACORN VICINITY   Halifax County (42)

Rosebank (Clarkton), SE side of State Rte. 632, .9 mi. NE of intersection with State Rtes. 634 and 626.

ACORN VICINITY   Westmoreland County (97)

Elba, .2 mi. W of State Rte. 604, at intersection with State Rte. 203.

Locust Farm, .1 mi. S of State Rte. 203, .2 mi. E of intersection with State Rte. 604.

AFTON VICINITY   Nelson County (63)

Hebron Baptist Church, .3 mi. E of State Rte. 151, 1.1 mi. S of intersection with State Rte. 631.

ALBERTA VICINITY   Brunswick County (13)

Hobson's Choice, N side of State Rte. 606, 1 mi. E of intersection with State
    Rte. 642.
House, E side of State Rte. 606, 1.9 mi. NW of intersection with State Rte. 628.

ALCOMA VICINITY   Buckingham County (15)

Merry Wood, .4 mi. SE of North River, .3 mi. N of State Rte. 56, .1 mi. NW of
    intersection with U.S. Rte. 60.
Mt. Rush, .1 mi. S of U.S. Rte. 60, .9 mi. SW of intersection with State Rte. 742.
Perry Hill, .6 mi. W of State Rte. 56, .1 mi. NW of intersection with State Rte.
    647.
Variety Shades, .4 mi. NE of State Rte. 649, .1 mi. N of intersection with State
    Rte. 56.
Westfield, 1.1 mi. N of intersection of State Rtes. 646 and 607, .9 mi. NW of
    intersection with U.S. Rte. 60.
Wheatland, .5 mi. SE of State Rte. 647, .2 mi. S of intersection with State Rte.
    56.

ALDIE VICINITY   Loudoun County (54)

Dover, S side of U.S. Rte. 50, opposite intersection with State Rte. 629.
Glengyle Farm, .1 mi. N of U.S. Rte. 50, 1.1 mi. SE of intersection with State
    Rte. 625.
Narrowgate, N side of U.S. Rte. 50, .2 mi. W of intersection with State Rte. 612.
Oak Hill, .2 mi. W of U.S. Rte. 15, 2 mi. N of intersection with U.S. Rte. 50.
Oakham, N side of U.S. Rte. 50, .2 mi. W of intersection with State Rte. 633.
Pine Ridge Farm, .2 mi. SE of Little River, S side of U.S. Rte. 50, .3 mi. E of
    intersection with State Rte. 612.

ALEXANDRIA

Bennett, Charles, House, 912 Cameron St.
City Hall, S side of Cameron St. between N. Royal and N. Fairfax Sts.
Fendall-Lee House, 614 Oronoco St.
Franklin and Armfield Slave Pen, 1315 Duke St.
Gilpin, Col. George, House, 206-08 King St.
Harper, John, Warehouse, 103 Prince St.
House, 224 N. Alfred St.
House, 112 S. Columbus St.
House, 805 Duke St.
House, 1207 Duke St.
House, 1621 Duke St.
House, 1707 Duke St.

House, 212 S. Pitt St.
House, 113 Prince St.
House, 115 Prince St.
House, 128 Prince St.
House, 808 Prince St.
House, 1020 Prince St.
House, 1108 Prince St.
House, 1111 Prince St.
House, 213 S. Royal St.
Johnston, Parson, House (Confederate Museum), 806 Prince St.
Laws, Bolitha, House, 1007 King St.
Piles, Lewis, House, 1115 Prince St.
Row Houses, 817-19 Prince St.
Row Houses, 214-18 S. Royal St.
Spring Gardens (Yates' Tavern), 414 Franklin St.
Warehouse, Tobacco, Swift Alley.
Washington, George, Tenement, 125 S. Pitt St.
Wolf House, 401 S. Lee St.
Young, Robert, House, 116 N. Payne St.

ALLEGHANY VICINITY   Alleghany County (3)

Crow's Tavern, SE side of intersection of State Rtes. 159 and 311, 3.4 mi. SE of
    intersection with State Rte. 602.

ALTAVISTA VICINITY   Campbell County (16)

Otterbourne, NE side of State Rte. 712, .2 mi. NW of intersection with U.S.
    Rte. 29.

ALTAVISTA VICINITY   Pittsylvania County (72)

Clement Hill, .2 mi. NW of U.S. Rte. 29, .9 mi. SW of intersection with State
    Rte. 43.

AMELIA   Amelia County (4)

Amelia County Courthouse, E side of State Rte. 1009, .1 mi. S of intersection
    with State Rtes. 1009 and 1007.
Evenholm, S side of intersection of U.S. Rte. 360 and State Rte. 656.

AMELIA VICINITY   Amelia County (4)

Eggleston-Hackett House, 1 mi. N of N end of State Rte. 638, 1.1 mi. NW of
    intersection with State Rte. 681.

Glebe, The, .4 mi. N of U.S. Rte. 360, .4 mi. NE of intersection with State Rte. 656.

Haw Branch, 2 mi. E of State Rte. 667, 1 mi. NE of intersection with State Rte. 681.

Sherwood, .3 mi. N of State Rte. 638, .3 mi. N of intersection with State Rte. 681.

AMHERST   Amherst County (5)

Amherst County Courthouse, SE end of State Rte. T1104, .1 mi. SE of intersection with U.S. Rte. 29.

Ascension Episcopal Church, SE side of U.S. Rte. 29.

Edgewood, .1 mi. S of intersection of U.S. Rte. 29 and State Rte. T1106.

Seven Oaks, NW side of U.S. Rte. 29, at intersection with State Rte. 643.

AMHERST VICINITY   Amherst County (5)

Edge Hill, .1 mi. W of State Rte. 663, .1 mi. SW of intersection with State Rte. 643 and U.S. Rte. 29.

Kenmore, .2 mi. S of State Rte. 643, 2 mi. NW of intersection with State Rte. 663 and U.S. Rte. 29.

Minor Hall (Glebe), .1 mi. E of State Rte. 151, .2 mi. NW of intersection with U.S. Rte. 29.

Poplar Grove, .7 mi. SE of State Rte. 661, 1.2 mi. S of intersection with State Rte. 660.

Sweet Briar House, .8 mi. NW of U.S. Rte. 29, 2.9 mi. S of intersection with U.S. Rte. 60.

AMSTERDAM   Botetourt County (12)

Stonelea, N side of State Rte. 735 at SW end, .7 mi. SW of intersection with State Rte. 655.

AMSTERDAM VICINITY   Botetourt County (12)

Fair View, .4 mi. W of U.S. Rte. 220, .3 mi. S of intersection with State Rte. 673.

Greenfield, .8 mi. W of U.S. Rte. 220, .7 mi. N of intersection with State Rte. 673.

Holladay, Lewis, House, .1 mi. W of U.S. Rte. 220, .7 mi. N of intersection with State Rte. 673.

McDonald, Bryan, Jr., House, .2 mi. N of State Rte. 779, .6 mi. S of intersection with State Rte. 630.

Sessler House, SW corner of intersection of State Rtes. 664 and 666, .8 mi. N of intersection with State Rte. 779.

Jones-McKenny House (New Store), .3 mi. N of State Rte. 636, .1 mi. NW of intersection with State Rte. 609.

Keswick, S side of State Rte. 636, .5 mi. SE of intersection with State Rte. 638.

Millwood, .1 mi. W of State Rte. 633, .4 mi. NW of intersection with State Rte. 609.

ANNANDALE — Fairfax County (30)

Oak Hill, 4800 Wakefield Chapel Rd.

APPOMATTOX — Appomattox County (6)

Appomattox County Clerk's Office, SW corner of intersection of State Rtes. T1023 and 131.

Appomattox County Courthouse, SW corner of intersection of State Rtes. T1023 and 131.

Appomattox County Jail, SW corner of intersection of State Rtes. T1023 and 131.

St. Ann's Episcopal Church, N side of State Rte. T631, .1 mi. NE of intersection with U.S. Rte. 460.

APPOMATTOX VICINITY — Appomattox County (6)

Bocock-Isbell House, .3 mi. N of State Rte. 24, 1.8 mi. E of intersection with State Rte. 656.

Bocock, Thomas, House, E side of State Rte. 616, 2.5 mi. N of intersection with State Rte. 608.

Eldon, .1 mi. NE of State Rte. 26, .3 mi. N of intersection with State Rte. 659.

Flood House, .2 mi. W of State Rte. 24, 1.3 mi. NE of intersection with State Rte. 656.

House (Falling River Community Center), .4 mi. E of State Rte. 643, .8 mi. S of intersection with State Rte. 691.

House, .1 mi. N of State Rte. 615, .9 mi. NE of intersection with State Rte. 686.

House, .1 mi. S of U.S. Rte. 460, .4 mi. W of intersection with State Rte. 613.

House, .6 mi. NE of State Rte. 711, .2 mi. NE of intersection with State Rte. 26.

House, S side of State Rte. 631, 1 mi. NE of intersection with State Rte. 634.

Martin House, N side of U.S. Rte. 460, .6 mi. W of intersection with State Rte. 26.

Peers, George T., House, .1 mi. W of State Rte. 24, .3 mi. N of intersection with State Rte. 627.

Red Knoll, W corner of intersection of State Rtes. 656 and 24, .5 mi. N of intersection with State Rte. 710.

Redfields, NE side of State Rte. 635, .8 mi. SE of intersection with State Rte. 1007.

Sackett, C. H., House, N side of U.S. Rte. 460, .4 mi. W of intersection with State Rte. 26.

Trent, William, House, SW side of State Rte. 634, .6 mi. SE of intersection with State Rte. 631.

Walnut Hill, .1 mi. NW of State Rte. 615, 1.5 mi. NE of intersection with State Rte. 616.

ARLINGTON   Arlington County (7)

Glebe, The, 4527 17th St.
Prospect Hill, 1230 S. Arlington Ridge Rd.

ARRINGTON VICINITY   Nelson County (63)

Believe It (Bellevette), SE side of State Rte. 757, .4 mi. S of intersection with State Rte. 655.

ARVONIA VICINITY   Buckingham County (15)

Mount Zion, .5 mi. W of Georgia Branch, N side of State Rte. 610, .3 mi. E of intersection with State Rte. 670.

Seven Islands, .1 mi. N of State Rte. 652, 2.5 mi. NW of intersection with U.S. Rte. 15.

Snowden, .2 mi. W of State Rte. 20, 2.8 mi. N of intersection with State Rte. 679.

ASHLAND VICINITY   Hanover County (43)

Brockspring, .1 mi. W of Lickinghole Creek, .3 mi. NE of State Rte. 661, .7 mi. SE of intersection with U.S. Rte. 1.

Medley Grove, .2 mi. N of State Rte. 54, 1.4 mi. NW of intersection with State Rte. 686.

Slash Church, W side of State Rte. 656, .3 mi. N of intersection with State Rte. 657.

Springfield, .2 mi. W of intersection of State Rtes. 686 and 54, .4 mi. NW of intersection with State Rte. 687.

ASPEN VICINITY   Charlotte County (20)

Cub Creek Church, N side of State Rte. 619, 1.3 mi. E of intersection with State Rte. 617.

House, W side of State Rte. 620, 2 mi. S of intersection with State Rte. 619.

Oaks, The, .5 mi. SW of State Rte. 649, .5 mi. SE of intersection with State Rte. 678.

Red Hill, S end of State Rte. 677, 1.1 mi. S of intersection with State Rte. 619.

Ridgeway, .8 mi. E of State Rte. 678, .7 mi. SE of intersection with State Rte. 649.

Staunton Hill, .2 mi. SE of State Rte. 619, 1.4 mi. SW of intersection with State Rte. 693.

Woodburn, .5 mi. E of S end of State Rte. 678, 1.8 mi. SE of intersection with State Rte. 649.

ATKINS VICINITY   Smyth County (87)

Rock House, .1 mi. W of Nicks Creek, S side of U.S. Rte. 11, .1 mi. W of intersection with State Rte. 622.

AUGUSTA SPRINGS   Augusta County (8)

Augusta Springs, .4 mi. E of Liptrap Run, .2 mi. NW of State Rte. 42, .5 mi. NE of intersection with Rte. 811.

AUSTINVILLE VICINITY   Wythe County (99)

Jackson, John, House, N side of State Rte. 69, 1.1 mi. E of intersection with State Rte. 636.

Jackson, Thomas, House, .4 mi. NW of State Rte. 69, .5 mi. NE of intersection with State Rte. 608.

Shot Tower, .1 mi. W of intersection of State Rte. 608 and U.S. Rte. 52, 2.3 mi. SE of intersection with State Rte. 619.

AXTON VICINITY   Henry County (45)

Gravely Tobacco Warehouse, W side of State Rte. 57, .3 mi. N of intersection with State Rte. 648.

AYLETT VICINITY   King William County (51)

Burlington, .7 mi. NE of State Rte. 600, 2.6 mi. NW of intersection with State Rte. 607.

Cownes, .4 mi. SE of State Rte. 600, .6 mi. NW of intersection with State Rte. 607.

Duncan, Capt. Silas, House, W side of State Rte. 600, .1 mi. SE of intersection with U.S. Rte. 360.

Edge Hill, .6 mi. SW of State Rte. 600, 1.4 mi. NW of intersection with U.S. Rte. 360.

Herring Creek Mill, SE side of State Rte. 607, .5 mi. SW of intersection with State Rte. 600.

House, E side of State Rte. 600, .1 mi. SE of intersection with U.S. Rte. 360.

Millwood, .1 mi. SW of State Rte. 607, .5 mi. SW of intersection with State Rte. 600.

Octagon, .2 mi. NW of State Rte. 608, .4 mi. NW of intersection with State Rte. 606.

Warsaw, .1 mi. SW of State Rte. 608, .4 mi. NW of intersection with State Rte. 606.

AYLETT VICINITY   King and Queen County (49)

Holly Hill, .2 mi. SW of U.S. Rte. 360, 1.6 mi. NE of intersection with State Rte. 600.

BACOVA VICINITY   Bath County (9)

House, E side of State Rte. 687, .5 mi. NE of intersection with State Rte. 679.

Warwickton (Hidden Valley Farm), 2.1 mi. N of State Rte. 621, 1.1 mi. N of intersection with State Rte. 39.

BALLSVILLE   Powhatan County (73)

House (Crenshaw House), E side of State Rte. 13, E of intersection with State Rte. 720.

BALLSVILLE VICINITY   Powhatan County (73)

Blenheim, S side of State Rte. 606, .2 mi. W of intersection with State Rte. 630.

Somerset, E side of State Rte. 630, .2 mi. S of intersection with U.S. Rte. 60.

BARBOURSVILLE VICINITY   Orange County (69)

Barboursville (and Ruins), .4 mi. NW of State Rte. 777, .5 mi. S of intersection with State Rte. 678.

Burlington, .2 mi. SE of State Rte. 738, 1 mi. NE of intersection with U.S. Rte. 33.

Campbellton, .2 mi. NE of U.S. Rte. 33, .4 mi. E of intersection with State Rte. 678.

Clifton (Klondike, Merriewood), .6 mi. NW of State Rte. 644, .8 mi. NE of intersection with State Rte. 655.

Edgewood, .1 mi. E of State Rte. 609, 1.4 mi. NW of intersection with State Rte. 644.

Fitzhugh House, E side of State Rte. 678, N corner of intersection with State Rte. 20.

Glendale, .8 mi. SW of State Rte. 609, 1.3 mi. NW of intersection with State Rte. 644.

Springdale, .4 mi. N of intersection of State Rtes. 609 and 644, 1.8 mi. NE of intersection with State Rte. 655.

Spring Forest (Blue Run Farm), .3 mi. N of State Rte. 655, .5 mi. NW of intersection with State Rte. 20.

BARHAMSVILLE VICINITY   New Kent County (64)

Brick House, exact location unknown, on Brick House Point.

Cedar Grove, .2 mi. SE of State Rte. 30, .4 mi. SW of intersection with State Rte. 600.

Eltham Site, .9 mi. N of State Rte. 33, .4 mi. SW of intersection with State Rte. 30.

River View, .3 mi. E of State Rte. 30, .5 mi. N of intersection with State Rte. 600.

BARNESVILLE VICINITY   Charlotte County (20)

House, N side of U.S. Rte. 360, .1 mi. W of intersection with State Rte. 608.

BASKERVILLE VICINITY   Mecklenburg County (59)

Alta Vista, .3 mi. W of State Rte. 4, .8 mi. S of intersection with State Rte. 708.

Edmonson House (Stony Cross), W side of intersection of State Rtes. 671 and 675, .4 mi. N of intersection with State Rte. 678.

Elm Hill, 1 mi. SE of State Rte. 4, .2 mi. SE of intersection with State Rte. 707.

Glen Grove, .3 mi. N of State Rte. 672, .4 mi. E of intersection with State Rte. 669.

House, .3 mi. SE of intersection of State Rtes. 708 and 669, .6 mi. S of intersection with U.S. Rte. 58.

House, NE corner of intersection of State Rtes. 4 and 674 and U.S. Rte. 58, .4 mi. S of intersection with State Rte. 676.

House, E side of State Rte. 658, .1 mi. N of intersection with State Rte. 670.

House, W side of State Rte. 674, .5 mi. S of intersection with State Rte. 669.

Mount Airy, .4 mi. SW of State Rte. 671, 1 mi. NW of intersection with State Rte. 675.

Tunstall House, S side of State Rte. 676, .5 mi. W of intersection with State Rte. 674.

Watson, Benjamin, House, W side of State Rte. 4, 2 mi. S of intersection with State Rte. 708.

BATTERY PARK   Isle of Wight County (47)

Todd House, N side of State Rte. 704, between State Rtes. 1001 and 1002.

BEAVERLETT VICINITY

Mathews County (58)

Poplar Grove, .5 mi. SW of intersection of State Rtes. 14 and 613, 1.1 mi. W of
   intersection with State Rte. 614.
Poplar Grove Mill, .6 mi. SW of intersection of State Rtes. 14 and 613, 1.1 mi. W
   of intersection with State Rte. 614.

BEDFORD

Bedford County (10)

Avenel, 300 Avenel St.
Bedford County Courthouse, 129 W. Main St.
Bedford Presbyterian Church, 100 block of Main St.
Boxwood Inn, 320 N. Bridge St.
First Methodist Church (St. Philip's Episcopal Church), 153 W. Main St.
Kingston, 512 Peaks St.
Masonic Hall, 501 E. Main St.
Wharton House, 319 N. Bridge St.

BEDFORD VICINITY

Bedford County (10)

Cedars, The, .1 mi. N of State Rte. 297, 1.5 mi. SE of intersection with State
   Rte. 43.
Fancy Farms, W side of State Rte. 43, .1 mi. N of intersection with State Rte.
   682.
Jeter House, .2 mi. S of State Rte. 675, .5 mi. E of intersection with State Rte.
   122.
Locust Hill, .3 mi. SE of intersection of State Rtes. 639 and 122, 2.5 mi. N of
   intersection with State Rte. 643.
Montpelier, S side of State Rte. 644, 1 mi. E of intersection with State Rte. 43.
Oakrest, N side of U.S. Rte. 460, 1.3 mi. W of intersection with State Rte. 122.
Otterburn, .1 mi. E of State Rte. 122, 1.6 mi. N of intersection with U.S. Rte.
   460.
Savenac, .3 mi. N of State Rte. 43, .8 mi. SE of intersection with State Rte. 722.
Three Otters, N side of State Rte. 838, .7 mi. W of intersection with State Rte. 43.
Wyoming, .4 mi. S of State Rte. 639, .6 mi. E of intersection with State Rte. 122.

BELMONT VICINITY

Spotsylvania County (89)

Cherry Grove, .7 mi. S of State Rte. 612, 1.8 mi. W of intersection with State
   Rte. 719.
Prospect Hill, .1 mi. N of State Rte. 612, .2 mi. W of intersection with State Rte.
   719.
Woodside, .4 mi. S of State Rte. 719, .7 mi. W of intersection with State Rte. 654.

319

Brown, Edward, House, E side of State Rte. 617, .5 mi. S of intersection with State Rte. 627.

Brown, Michael, House, .2 mi. NE of State Rte. 600, .3 mi. N of intersection with State Rte. 617.

BERRYVILLE   Clarke County (22)

Berryville Presbyterian Church, SW side of W. Main St., .1 mi. W of U.S. Rte. 340.

Clarke County Courthouse, SE side of Church St., opposite intersection with Academy St.

Clerk's Office and Jail, SE side of Church St., adjacent to courthouse on the SW side.

Crows Nest, 117 Church St.

Duncan Methodist Memorial Church, NE side E. Main St., .2 mi. SE of State Rte. 616.

Grace Episcopal Church, NE corner of intersection of Church and Barnett Sts.

House (The Nook), 106 E. Main St.

Smith, Treadwell, House (Hawthorne Building), NW corner of intersection of State Rte. 7 and U.S. Rte. 340.

Taylor House, SW corner of intersection of U.S. Rte. 340 and State Rte. 7.

BERRYVILLE VICINITY   Clarke County (22)

Anchorage, S side of U.S. Rte. 340, .4 mi. NE of intersection with State Rte. 641.

Arcadia, E side of State Rte. 612, .6 mi. N of intersection with State Rte. 7.

Audley, .8 mi. NE of State Rte. 7, .7 mi. E of intersection with State Rte. 613.

Balcutha, .4 mi. N of U.S. Rte. 340, .7 mi. NE of intersection with State Rte. 610.

Blakemare, NE side of U.S. Rte. 340, .2 mi. E of intersection with State Rte. 653.

Bloomfield, E side of State Rte. 641, .3 mi. NE of intersection with State Rte. 639.

Castleman, David, House (North Hill), .1 mi. S of State Rte. 7, .1 mi. W of intersection with State Rte. 603.

Castleman, William, House (White Haven), E side of State Rte. 603, .7 mi. NE of intersection with State Rte. 7.

Castleman's Ferry House, N side of State Rte. 603, .1 mi. E of intersection with State Rte. 7.

Castleman's Mill, W side of State Rte. 612, .7 mi. SE of intersection with U.S. Rte. 340.

Clermont, .2 mi. S of State Rte. 7, .7 mi. E of intersection with State Rte. 615.

Elmington, .3 mi. SE of U.S. Rte. 340, .4 mi. NE of intersection with State Rte. 611.

Elwood (Avenel), N side of State Rte. 657, .2 mi. E of intersection with State Rte. 636.

Fairfield, .2 mi. S of U.S. Rte. 340, .3 mi. NE of intersection with State Rte. 610.

Glen Allen, NE side of State Rte. 639, 1.8 mi. W of intersection with State Rte. 611.

Glendale Farm, N side of State Rte. 761, opposite intersection with State Rte. 632.

Helmsley, .2 mi. N of State Rte. 657, 1 mi. W of intersection with State Rte. 632.

Mansfield, .2 mi. W of State Rte. 641, .8 mi. N of intersection with U.S. Rte. 340.

Milton Valley, .4 mi. E of U.S. Rte. 340, .7 mi. SW of intersection with State Rte. 616.

Monterey Farm, .2 mi. NW of State Rte. 615, 1.8 mi. N of intersection with State Rte. 7.

Mount Hebron, .1 mi. W of State Rte. 613, 2.6 mi. S of intersection with State Rte. 7.

Norwood, .2 mi. S of State Rte. 7, .2 mi. E of intersection with S section of State Rte. 608.

Osborn, Decatur, House (Glenwood), .1 mi. S of State Rte. 7, opposite intersection with State Rte. 612.

Runnymeade, .4 mi. SE of State Rte. 612, .8 mi. SE of intersection with U.S. Rte. 340.

Smallwood House (Dan-Ridge Acres), .1 mi. W of State Rte. 613, .5 mi. S of intersection with State Rte. 7.

Soldiers Rest, .5 mi. NE of State Rte. T1005, .1 mi. SE of intersection with Church St.

Springsbury, .8 mi. S of S end of State Rte. 613, at intersection with State Rte. 618.

Upton, .7 mi. W of intersection with State Rte. 611.

Villa La Rue, E side of State Rte. 641, .7 mi. N of intersection with U.S. Rte. 340.

Ware, James, House (Riverside), .2 mi. N of State Rte. 603, .7 mi. NE of intersection with State Rte. 7.

Wee-Haw, .1 mi. W of State Rte. 611, .4 mi. N of intersection with State Rte. 639.

Wheat Farm, .2 mi. NW of State Rte. 608, .6 mi. NE of State Rte. 7.

Wickliffe Church, E side of State Rte. 609, .6 mi. NE of intersection with State Rte. 663.

Woodley, .7 mi. E of U.S. Rte. 340, .1 mi. SW of intersection with State Rte. 633.

BIG ISLAND VICINITY   Bedford County (10)

Hope Dawn, W side of State Rte. 761, 1.7 mi. NE of intersection with State Rte. 645.

Locust Grove, NE side of State Rte. 638, .6 mi. SE of intersection with State Rte. 122.

BIG STONE GAP   Wise County (98)

Ayers, Gen. Rufus A., House (Southwest Virginia Museum), 10 W. First St. N.

Fox House, 117 Shawnee Ave.

Tolliver, June, House, .1 mi. NE of U.S. Rte. 23, .1 mi. SE of intersection with U.S. Alt. Rte. 58.

BLACKRIDGE VICINITY   Mecklenburg County (59)

House, .4 mi. W of State Rte. 620, .8 mi. N of intersection with State Rte. 647.
House, SW side of State Rte. 625, .8 mi. SE of intersection with State Rte. 624.
Thomas-Rose House, E side of State Rte. 626, .9 mi. SE of intersection with
    State Rte. 774.

BLACKSBURG   Montgomery County (61)

Giles, Thomas, House, 114 N. Main St.
House, 400 Roanoke St.
House (Connor House), S corner of intersection of Wall and Water Sts.
Presbyterian Church (Odd Fellows Lodge), NE corner of Main and Lee Sts.

BLACKSBURG VICINITY   Montgomery County (61)

Flying Duck Farm, E side of State Rte. 723, 1.5 mi. S of intersection with State
    Rte. 785.
Green Acres, E side of State Rte. 723, .5 mi. N of intersection with State Rte. 603.
Henderson, Crose, House, SE side of State Rte. 785, 1.1 mi. NE of intersection
    with State Rte. 723.
House, NW side of State Rte. 785, .3 mi. NE of intersection with State Rte. 628.
House, N side of State Rte. 603, .2 mi. E of intersection with State Rte. 641.
House, SE side of State Rte. 785, 1.2 mi. NE of intersection with State Rte. 628.
Lavon, .5 mi. E of State Rte. 723, 1 mi. S of intersection with State Rte. 785.
McDonald Mill, SE side of State Rte. 785, 1.6 mi. NE of intersection with State
    Rte. 628.
Smithfield, .8 mi. S of State Rte. 685, 1 mi. W of city limits of Blacksburg.
Yellow Sulphur Springs Hotel, W side of State Rte. 643, .3 mi. S of intersection
    with State Rte. 642.

BLACKSTONE VICINITY   Nottoway County (68)

Oakwood, E side of State Rte. 606, .3 mi. N of intersection with State Rte. 692.

BLAIRS VICINITY   Pittsylvania County (72)

Beaver Tavern Kitchen, .1 mi. NE of U.S. Rte. 29, .6 mi. NE of intersection with
    State Rte. 720.

BLAKES VICINITY   Mathews County (58)

Hesse, W bank of Godfrey Bay, .8 mi. E of State Rte. 631, .4 mi. N of inter-
    section with State Rte. 198.

BLAND   Bland County (11)

Bland County Courthouse, SW side of State Rte. 98, .3 mi. SE of intersection
    with U.S. Rte. 21/52.
Sheriff's House and Jail, SW side of State Rte. 98, .2 mi. SE of intersection with
    U.S. Rte. 21/52.

BLAND VICINITY   Bland County (11)

Fairview, S side of State Rte. 42, 1.2 mi. E of intersection with State Rte. 604.
Green Meadows, .6 mi. NW of State Rte. 42, SW side of intersection with State
    Rte. 616.

BLUEMONT VICINITY   Loudoun County (54)

Welbourne, .1 mi. S of State Rte. 734, 1.2 mi. NW of intersection with State
    Rte. 611.

BLUE RIDGE VICINITY   Botetourt County (12)

Gross, Tom, House, SE side of State Rte. 738, 1.5 mi. SW of intersection with
    State Rte. 607.
House, 1.8 mi. SE of Curry Gap, SE side of U.S. Rte. 460, opposite intersection
    with State Rte. 767.
Lunsford House, N bank of Glade Creek, SE side of State Rte. 738, 1.3 mi. SW
    of intersection with State Rte. 607.

BON AIR VICINITY   Chesterfield County (21)

Alandale (Belgrade), .1 mi. N of State Rte. 147, 1.5 mi. SW of intersection with
    State Rte. 673.
Boxwood (Oak Hill), NE side of U.S. Rte. 60, .2 mi. NW of intersection with
    State Rte. 672.
Crow Spring Farm, .1 mi. N of U.S. Rte. 60, .6 mi. NE of intersection with State
    Rte. 678.
Moody's Tavern, S side of U.S. Rte. 60, .2 mi. W of intersection with State Rte.
    678.
Stanford Hill Farm, .4 mi. W of State Rte. 673, .5 mi. NW of intersection with
    State Rte. 147.
Windy Bend, S side of U.S. Rte. 60, 1 mi. W of intersection with State Rte. 678.

BOONES MILL VICINITY   Franklin County (34)

Arthur, John, House, N side of State Rte. 862, NW side of intersection with
    State Rte. 613.

323

Early House, .5 mi. SW of State Rte. 116, .7 mi. N of intersection with State Rte. 684.

Old Mansion House, .1 mi. SW of State Rte. 613, .3 mi. NW of intersection with U.S. Rte. 220.

Taylor, Mark, House, N side of State Rte. 613, .6 mi. NW of intersection with U.S. Rte. 220.

BOONESVILLE VICINITY   Albemarle County (2)

Brightberry, E side of State Rte. 629, .1 mi. N of intersection with State Rte. 624.

Headquarters, NW side of NW end of State Rte. 624, .2 mi. NW of intersection with State Rte. 629.

BOWLING GREEN   Caroline County (17)

Bowling Green Methodist Church, W side of State/U.S. Rte. 2/301, SW corner of intersection with State Rte. 207.

Glassellton, SW side of intersection of State Rte. 2 and U.S. Rte. 301.

BOWLING GREEN VICINITY   Caroline County (17)

Hampton Manor, .6 mi. N of State Rte. 641, .4 mi. NE of intersection with State Rte. 721.

BOYCE VICINITY   Clarke County (22)

Briars, The, .1 mi. SW of State Rte. 620, 1.6 mi. NW of intersection with State Rte. 652.

Chapel Hill, .7 mi. W of U.S. Rte. 340, .2 mi. SW of intersection with State Rte. 633.

Chapel Spring, S side of State Rte. 617, .2 mi. E of intersection with State Rte. 255.

Dearmont Hall, .4 mi. NW of State Rte. 644, at SW corner of intersection with U.S. Rte. 50.

House at New Market, N side of State Rte. 617, .2 mi. NE of intersection with State Rte. 620.

New Market, N side of State Rte. 617, .2 mi. NE of intersection with State Rte. 620.

Pagebrook, .2 mi. N of State Rte. 631, .6 mi. N of State Rte. 723.

BOYD TAVERN   Albemarle County (2)

Boyd Tavern, W side of intersection of State Rtes. 759 and 616.

Ash Lawn, .8 mi. NW of State Rte. 795, 1 mi. SW of intersection with State Rte.
    53.
Limestone, 1 mi. S of U.S. Rte. 250, .8 mi. NW of intersection with State Rte.
    616.
Morven, .8 mi. NW of intersection of State Rtes. 627 and 795, 2.6 mi. SW of
    intersection with State Rte. 53.
Morven Cottage, .9 mi. NW of intersection of State Rtes. 627 and 795, 2.6 mi.
    SW of intersection with State Rte. 53.

BOYDTON   Mecklenburg County (59)

Boyd, Alfred, Store, SW corner of intersection of State Rtes. T756 and T707.
Boyd's Tavern, NW corner of intersection of State Rte. 92 and U.S. Rte. 58.
Boydton Episcopal Church, SE corner of intersection of State Rtes. T1206 and
    T1209.
Boydton Methodist Church, W side of State Rte. T1202, SW corner of inter-
    section with State Rte. T756.
Cedar Crest, NE side of E end of State Rte. T1214.
House, exact location unknown.
Mecklenburg County Courthouse, W side of State Rte. T707, NW corner of inter-
    section with State Rte. T756.
Office Building, SE corner of intersection of State Rtes. T756 and T1202.
Presbyterian Meeting House, W side of State Rte. T1217, SW corner of inter-
    section with State Rte. 1204.
Tailor Shop, SE corner of intersection of State Rtes. T756 and T1202.
Tavern, N side of U.S. Rte. 58, NE corner of intersection with State Rte. 92.
Washington Tavern, SW corner of intersection of State Rtes. T756 and T707.

BOYDTON VICINITY   Mecklenburg County (59)

Berry Hill, .4 mi. NE of intersection of State Rtes. 718 and 826, 1.2 mi. W of
    intersection with State Rte. 717.
Burnett, Pleasant, House, W side of State Rte. 675, .5 mi. NE of intersection
    with U.S. Rte. 58.
China Grove, S side of State Rte. 707, 4.5 mi. SE of intersection with State Rte.
    615.
House, NW side of U.S. Rte. 58, 1.9 mi. NE of intersection with State Rtes. 92
    and 707.
Lofty Oaks, N side of U.S. Rte. 58, 1.1 mi. W of intersection with State Rte. 692.
Main Building, Old Randolph-Macon College, N side of intersection of State Rtes.
    705 and 756, 1.1 mi. SW of intersection with State Rte. 707.
President's House, Old Randolph-Macon College, N side of intersection of State
    Rte. 756 and U.S. Rte. 58, .9 mi. SW of intersection with State Rte. 688.
Professor's House, Old Randolph-Macon College, S side of U.S. Rte. 58, .1 mi. W
    of intersection with State Rte. 756.

Red Lawn Farm (Grymmes), .1 mi. E of State Rte. 693, .5 mi. NW of intersection with U.S. Rte. 58.

Steward's Hall, Old Randolph-Macon College, NW side of U.S. Rte. 58, .6 mi. SW of intersection with State Rte. 688.

Tallwood, .3 mi. W of State Rte. 826, 1.5 mi. N of intersection with State Rte. 718.

Wheatland, .1 mi. N of State Rte. 677, 1.3 mi. SW of intersection with State Rte. 691.

BRACEY VICINITY   Mecklenburg County (59)

Blandon House, .2 mi. NW of State Rte. 617, .6 mi. N of intersection with State Rte. 637.

Little Whitby, .3 mi. N of State Rte. 637, 1.4 mi. NW of intersection with State Rte. 617.

Rogers, George, House, .5 mi. SW of State Rte. 618, .3 mi. N of intersection with State Rte. 627.

St. Tammany, NW side of State Rte. 617, 1.1 mi. N of intersection with State Rte. 637.

Store, E side of State Rte. 618, .3 mi. N of intersection with State Rte. 627.

BRANDY STATION VICINITY   Culpeper County (24)

Arlington, .5 mi. W of State Rte. 685, 1.4 mi. W of intersection with State Rte. 687.

BREMO BLUFF   Fluvanna County (33)

Bremo Recess, .4 mi. NW of U.S. Rte. 15, .8 mi. N of intersection with State Rte. 656.

Glen Arvon, NE side of State Rte. 655, 2.2 mi. SE of intersection with State Rte. 656.

Glen Arvon, Servant's Quarters, NE side of State Rte. 655, 2.2 mi. SE of intersection with State Rte. 656.

Lower Bremo, 1 mi. W of State Rte. 656, at intersection with U.S. Rte. 15.

BREMO BLUFF VICINITY   Fluvanna County (33)

Spring Garden, S side of State Rte. 656, .9 mi. E of intersection with State Rte. 657.

BRIDGETOWN VICINITY   Northampton County (66)

Chatham, .7 mi. N of State Rte. 619, .1 mi. W of intersection with State Rte. 622.

Glebe of Hungars Parish, .1 mi. W of end of State Rte. 622, 1.3 mi. NW of intersection with State Rte. 619.

BRIDGEWATER

Brown House, 111 Main St.
House, 403 N. Main St.

BRIDGEWATER VICINITY

Miller House, .1 mi. NW of State Rte. 42, .4 mi. SW of intersection with State
Rte. 699.

BRISTOL

Akers House, SE corner of Gate City and Osborne Rds.
Dulaney House, 1209 W State St.
House, 639 Broad St.
House, 822 E. Mary St.
House, SW corner of Russell and Edmunds Sts.
Virginia Hotel, NW corner of Front and Sycamore Sts.

BROAD RUN POST OFFICE VICINITY

Stone Mill, S side of State Rte. 628, .1 mi. S of intersection with State Rte. 55.

BROADWAY VICINITY

Chenault House, N end of State Rte. 804, .4 mi. N of intersection with State
Rte. 809.
House, S side of State Rte. 784, .6 mi. W of intersection with State Rte. 617.
Shank House, .3 mi. E of State Rte. 42, 1 mi. S of intersection with State Rte.
786.
Tunker House, .1 mi. S of State Rte. 786, .2 mi. E of intersection with State
Rte. 42.

BRODNAX VICINITY

House, .1 mi. N of State Rte. 623, 1.4 mi. NW of intersection with U.S. Rte. 58.
House, S side of U.S. Rte. 58, .8 mi. E of intersection with State Rte. 623.
Log Cabin, NE side of State Rte. 623, 1.2 mi. NW of intersection with U.S. Rte. 58.

BROWNSBURG

Carson House, SW corner of intersection of State Rtes. 724 and 252.
House, SW corner of intersection of State Rtes. 252 and 762.
McChesney House, NW corner of intersection of State Rtes. 252 and 762.

Bellevue, N side of State Rte. 724, .5 mi. NW of intersection with State Rte. 726.

House (Camp Briar Wood), .8 mi. W of State Rte. 620, 1 mi. N of intersection with State Rte. 726.

Kennedy House, .5 mi. S of State Rte. 606, 1.5 mi. SE of intersection with State Rte. 604.

Kennedy Mill, W side of intersection of State Rtes. 604 and 606, .8 mi. NE of intersection with State Rte. 721.

Level Loop, SW side of State Rte. 724, .9 mi. W of intersection with State Rte. 729.

McFadden House, N side of State Rte. 606, .8 mi. NE of intersection with State Rte. 721.

Mulberry Grove, S side of State Rte. 724, 1 mi. SE of intersection with State Rte. 252.

New Providence Presbyterian Church, SW corner of intersection of State Rtes. 726 and 252, .9 mi. N of intersection with State Rte. 606.

Stuart House, .1 mi. W of State Rte. 602, .4 mi. N of intersection with State Rte. 724.

Wilson House (Holbrook Farm), .2 mi. SE of State Rte. 717, .3 mi. E of intersection with State Rte. 724.

BRUINGTON VICINITY   King and Queen County (49)

Brewington, .2 mi. E of State Rte. 14, .7 mi. S of intersection with State Rte. 631.

Bruington Church, 1 mi. W of Garnetts Creek, W side of State Rte. 14.

Erin (Bruington Parsonage), .1 mi. N of State Rte. 631, .1 mi. E of intersection with State Rte. 14.

Locust Hill, .9 mi. W of Garnetts Creek, .1 mi. E of State Rte. 14.

Smyrna Church, S side of State Rte. 620, opposite intersection with State Rte. 631.

BUCHANAN   Botetourt County (12)

Buchanan Presbyterian Church, W side of Main (High), St., between Washington and Pine Sts.

Douthat House, W side of Water (Lower) St., between Pine and Washington Sts.

Hotel Botetourt, NW corner of Water (Lower) and Washington Sts.

Trinity Episcopal Church, E side Main (High) St., between Washington and Bedford Sts.

Valentine House, E side Main (High) St., between Bedford and Exchange Sts.

Wilson Warehouse, N corner of intersection of Water (Lower) and Washington Sts.

BUCHANAN VICINITY   Botetourt County (12)

Finney House, .2 mi. NW of U.S. Rte. 11, .6 mi. N of intersection with State Rte. 43.

Greyledge, .4 mi. N of State Rte. 611, 1 mi. N of intersection with U.S. Rte. 11 (I-81).

Spreading Springs Farm, SE side of U.S. Rte. 11, .9 mi. NE of intersection with State Rte. 622.

BUCKINGHAM

Buckingham County Courthouse, N side of U.S. Rte. 60, SW side of intersection with State Rte. 633.

Buckingham Hotel, SE corner of intersection of U.S. Rte. 60, .3 mi. NE of intersection with State Rte. 638.

Buckingham Inn, S side of U.S. Rte. 60, .1 mi. SW of intersection with State Rte. 633.

Forbes House, S side of U.S. Rte. 60, .1 mi. NE of intersection with State Rte. 633.

Leach House, .1 mi. N of U.S. Rte. 60, .3 mi. NE of intersection with State Rte. 633.

Presbyterian Manse, S side of U.S. Rte. 60, .2 mi. NE of intersection with State Rte. 633.

Rose Terrace, S side of U.S. Rte. 60, E side of intersection with State Rte. 638.

Tavern, S side of U.S. Rte. 60, .1 mi. SW of intersection with State Rte. 633.

Trenton, .1 mi. N of U.S. Rte. 60, E side of intersection with State Rte. 638.

Trinity Presbyterian Church, .1 mi. N of intersection of U.S. Rte. 60 and State Rte. 638.

West View, N side of U.S. Rte. 60, .2 mi. NE of intersection with State Rte. 633.

Woodside, .4 mi. S of U.S. Rte. 60, .5 mi. E of intersection with State Rte. 633.

BUCKINGHAM VICINITY

Algoma, N side of State Rte. 653, 1.1 mi. NE of intersection with State Rte. 602.

Col Alto, S side of State Rte. 601, .2 mi. NW of intersection with State Rte. 602.

Hermitage, .2 mi. S of State Rte. 652, 1.2 mi. SE of intersection with State Rte. 667.

House, .1 mi. N of State Rte. 604, .3 mi. E of intersection with State Rte. 668.

Magnolia Hill, SE side of State Rte. 729, .6 mi. E of intersection with State Rte. 605.

Mount Pleasant, .5 mi. SE of State Rte. 602, 1.6 mi. N of intersection with State Rte. 659.

Mt. Hermon Baptist Church, NW corner of intersection of State Rtes. 606 and 604, 2.2 mi. W of intersection with State Rte. 667.

Old Hundred Farm, .1 mi. E of State Rte. 652, .1 mi. SE of intersection with State Rte. 607.

Rolfeton, N side of NE end of State Rte. 749, 1.1 mi. NE of intersection with State Rte. 648.

Shepherd House, N side of State Rte. 690, .2 mi. SE of intersection with U.S. Rte. 60.

Traveler's Rest, N side of N end of State Rte. 604, .5 mi. N of intersection with State Rte. 693.

Twin Oaks, .2 mi. N of State Rte. 604, .2 mi. E of intersection with State Rte. 605.

BUENA VISTA

Green Forest, 723 W. 29th St.

Southern Seminary, Main Building, intersection of Ivy and Park Aves.

BUENA VISTA VICINITY   Rockbridge County (82)

Fruit Hill, .3 mi. W of State Rte. 671, .7 mi. S of intersection with State Rte. 700.

Hamilton Galbrith House, SE side of State Rte. 608, .4 mi. SW of intersection with State Rte. 699.

Hamilton, John, House, .2 mi. SW of State Rte. 699, .8 mi. SE of intersection with State Rte. 608.

Jordan Furnace, SE side of State Rte. 608, .1 mi. SW of intersection with State Rte. 631.

Jordan Furnace Commissary, W corner of intersection of State Rtes. 608 and 631, .8 mi. SE of intersection with State Rte. 704.

Jordan House, W corner of intersection of State Rtes. 608 and 631, .8 mi. SE of intersection with State Rte. 704.

Rose Hill, 1.5 mi. NW of State Rte. 671, .6 mi. NW of intersection with State Rte. 698.

Rose Lawn, NW side of State Rte. 608, .8 mi. SW of intersection with State Rte. 699.

Tuscan Villa, .3 mi. S of State Rte. 608, 1.1 mi. SW of intersection with State Rte. 631.

BUFFALO JUNCTION VICINITY   Mecklenburg County (59)

Cold Hill, S side of State Rte. 731, .4 mi. W of intersection with State Rtes. 767 and 732.

Rebel Hill, NW corner of intersection of State Rte. 732 and U.S. Rte. 58, .6 mi. NW of intersection with U.S. Rte. 58 and State Rte. 735.

River Side Farm, NE side of State Rte. 722, .1 mi. SE of intersection with State Rte. 749.

White House, N side of State Rte. 602, .1 mi. W of intersection with State Rte. 735.

White House, Old, N side of State Rte. 602, .2 mi. W of intersection with State Rte. 735.

BUMPASS   Louisa County (55)

Bumpass House, W side of intersection of State Rtes. 601 and 701, .4 mi. S of
    intersection of State Rte. 652.

BUMPASS VICINITY   Louisa County (55)

Bear Castle, .4 mi. NE of State Rte. 690, 1.2 mi. SE of intersection with State
    Rte. 614.
Elk Creek Baptist Church, NE side of State Rte. 652, .4 mi. NW of intersection
    with State Rte. 614.
Ellerslie, .2 mi. NE of State Rte. 614, .4 mi. N of intersection with State Rte. 690.
Jerdone Castle, .6 mi. NE of State Rte. 652, .4 mi. NW of intersection with State
    Rte. 622.

BURGESS VICINITY   Dinwiddie County (27)

Evergreens, The, .4 mi. E of Gravelly Run, .1 mi. S of U.S. Rte. 1, 1 mi. SW of
    intersection with State Rte. 660.
House, .1 mi. S of State Rte. 613, 1 mi. W of intersection with State Rte. 631.
Steers' Mill, W side of State Rte. 670, .3 mi. N of intersection with State Rte. 613.

BURKES GARDEN VICINITY   Tazewell County (93)

Wynne, John, House, NE side of State Rte. 61, 4.5 mi. W of intersection with
    State Rte. 623.

BURKEVILLE VICINITY   Nottoway County (68)

Inverness, S side of State Rte. 624, 1.1 mi. E of intersection with State Rte. 723.

CABIN POINT   Surry County (91)

Clerestory House, W side of State Rte. 10, opposite intersection with State Rte.
    613.
House, E side of State Rte. 10, immediately S of intersection with State Rte. 613.

CABIN POINT VICINITY   Surry County (91)

Montpelier, .2 mi. S of State Rte. 602, 1.6 mi. E of intersection with State Rte.
    611.

CALLANDS   Pittsylvania County (72)

First Pittsylvania County Jail, E side of State Rte. 969, .5 mi. NW of intersection
    with State Rte. 57.
Old Clerk's Office (Moorman House), W side of State Rte. 969, .5 mi. NW of
    intersection with State Rte. 57.

CALLANDS VICINITY   Pittsylvania County (72)

Arnn Store, N side of State Rte. 57, .4 mi. E of intersection with State Rte. 969.
Moorman, Achilles H., House, .1 mi. W of State Rte. 969, .5 mi. NW of inter-
    section with State Rte. 57.
Swanson House, .2 mi. S of S end of State Rte. 1127, .2 mi. S of intersection
    with State Rte. 932.

CALLAWAY VICINITY   Franklin County (34)

Price, Cyrus, House, NE side of State Rte. 643, .2 mi. NW of intersection with
    State Rte. 744.

CAPEVILLE VICINITY   Northampton County (66)

Milford, .2 mi. E of State Rte. 600, 2.8 mi. N of intersection with State Rte.
    683.

CARET VICINITY   Essex County (29)

Greenway, .1 mi. N of State Rte. 627, 4.4 mi. W of State Rte. 717.
Lily Mount, .5 mi. SW of U.S. Rte. 17, 1.3 mi. NW of intersection with State
    Rte. 624.
Mahockney, .3 mi. W of State Rte. 627, .4 mi. W of intersection with State Rte.
    716.
Paynefield, .4 mi. SE of State Rte. 627, .7 mi. W of intersection with State Rte.
    716.
Rockland, .3 mi. N of State Rte. 627, 1.7 mi. W of intersection with State Rte.
    716.

CARROLLTON   Isle of Wight County (47)

Carroll's Shop, E corner of intersection of State Rtes. 665 and 670.

CARROLLTON VICINITY
Isle of Wight County (47)

House, E side of State Rte. 10/32, .6 mi. S of intersection with State Rte. 604.

CARRSVILLE VICINITY
Isle of Wight County (47)

House, E side of U.S. Rte. 258, .3 mi. N of intersection with U.S. Rte. 58.
House Site, .3 mi. E of State Rte. 641, .8 mi. NE of intersection with State Rte. 696.
Oak Crest, NE side of State Rte. 616, 1.6 mi. SE of intersection with U.S. Rte. 58.

CARSON VICINITY
Dinwiddie County (27)

Tabernacle Church, E side of State Rte. 667, 1.4 mi. S of intersection with State Rte. 703.

CARTERSVILLE
Cumberland County (25)

Baptist Parsonage, NW side of State Rte. 649, .1 mi. NE of intersection with State Rte. 45.
Deanery, .1 mi. NW of intersection of State Rtes. 649 and 45.
Palmore, SE side of State Rte. 665, .1 mi. N of intersection with State Rte. 45.
St. James Episcopal Church, W side of State Rte. 45, .2 mi. SW of intersection with State Rte. 649.

CARTERSVILLE VICINITY
Cumberland County (25)

Chantilly, NW side of State Rte. 45, .5 mi. SW of intersection with State Rte. 649.
Morven, NW side of State Rte. 45, .7 mi. SW of intersection with State Rte. 649.

CASANOVA VICINITY
Fauquier County (31)

Weston, at end of State Rte. 747, 1 mi. E of Casanova.

CASCADE VICINITY
Pittsylvania County (72)

Bachelor's Hall, .5 mi. W of Childress Creek, E side of State Rte. 863, .8 mi. NE of intersection with State Rte. 874.
Berry Hill, SE side of State Rte. 863, .3 mi. W of intersection with State Rte. 880.
Cherry Hill, SW corner of intersection of State Rtes. 870 and 872, 2.3 mi. SE of intersection with U.S. Rte. 58.
Micheaux, .3 mi. NW of State Rte. 859, .8 mi. SE of intersection with State Rte. 622.

Oak Hill, .1 mi. S of intersection of State Rtes. 863 and 862, 2.4 mi. SE of intersection with State Rte. 621.

Oak Ridge (The Pink House), SE side of State Rte. 863, .2 mi. NE of intersection with State Rte. 874.

Windsor, .2 mi. E of State Rte. 861, 2.3 mi. S of intersection with State Rte. 621.

CASTLETON VICINITY   Rappahannock County (79)

Alta-Vista, .2 mi. W of State Rte. 626, .8 mi. N of intersection with State Rte. 618.

CATAWBA   Halifax County (42)

House, SE side of State Rte. 603, .1 mi. SW of intersection with State Rte. 644.

CATAWBA VICINITY   Roanoke County (81)

Brillhart, Daniel, House, S side of State Rte. 624, 1.4 mi. W of intersection with State Rte. 697.

Doosing House, N side of State Rte. 785, 1.9 mi. NE of intersection with State Rte. 697.

Woods House, S side of State Rte. 785, 6.8 mi. NE of intersection with State Rte. 697.

CENTER CROSS VICINITY   Essex County (29)

Colnbrook, .6 mi. SW of State Rte. 602, .3 mi. SE of intersection with U.S. Rte. 17.

Greenfield, .1 mi. S of State Rte. 684, .9 mi. W of intersection with U.S. Rte. 17.

South Hill, .1 mi. E of State Rte. 656, .5 mi. E of intersection with State Rte. 644.

CENTREVILLE   Fairfax County (30)

Centreville Methodist Church, 13941 Braddock Rd.

Level Green, 14000 Stull Rd.

Royal Oaks, E side of Braddock Rd., .1 mi. N of intersection with U.S. Rte. 29.

CENTREVILLE VICINITY   Fairfax County (30)

Cabell's Mill and Miller's House, 5235 Centreville Rd.

CERES VICINITY   Bland County (11)

Crabtree, John, House, SE side of State Rte. 42, 1.1 mi. SW of intersection with
    State Rte. 625.

CHAMPLAIN VICINITY   Essex County (29)

Blandfield, 1.2 mi. NW of U.S. Rte. 17, 1.4 mi. SE of intersection with State
    Rte. 631.
Linden, .2 mi. SW of U.S. Rte. 17, .7 mi. SE of intersection with State Rte. 631.
Poverty Ridge, .3 mi. NE of U.S. Rte. 17, .8 mi. SE of intersection with State
    Rte. 631.
St. Matthew's Episcopal Church, E side of State Rte. 633, .1 mi. N of inter-
    section with U.S. Rte. 17.

CHANCE   Essex County (29)

Glencairn, .2 mi. S of U.S. Rte. 17, .4 mi. N of intersection with State Rte. 637.

CHANCELLOR VICINITY   Spotsylvania County (89)

Beauclaire, .1 mi. W of Long Branch, .5 mi. SW of State Rte. 620, 1.9 mi. E of
    intersection with State Rte. 639.

CHANTILLY VICINITY   Fairfax County (30)

Ayre House, 13110 Lee-Jackson Hwy.
Hermitage, 14530 Lee Rd.
Leeton, 4619 Centreville Rd.
Mitchell's Tavern, 13623 Lee-Jackson Hwy.
Tunlaw, Dulles International Airport Vicinity.

CHARLES CITY   Charles City County (19)

Charles City County Jail, S side of State Rte. 5, .2 mi. SW of intersection with
    State Rte. 155.

CHARLES CITY VICINITY   Charles City County (19)

Belle Air, .4 mi. N of State Rte. 5, .4 mi. E of intersection with State Rte. 155.
Colesville, .2 mi. N of State Rte. 5, .2 mi. E of intersection with State Rte. 618.
Edna's Mill, NW side of State Rte. 609, 1 mi. SE of intersection with State Rte.
    600.

Edna's Mill House, SE side of State Rte. 609, 1 mi. SE of intersection with State Rte. 600.

House (Burlington), S side of State Rte. 5, .6 mi. E of intersection with State Rte. 619.

Kittiewan, 1.3 mi. S of State Rte. 619, 1 mi. S of intersection with State Rte. 5.

Mount Sterling, .2 mi. NE of State Rte. 155, 1.6 mi. S of intersection with State Rte. 629.

Mount Sterling Outbuildings, .2 mi. NE of State Rte. 155, 1.6 mi. S of intersection with State Rte. 629.

Oak Hill, .4 mi. E of State Rte. 5, 1.9 mi. E of intersection with State Rte. 619.

Poplar Springs, .4 mi. S of State Rte. 615, 2 mi. E of intersection with State Rte. 614.

River Edge, .4 mi. S of State Rte. 5, .4 mi. E of intersection with State Rte. 618.

Tettington, E side of State Rte. 613, .3 mi. SW of intersection with State Rte. 617.

Toma Hund, 1.1 mi. S of State Rte. 5, 2.7 mi. SE of intersection with State Rte. 623.

Upper Shirley, .1 mi. NW of State Rte. 608, 1.4 mi. W of intersection with State Rte. 5.

Upper Weyanoke, .4 mi. W of State Rte. 619, 3.5 mi. S of intersection with State Rte. 5.

Westover Church, .3 mi. S of State Rte. 5, .4 mi. E of intersection with State Rte. 609.

CHARLOTTE COURT HOUSE   Charlotte County (20)

Charlotte County Courthouse, E side of intersection of State Rtes. 40 and 47.

Diamond Hill, N side of State Rte. 40, .1 mi. W of intersection with State Rte. 47.

House, S side of State Rte. 40, SW corner of intersection with State Rte. 47.

Marshall, Judge Hunter, House (Charlotte County Public Library), W side of State Rte. 47, SW corner of intersection with State Rte. 40.

Masonic Lodge, NW side of intersection of State Rtes. 40 and 47.

Mt. Tirzah Baptist Church, E side of State Rte. 47, .1 mi. N of intersection with State Rte. T1103.

Old County Records Office, E side of State Rte. 47, SE corner of intersection with State Rte. 40.

Presbyterian Manse, S side of State Rte. 40, .5 mi. W of intersection with State Rte 47.

Rose (Wynyard), .3 mi. N of State Rte. 40, .3 mi. W of intersection with State Rte. 47.

Store, NW side of intersection of State Rtes. 40 and 47.

Tankersley Tavern, NW side of intersection of State Rtes. 40 and 47.

Village Presbyterian Church, W side of State Rte. 47, .1 mi. SE of intersection with State Rte. 40.

Ville View, .3 mi. NW of State Rte. 40, .5 mi. W of intersection with State Rte. 47.

Watkins Office, NW side of intersection of State Rtes. 40 and 47.

Watkins Tavern, SE side of State Rte. 40, .1 mi. NE of intersection with State Rte. 47.

Arcadia, .5 mi. SW of State Rte. 47, 1 mi. SE of intersection with State Rte. 40.
Edgehill, .6 mi. SE of State Rte. 656, .4 mi. S of intersection with State Rte. 604.
Greenfield, .1 mi. E of State Rte. 656, .6 mi. N of intersection with State Rte. 40.
House, .3 mi. W of State Rte. 746, .4 mi. N of intersection with State Rte. 619.
Moldavia, .3 mi. NW of State Rte. 40, 1 mi. NE of intersection with State Rte. T1103.
Wardsfork, .3 mi. E of State Rte. 40, .5 mi. SE of intersection with State Rte. 682.
Woodfork, E side of State Rte. 650, 2.8 mi. NW of intersection with State Rte. 47.

CHARLOTTESVILLE   Albemarle County (2)

Albemarle County Courthouse, Court Square
Albemarle Female Institute, NE corner of intersection of E. Jefferson and Tenth Sts.
Farm, The, 1201 E. Jefferson St.
House, 1215 W. Main St.
Jones, Col. John R., House, 109 E. Jefferson St.
Lewis, Nicholas, House, 309 Twelfth St.
Locust Grove, 810 Locust Ave.
Montebello, 1 Montebello Cle.
Oaklawn, SW corner of Cherry and Ninth Sts.

CHARLOTTESVILLE VICINITY   Albemarle County (2)

Birdwood, .2 mi. S of U.S. Rte. 250, .5 mi. NW of intersection with U.S. (BYP) Rte. 29.
Brookhill, .5 mi. SE of U.S. Rte. 29, .5 mi. NE of intersection with State Rte. 643.
Buena Vista, W side of State Rte. 20, 1.6 mi. NE of intersection with U.S. Rte. 250.
Dunlora, 1.4 mi. NE of State Rte. 631, .8 mi. SE of intersection with U.S. Rte. 29.
Edgemont, .3 mi. NW of intersection of State Rtes. 612 and 20, .9 mi. NE of intersection with State Rte. 621.
Franklin, .3 mi. E of State Rte. 20, 1.3 mi. NE of intersection with U.S. Rte. 250.
Hollymead, .9 mi. SE of U.S. Rte. 29, 1.4 mi. NE of intersection with State Rte. 643.
Land's End, .3 mi. S of State Rte. 784, .3 mi. W of intersection with State Rte. 600.
Michie Tavern, SW side of State Rte. 53, .8 mi. SE of intersection with State Rte. 20.
Old Ordinary (Burnley's Tavern), W side of State Rte. 20, 2 mi. NE of intersection with U.S. Rte. 250.
Red Hills, .2 mi. E of State Rte. 643, 1.9 mi. E of intersection with U.S. Rte. 29.

Ridgeway, .8 mi. NW of State Rte. 20, 3.3 mi. NE of intersection with U.S. Rte. 250.

Riggory, The, .1 mi. SE of State Rte. 20, .2 mi. NE of intersection with State Rte. 649.

Rock House (Cochran's Mill), .2 mi. SE of State Rte. 20, .3 mi. NE of intersection with State Rte. 649.

Sunnyside, SW side of State Rte. 654, .4 mi. NW of intersection with U.S. Rte. 29.

Tufton, .3 mi. N of State Rte. 732, .6 mi. E of intersection with State Rte. 53.

Tufton Stone Wing, .3 mi. N of State Rte. 732, .6 mi. E of intersection with State Rte. 53.

Windie Knowe, E side of State Rte. 20, 2.5 mi. NE of intersection with U.S. Rte. 250.

CHASE CITY VICINITY   Mecklenburg County (59)

House, NE side of State Rte. 47, .8 mi. SE of intersection of State Rtes. 622 and 662.

House, E side of State Rte. 92, 1.5 mi. SE of intersection with State Rte. 688.

House, .2 mi. E of State Rte. 92, 1.3 mi. SE of intersection with State Rte. 688.

Reveille, SE side of State Rte. 685, 1 mi. S of intersection with State Rte. 49.

CHATHAM   Pittsylvania County (72)

Blue Cottage, E side of State Rte. T1408, .1 mi. N of intersection with State Rte. 832.

Davis Tavern, E side of U.S. Rte. 29, .2 mi. N of intersection with State Rte. 832.

Morea (Quencus Manor), W side of State Rte. 29, .1 mi. S of intersection with State Rte. T1403.

Pittsylvania County Clerk's Office, Court Place.

Weir, Hugh, House, S side of State Rte. T1405, .1 mi. E of intersection with U.S. Rte. 29.

CHATHAM VICINITY   Pittsylvania County (72)

Belle Grove, .5 mi. N of State Rte. 703, 1.1 mi. NE of intersection with U.S. Rte. 29.

Cabell-Shelton House (Cedar Hill), E side of State Rte. 649, 1.3 mi. SE of intersection with State Rte. 691.

Cherbourg Cottage, S side of State Rte. 691, 1 mi. E of intersection with State Rte. 649.

Coles Hill, .1 mi. NE of State Rte. 690, .6 mi. SE of intersection with State Rte. 685.

Eldon, N side of intersection of Rtes. 685 and 703, 1 mi. E of intersection with U.S. Rte. 29.

First Pittsylvania County Clerk's Office, W side of State Rte. 799, .8 mi. NW of intersection with State Rte. 57.

House (Hargraves House), N side of intersection of State Rtes. 689 and 695, 1.8 mi. NE of intersection with State Rte. 649.

Little Cherrystone (Wooding), .1 mi. N of State Rte. 703, .1 mi. N of intersection with State Rte. 832.

Mountain View, .5 mi. S of State Rte. 703, .5 mi. W of intersection with State Rte. 704.

Oakland, .1 mi. W of U.S. Rte. 29, .4 mi. S of intersection with State Rte. 704.

Pineville (Pinecrest Farm), .3 mi. W of State Rte. 649, .1 mi. SE of intersection with State Rte. 691.

CHECK VICINITY   Floyd County (32)

Jack House, SW side of State Rte. 648, 1.5 mi. E of intersection with U.S. Rte. 221.

Paul House, NW side of State Rte. 651, .9 mi. SW of intersection with State Rte. 641.

CHERITON VICINITY   Northampton County (66)

Town Fields, .2 mi. NW of State Rte. 640, 1.6 mi. SW of intersection with State Rte. 639.

CHESTER VICINITY   Chesterfield County (21)

Clay House, S side of intersection of State Rte. 618, .3 mi. E of intersection with U.S. Rte. I-95.

Halfway House, E side of U.S. Rte. 1/301, 1.2 mi. N of intersection with State Rte. 616.

Hedgelawn, .2 mi. N of State Rte. 637, .3 mi. N of intersection with State Rte. 145.

CHESTERFIELD   Chesterfield County (21)

Castlewood, SE side of State Rte. 903, .1 mi. NE of intersection with State Rte. 10.

Greenyard, .2 mi. W of State Rte. 10, .3 mi. S of intersection with State Rte. 145.

Magnolia Grange, S side of State Rte. 10, .1 mi. E of intersection with State Rte. 655.

Wrexham, SE corner of intersection of State Rtes. 145 and 10.

CHESTERFIELD VICINITY   Chesterfield County (21)

Belmont Manor, NW side of State Rte. 651, .5 mi. SW of intersection with State Rte. 643.

Brown-Clay House, .2 mi. E of State Rte. 649, 1.8 mi. NE of intersection with State Rtes. 604 and 651.

CHRISTIANSBURG   Montgomery County (61)

Bank of Christiansburg, 4 E. Main St.
Christiansburg Presbyterian Church, 100 block W. Main St.
Clark-Montague-Crush House, 109 E. Main St.
Masonic Hall, 22 S. Franklin St.
Montgomery County Courthouse, SE corner of S. Franklin and E. Main Sts.
Phlegar-Taylor House, 20 S. Franklin St.

CHUCKATUCK   Nansemond County (62)

House, SE corner of intersection of State Rtes. 125 and 10/32.
House, NE corner of intersection of State Rtes. 125 and 10/32.

CHUCKATUCK VICINITY   Nansemond County (62)

House, N side of intersection of State Rtes. 601 and 603.
St. John's Episcopal Church, N side of State Rte. 125, .5 mi. SE of intersection with State Rte. 628.

CHULA VICINITY   Amelia County (4)

Dykeland, .1 mi. S of State Rte. 636, 1.1 mi. W of intersection with State Rte. 604.
Egglestetton, .1 mi. N of State Rte. 630, .6 mi. W of intersection with State Rte. 609.
Giles Mill, E side of State Rte. 609, 2.2 mi. N of intersection with State Rte. 616.
Grub Hill Church (St. John's Episcopal Church), W side of State Rte. 609, .3 mi. SW of intersection with State Rte. 636.
Wigwam, .2 mi. N of State Rte. 637, .3 mi. NE of intersection with State Rte. 636.

CHURCH ROAD VICINITY   Dinwiddie County (27)

Denmark, N side of N end of State Rte. 736, .3 mi. NW of intersection with State Rte. 611.

Castle Hill, .8 mi. NW of State Rte. 231, 2 mi. NE of intersection with State Rte. 600.

Cismont Manor, .4 mi. NW of State Rte. 22, .3 mi. SW of intersection with State Rte. 648.

Cloverfields, .5 mi. NW of State Rte. 22, 1.1 mi. SW of intersection with State Rte. 231.

Cloverfields Cottage, .5 mi. NW of State Rte. 22, 1.1 mi. SW of intersection with State Rte. 231.

Cloverfields Outbuildings, .5 mi. NW of State Rte. 22, 1.1 mi. SW of intersection with State Rte. 231.

Fairmont, .1 mi. N of intersection of State Rtes. 20 and 600, 5.2 mi. NW of intersection with State Rte. 231.

Findowrie (Aspen Grove), .5 mi. SW of State Rte. 600, 1.3 mi. S of intersection with State Rte. 22.

Glebe of St. Anne's Parish, .6 mi. NW of State Rte. 22, 1.1 mi. SW of intersection with State Rte. 231.

Grace Church, SE side of State Rte. 231, .5 mi. NE of intersection with State Rtes. 231 and 600.

Hopedale (Holly Fork), .2 mi. NW of State Rte. 231, .2 mi. NE of intersection with State Rte. 740.

Maxfield, S side of SE end of State Rte. 647, 1.3 mi. SE of intersection with State Rte. 22.

Merrie Mill, SW side of State Rte. 783, .5 mi. SE of intersection with State Rte. 231.

Piedmont Manor, .4 mi. SE of State Rte. 20, .8 mi. NE of intersection with State Rte. 641.

Blue Creek Manor, S corner of intersection of State Rtes. T1105 and T1109.

Clarksville Presbyterian Church (now Second Baptist Church), N corner of intersection of U.S. Rte. 15 and State Rte. T1104.

House, E corner of intersection of State Rte. T1108 and U.S. Rte. 15.

House, N corner of intersection of State Rtes. T750 and 49.

House, NW side of State Rte. T1108, .1 mi. NE of intersection with State Rte. T1105.

House, S corner of intersection of State Rtes. T1103 and T1107.

House, SE side of State Rte. 49, .1 mi. SW of intersection with State Rte. T1107.

House, SW side of State Rte. T1107, .1 mi. SE of intersection with State Rte. T1103.

House, SW side of State Rte. T1107, .1 mi. SE of intersection with State Rte. 49.

House, .2 mi. NW of State Rte. 49, .3 mi. NE of intersection with State Rte. T1106.

Moss Factory Tenement House, NW side of intersection of State Rtes. 49 and T1107.

Moss Tobacco Factory, NW side of intersection of U.S. Rte. 58 and State Rte. T1107.

Sheldale, E corner of intersection of State Rtes. T1106 and T1123.

Sunnyside, NW corner of intersection of State Rte. 723 and U.S. Rte. 15.

CLARKSVILLE VICINITY   Mecklenburg County (59)

Cedar Grove, .5 mi. S of State Rte. 724, .9 mi. SE of intersection with State Rte. 723.

House, NE side of State Rte. 857, .5 mi. NW of intersection with U.S. Rte.15.

Midway, .4 mi. SW of State Rte. 700, .1 mi. W of intersection with U.S. Rte. 15.

Mistletoe Castle, SE side of intersection of State Rte. 702 and U.S. Rte. 58, 1.1 mi. E of intersection with U.S. Rte. 15.

Oakley, .1 mi. N of State Rte. 640, .8 mi. SW of intersection with State Rte. 609.

Prestwould Outbuildings, .9 mi. SW of U.S. Rte. 15, .4 mi. NW of intersection with State Rte. 49.

Wheatland, .4 mi. N of State Rte. 640, .6 mi. NW of intersection with State Rte. 699.

CLAYVILLE VICINITY   Powhatan County (73)

Genito Ordinary, NW side of State Rte. 604, .2 mi. SW of intersection with State Rte. 603.

Grace Church, NE side of State Rte. 603, .5 mi. NW of intersection with State Rte. 604.

Paxton, N side of intersection of State Rtes. 603 and 604, .8 mi. W of intersection with State Rte. 610.

Seven Oaks, .1 mi. E of State Rte. 610, .3 mi. N of intersection with State Rte. 602.

CLIFFORD   Amherst County (5)

St. Mark's Church, E side of State Rte. 151, .2 mi. S of intersection with State Rte. 610.

Winton, .1 mi. W of State Rte. 151, .4 mi. S of intersection with State Rte. 610.

CLIFFORD VICINITY   Amherst County (5)

Fair View, .4 mi. SE of State Rte. 778, .2 mi. SW of intersection with State Rte. 621.

Geddes (Naked Creek), .3 mi. N of State Rte. 700, .4 mi. N of intersection with State Rte. 662.

House, SE side of State Rte. 619, 1.6 mi. SW of intersection with State Rte. 735.

Long Ridge, .4 mi. S of U.S. Rte. 60, 1 mi. W of intersection with State Rte. 631.

Mountain View, .2 mi. N of U.S. Rte. 29, .2 mi. NE of intersection with State Rte. 610.

Tusculum, .4 mi. W of U.S. Rte. 29, .3 mi. SW of intersection with State Rte. 610.

CLINCHPORT VICINITY   Scott County (85)

Brick Church (Rye Cove Primitive Baptist Church), N side of State Rte. 65, .9 mi. NE of intersection with State Rte. 647.

CLINTWOOD   Dickenson County (26)

Dickenson County Courthouse, NW side of intersection of State Rtes. T1001 and T607.

CLOVER VICINITY   Halifax County (42)

Black Walnut, .2 mi. W of State Rte. 600, 1.4 mi. N of intersection with U.S. Rte. 360.

House, SE side of State Rte. 621, .6 mi. SW of intersection with State Rtes. 603 and 746.

House, NW side of State Rte. 621, .6 mi. SW of intersection with State Rtes. 603 and 746.

House, .2 mi. SE of State Rte. 621, .8 mi. SW of intersection with State Rtes. 603 and 746.

Mt. Laurel Episcopal Church, SE side of State Rte. 621, .8 mi. SW of intersection with State Rtes. 603 and 746.

Mt. Laurel Mill, .1 mi. W of State Rte. 780, .5 mi. N of intersection with State Rte. 746.

CLUSTER SPRINGS VICINITY   Halifax County (42)

House, W side of State Rte. 707, .5 mi. S of intersection with State Rte. 658.

House, .1 mi. S of State Rte. 658, .4 mi. S of intersection with State Rte. 704.

House, NE side of State Rte. 741, 2 mi. SE of intersection with State Rte. 658.

COBHAM VICINITY   Albemarle County (2)

Turkey Hill (Keswick), .7 mi. NE of State Rte. 640, .6 mi. NW of intersection with State Rte. 231.

Walker Mill, NW side of State Rte. 231, 2.6 mi. NE of intersection with State Rte. 615.

COLOGNE VICINITY   King and Queen County (49)

Buena Vista, SW side of State Rte. 14, .1 mi. SE of intersection with State Rte.
    601.

COLONIAL BEACH VICINITY   Westmoreland County (97)

Shellfield, .1 mi. N of State Rte. 205, 1.4 mi. NE of intersection with State
    Rte. 758.

COLONIAL HEIGHTS   Chesterfield County (21)

Conjurors Neck, .2 mi. N of NE end of Conduit Rd., 2.9 mi. NE of intersection
    with U.S. Rte. I-95.

COLUMBIA   Fluvanna County (33)

St. John's Episcopal Church, NW side of State Rte. T1104, between State Rtes.
    6 and T1101.

COLUMBIA VICINITY   Fluvanna County (33)

Oaks, The, N side of State Rte. 603, 1.4 mi. SE of intersection with State Rte.
    601.
Point of Fork, .3 mi. E of State Rte. 656, .2 mi. S of intersection with State
    Rte. 6.

CORBIN   Caroline County (17)

Grace Episcopal Church, E side of State Rte. 2, .2 mi. S of intersection with
    State Rte. 610.

CORBIN VICINITY   Caroline County (17)

Locust Hill, SE side of State Rte. 606, 1.5 mi. SW of intersection with State
    Rte. 607.
Mill Hill, .1 mi. NE of State Rte. 609, .5 mi. SE of intersection with State Rte.
    607.
Santee, .6 mi. N of State Rte. 610, 1.9 mi. NE of intersection with State Rte. 2.
South Brook, NE side of State Rte. 609, .2 mi. N of intersection with State
    Rte. 606.

COURTLAND   Southampton County (88)

Kello, Samuel, House (Reese House), SW corner of U.S. Rte. 58 and State Rte.
    611.
Mahone Hotel, N side of U.S. Rte. 58, 500 ft. N of intersection with State Rte.
    1510.
Rochelle House, N side of U.S. Rte. 58, 500 ft. S of intersection with State Rte.
    1510.
Southampton County Courthouse, S side of U.S. Rte. 58, opposite State Rte.
    1510.

COURTLAND VICINITY   Southampton County (88)

Beechwood, .1 mi. S of State Rte. 646, .1 mi. E of intersection with State Rte.
    643.
Ricks, Robert, House, .1 mi. E of State Rte. 616, .9 mi. NE of intersection with
    State Rte. 728.

COVINGTON

Alleghany County Courthouse, NW corner of Court and Main Sts.
Bishop House, 214 Riverside Ave. W.
Clark House, 212 Riverside Ave. W.
House, 130 Riverside Ave. W.
House, SE corner of Main and Court Sts.

COVINGTON VICINITY   Alleghany County (3)

High House, N side of U.S. Rte. 60, .4 mi. N of intersection with State Rte. 600.
Humpback Bridge, .1 mi. S of U.S. Rte. 60, .6 mi. SW of intersection with State
    Rte. 651.
Milton Hall, .4 mi. NW of State Rte. 600, N side of intersection with U.S. Rte.
    I-64.
Rose Dale, 504 Midland Trail Rd.

CRAIG SPRINGS   Craig County (23)

Craig Springs, N side of State Rte. 658, .2 mi. W of intersection with State Rte.
    635.

CRITZ VICINITY
Patrick County (71)

Poplar Grove, .2 mi. NW of State Rte. 626, .4 mi. N of intersection with State Rte. 701.

Reynolds House, E side of State Rte. 798, .5 mi. N of intersection with State Rte. 626.

CROUCH VICINITY
King and Queen County (49)

Smith, Thomas, Sr., House, SW side of State Rte. 612, .2 mi. NW of intersection with State Rte. 617.

CROZET VICINITY
Albemarle County (2)

Cedars, The, N side of U.S. Rte. 250, .2 mi. W of intersection with State Rte. 689.

Long House, S side of U.S. Rte. 250, .2 mi. W of intersection with State Rte. 689.

Mountain View, W side of State Rte. 684, .3 mi. S of intersection with State Rte. 691.

Seven Oaks, .1 mi. N of U.S. Rte. 250, .8 mi. W of intersection with State Rte. 689.

Seven Oaks, Old House, .1 mi. N of U.S. Rte. 250, .8 mi. W of intersection with State Rte. 689.

Temple Hill, N side of State Rte. 682, .7 mi. SW of intersection with State Rte. 787.

CROZIER VICINITY
Goochland County (38)

Contention, W side of State Rte. 628, 1.3 mi. S of intersection with State Rte. 6.

Dover, E side of State Rte. 642, 1 mi. N of intersection with State Rte. 6.

Dover Stable, E side of State Rte. 642, .5 mi. N of intersection with State Rte. 6.

Sabot Hill Barn, .2 mi. N of State Rte. 6, .6 mi. SE of intersection with State Rte. 642.

CULPEPER
Culpeper County (24)

Culpeper County Courthouse, 156 Davis St.

Hill Mansion, 501 East St.

St. Stephen's Episcopal Church, E side of East St., between Davis and Cameron Sts.

CULPEPER VICINITY
Culpeper County (24)

Forest Grove, .1 mi. SE of State Rte. 720, 1 mi. S of intersection with State Rte. 686.

Green Valley (Val Verde), .5 mi. W of intersection of State Rte. 15 and U.S. Rte. 692, 2.3 mi. SW of intersection with State Rte. 686.

Greenwood, SE side of U.S. Rte. 15, 1 mi. SW of intersection with U.S. Rte. 29.
Redwood, .5 mi. S of U.S. Rte. 522, 1.3 mi. NW of intersection with U.S. Rte. 29.
Wheatland Farm, .6 mi. SE of State Rte. 699, 1 mi. E of intersection with U.S. Rte. 15/29.

CUMBERLAND   Cumberland County (25)

Center Presbyterian Church, NW side of U.S. Rte. 60, .4 mi. SW of intersection with State Rte. 600.
Cumberland County Jail, W side of intersection of U.S. Rte. 60 and State Rte. 600.

CUMBERLAND VICINITY   Cumberland County (25)

Brick House (Trenton), .5 mi. NW of intersection of State Rtes. 628 and 629, 1 mi. SW of intersection with State Rte. 666.
Grace Episcopal Church, N side of State Rte. 632, .6 mi. SW of intersection with U.S. Rte. 60.
Hors Du Monde, .4 mi. S of State Rte. 600, .4 mi. SW of intersection with State Rte. 620.
Inglewood, W side of State Rte. 627, 1 mi. NW of intersection with State Rtes. 629 and 622.
Langhorne House, .1 mi. NW of State Rte. 45, 1.5 mi. SW of intersection with State Rte. 633.
Langhorne Tavern, .1 mi. SE of State Rte. 45, 1.5 mi. SW of intersection with State Rte. 633.
Locust Level, .1 mi. S of intersection of State Rtes. 631 and 45, .6 mi. S of intersection with State Rte. 669.
West Hill, W side of State Rte. 600, .8 mi. S of intersection with State Rte. 638.

CUMNOR VICINITY   King and Queen County (49)

Fair Oaks, E side of State Rte. 617, 1.4 mi. S of intersection with State Rte. 616.
Liberty Hall, SW corner of intersection of State Rtes. 617 and 616, 1.8 mi. E of intersection with State Rte. 600.
Mattaponi Church, .1 mi. NW of State Rte. 14, .5 mi. SW of intersection with State Rte. 618.
Plain Dealing, .6 mi. N of State Rte. 612, .2 mi. N of intersection with State Rte. 617.
Rose Garden, W side of State Rte. 617, .9 mi. S of intersection with State Rte. 616.
Spring Hill, .2 mi. N of State Rte. 612, 1.2 mi. NE of intersection with State Rte. 630.
Woodlawn, 1.2 mi. N of State Rte. 617, 1.4 mi. NW of intersection with State Rte. 614.

DALEVILLE VICINITY

Botetourt County (12)

Daleville College Administration Building, .2 mi. S of U.S. Rte. 220, .4 mi. S of intersection with State Rte. 779.

Daleville College Normal Building, W side of U.S. Rte. 220, .6 mi. S of intersection with State Rte. 779.

Gish, Christian, House, W side of U.S. Rte. 220, .5 mi. S of intersection with State Rte. 779.

Gish-Nininger House, .2 mi. S of U.S. Rte. 220, .4 mi. S of intersection with State Rte. 779.

Nininger Hall, .1 mi. S of U.S. Rte. 220, .4 mi. S of intersection with State Rte. 779.

Whitehouse, The, .2 mi. E of U.S. Rte. 11, .6 mi. S of intersection with State Rte. 654.

DAMASCUS VICINITY

Washington County (96)

House, W side of intersection of State Rtes. 711 and 710, .9 mi. S of intersection with State Rte. 783.

DANIELTOWN VICINITY

Brunswick County (13)

Mt. Donum Outbuilding, .6 mi. NE of N tributary of Sturgeon Creek, .1 mi. S of State Rte. 643, 1.5 mi. E of intersection with State Rte. 644.

Rocky Run Methodist Church, .1 mi. W of S end of State Rte. 616, .2 mi. E of intersection with State Rte. 689.

Roslin, .6 mi. N of State Rte. 643, 1.5 mi. E of intersection with State Rte. 644.

DANVILLE

Church of the Epiphany, 781 Main St.

Danville Technical Institute, SW corner of Kemper Rd. and S. Main St.

House, 862 Main St.

House, S corner of intersection of Main and Ridge Sts.

House, SW side of U.S. Rte. 58, 1.2 mi. W of intersection with State Rte. 51.

Lanier House, 770 Main St.

Schoolfield, John H., House, 944 Main St.

Stratford College, 1189 Main St.

Sutherlin House (Confederate Memorial), SE side of U.S. Rte. 29, .2 mi. NE of intersection with State Rte. 86.

DANVILLE VICINITY

Pittsylvania County (72)

Bent Oaks, SW corner of intersection of State Rte. 873 and U.S. Rte. 58, .6 mi. W of intersection with State Rte. 968.

DARLINGTON HEIGHTS   Prince Edward County (74)

Haverhill, at S end of State Rte. 733, .7 mi. S of intersection with State Rte. 657.

DARLINGTON HEIGHTS VICINITY   Prince Edward County (74)

Buffalo Church, W side of State Rte. 659, .3 mi. S of intersection with State Rte. 658.

DAYTON   Rockingham County (83)

Harrison House, NW side of State Rte. 42, .2 mi. NE of intersection with State Rte. T775.

DEEP CREEK

Hendren-Creekmur House, W side of George Washington Hwy. (U.S. Rte. 17), .2 mi. N of intersection with Shell Rd., near Chesapeake.

DELAPLANE VICINITY   Fauquier County (31)

Ashland, .1 mi. W of State Rte. 712, .5 mi. N of intersection with U.S. Rte. 17.
Ashleigh, .2 mi. SW of U.S. Rte. 17, .2 mi. S of intersection with State Rte. 731.
Aspen Dale, .2 mi. S of State Rte. 55, 1.6 mi. W of intersection with U.S. Rte. 17.
Carrington, .2 mi. S of State Rte. 729, 1.7 mi. S of intersection with State Rte. 55.
Cool Spring Methodist Church, N side of State Rte. 731, .6 mi. W of intersection with U.S. Rte. 17.
Emmanuel Episcopal Church, NE corner of intersection of U.S. Rte. 17 and State Rte. 713.
Grove, The, E side of U.S. Rte. 17, .6 mi. S of intersection with State Rte. 713.
Waverly, .2 mi. SE of State Rte. 731, .6 mi. W of intersection with U.S. Rte. 17.
Woodside, .1 mi. S of State Rte. 713, .6 mi. NE of intersection with U.S. Rte. 17.
Yew Hill, NW corner of intersection of U.S. Rte. 17 and State Rte. 731.

DENDRON VICINITY   Surry County (91)

Cedar Ridge, N side of State Rte. 604, 2 mi. SE of intersection with State Rte. 617.

DENNISTON VICINITY   Halifax County (42)

Denniston Tavern, NW side of State Rte. 711, 1.5 mi. NE of intersection with State Rte. 707.

Berryman House, .5 mi. E of State Rte. 743, 1.9 mi. E of intersection with State Rte. 622.

Brown, Beverly, II, House, N side of State Rte. 617, 1.8 mi. E of intersection with U.S. Rte. 15.

Cacerta, E side of U.S. Rte. 15, 2 mi. S of intersection with State Rte. 621.

Caryswood (Page, Edward Trent, House), .8 mi. E of State Rte. 667, 1.8 mi. N of intersection with State Rte. 650.

Chellowe, W side of State Rte. 623, 1 mi. SW of intersection with U.S. Rte. 60.

Clermont, .5 mi. S of State Rte. 617, 5 mi. E of intersection with U.S. Rte. 15.

Clifton, S side of State Rte. 636, .3 mi. W of intersection with U.S. Rte. 15.

Francisco, Peter, House, .9 mi. S of S end of State Rte. 629, .4 mi. S of intersection with U.S. Rte. 60.

Rosny, .4 mi. N of State Rte. 629, 3 mi. SE of intersection with U.S. Rte. 15.

Saratoga, .4 mi. W of intersection of State Rtes. 600 and 623, 2.9 mi. E of intersection with U.S. Rte. 15.

Union Hill, N side of State Rte. 650, 1 mi. NE of intersection with State Rte. 626.

West, John S., Tavern, N side of State Rte. 617, 1.8 mi. E of intersection with U.S. Rte. 15.

DINWIDDIE   Dinwiddie County (27)

Calvary Episcopal Church, E side of State Rte. 619, SE corner of intersection with U.S. Rte. 1.

Dinwiddie County Courthouse, W side of State Rte. 619, SW corner of intersection with U.S. Rte. 1.

Lebanon Methodist Church, .1 mi. S of U.S. Rte. 1, W side of intersection with State Rte. 619.

Ridgeway, .1 mi. N of U.S. Rte. 1, W side of intersection with State Rte. 619.

Scott's Law Office, N side of U.S. Rte. 1, .1 mi. W of intersection with State Rte. 619.

DISPUTANTA VICINITY   Prince George County (75)

Aberdeen, .1 mi. W of State Rte. 10, .3 mi. NW of intersection with State Rte. 625.

Brandon Church, N side of intersection of State Rtes. 1201 (Rte. 611) and 10, .4 mi. E of intersection with State Rte. 614.

House, .2 mi. N of State Rte. 611, 1.5 mi. E of intersection with State Rte. 625.

Lees Mill, E side of State Rte. 156, 1.4 mi. SW of intersection with State Rte. 626.

Old Town, .4 mi. NE of State Rte. 666, 1.4 mi. N of intersection with State Rte. 616.

DITCHLEY VICINITY

Northumberland County (67)

Cobbs Hall, at end of State Rte. 690, .7 mi. E of intersection with State Rte. 669.
Morattico Baptist Church, W side of State Rte. 679, .1 mi. NW of intersection with State Rte. 200.

DIXIE VICINITY

Fluvanna County (33)

Hill Grove, .2 mi. N of State Rte. 628, .6 mi. N of intersection with State Rte. 6.

DOGUE VICINITY

King George County (50)

Bleak Hill, W side of State Rte. 637, .5 mi. S of intersection with State Rte. 3.
Millbank, at S end of State Rte. 631, 1.3 mi. S of intersection with State Rte. 607, .8 mi. W of intersection with U.S. Rte. 301.
Powhatan, .6 mi. NW of State Rte. 610, .5 mi. NE of intersection with State Rte. 607.
Rokeby, .6 mi. N of State Rte. 3, .2 mi. NE of intersection with State Rte. 607.

DOSWELL VICINITY

Hanover County (43)

Doswell House, .1 mi. S of State Rte. 685, .5 mi. SW of intersection with State Rte. 684.

DOWNINGS VICINITY

Richmond County (80)

Woodford, approx. 7 mi. from Downings, exact location unknown.

DRAKES BRANCH VICINITY

Charlotte County (20)

Do Better, N side of State Rte. 643, .4 mi. SW of intersection with State Rte. 642.
House, 1.3 mi. E of State Rte. 47, 1.5 mi. N of intersection with State Rte. 59.
Ingleside, 1.5 mi. NE of State Rte. 47, 1.5 mi. N of intersection with State Rte. 59.
Pine Grove, N side of State Rte. 59, 1.1 mi. E of intersection with State Rte. 654.

DRAPER VICINITY

Pulaski County (78)

Honaker House, E side of service road for U.S. Rte. I-81, 1 mi. NE of intersection with State Rte. 658.

351

Darden House, .4 mi. NE of State Rte. 629, .2 mi. N of intersection with State Rte. 125.

Glebe Church, N side of State Rte. 337, .2 mi. E of intersection with State Rte. 125.

DUBLIN   Pulaski County (78)

House, SE side of State Rte. T747, .1 mi. NE of intersection with State Rte. T746.

DUBLIN VICINITY   Pulaski County (78)

Anderson, William, House, .7 mi. S of State Rte. 627, 1.6 mi. E of intersection with State Rte. 100.

Back Creek Farm, .5 mi. SW of State Rte. 100, .8 mi. NW of intersection with State Rte. 627.

Belhampton, .4 mi. N of State Rte. 627, 2.5 mi. E of intersection with State Rte. 100.

Belspring Presbyterian Church (now residence), E side of State Rte. 677, .1 mi. E of intersection with State Rte. 600.

Ingles Ferry, N side of N end of State Rte. 611, .9 mi. N of intersection with State Rte. 624.

Oakshade, N side of State Rte. 628, 1.5 mi. NW of intersection with State Rte. 100.

Sifford House, S side of State Rte. 600, 5.4 mi. NW of intersection with U.S. Rte. 11.

DUNNSVILLE   Essex County (29)

Hundley Hall, NE side of State Rte. 1101, .1 mi. SE of intersection with State Rte. 611.

Rappahannock Christian Church, NE corner of intersection of State Rtes. 1101 and 611.

DUNNSVILLE VICINITY   Essex County (29)

Bellevue, .6 mi. SE of State Rte. 611, 2.9 mi. NE of intersection with U.S. Rte. 17.

Fairview, W side of State Rte. 616, 1 mi. N of intersection with State Rte. 611.

Woodland, NE side of U.S. Rte. 17, .7 mi. NW of intersection with State Rte. 611.

EARLYSVILLE   Albemarle County (2)

Buck Mountain Church, E side of State Rte. 743.

EARLYSVILLE VICINITY   Albemarle County (2)

Bel Aire, NW side of State Rte. 606, 2.4 mi. NE of intersection with State Rte.
    649.
Clover Hill, .3 mi. W of State Rte. 743, 1.4 mi. SW of intersection with State
    Rte. 643.
Wakefield, .9 mi. NE of State Rte. 743, .1 mi. SE of intersection with State
    Rte. 660.

EASTVILLE   Northampton County (66)

Christ Episcopal Church, W side of U.S. Rte. 13, .2 mi. N of intersection with
    State Rte. 631.
Ingleside, .2 mi. SE of State Rte. 631, .4 mi. E of intersection with U.S. Rte. 13.
Park Hall, .1 mi. S of State Rte. 631, .1 mi. E of intersection with U.S. Rte. 13.

EASTVILLE VICINITY   Northampton County (66)

Brickhouse, .4 mi. NW of State Rte. 674, .4 mi. NW of intersection with U.S.
    Rte. 13.
Elkington, .5 mi. NW of NW end of State Rte. 665, .4 mi. NW of intersection
    with State Rtes. 666 and 634.
Old Castle, S end of State Rte. 665, 1.5 mi. SW of intersection with State Rte.
    634.
Oak Grove, 1.2 mi. N of State Rte. 630, 1.3 mi. NW of intersection with U.S.
    Rte. 13.
Pembroke, N side of State Rte. 630, 2.6 mi. NW of intersection with U.S. Rte. 13.
Westover, .5 mi. NE of State Rte. 630, .8 mi. NW of intersection with U.S. Rte.
    13.
White Cliffs, .3 mi. NE of State Rte. 666, 1.2 mi. NW of intersection with State
    Rte. 634.

ELK HILL   Goochland County (38)

Elk Hill, .5 mi. E of State Rte. 608, 1.5 mi. SW of intersection with State Rte. 6.

ELKTON VICINITY

Rockingham County (83)

Kite House, SW side of State Rte. 623, .6 mi. SE of intersection with State Rte. 759.

Miller, Adam, House, .1 mi. W of U.S. Rte. 340, .2 mi. N of intersection with State Rte. 633.

ELLISTON VICINITY

Montgomery County (61)

Big Spring, .1 mi. NE of U.S. Rte. 11/460, .4 mi. S of intersection with State Rte. 631.

EMPORIA

Greensville County (41)

Butt's Tavern, S end of Reese Ave., at intersection with Park Ave.
Greensville County Clerk's Office, NE corner of E. Main St. and Brunswick Ave.
Greensville County Courthouse, E. Main St., N of Brunswick Ave.
Village View, 221 Briggs St.

EPWORTH VICINITY

King William County (51)

Brighton, .4 mi. S of State Rte. 608, .5 mi. E of intersection with State Rte. 607.
Edge Hill (Plain View), .4 mi. N of State Rte. 628, 1.6 mi. SW of intersection with State Rte. 608.
Greenmont, .2 mi. SW of State Rte. 600, .4 mi. NW of intersection with State Rte. 628.
Smyrna, .1 mi. S of State Rte. 604, .2 mi. SE of intersection with State Rte. 614.
Wakefield, .5 mi. SW of State Rte. 600, 1 mi. NW of intersection with State Rte. 609.

ESMONT VICINITY

Albemarle County (2)

Esmont, .3 mi. W of State Rte. 627, .6 mi. N of intersection with State Rte. 6.
Esmont, Outbuildings, .3 mi. W of State Rte. 627, .6 mi. N of intersection with State Rte. 6.
Hampstead (Belle Gate Farm), .4 mi. W of State Rte. 715, .6 mi. N of intersection with State Rte. 6.
Hampstead (Belle Gate Farm), Outbuilding, .4 mi. W of State Rte. 715, .6 mi. N of intersection with State Rte. 6.
Mountain Grove, .2 mi. E of State Rte. 717, .6 mi. NE of intersection with State Rte. 755.
Tallwood, .1 mi. NW of State Rte. 627, 1 mi. N of intersection with State Rte. 715.
Woodville, .3 mi. W of State Rte. 627, .1 mi. NW of intersection with State Rte. 715.

EVINGTON VICINITY   Campbell County (16)

Federal Hill, .3 mi. SW of State Rte. 623, .7 mi. N of intersection with State
    Rte. 297.

EWING   Lee County (53)

Fulkerson, Dow, House, N side of U.S. Rte. 58, .1 mi. SW of intersection with
    State Rte. 724.

EWING VICINITY   Lee County (53)

Ball, Smith, House, N side of State Rte. 684, .2 mi. NW of intersection with U.S.
    Rte. 58.
Ely, William, House, N side of U.S. Rte. 58, .1 mi. W of intersection with State
    Rte. 690.
Ewing, William Smith, House (McLin House), N side of U.S. Rte. 58, .1 mi. NE
    of intersection with State Rte. 682.

EXMORE VICINITY   Northampton County (66)

End View, .2 mi. E of State Rte. 618, .5 mi. SW of intersection with State Rte.
    607.

FABER VICINITY   Nelson County (63)

Waveland, .5 mi. SE of State Rte. 632, .3 mi. N of intersection with State Rte. 6.

FAIRFAX

Draper, Dr. S., House, 10364 E. Main St.
Earp's Ordinary, 10386 E. Main St.
Fairfax County Courthouse, 4000 Chain Bridge Rd.
Ford, Antonia, House, 3977 Chain Bridge Rd.
Gunnell, Joshua Coffer, House, 4023 Chain Bridge Rd.

FAIRFIELD   Rockbridge County (82)

House, W corner of intersection of State Rte. 710 and U.S. Rte. 11.
Methodist Parsonage, W corner of intersection of State Rte. 710 and U.S. Rte. 11.

Associate Reformed Presbyterian Church, SE side of U.S. Rte. 11, .2 mi. SW of intersection with State Rte. 716.

Cherry Grove, NW side of U.S. Rte. 11, .9 mi. SW of intersection with State Rte. 710.

Mackey House, 1 mi. E of State Rte. 716, 1 mi. S of intersection with U.S. Rte. 11.

Maple Hall (First House), .1 mi. N of U.S. Rte. 11, .5 mi. SW of intersection with State Rte. 716.

Maple Hall (Second House), NW side of intersection of State Rte. 785 and U.S. Rte. 11, .5 mi. SW of intersection with State Rte. 716.

Rocky Hollow, .5 mi. SE of State Rte. 711, .4 mi. SE of intersection with State Rte. 706.

Timber Ridge Plantation, W side of State Rte. 785, .1 mi. S of intersection with U.S. Rte. 11.

Timber Ridge Presbyterian Church, SE side of U.S. Rte. 11, .3 mi. SW of intersection with State Rte. 716.

Treavy House, N corner of intersection of State Rtes. 712 and 710.

FALMOUTH   Stafford County (90)

Belmont, N side of State Rte. 1001, .4 mi. SE of intersection with U.S. Rte. 17.
Carlton, 501 Melcher's Dr.

FALMOUTH VICINITY   Stafford County (90)

Berea Baptist Church, NE corner of intersection of State Rtes. 750 and 654, immediately E of intersection of U.S. Rte. 17 and State Rte. 654.

FANCY GAP VICINITY   Carroll County (18)

Allen, Sidna, House, E side of U.S. Rte. 52, .1 mi. NE of intersection with State Rte. 685.

Puckett's Cabin, N side of Blue Ridge Pkwy., S side of State Rte. 608, .5 mi. SE of intersection with State Rte. 641.

FARMVILLE VICINITY   Prince Edward County (74)

Appomattox Presbyterian Church, SE corner of intersection of U.S. Rte. 460 and State Rte. 645.

Brown's Presbyterian Church, SE side of State Rte. 638, 1.3 mi. NE of intersection with State Rte. 653.

Chatham, E side of State Rte. 603, .1 mi. N of intersection with U.S. Rte. 460.

Hay Market, .3 mi. NE of U.S. Rte. 460, .9 mi. S of intersection with State Rte. 45, .1 mi. E of Farmville's E boundary.

Locust Grove, .5 mi. N of State Rte. 658, 2.1 mi. W of intersection with State Rte. 643.

FARNHAM VICINITY   Richmond County (80)

Farnham Baptist Church, S side of State Rte. 608, .5 mi. SW of intersection with State Rte. 3.

FERNCLIFF VICINITY   Louisa County (55)

Hall's Tavern, W corner of intersection of State Rtes. 689 and 615, .5 mi. NW of intersection with U.S. Rte. 250.

House, W side of State Rte. 649, .4 mi. N of intersection with State Rte. 640.

Locust Hill, NE side of State Rte. 600, .6 mi. N of intersection with State Rte. 627.

Mill View, .7 mi. SE of State Rte. 613, 2 mi. NE of intersection with U.S. Rte. 250.

Prospect Hill, .1 mi. NW of State Rte. 613, 3 mi. NE of intersection with U.S. Rte. 250.

Spring Grove, .4 mi. N of State Rte. 600, 1.2 mi. NW of intersection with State Rte. 627.

FERRUM VICINITY   Franklin County (34)

Bleak Hill, .1 mi. SE of State Rte. 640, .2 mi. NE of intersection with State Rte. 602.

Wade, Benjamin, House, E side of State Rte. 767, 3.9 mi. S of intersection with State Rte. 623.

FIELDALE VICINITY   Henry County (45)

Hillcroft, NE corner of intersection of State Rtes. 609 and 683, 1.4 mi. S of intersection with State Rte. 681.

FIFE VICINITY   Goochland County (38)

Perkins Baptist Church, N side of State Rte. 606, .7 mi. NE of intersection with State Rte. 610.

Tinsleyville Tavern, SE side of State Rte. 603, .1 mi. S of intersection with State Rte. 667.

Ammen, Benjamin, House, NW corner of U.S. Rte. 220 and Back St.

Big Spring, NE corner of Back and Water Sts., and Market House, SE corner of
   Back and Water Sts.

Blacksmith Shop, S side of W. Main St., between Catawba and Roanoke Sts.

Botetourt County Courthouse, NW corner Main and Roanoke Sts.

Carper House, 202 Carper St.

Chair Factory, 19 Murray St.

Christian-Holmes House, 312 Back St.

Fellers, Wallace, House, 137 Church St.

Figgatt, Capt. James H., House, 20 Main St.

Fincastle Herald Office, S side of Main St., between Roanoke and Catawba Sts.

Fincastle Methodist Church, E side of Church St., between Academy St. and
   Griffin Alley.

Fincastle Presbyterian Church, NW corner Church and Back Sts.

First Baptist Church, S side of State Rte. 606, .1 mi. SE of intersection with
   State Rte. T1210.

Gray's Folly (Prospect), E of Church St., in SE Fincastle.

Hayth's Hotel, 13-19 Roanoke St.

House, 119 Jefferson St.

House, 201 Main St.

Jail, W. Main St., between Catawba and Roanoke Sts.

Kyle, Robert, House and Store, 101 Main St.

Kyle, William and David, House, 123 Main St.

Peck-Figgatt House, 322 Main St.

Potter's Shop, 312 Back St.

Price House, 25 Main St.

St. Mark's Episcopal Church, W side of Roanoke St., between Griffin Alley and
   Murray St.

Simmons House, 302 Main St.

Thompson-Carper House, 110 Roanoke St.

Western Hotel, SW corner of Back and Roanoke Sts.

FINCASTLE VICINITY   Botetourt County (12)

Glencoe, .2 mi. SE of State Rte. 681, 1.1 mi. NE of intersection with State Rte.
   630.

Grove Hill, .4 mi. N of State Rte. 606, .3 mi. E of intersection with State Rte.
   600.

Hawthorn Hall, N side of State Rte. 600, .4 mi. W of intersection with State Rte.
   668.

Mineral Spring House, S side of State Rte. 606, 1.4 mi. E of intersection with
   State Rte. 630.

Promised Land, .4 mi. W of State Rte. 655, .2 mi. N of intersection with U.S.
   Rte. 220.

Santillane, .2 mi. W of U.S. Rte. 220, .3 mi. S of intersection with State Rte. 606.

Spring House, W side of U.S. Rte. 220, .2 mi. N of intersection with State Rte. 1204.

Wheatland Manor, NE side of State Rte. 639, .2 mi. SE of intersection with State Rte. 732.

Willoma, .5 mi. W of State Rte. 220, .3 mi. S of intersection with State Rte. 655.

FINE CREEK MILLS VICINITY
Powhatan County (73)

Greenwood, .1 mi. N of State Rte. 711, 1 mi. E of intersection with State Rte. 615.

FISHERVILLE VICINITY
Augusta County (8)

Old Stone Fort (William Johnson House), .1 mi. W of State Rte. 608, 1.4 mi. N of intersection with State Rte. 796.

FLINT HILL VICINITY
Rappahannock County (79)

Clifton, E side of State Rte. 729, .8 mi. SE of intersection with State Rte. 522.

Locust Grove, .4 mi. E of U.S. Rte. 522, .8 mi. N of intersection with State Rte. 647.

FLOYD
Floyd County (39)

Floyd County Courthouse, NE corner of intersection of State Rte. 8 and U.S. Rte. 221.

Floyd Methodist Church, NW side of intersection of U.S. Rte. 221 and State Rte. T615.

Floyd Presbyterian Church, S side of U.S. Rte. 221, .2 mi. E of intersection with State Rte. 8.

House, S side of U.S. Rte. 221, .2 mi. W of intersection with State Rte. 8.

Stuart House, W side of State Rte. 8, .3 mi. N of intersection with U.S. Rte. 221.

FLOYD VICINITY
Floyd County (32)

Eberle Mill, S side of State Rte. 714, .3 mi. NE of intersection with State Rte. 8.

West Fork Primitive Baptist Church, N side of U.S. Rte. 221, .3 mi. W of intersection with State Rte. 726.

FOREST VICINITY
Bedford County (10)

Cedars, The, NW side of State Rte. 811, .6 mi. W of intersection with State Rte. 623.

Elk Hill, .2 mi. W of State Rte. 663, 3.9 mi. NW of intersection with U.S. Rte. 460.

House, S side of State Rte. 666, 2.8 mi. SW of intersection with U.S. Rte. 460.

Liberty Hall, N side of State Rte. 297, .3 mi. W of intersection with State Rte. 811.

Perrow Place (Berkeley), .2 mi. SW of State Rte. 663, 3.1 mi. NW of intersection with U.S. Rte. 460.

St.˙ Stephen's Episcopal Church, NE side of State Rte. 663, .5 mi. NW of intersection with State Rte. 662.

Woodburne, .1 mi. W of State Rte. 609, .3 mi. N of intersection with U.S. Rte. 460.

FORK UNION   Fluvanna County (33)

Fork Union Baptist Church, E side of U.S. Rte. 15, N of intersection with State Rte. 652, adjacent to Fork Union Military Academy.

FORK UNION VICINITY   Fluvanna County (33)

Melrose, SW side of State Rte. 640, .1 mi. S of intersection with State Rte. 650.

Mount Airy, E side of S end of State Rte. 646, 3.8 mi. S of intersection with State Rte. 6.

FORT DEFIANCE VICINITY   Augusta County (8)

Belvidere, .1 mi. SW of State Rte. 777, 1.2 mi. SE of intersection with U.S. Rte. I-81.

FORT LEE VICINITY   Henrico County (44)

Varina Farm, .9 mi. S of S end of Varina Rd., 1.6 mi. SE of intersection with Kingsland Rd.

FOSTERS FALLS VICINITY   Wythe County (99)

Graham, Major David, House, .2 mi. W of intersection of State Rtes. 626 and 619, 1.4 mi. N of intersection with State Rte. 752.

FRANKLIN VICINITY   Southampton County (88)

Bowers House, .4 mi. E of State Rte. 635, .6 mi. NE of intersection with State Rte. 611.

FRANKTOWN   Northampton County (66)

Crystal Palace, S corner of intersection of State Rtes. 618 and 609.

FRANKTOWN VICINITY   Northampton County (66)

Wellington, .2 mi. N of State Rte. 609, .8 mi. W of intersection with State Rte.
    610.

FREDERICKS HALL VICINITY   Louisa County (55)

Fredericks Hall, E side of State Rte. 656, .5 mi. SW of intersection with State
    Rte. 618.
Hermitage, The, E side of State Rte. 656, 1 mi. SW of intersection with State
    Rte. 689.
Hope's Tavern, E side of U.S. Rte. 33, .5 mi. SE of intersection with State Rte.
    609.
Oaksby, .7 mi. NW of State Rte. 609, 2.2 mi. SW of intersection with State Rte.
    618.
Pottie, George, House, SE side of State Rte. 650, 1.1 mi. NE of intersection with
    State Rte. 680.
Woodlawn, .1 mi. E of State Rte. 650, .8 mi. NE of intersection with State Rte.
    680.

FREDERICKSBURG

Allen, James, House, 1008 Princess Anne St.
Allen, John, House, 1106 Princess Anne St.
Baylor-Wells House, 818 Sophia St.
Brayhead, 117 Lee Dr.
Carter House, 1100 Charles St.
Chew House (Stoner's Museum), 1202 Prince Edward St.
Chimneys, The, 623 Caroline St.
Clear View, 420 Forbes St.
Corbin House, NW corner of Charles and Lewis Sts.
Dabney, Herndon, House (The National Bank of Fredericksburg), SW corner of
    Princess Anne and George Sts.
Dick, Charles, House, 1107 Princess Anne St.
Dixon-Maury House, 214 Caroline St.
Duncan, Alexander, House (Oxford Shop), SW corner of Caroline and William Sts.
Ellis, Robert, House, 718 Princess Anne St.
First Christian Church, 1115 Caroline St.
Fredericksburg Baptist Church, SE corner of Amelia and Princess Anne Sts.
Fredericksburg Charity School, 1119 Caroline St.
Fredericksburg City Hall, E corner of intersection of Princess Anne and William
    Sts.

Fredericksburg Courthouse, E side of Princess Anne St., between George and Hanover Sts.

Fredericksburg Presbyterian Church, SE corner of Princess Anne and George Sts.

Goodwin, Arthur, House, 1202 Charles St.

Gordon, Basil, House, SW corner of Caroline and Lewis Sts.

Hackley-Monroe House, 301 Caroline St.

House, 300 Caroline St.

House, 309 Caroline St.

House, 611 Caroline St.

House (Betty Washington Inn), 1112 Charles St.

Lewis-Daniel House, 1300 Charles St.

Lewis, George, House (Steamboat House), 1116 Prince Edward St.

Lewis, John, House, 801 Hanover St.

Macky, John, House (Macky's Folly), 1201 Princess Anne St.

Masonic Lodge No. 4, NW corner of Princess Anne and Hanover Sts.

Mercer, Dr. Hugh, Apothecary Shop, 1020 Caroline St.

Methodist Church, 310 Hanover St.

Millstones, 1200 William St.

Monroe, James, Law Office, S side of Charles St., between George and William Sts.

Mortimer, Dr. Charles, House, 213 Caroline St.

Mortimer, Dr. Charles, House, 303 Caroline St.

St. George's Episcopal Church, NW corner of Princess Anne and George Sts.

St. George's Parish House and School, N side of Princess Anne St., between Commerce or William and George Sts.

St. Mary's Catholic Church, S side of Caroline St., between Charlotte and Hanover Sts.

Scotia, 1204 Charles St.

Sligo, 1100 Dixon St.

Smithsonia (Female Orphan Asylum), 307 Amelia St.

Stevenson, Charles L., House, 303 Amelia St.

Stone-Marye House, 1111 Princess Anne St.

Wellford, Dr. Robert, House, 1501 Caroline St.

Wilford, Dr. Carter, House, 408 Hanover St.

Williams, John, House, 211 Caroline St.

Willis Warehouse, 826-28 Caroline St.

Yates-Carmichael House, 309 Hanover St.

FREDERICKSBURG VICINITY   Spotsylvania County (89)

Belvidere, .7 mi. NE of U.S. Rte. 17, .8 mi. NE of intersection with State Rte. 2.

Breeze Land, .5 mi. S of State Rte. 208, 1.1 mi. SW of intersection with U.S. Rte. 1.

Fall Hill, .4 mi. NW of State Rte. 639, .7 mi. W of intersection with U.S. Rte. 1.

La-Vue, .9 mi. S of State Rte. 608, 1.2 mi. S of intersection with State Rte. 636.

Nottingham, .4 mi. NW of U.S. Rte. 17, .8 mi. NE of intersection with State Rte. 2.

St. Julian, .6 mi. W of State Rte. 2, .8 mi. S of intersection with U.S. Rte. 17.
Sherwood Forest, .1 mi. W of State Rte. 3, .7 mi. SE of intersection with State
   Rte. 601.

FREEMAN VICINITY   Brunswick County (13)

House, W side of State Rte. 712, .3 mi. N of intersection with State Rte. 608.
Smoky Ordinary, Dependency, NW side of State Rte. 712, .5 mi. NE of intersection with State Rte. 634.

FRIES VICINITY   Grayson County (39)

First Court of Grayson County, SW side of State Rte. 651, .6 mi. NW of intersection with State Rte. 805.
Spring Valley Post Office, SE side of State Rte. 777, .5 mi. NE of intersection
   with State Rte. 805.

FRONT ROYAL   Warren County (94)

Ardham, NE corner of intersection of Jackson Lane and S. Commerce St.
Bel Aire, SW corner of intersection of Braxton and Happy Creek Rds.
Colonial, The, 25 S. Royal Ave.
Front House, E side of Chester St., between Peyton and Manassas Sts.
Jones-Clarke House, 10 High St.
Warren County Courthouse, S side of intersection of E. Main and Crescent Sts.
Weaver House, E side of Royal Ave., between Peyton Ave. and Crescent St.

FRONT ROYAL VICINITY   Warren County (94)

Chapel Hill, .1 mi. W of U.S. Rte. 522/340, .9 mi. NE of intersection with State
   Rte. 655.
Erin, .1 mi. NE of U.S. Rte. 522/340, .3 mi. NE of intersection with State Rte.
   639
Guard Hill, W side of intersection of State Rte. 637 and U.S. Rte. 522/340,
   .5 mi. N of intersection with State Rte. 55.
McKay, Robert, House, N side of State Rte. 627, .1 mi. W of intersection with
   U.S. Rte. 522/340.
Mountain Home, N side of U.S. Rte. 522, 1.3 mi. SE of intersection with State
   Rte. 604.
River Bend, .6 mi. NW of intersection of State Rte. 607 and U.S. Rte. 340,
   3.5 mi. SW of intersection with Skyline Drive.
Riverside, W side of U.S. Rte. 522/340, 2.4 mi. N of intersection with State
   Rte. 55.

GALAX VICINITY   Grayson County (39)

Old Town Clerk's Office (U.S. Post Office), SW corner of intersection of State
   Rtes. 634 and 640, .6 mi. W of intersection with State Rte. 780.
Old Town Courthouse, N side of intersection of State Rte. 634 and 640, .6 mi.
   W of intersection with State Rte. 780.

GATE CITY   Scott County (85)

Jail (Scott County Health Department), N corner of intersection of State Rtes.
   665 and 71.
Scott County Courthouse, N corner of intersection of State Rtes. 665 and 71.

GLADE SPRING VICINITY   Washington County (96)

Brook Hall, S side of U.S. Rte. 11, .8 mi. SW of intersection with State Rte. 767.
DeBusk Mill, NE corner of intersection of State Rtes. 605 and 733, .6 mi. SE of
   intersection with State Rte. 732.
Fort Kilmakronen, .1 mi. SE of State Rte. 751, .8 mi. S of intersection with
   U.S. Rte. 11.
House, N side of State Rte. 762, 2.4 mi. NE of intersection with State Rte. 608.
Rush Creek Primitive Baptist Church, S side of State Rte. 605, .1 mi. SW of
   intersection with State Rte. 733.

GLADYS VICINITY   Campbell County (16)

Oak Dale, .3 mi. NE of State Rte. 650, 1.2 mi. N of intersection with State Rte.
   652.
Rock House, E side of State Rte. 651, .8 mi. S of intersection with State Rte.
   652.
Shady Grove, NW side of State Rte. 650, .5 mi. N of intersection with State Rte.
   652.

GLASGOW   Rockbridge County (82)

Sallings House, NE side of State Rte. T1103, .2 mi. NW of intersection with
   State Rte. 130.

GLASGOW VICINITY   Rockbridge County (82)

Beggs-Weaver House and Mill, SW side of State Rte. 671, .1 mi. NW of intersection with State Rte. 608.
Cherry Hill (Marlbrook Farm), .1 mi. S of State Rte. 608, .4 mi. W of intersection with State Rte. 688.

Falling Spring Presbyterian Church, N side of intersection of State Rtes. 679 and 680, .8 mi. W of intersection with State Rte. 608.

Falling Spring Presbyterian Manse, N side of State Rte. 680, .1 mi. W of intersection with State Rte. 679.

Fancy Hill, SE side of U.S. Rte. 11, .2 mi. NE of intersection with State Rte. 680.

Hickory Hill, .5 mi. NW of State Rte. 608, .5 mi. NE of intersection with State Rte. 684.

Penrobin, .4 mi. N of State Rte. 680, .2 mi. N of intersection with State Rte. 679.

Pleasant View, S side of State Rte. 679, .8 mi. N of intersection with State Rte. 680.

Round View, E side of State Rte. 679, .2 mi. NW of intersection with State Rte. 608.

Trimble, Alexander, House, NW side of U.S. Rte. 11, .3 mi. SW of intersection with State Rte. 680.

Vinard Hill Farm, NW side of State Rte. 608, .8 mi. NE of intersection with State Rte. 679.

Willow Grove, W side of U.S. Rte. 501, .4 mi. NE of intersection with State Rte. 130.

GLEN WILTON VICINITY   Botetourt County (12)

River Ridge Farm, .2 mi. NW of State Rte. 633, 1.4 mi. NE of intersection with State Rte. 622.

GLENNS VICINITY   Gloucester County (37)

Dragon Ordinary, .2 mi. SW of State Rte. 33, 1.4 mi. W of intersection with U.S. Rte. 17 and State Rte. 601.

GLOUCESTER   Gloucester County (37)

Debtor's Jail, Court Square.
Gloucester County Clerk's Office (now Treasurer's Office), Court Square.

GLOUCESTER VICINITY   Gloucester County (37)

Airville, .2 mi. SE of State Rte. 629, .3 mi. S of intersection with State Rte. 626.

Airville, Outbuildings, .2 mi. SE of State Rte. 629, .3 mi. S of intersection with State Rte. 626.

Church Hill, .2 mi. SE of State Rte. 14, .1 mi. NE of intersection with State Rte. 604.

Roaring Spring, .3 mi. E of State Rte. 616, 1.2 mi. N of intersection with U.S. Rte. 17.

Summerville Ice House, .2 mi. E of State Rte. 616, .8 mi. SW of intersection with U.S. Rte. 17.

GOOCHLAND   Goochland County (38)

Brightly, E side of U.S. Rte. 522 and State Rte. 6, .6 mi. S of intersection with
State Rte. 631.
Goochland County Clerk's Office, E side of U.S. Rte. 522, .1 mi. S of inter-
section with State Rte. 631.
Goochland County Jail, E side of U.S. Rte. 522, .1 mi. S of intersection with
State Rte. 631.

GOOCHLAND VICINITY   Goochland County (38)

Bolling Hall, 1 mi. SE of State Rte. 600, 1.9 mi. SW of intersection with State
Rte. 6.
Byrd Presbyterian Church, E side of State Rte. 614, .2 mi. N of intersection
with State Rte. 602.
Longwood (Rebel Hill), 1 mi. SW of State Rte. 632, .2 mi. E of intersection
with State Rte. 634.
Reed Marsh, .1 mi. SW of intersection of State Rte. 6 and U.S. Rte. 522, .7 mi.
N of intersection with State Rte. 631.
Rose Retreat, .2 mi. E of U.S. Rte. 522, 1.4 mi. N of intersection with State
Rte. 632.

GOODE VICINITY   Bedford County (10)

Bellevue, .3 mi. E of State Rte. 643, .5 mi. N of intersection with State Rte. 762.
Ivy Cliff, E side of State Rte. 709, 3 mi. SW of intersection with State Rte. 811.
Lochwood Hall, NW corner of intersection of U.S. Rte. 460 and State Rte. 668,
.3 mi. N of intersection with State Rte. 840.
Otter Hill, .5 mi. SW of State Rte. 668, 3.2 mi. S of intersection with State Rte.
297.

GORDONSVILLE   Orange County (69)

Gordon Inn, NE corner of intersection of U.S. Rtes. 15 and 33.
Presbyterian Church, E side of U.S. Rte. 15/33, .4 mi. SE of intersection with
State Rte. 231.

GORDONSVILLE VICINITY   Louisa County (55)

Annadale, .3 mi. NE of State Rte. 231, .1 mi. N of intersection with U.S. Rte. 33.
Beaumont, .1 mi. E of State Rte. 231, .5 mi. N of intersection with State Rte.
646.
Hopewell, .5 mi. E of State Rte. 231, 1.8 mi. SW of intersection with U.S. Rtes.
33 and 14.

Jordan, .5 mi. NW of U.S. Rte. 15, 1.5 mi. NE of intersection with State Rte. 231.

Montebello, .6 mi. W of State Rte. 645, .1 mi. S of intersection with U.S. Rte. 33.

Monteith, .2 mi. N of U.S. Rte. 33, 1 mi. W of intersection with State Rte. 646.

Thistlewood (Egypt, Carleton), .1 mi. N of U.S. Rte. 33, 1.3 mi. W of intersection with State Rte. 646.

Toll House, W side of State Rte. 231, .8 mi. NW of intersection with U.S. Rte. 33.

GOSHEN VICINITY   Rockbridge County (82)

Rockbridge Alum Springs, .3 mi. S of State Rte. 633, 1.5 mi. W of intersection with State Rte. 780.

Walnut Hill Hotel, W side of State Rte. 601, 1.6 mi. S of intersection with State Rte. 615.

Youell House, E side of State Rte. 601, .9 mi. N of intersection with State Rte. 615.

GRAFTON VICINITY   York County (100)

Grafton Christian Church, S side of State Rte. 622, .2 mi. W of intersection with U.S. Rte. 17.

GREAT FALLS VICINITY   Fairfax County (30)

Cornwell Farm, 9414 Old Georgetown Pike.

GREENWOOD VICINITY   Albemarle County (2)

Mirador, .1 mi. SE of State Rte. 691, 1.2 mi. S of intersection with State Rte. 690.

GRESSITT VICINITY   King and Queen County (49)

Belle Vue, 1.3 mi. SW of State Rte. 605, 1.2 mi. NW of intersection with State Rte. 601.

GRUNDY   Buchanan County (14)

Buchanan County Courthouse, SE corner of State Rte. T1003 and U.S. Rte. 460, .1 mi. S of intersection with State Rte. 83.

Providence Presbyterian Church, .2 mi. NE of State Rte. 700, .3 mi. N of intersection with U.S. Rte. 250.

Roseneath, .3 mi. NE of U.S. Rte. 522, 1.9 mi. NE of intersection with U.S. Rte. 250.

HADENSVILLE VICINITY   Goochland County (38)

Mt. Gilead Baptist Church, W corner of intersection of State Rtes. 605 and 603, 2.8 mi. NW of intersection with State Rte. 609.

Wysteria Hall, W side of State Rte. 606 at intersection with State Rte. 629, .9 mi. N of intersection with State Rte. 609.

HAGUE   Westmoreland County (97)

Hague House, N side of State Rte. 719, .1 mi. E of intersection with State Rte. 202.

Linden (Kitchen Dependency), .2 mi. S of State Rte. 202, .2 mi. E of intersection with State Rte. 612.

HAGUE VICINITY   Westmoreland County (97)

Auburn, .8 mi. N of State Rte. 202, .8 mi. SE of intersection with State Rte. 612.

Centreville, SW side of State Rte. 710, .1 mi. SE of State Rte. 611, 1.5 mi. NE of intersection with State Rte. 202.

Kirnan, NE side of State Rte. 710, .1 mi. SE of State Rte. 611, .5 mi. NE of intersection with State Rte. 202.

Wilton, .2 mi. NE of State Rte. 666, .9 mi. N of intersection with State Rte. 606.

HALIFAX   Halifax County (42)

Bondbrook, N side of U.S. Rte. 360, .8 mi. W of intersection with U.S. Rte. 501.

Giant Poplars, S side of U.S. Rte. 360, .7 mi. W of intersection with U.S. Rte. 501.

Grand Oaks, N side of U.S. Rte. 360, .1 mi. W of intersection with U.S. Rte. 501.

Halifax Methodist Church, N side of intersection of U.S. Rte. 360 and State Rte. T652.

House, NW side of U.S. Rte. 360/501, .3 mi. NE of intersection with State Rte. 651.

House, NW side of U.S. Rte. 360/501, .4 mi. NE of intersection with State Rte. 651.

Masonic Lodge, N side of U.S. Rte. 360, .1 mi. W of intersection with U.S. Rte. 501.

Rectory of St. John's Episcopal Church, S side of U.S. Rte. 360, .6 mi. W of intersection with U.S. Rte. 501.

St. John's Episcopal Church, N side of U.S. Rte. 360, .3 mi. W of intersection with U.S. Rte. 501.

HALIFAX VICINITY   Halifax County (42)

House, .8 mi. SW of U.S. Rte. 501, 2.3 mi. NW of intersection with U.S. Rte. 360.

House, .4 mi. NW of State Rte. 651, .6 mi. E of intersection with State Rte. 783.

Round Hill, .4 mi. NW of State Rte. 832, 1 mi. N of intersection with State Rte. 360.

Terry, William, House, .2 mi. E of State Rte. 626, .7 mi. N of intersection with U.S. Rte. 360.

Woodside, SE side of U.S. Rte. 360, .3 mi. SW of intersection with State Rte. 652.

HALLWOOD VICINITY   Accomack County (1)

Wessell's Root Cellar, .3 mi. E of State Rte. 701, .1 mi. N of intersection with State Rte. 692.

HAMILTON VICINITY   Cumberland County (25)

Ampthill, W side of State Rte. 602, 3 mi. N of intersection with State Rte. 45.

Clifton, 1.1 mi. NE of intersection of State Rtes. 605 and 690, .8 mi. NW of intersection with State Rte. 45.

Elkora, .4 mi. NE of State Rte. 602, 4 mi. N of intersection with State Rte. 45.

Flannagan's Mill (Trice's Mill), SE side of State Rte. 612, .3 mi. SW of intersection with State Rte. 690.

Fork of Willis Church, W side of State Rte. 690, .3 mi. S of intersection with State Rte. 602.

Glentivar, W side of State Rte. 602, 1 mi. N of intersection with State Rte. 45.

Morningside, .3 mi. S of State Rte. 690, .4 mi. W of intersection with State Rte. 611.

Mount Elba, SE side of S end of State Rte. 700, 1 mi. S of intersection with State Rte. 690.

Oakland, 1 mi. NE of State Rte. 690, .9 mi. NW of intersection with State Rte. 612.

Pleasant Grove (Clifton), .1 mi. E of State Rte. 612, .9 mi. S of intersection with State Rte. 690.

Thomas Chapel, NW side of State Rte. 45, .4 mi. SW of intersection with State Rte. 697.

Viewmont, .1 mi. E of State Rte. 608, .3 mi. S of intersection with State Rte. 612.

Administration Building, Hampden-Sydney College.
Alamo, The, Hampden-Sydney College.
College Presbyterian Church, Hampden-Sydney College.
Cradle, Hampden-Sydney College.
Cushing Hall, Hampden-Sydney College.
Eastecourt, Hampden-Sydney College.
Graham Hall, Hampden-Sydney College.
Hampden House, Hampden-Sydney College.
Middlecourt, Hampden-Sydney College.
Penshurst, Hampden-Sydney College.
Venable Hall, Hampden-Sydney College.

HAMPTON

Finn, Capt. Thomas, House (Copeland-Finn-Drummond House), 300-A Harris
    Creek Rd.
Fort Wool, Island, 1 mi. S of Fortress Monroe, at the entrance to Hampton
    Roads Harbor between Willoughby Spit and Old Point Comfort.
Mansion House, Hampton Institute, S side of U.S. Rte. 60, 1 mi. W of inter-
    section with Mallory St.
Memorial Church, Hampton Institute, S side of U.S. Rte. 60, 1 mi. W of inter-
    section with Mallory St.
Old Point Comfort Lighthouse, Fenwick Rd.
Roseland Manor (Strawberry Banks Manor House), .1 mi. S of National Ave. at
    intersection with S. Mallory Ave.
St. John's Church, NW corner of West Queen and Court Sts.
Virginia Hall, Hampton Institute, S side of U.S. Rte. 60, 1 mi. W of intersection
    with Mallory St.

HANOVER   Hanover County (43)

Hanover County Jail, NE side of intersection of U.S. Rte. 301 (State Rte. 2) and
    State Rte. 1002.

HANOVER VICINITY   Hanover County (43)

Dundee, .5 mi. S of State Rte. 605, .1 mi. SE of intersection with State Rte. 326.
Signal Hill, .1 mi. E of State Rte. 2 (U.S. Rte. 301), .6 mi. S of intersection with
    State Rte. 605.

HARMONY VICINITY   Halifax County (42)

Holt, Timothy, House, E side of State Rte. 713, .6 mi. S of intersection with
    State Rte. 711.

HARRISONBURG   Rockingham County (83)

Homeland, 725 S. High St.
Morrison House, NW corner of intersection of W. Market and N. Liberty Sts.
Rockingham County Courthouse, Courthouse Square.
Warren Hotel, Courthouse Square.

HARRISONBURG VICINITY   Rockingham County (83)

Smithland, SW corner of intersection of U.S. Rte. 11 and State Rte. 720, .8 mi.
    N of intersection with State Rte. 718.

HARTFIELD VICINITY   Middlesex County (60)

Barn Elms, 1.5 mi. S of State Rte. 3, .4 mi. SE of intersection with State Rte. 33.
Methodist Lower Church, .1 mi. S of State Rte. 3/33, .4 mi. W of intersection
    with State Rte. 626.
Wilton, .1 mi. W of State Rte. 3, 1 mi. SE of intersection with State Rte. 630.
Woodstock, 1.2 mi. SW of State Rte. 629, .5 mi. S of intersection with State
    Rte. 3/33.

HAYMARKET   Prince William County (76)

St. Paul's Episcopal Church, W side of Fayette St., .2 mi. S of intersection with
    State Rte. 55.

HAYMARKET VICINITY   Prince William County (76)

Buckland Hall, SE side of State Rte. 684, .5 mi. S of intersection with U.S. Rte.
    29/211.
Waverly Plantation, .2 mi. W of U.S. Rte. 15, 1.7 mi. N of intersection with
    State Rte. 55.

HEATHSVILLE   Northumberland County (67)

Hughlett's Tavern, E side of State Rte. 1002, .1 mi. E of intersection with U.S.
    Rte. 360.
Northumberland County Courthouse, E side of U.S. Rte. 360, at intersection
    with State Rte. 1002.
Springfield, W side of State Rte. 601, .3 mi. N of intersection with U.S. Rte. 360.

HEATHSVILLE VICINITY   Northumberland County (67)

Coan Hall Smokehouse, .1 mi. W of State Rte. 630, 1.5 mi. N of intersection
with State Rte. 631.
Mantua, 1 mi. NW of N end of State Rte. 634, .6 mi. N of intersection with
State Rte. 629.

HELMET VICINITY   King and Queen County (49)

Oakley, .1 mi. N of State Rte. 623, 2 mi. E of intersection with State Rte. 635.
Upper King and Queen Baptist Church, NE side of State Rte. 635, .3 mi. N of
intersection with State Rte. 623.

HERNDON VICINITY   Fairfax County (30)

Dranesville Methodist Church, 11711 Leesburg Pike.
Dunbarton, 910 Seneca Rd.
Frying Pan Church, 2615 Centreville Rd.
Holly Knoll, 12000 Leesburg Pike.
Ivy Chimneys, 11706 Leesburg Pike.
Mayfield, 11700 Leesburg Pike.

HENRY VICINITY   Charlotte County (20)

Mapleton (Kentwood), .5 mi. SW of State Rte. 40, .5 mi. W of intersection with
State Rte. 654.

HIGHTOWN   Highland County (46)

Hevener, Jacob, Store, N corner of intersection of U.S. Rte. 250 and State Rte.
640.

HIGHTOWN VICINITY   Highland County (46)

Campbell House, W side of State Rte. 640, 2.5 mi. S of intersection with U.S.
Rte. 250.

HILLSVILLE   Carroll County (18)

Carroll County Courthouse, E side of U.S. Rte. 52, .1 mi. NW of intersection
with State Rte. 701.
Cook House, .3 mi. SW of U.S. Rte. 52, .1 mi. NW of intersection with State
Rte. 701.

HILLSVILLE VICINITY Carroll County (18)

Carroll House, N side of U.S. Rte. 58, .9 mi. SE of intersection with State Rte. 668.

Kinzer House, E side of State Rte. 669, .1 mi. SE of intersection with U.S. Rte. 221 and State Rte. 100.

HOLLINS COLLEGE Roanoke County (81)

East Dormitory, Hollins College, .3 mi. N of U.S. Rte. 11/220, .7 mi. NE of intersection with State Rte. 601.

Main Building, Hollins College, .3 mi. N of U.S. Rte. 11/220, .6 mi. NE of intersection with State Rte. 601.

West Dormitory, Hollins College, .2 mi. N of Rte. 11/220, .6 mi. NE of intersection with State Rte. 601.

HOPEWELL

St. John's Church, E side of intersection of Cedar Lane and Maplewood.

HOPEWELL VICINITY Prince George County (75)

Evergreen, .1 mi. W of State Rte. 644, .4 mi. N of intersection with State Rte. 10/156.

House, .2 mi. E of State Rte. 641, 2.4 mi. SE of intersection with State Rte. 10.

House, .2 mi. S of State Rte. 641, 2 mi. SE of intersection with State Rte. 10.

Kippax, .1 mi. SW of State Rte. 648, .2 mi. N of intersection with State Rte. 36.

Roseneath, .1 mi. S of State Rte. 646, 1.7 mi. E of intersection with State Rte. 156.

Tar Bay, .9 mi. N of State Rte. 641, .3 mi. NE of intersection with State Rte. 10.

Weston Manor, .4 mi. W of State Rte. 10.

HOWARDSVILLE Albemarle County (2)

Westcote (Summer Hill), .2 mi. W of State Rte. 602, .1 mi. W of intersection with State Rte. 626.

HOWARDSVILLE VICINITY Albemarle County (2)

Monticola, .4 mi. E of State Rte. 602, .6 mi. N of intersection with State Rte. 724.

Monticola, Outbuildings, .4 mi. E of State Rte. 602, .6 mi. N of intersection with State Rte. 724.

HUNTLY VICINITY

Rappahannock County (79)

Wakefield Manor, .5 mi. W of U.S. Rte. 522, .3 mi. S of intersection with State Rte. 664.

HUSTLE VICINITY

Essex County (29)

Oakalona, .1 mi. N of State Rte. 637, 3 mi. W of intersection with U.S. Rte. 17.

INDEPENDENCE

Grayson County (39)

Grayson County Courthouse, NE corner of intersection of Liberty Ave. and Main St.
Montarosa, NE corner of State Rte. T1101 and U.S. Rte. 21.

INDEPENDENCE VICINITY

Grayson County (39)

Hale House, NW side of intersection of State Rte. 666 and U.S. Rte. 21, 2.7 mi. NE of intersection with State Rte. 667.

ISLE OF WIGHT

Isle of Wight County (47)

House, .1 mi. NW of State Rte. 258, .3 mi. NE of intersection with State Rte. 637.
Isle of Wight County Clerk's Office, .1 mi. NW of U.S. Rte. 258, .3 mi. NE of intersection with State Rte. 637.

ISLE OF WIGHT VICINITY

Isle of Wight County (47)

Cedar Acres, .3 mi. S of State Rte. 644, .1 mi. W of intersection with State Rte. 637.
House, W side of State Rte. 654, .2 mi. N of intersection with State Rte. 644.
House, .1 mi. NE of State Rte. 600, .4 mi. NE of intersection with State Rte. 652.
Seeds House, .1 mi. N of State Rte. 637, .4 mi. SE of intersection with State Rte. 644.

IVOR VICINITY

Southampton County (88)

Clements, .2 mi. S of State Rte. 620, .3 mi. SE of intersection with State Rte. 617.

IVY VICINITY Albemarle County (2)

Bloomfield, .1 mi. W of State Rte. 677, .5 mi. S of intersection with U.S. Rte. 250.

Malvern, .3 mi. W of State Rte. 708, .3 mi. N of intersection with State Rte. 637.

Spring Hill, .6 mi. SW of intersection of State Rtes. 786 and 637, .3 mi. SW of intersection with U.S. Rte. 250.

JAMAICA VICINITY Middlesex County (60)

Glebe Landing Church, W side of State Rte. 606, .1 mi. S of intersection with U.S. Rte. 17.

JAMES STORE VICINITY Gloucester County (37)

Exchange, N side of SE end of State Rte. 680, 1.6 mi. SE of intersection with State Rte. 14.

Exchange Ice House, S side of SE end of State Rte. 680, 1.6 mi. SE of intersection with State Rte. 14.

Midlothian, 1.1 mi. SE of State Rte. 14, .3 mi. SW of intersection with State Rte. 602.

Midlothian Ice House, 1.1 mi. SE of State Rte. 14, .3 mi. SW of intersection with State Rte. 602.

Newstead, .2 mi. E of State Rte. 622, 1.7 mi. NE of intersection with State Rte. 14.

Waverly Ice House, S side of State Rte. 694, 1.4 mi. E of intersection with State Rte. 14.

JARRATT VICINITY Sussex County (92)

Fortsville, S side of State Rte. 612, 1.5 mi. SE of intersection with State Rte. 611.

House, S side of State Rte. 631, .1 mi. W of intersection with State Rte. 645.

House, .1 mi. N of State Rte. 631, .6 mi. W of intersection with State Rte. 635.

House, S side of State Rte. 612, 1.6 mi. NW of intersection with State Rte. 611.

JAVA VICINITY Pittsylvania County (72)

Candy House, N side of State Rte. 832, 1.1 mi. W of intersection with State Rte. 698.

Elkhorn, .4 mi. SW of State Rte. 680, .6 mi. NW of intersection with State Rte. 832.

Grasty House, NE corner of intersection of State Rtes. 640 and 40, .5 mi. N of intersection with State Rte. 979.

Jones House, E side of State Rte. 680, 1 mi. N of intersection with State Rte. 666.

Sharswood, S side of State Rte. 40, .3 mi. E of intersection with State Rte. 640.

Woodlawn, E side of State Rte. 698, 1.8 mi. E of intersection with State Rte. 729.

JEFFERSON VICINITY   Powhatan County (73)

Belmead (St. Emma's Industrial and Agricultural School), .4 mi. NW of NW end of State Rte. 663, .5 mi. NW of intersection with State Rte. 600.

Elioch, .4 mi. S of State Rte. 711, 1 mi. E of intersection with State Rte. 614.

Jefferson Landing, at NW end of State Rte. 618 extended, 3 mi. NW of intersection with U.S. Rte. 522.

St. Luke's Episcopal Church, S side of State Rte. 711, immediately W of intersection with State Rte. 615.

Subletts, NE side of State Rte. 711, .7 mi. E of intersection with State Rte. 614.

Tavern, 1.4 mi. N of Fine Creek, NW side of U.S. Rte. 522, .1 mi. E of intersection with State Rte. 618.

JEFFERSONTON   Culpeper County (24)

Jeffersonton Baptist Church, S side of State Rte. 802, .1 mi. E of intersection with State Rte. 621.

Old Stage Tavern, SE corner of intersection of State Rtes. 621 and 802.

JEFFERSONTON VICINITY   Culpeper County (24)

Presqu' Isle, 1.6 mi. S of State Rte. 710, .3 mi. SW of intersection with State Rte. 621.

JERSEY VICINITY   King George County (50)

Nanzatico, at end of State Rte. 650, 1.7 mi. S of State Rte. 627, 3 mi. E of U.S. Rte. 301.

White Plains, NW side of U.S. Rte. 301, 1 mi. N of intersection of State Rtes. 660 and 625.

JETERSVILLE VICINITY   Amelia County (4)

Chestnut Row, .3 mi. S of State Rte. 681, .2 mi. NW of intersection with State Rte. 667.

House, E side of State Rte. 621, .2 mi. N of intersection with State Rte. 644.

JONESVILLE   Lee County (53)

Lee County Courthouse, NW corner of intersection of U.S. Rte. 58 and State
    Rte. T1205.
Morgan House, S side of U.S. Rte. 58, .3 mi. W of intersection with State Rte. 70.

JONESVILLE VICINITY   Lee County (53)

Allen House, .4 mi. E of State Rte. 654, .7 mi. S of intersection with State Rte.
    614.
Browning-Wynn Mill, W side of State Rte. 647, .7 mi. N of intersection with
    State Rte. 745.
DeVault, Blanc, House, NW side of State Rte. 612, .9 mi. SW of intersection
    with State Rte. 70.
Methodist Camp Ground, NW corner of intersection of State Rte. 652 and U.S.
    Rte. 58, .1 mi. W of intersection with State Rte. 745.
Thompson Settlement Church, N side of State Rte. 665, .5 mi. E of intersection
    with State Rte. 758.

JORDAN MINES VICINITY   Alleghany County (3)

Humphrey House, S side of State Rte. 616, 1 mi. NE of intersection with State
    Rte. 617.

KEENE VICINITY   Albemarle County (2)

Bellair, .9 mi. S of State Rte. 708, 1.6 mi. SE of intersection with State Rte. 627.
Brookhill, .1 mi. E of State Rte. 20, 1.2 mi. N of intersection with State Rte. 708.
Christ Church (Glendower), NW side of State Rte. 713, .4 mi. SW of intersection
    with State Rte. 712.
Enniscorthy, .4 mi. SW of State Rte. 627, .1 mi. S of intersection with State
    Rte. 712.
Enniscorthy Cabin, .4 mi. SW of State Rte. 627, .1 mi. S of intersection with
    State Rte. 712.
Estouteville (Calycanthus Hill), .7 mi. N of State Rte. 712, 1.5 mi. NW of inter-
    section with State Rtes. 715 and 20.
Estouteville, Outbuildings, .7 mi. N of State Rte. 712, 1.5 mi. NW of intersection
    with State Rtes. 715 and 20.
Glendower, .4 mi. SW of State Rte. 20, .1 mi. SE of intersection with State
    Rte. 713.
Glendower (Old House), .4 mi. SW of State Rte. 20, .1 mi. SE of intersection
    with State Rte. 713.
Plain Dealing, .2 mi. W of State Rte. 713, .5 mi. N of intersection with State
    Rte. 712.

Redlands, .6 mi. NE of State Rte. 708, .1 mi. E of intersection with State Rte. 627.

Round Top, 1.2 mi. E of State Rte. 20, .3 mi. N of intersection with State Rte. 708.

KENBRIDGE VICINITY   Lunenburg County (56)

Ben Lomond, .8 mi. NW of State Rte. 40, .7 mi. NE of intersection with State Rte. 649.

Brickland, .1 mi. N of State Rte. 613, .3 mi. W of intersection with State Rte. 138.

Flat Rock, N side of State Rte. 655, .1 mi. W of intersection with State Rte. 637.

House, NW corner of intersection of State Rtes. 753 and 138, .9 mi. S of intersection with State Rte. 619.

Laurel Branches, E side of State Rte. 646, .6 mi. S of intersection with State Rte. 647.

Loch Lomond, .2 mi. NE of State Rte. 40, .5 mi. NE of intersection with State Rte. 600.

New Woodlawn, E side of State Rte. 138, .3 mi. S of intersection with State Rte. 619.

Old Woodlawn, E side of State Rte. 138, .2 mi. S of intersection with State Rte. 619.

Pleasant Hill, .6 mi. S of State Rte. 607, 1.9 mi. S of intersection with State Rte. T1111.

Woodlawn, .6 mi. W of State Rte. 607, 1.3 mi. S of intersection with State Rte. T1111.

KEOKEE VICINITY   Lee County (53)

Seminary Methodist Church, SE side of intersection of U.S. Rte. (Alt.) 58 and State Rte. 708, 1.2 mi. E of intersection with State Rte. 622.

KESWICK VICINITY   Albemarle County (2)

East Belmont, 1 mi. NW of intersection of State Rtes. 616 and 22, .2 mi. NE of intersection with State Rte. 731.

Tall Oaks, .4 mi. NW of State Rte. 22, .7 mi. NE of intersection with State Rte. 616.

KILMARNOCK   Northumberland County (67)

Clifton, Clifton Ave., .3 mi. E of intersection with State Rte. 200.

KILMARNOCK VICINITY   Lancaster County (52)

Corotoman (Overseer's House), .1 mi. NW of State Rte. 699, .2 mi. NW of intersection with State Rte. 675.

KING AND QUEEN COURT HOUSE

King and Queen County (49)

King and Queen County Clerk's Office, S side of State Rte. 14, W side of intersection with State Rtes. 681 and 655.
King and Queen County Courthouse, W side of intersection of State Rtes. 681 and 655.

KING AND QUEEN COURT HOUSE VICINITY

King and Queen County (49)

Pleasant Green, .1 mi. E of State Rte. 617, 1.9 mi. NE of intersection with State Rte. 14.

KING GEORGE

King George County (50)

King George County Courthouse, N side of State Rte. 3.
St. John's Episcopal Church, N side of State Rte. 3.

KING GEORGE VICINITY

King George County (50)

Ashland, N side of State Rte. 205, opposite intersection with State Rte. 622.
Comorn, N side of State Rte. 677, .2 mi. NW of intersection with State Rte. 3.
Indiantown, NW corner of intersection of State Rtes. 206 and 210.
Mount Stuart, N side of State Rte. 218, opposite intersection with State Rte. 210.
Office Hall, NE corner of intersection of State Rte. 3 and U.S. Rte. 301.

KING WILLIAM VICINITY

King William County (51)

Aspen Grove, .9 mi. SE of State Rte. 629, .4 mi. S of intersection with State Rte. 30.
Auburn, .1 mi. W of State Rte. 629, .3 mi. S of intersection with State Rte. 618.
Broadneck, .6 mi. S of State Rte. 618, 1 mi. W of intersection with State Rte. 629.
Brooklyn, .3 mi. SW of State Rte. 618, 2.6 mi. NW of intersection with State Rte. 629.
Canton, SE side of State Rte. 641, .1 mi. NE of intersection with State Rte. 30.
Cool Spring, .2 mi. S of State Rte. 30, .4 mi. SE of intersection with State Rte. 629.
Endfield, E side of State Rte. 629, .4 mi. N of intersection with State Rte. 664.
Flot Beck, .2 mi. N of E end of State Rte. 618, .6 mi. SE of intersection with State Rte. 629.
Jerusalem Christian Church, W side of State Rte. 633, 2.3 mi. S of King William.
Longwood, .5 mi. S of State Rte. 637, .6 mi. E of intersection with State Rte. 619.
Malbourne, .1 mi. S of State Rte. 30, .8 mi. E of intersection with State Rte. 633.

Montebello, .5 mi. SW of State Rte. 632, .3 mi. SE of intersection with State Rte. 629.

Mount Pisgah, .4 mi. NE of State Rte. 600, 1 mi. N of intersection with State Rte. 30.

New Farm, .7 mi. NE of State Rte. 617, .4 mi. NW of intersection with State Rte. 30.

North Point Farm, 1.3 mi. NE of State Rte. 617, .7 mi. NW of intersection with State Rte. 30.

Woodberry, .2 mi. NE of E end of State Rte. 664, 1.7 mi. E of intersection with State Rte. 629.

KINSALE   Westmoreland County (97)

Great House, .2 mi. S of State Rte. 203.

KINSALE VICINITY   Westmoreland County (97)

Ayrfield, .2 mi. W of State Rte. 606, .9 mi. S of intersection with State Rte. 610.

Grove, The, .1 mi. E of State Rte. 607, .5 mi. N of intersection with State Rte. 203.

LA CROSSE VICINITY   Mecklenburg County (59)

House, S side of U.S. Rte. 58, 1 mi. NE of intersection with State Rte. 644.

LACEY SPRING VICINITY   Rockingham County (83)

Bethlehem Church, W corner of intersection of State Rte. 798 and U.S. Rte. 11, 1.1 mi. NE of intersection with State Rte. 259.

LAHORE VICINITY   Orange County (69)

Fairview (Green Meadows), E side of State Rte. 649, 1.5 mi. S of intersection with State Rte. 629.

LANCASTER   Lancaster County (52)

Lancaster County Courthouse, N side of State Rte. 3, .1 mi. E of intersection with State Rte. 600.

Old Lancaster Jail, S side of State Rte. 3, opposite Courthouse.

LANCASTER VICINITY

White Marsh Methodist Church, SW side of State Rte. 3, .4 mi. SE of intersection with State Rte. 605.

LANESVILLE VICINITY

Colosse Baptist Church, N side of State Rte. 30, .9 mi. NW of intersection with State Rte. 640.

Foxes, .8 mi. SE of SE end of State Rte. 643, 2 mi. SE of intersection with State Rte. 640.

Frazier's Ferry (Wakuma), S side of NE end of State Rte. 640, .4 mi. NE of intersection with State Rte. 643.

Marl Hill, .1 mi. SW of State Rte. 30, .7 mi. SE of intersection with State Rte. 626.

LANEVIEW VICINITY

Plainview, .1 mi. N of State Rte. 600, 1.6 mi. NE of intersection with U.S. Rte. 17.

LAWRENCEVILLE

Brunswick County Courthouse, E side of U.S. Rte. 58, .1 mi. N of intersection with State Rte. T713.

LAWRENCEVILLE VICINITY

Brunswick Springs, .2 mi. E of State Rte. 670, .7 mi. S of intersection with State Rte. 606.

Fort Christanna, .2 mi. N of State Rte. 686, .6 mi. W of intersection with State Rte. 46.

Raise-a-Pint, .1 mi. N of State Rte. 638, .2 mi. N of intersection with U.S. Rte. 58.

Woodslawn, .1 mi. S of State Rte. 681, .4 mi. NW of intersection with U.S. Rte. 58.

Woodslawn, Outbuildings, .1 mi. S of State Rte. 681, .4 mi. NW of intersection with U.S. Rte. 58.

LEBANON

Alderson, Dr. Chris, House, NW corner of intersection of U.S. Rte. 19 and State Rte. T701.

Alexander, David B., House, N side of U.S. Rte. 19, .1 mi. W of intersection with State Rte. T701.

Russell County Courthouse, NE corner of Main St. and Court Ave.

Dickenson, Henry, House, N side of U.S. Rte. Alt./58, .8 mi. W of intersection with State Rte. 71.

Gilmore (Gilmer), William, House, S side of U.S. Rte. 19, .1 mi. E of intersection with State Rte. 658.

Hanson, David, House, W side of U.S. Rte. Alt./58 and U.S. Rte. 19, .7 mi. S of intersection with State Rte. 614.

Hendricks, Fullen, House, N side of U.S. Rte. 19, .9 mi. NE of intersection with State Rte. 654.

Munsey, David, House (Waggoner House), NW side of State Rte. 71, .4 mi. SW of intersection with State Rte. 82.

Price-Duty-Broom House, E side of U.S. Rte. 19, 1.4 mi. S of intersection with State Rte. 660.

LEE MONT VICINITY   Accomack County (1)

Hills Farm, .9 mi. N of State Rte. 661, .2 mi. NW of intersection with State Rte. 658.

LEESBURG   Loudoun County (54)

Exeter, 1.2 mi. E of intersection of Church and Market Sts.

House, 30 E. Loudoun St.

Laurel Brigade Inn, 20 W. Market St.

Leesburg Academy (County Administration Building), N side of Market St., between King and Church Sts.

Loudoun County Courthouse, NE corner of the intersection of King and Market Sts.

Osburn's Tavern, 7 E. Loudoun St.

LEESBURG VICINITY   Loudoun County (54)

Belmont, .4 mi. SW of State Rte. 7, .8 mi. SE of intersection with State Rte. 659.

Church of Our Savior, NE corner of intersection of U.S. Rte. 15 and State Rte. 650.

Clapham's Ferry House, N side of E end of State Rte. 657, .8 mi. E of intersection with State Rte. 662.

Morven Park, .8 mi. N of State Rte. 698, .3 mi. NW of intersection with Morven Park Rd.

Oatlands, .4 mi. SE of U.S. Rte. 15, .3 mi. S of intersection with State Rte. 651.

Rokeby, .3 mi. W of State Rte. 650, .9 mi. S of intersection with U.S. Rte. 15.

Shadow Mountain, W side of U.S. Rte. 15, .5 mi. S of intersection with State Rte. 704.

Woodburn, W side of State Rte. 704, opposite intersection with State Rte. 769.

LEON VICINITY

Mountain Prospect, S end of State Rte. 716, .9 mi. SW of intersection with U.S. Rte. 29.

LENNIG VICINITY

House, NW side of State Rte. 603, .8 mi. NE of intersection with State Rte. 626.

LEXINGTON

Castle, The, 8 Randolph St.
Col Alto, SE corner of E. Nelson St. and Spotswood Dr.
Darst-Pendleton House, 111 Lee Ave.
Darst, Samuel, House, 109 Lee Ave.
Darst, Samuel, House, NE corner of Main and Washington Sts.
Dorman House (Episcopal Rectory), 107 Lee Ave.
Graham-Jackson House, 8 E Washington St.
Halestones, 101 E. Washington St.
Lexington Presbyterian Church, SW corner of Main and Nelson Sts.
Mulberry Hill, 115 Liberty Hall Rd.
Presbyterian Manse, 6 White St.
President's House, 2 University Pl.
Reid-White House, 208 W. Nelson St.

LEXINGTON VICINITY

Fairdale Manor, .2 mi. NE of State Rte. 671, .8 mi. SE of intersection with State Rte. 701.
Hall House, W side of State Rte. 612, .4 mi. SW of intersection with State Rte. 677.
Hidden House Farm, 1.3 mi. N of U.S. Rte. 60, 1.8 mi. E of intersection with State Rte. 699.
Liberty Hall Academy, .3 mi. NE of U.S. Rte. 60, .1 mi. SE of intersection with State Rte. 666.
Little Stono, W side of State Rte. 671, .2 mi. S of intersection with State Rte. 735.
Long House, NW side of State Rte. 612, .2 mi. SW of intersection with State Rte. 677.
Monmouth Church, NE side of intersection of U.S. Rte. 60 and State Rte. 669.
New Monmouth Church, E side of U.S. Rte. 60, 1.5 mi. N of intersection with State Rte. 639.
Spring Meadow, .2 mi. NW of State Rte. 251, 1.5 mi. SW of intersection with U.S. Rte. 11.
Thorn Hill, .2 mi. NW of State Rte. 251, .4 mi. NE of intersection with State Rte. 764.

Wallace House, N side of intersection of State Rtes. 677, 675 and 251, .9 mi. W of intersection with State Rte. 670.

West Wood, SW side of State Rte. 672, .1 mi. W of intersection with State Rte. 670.

LIGHTFOOT James City County (48)

Walsh House, W side of intersection of U.S. Rte. 60, .1 mi. N of intersection with State Rte. 614.

LIGHTFOOT VICINITY James City County (48)

Harris House, S side of State Rte. 633, 1.6 mi. SW of intersection with State Rte. 614.

LINCOLN VICINITY Loudoun County (54)

Cornerstone Farm, SW corner of intersection of State Rtes. 622 and 729.

Evergreen Farm, E side of State Rte. 722, .4 mi. S of intersection with State Rte. 723.

Green Hill, N side of State Rte. 622, .4 mi. SW of intersection with State Rte. 704.

Oakland Green, .1 mi. E of State Rte. 841, .7 mi. S of intersection with State Rte. 727.

LINVILLE Rockingham County (83)

Kratzer-Sipe House, W side of intersection of State Rtes. 753 and 721, .4 mi. W of intersection with State Rte. 948.

LINVILLE VICINITY Rockingham County (83)

Beery House, .3 mi. E of State Rte. 42, .5 mi. S of intersection with State Rte. 721.

Lincoln House, E side of State Rte. 42, .8 mi. N of intersection with State Rte. 782.

LITHIA VICINITY Botetourt County (12)

Arch Mill Farm, .1 mi. SE of intersection of State Rte. 641 and U.S. Rte. 11, .5 mi. N of intersection with U.S. Rte. I-81.

384

LITTLE PLYMOUTH   King and Queen County (49)

Cedarlane, W side of State Rte. 614, .2 mi. NE of intersection with State Rte. 14.
Little Plymouth, SW corner of intersection of State Rtes. 14 and 614.

LITTLE PLYMOUTH VICINITY   King and Queen County (49)

Edgehill, .2 mi. NE of State Rte. 14, 2.5 mi. NW of intersection with State Rte.
   614.
Garrett Hill, .2 mi. NE of State Rte. 14, 2.6 mi. NW of intersection with State
   Rte. 614.

LITTLETON VICINITY   Sussex County (92)

Little Town, S side of State Rte. 622, 1.1 mi. W of intersection with State Rte. 35.

LIVELY VICINITY   Lancaster County (52)

Fox Hill Plantation, .2 mi. W of State Rte. 201, 2.2 mi. SW of intersection with
   State Rte. 3.
Mitchell, John, House, .6 mi. SE of State Rte. 620, .6 mi. S of intersection with
   State Rte. 3.

LOCUST DALE VICINITY   Madison County (57)

Chilmark, .5 mi. N of State Rte. 614, 1.5 mi. SE of intersection with U.S. Rte. 15.
Forest View, .1 mi. W of U.S. Rte. 15, .9 mi. S of intersection with State Rte.
   634.
Glendalough, .8 mi. W of State Rte. 634, 1 mi. N of intersection with U.S. Rte.
   15.
Indian Trace, .3 mi. NE of State Rte. 634, .5 mi. N of intersection with U.S.
   Rte. 15.
Meander Farm, 2 mi. NW of U.S. Rte. 15, 1 mi. NE of intersection with State
   Rte. 614.
River Bend Farm, .5 mi. E of U.S. Rte. 15, .6 mi. NE of intersection with State
   Rte. 614.

LOCUST GROVE   Orange County (69)

Robinson's Tavern, NE side of intersection of State Rtes. 611 and 20.

LOCUST GROVE VICINITY

Orange County (69)

Indiantown Mill, SW side of State Rte. 603, .9 mi. N of intersection with State Rte. 614.

LORETTO VICINITY

Essex County (29)

Edenetta, .6 mi. S of U.S. Rte. 17, 1 mi. SE of intersection with State Rte. 638.
Rose Mount, W side of State Rte. 635, .5 mi. S of intersection with U.S. Rte. 17.
Wheatland, .1 mi. N of State Rte. 638, 1 mi. N of intersection with U.S. Rte. 17.

LORNE VICINITY

Caroline County (17)

Elson Green, .1 mi. W of State Rte. 651, 1.2 mi. SE of intersection with State Rte. 2.
Grove, The, E side of State Rte. 651, 1.1 mi. SE of intersection with State Rte. 2.
Mt. Gideon, .1 mi. S of State Rte. 651, 1.4 mi. SE of intersection with State Rte. 2.
Rock Spring, .2 mi. SE of State Rte. 677, .4 mi. S of intersection with State Rte. 693.

LORTON VICINITY

Fairfax County (30)

La Grange, 9501 Old Colchester Rd.
Mount Air, 8600 Accotink Rd.

LOTTSBURG VICINITY

Northumberland County (67)

Wheatland, .3 mi. E of State Rte. 624, 2 mi. N of intersection with U.S. Rte. 360.

LOUISA

Louisa County (55)

Louisa County Courthouse, SW corner of intersection of State Rte. 659 and U.S. Rte. 33.
Louisa County Jail, W side of State Rte. 659, S of U.S. Rte. 33.
Louisa Methodist Church, SE corner of U.S. Rte. 33 and State Rte. 659.
Louisa Station and Freight Room, E side of Church Ave., N of intersection with Main St.
St. James Church, SW corner of Ellisville Dr. and West St.

LOUISA VICINITY

Louisa County (55)

Ben Ghoil, .1 mi. NW of State Rte. 628, .5 mi. NE of intersection with U.S. Rte. 33.

Bloomington, .2 mi. E of State Rte. 646, .7 mi. SE of intersection with State Rte. 604.

Byrd Mill, E side of State Rte. 649, .5 mi. S of intersection with State Rte. 632.

Daniel House, .1 mi. W of State Rte. 628, 4.6 mi. NE of intersection with U.S. Rte. 33 and State Rte. 22.

Edgelawn, .2 mi. E of State Rte. 644, 3.2 mi. S of intersection with U.S. Rte. 33.

Elmwood, .1 mi. W of State Rte. 628, 6.3 mi. NE of intersection of U.S. Rte. 33 and State Rte. 22.

Goldmine Church, N side of State Rte. 613, .6 mi. NW of intersection with State Rte. 628.

Honey Grove (Happy Valley), .6 mi. W of State Rte. 669, 1 mi. N of intersection with State Rte. 742.

Woodbourne (Woodburn), .5 mi. E of State Rte. 659, .5 mi. S of intersection with State Rte. 630.

LOVETTSVILLE VICINITY   Loudoun County (54)

St. Paul's Lutheran Church, W side of State Rte. 671, .7 mi. S of intersection with State Rte. 686.

LOVINGSTON   Nelson County (63)

Public Office Building, .2 mi. E of U.S. Rte. 29, .3 mi. N of intersection with State Rte. 56.

LOWRY VICINITY   Bedford County (10)

Knollwood Farm, .8 mi. SE of State Rte. 718, .6 mi. SW of intersection with State Rte. 671.

Locust Hill Farm, E side of State Rte. 715, .8 mi. S of intersection with State Rte. 297.

Merriman Manor, W side of State Rte. 715, .1 mi. S of intersection with State Rte. 803.

LUNENBURG   Lunenburg County (56)

Hotel Gary, SW corner of intersection of State Rtes. 40/49 and 675.

House, S side of State Rte. 40/49, .2 mi. E of intersection with State Rte. 675.

Lunenburg County Courthouse, N side of intersection of State Rtes. 675 and 40/49.

Lunenburg Methodist Church, S side of State Rte. 40/49, .3 mi. E of intersection with State Rte. 675.

Lunenburg State Inn, N side of intersection of State Rtes. 40/49 and 675.

House, E side of State Rte. 671, .9 mi. S of intersection with State Rte. 672.
House, .3 mi. E of State Rte. 672, .8 mi. SW of intersection with State Rte. 671.
Love's Mill, .2 mi. SW of State Rte. 671, 1 mi. S of intersection with State Rte.
  672.

LURAY   Page County (70)

Aventine Hall, 143 S. Court St.
Eagle Tavern (Luray Museum), between 211 and 219 W. Main St.
House, 138 E. Main St.
Laurance Hotel, SE corner of W. Main and Court Sts.
Page County Courthouse, 116 S. Court St.
Ruffin, John, House, 102 W. Main St.

LURAY VICINITY   Page County (70)

Heiston-Strickler House, .2 mi. W of State Rte. 765, .2 mi. N of intersection with
  State Rte. 675.
Locust Dell, .1 mi. NE of State Rte. 641, .2 mi. SE of intersection with State
  Rte. 640.
Mill Creek Baptist Church, N side of State Rte. 766, .3 mi. W of intersection
  with U.S. Rte. 211.
Mill Creek Primitive Baptist Church, SE side of State Rte. 766, .6 mi. SW of
  intersection with U.S. Rte. 211.
White House, N side of State Rte. 646, .1 mi. NW of intersection with U.S. Rte.
  211.
Willow Grove, N side of State Rte. 642, .1 mi. SE of intersection with U.S. Rte.
  340.

LYNCHBURG

Academy of Music, 522-26 Main St.
Cralle's Folly, SE corner of Tenth and Wise Sts.
Early, Bishop John, House, 3890 Peakland Pl.
Garland, Samuel, Jr., House, SW corner of intersection of Madison and Third Sts.
Harris House, 626 Franklin St.
Hollins, House, 474 McIvor St.
Holy Cross Roman Catholic Church, 700 Clay St.
Hoyle-Harper House, 203 Federal St.
Lynchburg Courthouse, Court St.
Miller-Claytor House, W side of Ash St., N of Rivermont Ave., Riverside Park.
Moorman House, 4067 Fort Ave.
Quaker Meeting House, S side of Fort Ave., SW side of intersection with San-
  dusky Dr.

Roane-Rodes House, 1008 Harrison St.

Sandusky, N side of Sandusky Dr., .6 mi. NW of intersection with Fort Ave.

Simpson-Guggenheimer House, 1902 Grace St.

Spring Hill Tobacco Warehouse, NW corner of Commerce and Twelfth Sts.

Warwick House, 720 Court St.

Western Hotel, 501 Madison St.

Wills-Glass House, 605 Clay St.

LYNCHBURG VICINITY   Campbell County (16)

Graves Mill, N side of State Rte. 126, .7 mi. SW of intersection with State Rte. 675.

Rock Castle Farm, .3 mi. NE of State Rte. 126, .2 mi. SE of intersection with State Rte. 675.

Roseland, N side of State Rte. 126, .2 mi. W of intersection with State Rte. 675.

MACON VICINITY   Powhatan County (73)

Finches Mill, .1 mi. S of S end of State Rte. 625, .8 mi. S of intersection with State Rte. 637.

Red Hill, .1 mi. N of State Rte. 13, .4 mi. W of intersection with State Rte. 609.

MADISON   Madison County (57)

Carpenter, Samuel, Tavern, SW side of intersection of State Rte. 657 and U.S. Rte. 29.

Rock Hill, .1 mi. W of U.S. Rte. 29, 3.3 mi. S of intersection with State Rte. 662.

MADISON VICINITY   Madison County (57)

Hebron Lutheran Church, NE side of intersection of State Rtes. 638 and 653, 1 mi. NE of intersection with State Rte. 231.

MADISON MILLS VICINITY   Madison County (57)

Edgewood, .6 mi. S of State Rte. 620, 1 mi. SW of intersection with State Rte. 230.

Hilton, .3 mi. SW of State Rte. 230, .2 mi. W of intersection with State Rte. 620.

MADISONVILLE   Charlotte County (20)

Harvey's Store, W side of State Rte. 47, .2 mi. N of intersection with State Rte.
    649.
Harvey's Tavern, E side of State Rte. 47, .2 mi. N of intersection with State Rte.
    649.

MADISONVILLE VICINITY   Charlotte County (20)

High Hill, N side of State Rte. 615, 1.2 mi. W of intersection with State Rte. 47.

MAIDENS VICINITY   Goochland County (38)

Aspenwall, .4 mi. SE of State Rte. 634, 1 mi. NE of intersection with State Rte. 6.

MANAKIN VICINITY   Goochland County (38)

Brooke, Joe, House, .4 mi. N of State Rte. 6, 1.4 mi. NW of intersection with
    State Rte. 662.
Tuckahoe, .9 mi. S of State Rte. 650, .6 mi. E of intersection with State Rte. 647.

MANASSAS   Prince William County (76)

Prince William County Courthouse, NW corner of intersection of Lee Ave. and
    N. Grant St.

MANASSAS VICINITY   Prince William County (76)

Fourth Prince William County Courthouse, N side of State Rte. 619, at inter-
    section with State Rte. 678.
Hatcher's Memorial Baptist Church (formerly St. James Episcopal Church), E
    side of State Rte. 678, .1 mi. S of intersection with State Rte. 619.

MANGOHICK VICINITY   King William County (51)

Bear Garden, .8 mi. E of State Rte. 601, 1.6 mi. S of intersection with State
    Rte. 30.
Mill (Gravatt's Mill), S side of State Rte. 614, 1 mi. W of intersection with State
    Rte. 615.
Wyoming, .1 mi. NW of State Rte. 615, 2.2 mi. S of intersection with State Rte.
    652.

390

Belleview, E side of State Rte. 605, .2 mi. N of intersection with State Rte. 649.
Chericoke, N side of SW end of State Rte. 666, 1 mi. SW of intersection with
    State Rte. 600.
Dunluce, .5 mi. SE of State Rte. 613, .8 mi. N of intersection with State Rte. 618.
Grove, The (Wormeley Grove), .3 mi. E of E end of State Rte. 602, .3 mi. E of
    intersection with State Rte. 604.
Manskin Lodge, 1.5 mi. NE of State Rte. 604, 2.2 mi. NW of intersection with
    U.S. Rte. 360.
Marl Hill, .2 mi. W of U.S. Rte. 360, 1.2 mi. N of intersection with State Rte. 618.
Mt. Columbia, .5 mi. NE of State Rte. 649, 2.2 mi. W of intersection with State
    Rte. 605.
Pleasant Green, .9 mi. S of State Rte. 605, 1 mi. W of intersection with State
    Rte. 611.
Queenfield, .3 mi. NE of State Rte. 604, 1 mi. NW of intersection with U.S. Rte.
    360.
Sharon Baptist Church, W side of State Rte. 662, .2 mi. NE of intersection with
    U.S. Rte. 360.

MAPLE GROVE VICINITY   Rockbridge County (82)

Elder House, N side of State Rte. 654, 1.5 mi. W of intersection with State Rte.
    770.
Hillrock, N side of U.S. Rte. 60, .1 mi. E of intersection with State Rte. 629.
House, SE side of State Rte. 646, .4 mi. S of intersection with U.S. Rte. 60.
Oxford Presbyterian Church, SW side of State Rte. 677, .4 mi. NW of inter-
    section with State Rte. 612.
Trimble, Moses, House, N side of U.S. Rte. 60, 1.2 mi. E of intersection with
    State Rte. 646.

MARION   Smyth County (87)

House, S side of intersection of Main St. and Action Pl.
Smyth County Courthouse, E corner of intersection of E. Main and S. Church Sts.

MARION VICINITY   Smyth County (87)

Preston, John, House (Wilderness Road Trading Post), E side of State Rte. 645,
    .1 mi. S of intersection with U.S. Rte. 11.

MARTINSVILLE

Greenwood, 1101 Mulberry Rd.
Henry County Courthouse, N side of Main St., between Jones and Franklin Sts.
Smith House, 33 W. Church St.

MARTINSVILLE VICINITY   Henry County (45)

Beaver Creek, E side of State Rte. 108, 1.3 mi. N of intersection with State Rte. 667.
New Leatherwood Primitive Baptist Church, E side of State Rte. 657, .5 mi. N of intersection with State Rte. 57.

MASSIES MILL   Nelson County (63)

Level Green, W side of State Rte. 679, .2 mi. NW of intersection with State Rte. 666.

MASSIES MILL VICINITY   Nelson County (63)

Willow Brook, .4 mi. E of State Rte. 151, .1 mi. N of intersection with State Rte. 666.

MATHEWS   Mathews County (58)

Disciples Meeting House, SE side of intersection of State Rtes. 611 and 14.
Hurricane Hall, E side of State Rte. 14, .3 mi. S of intersection with State Rte. 1001.
Mathews County Clerk's Office, SW corner of intersection of State Rtes. 1002 and 611.
Mathews County Courthouse, SW corner of intersection of State Rtes. 611 and 1002.
Mathews County Sheriff's Office, NE corner of intersection of State Rtes. 1001 and 1003.
Miller House, SW corner of intersection of State Rtes. 1001 and 14.
Westville Baptist Church, E side of State Rte. 14, .1 mi. S of intersection with State Rte. 198.

MATHEWS VICINITY   Mathews County (58)

Springdale, .1 mi. W of State Rte. 14, .5 mi. S of intersection with State Rte. 611.
Spring Hill, .1 mi. W of State Rte. 14, .8 mi. S of intersection with State Rte. 611.

MATOACA VICINITY   Chesterfield County (21)

Bellevue, .2 mi. S of State Rte. 36, .4 mi. E of intersection with State Rte. 722.
Olive Hill, .5 mi. S of State Rte. 36, .7 mi. W of intersection with State Rte. 600.

MATTAPONI VICINITY   King and Queen County (49)

Brookshire, .3 mi. W of State Rte. 661, .3 mi. S of intersection with State Rte. 33.

Anchor & Hope Plantation, .9 mi. NW of State Rte. 121, 1 mi. S of intersection with State Rte. 610.

Fort Chiswell Plantation, S side of U.S. Rte. 11, .6 mi. E of intersection with U.S. Rte. 52 and State Rte. 121.

Mansion House (James McGavock House), E side of State Rte. 121, .3 mi. S of intersection with State Rte. 610.

MAYO   Halifax County (42)

Mayo, N side of State Rte. 887, .2 mi. E of intersection with State Rte. 96.

MAYO VICINITY   Halifax County (42)

Violet Glen, N side of State Rte. 602, .9 mi. NE of intersection with State Rte. 740.

Woodland Heights (Snowball Gate), SE side of State Rte. 866, .1 mi. SW of intersection of U.S. Rte. 501.

McDOWELL   Highland County (46)

Hull House, NE corner of intersection of State Rtes. 654 and 645, .1 mi. N of intersection with U.S. Rte. 250.

McDowell Presbyterian Church, W corner of intersection of State Rte. 678 and U.S. Rte. 250, .3 mi. SE of intersection with State Rte. 645.

Mansion House, N side of State Rte. 645, .2 mi. E of intersection with U.S. Rte. 250.

McGAHEYSVILLE VICINITY   Rockingham County (83)

Bonny Brook Farm, SE side of U.S. Rte. 33, .4 mi. NE of intersection with State Rte. 648.

Lethe, W side of State Rte. 652, 1 mi. S of intersection with State Rte. 650.

Three Springs Farm, W side of State Rte. 652, .4 mi. S of intersection with State Rte. 650.

McKENNY VICINITY   Dinwiddie County (27)

Harper House, .3 mi. W of State Rte. 638, 1.8 mi. NW of intersection with State Rte. 612.

Manson's Church, NE side of State Rte. 651, 1.9 mi. NW of intersection with State Rte. 650.

Sappony Episcopal Church, E side of E end of State Rte. 655, .6 mi. E of intersection with State Rtes. 646 and 692.

Worsham House, E side of State Rte. 613, .8 mi. N of intersection with State Rte. 638.

McLEAN   Fairfax County (30)

Bienvenue, 6800 Churchill Rd.

St. John's Episcopal Church, S side of Chain Bridge Rd., between Old Dominion Dr. and Brawner St.

Salona (Smoot House), 1214 Buchanan St.

McLEAN VICINITY   Fairfax County (30)

Drover's Rest, 8526 Georgetown Pike.

Spring Hill, 1121 Spring Hill Rd.

MEADOWVIEW VICINITY   Washington County (96)

Astin House, SW corner of intersection of U.S. Rte. 11, State Rtes. 803 and 80, 1 mi. S of intersection with State Rte. 609.

MECHANICSBURG VICINITY   Bland County (11)

House, NW side of State Rte. 42, 2 mi. NE of intersection with State Rte. 738.

MECHANICSVILLE VICINITY   Hanover County (43)

Cedar Grove, .5 mi. W of State Rte. 638, .6 mi. S of intersection with State Rte. 639.

Hogan House (Selvyn Farm), .4 mi. SE of State Rte. 615, .4 mi. SW of intersection with State Rte. 156.

Immanuel Church, S side of State Rte. 606, .3 mi. E of intersection with State Rte. 628.

MEHERRIN VICINITY   Prince Edward County (74)

Falkland, N side of State Rte. 632, 2.3 mi. NW of intersection with State Rte. 630.

Linden, .5 mi. SW of State Rte. 630, 2.3 mi. NW of intersection with State Rte. 632.

Mount Vernon, .3 mi. E of U.S. Rte. 15, 2.8 mi. S of intersection with State Rte. 634.

MEREDITHVILLE VICINITY   Brunswick County (13)

Millville, S side of State Rte. 618, .8 mi. SE of intersection with U.S. Rte. 1.

MERRY POINT VICINITY   Lancaster County (52)

Spring Hill, N side of State Rte. 604 at S terminus of Merry Point–Ottoman
    Wharf Ferry, .1 mi. E of intersection with State Rte. 610.

MIDDLEBROOK VICINITY   Augusta County (8)

Arbor Hill, N side of State Rte. 695, .3 mi. W of intersection with State Rte. 252.
Bethel Green, SW side of State Rte. 701, .5 mi. S of intersection with State Rte.
    695.
Locust Grove, NW side of State Rte. 252, 1.1 mi. SW of intersection with State
    Rte. 726.
McChesney House, .2 mi. NW of State Rte. 252, .7 mi. NE of intersection with
    State Rte. 876.
Sugar Loaf Farm, .4 mi. NW of State Rte. 695, .1 mi. SW of intersection with
    State Rte. 710.

MIDDLEBURG   Loudoun County (54)

Asbury Methodist Episcopal Church, NE corner of Madison and Jay Sts.
Hill, The, E side of State Rte. 766, .2 mi. S of intersection with U.S. Rte. 50.

MIDDLEBURG VICINITY   Loudoun County (54)

Benton, .1 mi. E of State Rte. 744, .2 mi. E of intersection with State Rte. 745.
Crednal, .2 mi. N of State Rte. 743, 1 mi. NW of intersection with State Rte. 611.

MIDDLETOWN   Frederick County (35)

St. Thomas Episcopal Church, S corner of intersection of State Rtes. 1102 and
    1105.

MIDDLETOWN VICINITY   Frederick County (35)

Monte Vista Farm, .6 mi. SE of U.S. Rte. 11, 1 mi. SW of intersection with State
    Rte. 627.

House, N side of U.S. Rte. 60, .1 mi. NW of intersection with State Rte. 754.
Sycamores, The, NW corner of intersection of State Rte. 1003 and U.S. Rte. 60.

MIDLOTHIAN VICINITY   Chesterfield County (21)

Aetna Hill, .3 mi. E of State Rte. 1007, .4 mi. N of intersection with State Rte. 1003.
Cole's Free School, .3 mi. SW of State Rte. 677, 1.4 mi. NE of intersection with U.S. Rte. 60.
Cole's Tavern, Barn, and Kitchen, NE corner of intersection of State Rte. 147 and U.S. Rte. 60, 1.6 mi. E of intersection with State Rte. 677.
Hallsborough Tavern, NW corner of intersection of State Rte. 607 and U.S. Rte. 60, 2 mi. W of intersection with State Rte. 667.
House, N side of State Rte. 677, 1 mi. NE of intersection with U.S. Rte. 60.
House, .2 mi. NE of State Rte. 653, .7 mi. S of intersection with State Rte. 688.
Ivymont, S side of U.S. Rte. 60, .1 mi. W of intersection with State Rte. 707.
Melrose, N side of State Rte. 677, 1.2 mi. NE of intersection with U.S. Rte. 60.
Moody House, .2 mi. W of State Rte. 653, .4 mi. SE of intersection with U.S. Rte. 60.
Railey Hill, E side of State Rte. 624, .1 mi. S of intersection with U.S. Rte. 60.
St. Leger, E side of State Rte. 652, 1.4 mi. S of intersection with State Rte. 604.
Trabue's Tavern, N side of State Rte. 677, 1.2 mi. NE of intersection with U.S. Rte. 60.
Trabue's Tavern, Outbuildings, N side of State Rte. 677, 1.2 mi. NE of intersection with U.S. Rte. 60.

MILL GAP VICINITY   Highland County (46)

House, E side of State Rte. 604, .5 mi. S of intersection with State Rte. 84.

MILLBORO SPRINGS VICINITY   Bath County (9)

Green Valley Farm, W side of intersection of State Rtes. 678 and 629, 6.5 mi. NE of intersection with State Rte. 625.
Windy Grove Presbyterian Church, W side of intersection of State Rtes. 678 and 39, .6 mi. NW of intersection with U.S. Rte. 42.

MILLERS TAVERN VICINITY   Essex County (29)

Beaver's Hill, .4 mi. N of State Rte. 620, at the intersection of State Rte. 625.
Cherry Walk, .1 mi. W of State Rte. 620, 2.3 mi. N of intersection with U.S. Rte. 360.

Laurel Grove, .5 mi. NE of State Rte. 620, .8 mi. N of intersection with U.S. Rte. 360.

Retreat, .4 mi. NE of State Rte. 621, .8 mi. NW of intersection with U.S. Rte. 360.

St. Paul's Episcopal Church, N side of U.S. Rte. 360 at Essex Co. line, 1.4 mi. W of intersection with State Rte. 620.

Shelba, .5 mi. W of State Rte. 620, .8 mi. N of intersection with U.S. Rte. 360.

Wayland, .2 mi. W of State Rte. 622, 1.1 mi. N of intersection with State Rte. 621.

Wood Farm, .4 mi. NW of U.S. Rte. 360, 2.8 mi. NE of intersection with State Rte. 620.

Woodlawn, SE side of U.S. Rte. 360, 2 mi. NE of intersection with State Rte. 620.

Woodville, .6 mi. NW of U.S. Rte. 360, 2 mi. NE of intersection with State Rte. 620.

MILLERS TAVERN VICINITY   King and Queen County (49)

Davis House, S side of U.S. Rte. 360, .2 mi. W of intersection with State Rte. 620.

Fleetwood, .2 mi. NW of U.S. Rte. 360, .3 mi. SW of intersection with State Rte. 622.

Mann House, .1 mi. SW of State Rte. 620, 1.6 mi. S of intersection with U.S. Rte. 360.

MILLWOOD   Clarke County (22)

Christ Episcopal Church, W side of State Rte. 255, .2 mi. NE of intersection with State Rte. 723.

Morgan, Daniel, Mill (Millwood Mill), SW side of State Rte. 723, opposite intersection with State Rte. 255.

Old Christ Church, .4 mi. NE of Spout Run, NW side of State Rte. 255, .3 mi. NE of intersection with State Rte. 723.

MILLWOOD VICINITY   Clarke County (22)

Clay Hill, N side of State Rte. 651, .9 mi. SE of intersection with State Rte. 255.

Gaywood, .2 mi. E of State Rte. 625, 1.4 mi. S of intersection with U.S. Rte. 50.

Gibson House (Mar-tu-con Farm), .3 mi. NW of State Rte. 622, .9 mi. S of intersection with U.S. Rte. 50.

Goshen, .1 mi. S of State Rte. 622, .8 mi. E of intersection with State Rte. 625.

Long Branch, .8 mi. S of State Rte. 626, .2 mi. W of intersection with State Rte. 624.

Longwood, .2 mi. E of State Rte. 620, .4 mi. N of intersection with State Rte. 255.

Old Baptist Meeting House, E side of State Rte. 625, .2 mi. S of intersection with State Rte. 622.

Red Gate Farm, .2 mi. SE of State Rte. 624, .6 mi. SW of intersection with State Rte. 622.

Riverside, S side of U.S. Rte. 50, .5 mi. E of intersection with State Rte. 723.

Rosney, .2 mi. W of State Rte. 624, .3 mi. S of intersection with U.S. Rte. 50.

Shan Hill, .3 mi. E of State Rte. 651, 1.1 mi. SE of intersection with State Rte. 255.

Vineyard, The, .1 mi. E of State Rte. 621, 1 mi. N of intersection with State Rte. 723.

MINERAL VICINITY   Louisa County (55)

Sunning Hill, .1 mi. NW of U.S. Rte. 522, 2.4 mi. N of intersection with State Rte. 208.

MINT SPRING VICINITY   Augusta County (8)

Annandale, .4 mi. SE of U.S. Rte. 11, .8 mi. NE of intersection with State Rte. 654.

Chapel Hill, .1 mi. NE of State Rte. 654, 1.2 mi. SE of intersection with U.S. Rte. I-81.

MITCHELLS VICINITY   Culpeper County (24)

Horeshoe Farm, .8 mi. S of State Rte. 614, .6 mi. W of intersection with State Rte. 721.

MOLLUSK VICINITY   Lancaster County (52)

Chowning's Ferry, .2 mi. S of State Rte. 627, .2 mi. W of intersection with State Rte. 626.

Midway, .8 mi. W of State Rte. 354, .1 mi. N of intersection with State Rte. 681.

Monaskon, .1 mi. S of State Rte. 681, 1 mi. SE of intersection with State Rte. 354.

MONROE VICINITY   Amherst County (5)

Cloverdale Farm, .1 mi. E of State Rte. 130, 1 mi. SE of intersection with State Rte. 652.

MONTEREY   Highland County (46)

Bell, James, House, NE side of U.S. Rte. 250, .2 mi. NW of intersection with U.S. Rte. 220.

Highland County Courthouse, SW side of U.S. Rte. 250, .2 mi. NW of intersection with U.S. Rte. 220.

Shoemake House, NE side of U.S. Rte. 250, .2 mi. NW of intersection with U.S. Rte. 220.

MONTEREY VICINITY

Highland County (46)

Seybert Hills Slave Quarters, E side of State Rte. 629, .4 mi. N of intersection with State Rte. 631.

Toll House, W side of U.S. Rte. 250, .8 mi. S of intersection with State Rte. 629.

MONTPELIER VICINITY

Hanover County (43)

Lombardy Farm, .4 mi. SW of U.S. Rte. 33, .8 mi. S of intersection with State Rte. 657.

Long Row, E side of State Rte. 658, 1.3 mi. N of intersection with State Rte. 683.

Meadow, The, SE corner of intersection of State Rtes. 668 and 683, 1.1 mi. E of intersection with State Rte. 658.

Oakland, .5 mi. NW of State Rte. 631, 1.2 mi. NE of intersection with State Rte. 674.

Taylors Creek, .3 mi. NW of State Rte. 610, 1.6 mi. S of intersection with State Rte. 691.

MONTPELIER STATION VICINITY

Orange County (69)

Montpelier, 1 mi. SE of intersection of State Rtes. 20 and 693.

MONTROSS

Westmoreland County (97)

Westmoreland County Courthouse, N side of intersection of State Rtes. 3 and 622.

MONTVALE VICINITY

Bedford County (10)

Gross House, .4 mi. SE of State Rte. 607, .5 mi. SW of intersection with U.S. Rte. 460.

Locust Level, SW side of U.S. Rte. 460, .4 mi. NW of intersection with State Rte. 695.

MOUNT CRAWFORD VICINITY   Rockingham County (83)

Barn, .1 mi. W of Cooks Creek, E side of U.S. Rte. 11, .5 mi. S of intersection with State Rte. 727.
House, W side of U.S. Rte. 11, .5 mi. S of intersection with State Rte. 727.

MOUNT JACKSON   Shenandoah County (86)

Town House, W side of U.S. Rte. 11, NW corner of intersection with State Rte. 263.
Union Church, W side of U.S. Rte. 11, NW corner of intersection with State Rte. 263.

MOUNT JACKSON VICINITY   Shenandoah County (86)

Byrd, Moance, House, N side of State Rte. 616, .5 mi. E of intersection with U.S. Rte. 11.

MOUNT HOLLY VICINITY   Westmoreland County (97)

Glebe, The, .1 mi. N of State Rte. 703, 1.3 mi. NE of intersection with State Rte. 625.
Laurel Springs, NE corner of intersection of State Rtes. 202 and 621.
Nominy Church, N side of State Rte. 202, .3 mi. W of intersection with State Rte. 662.
Spring Grove, N side of State Rte. 202, .2 mi. SE of intersection with State Rte. 621.

MOUNT SOLON VICINITY   Augusta County (8)

Crone House, N side of State Rte. 747, .3 mi. E of intersection with State Rte. 613.
Mossy Creek Presbyterian Church, W side of State Rte. 613, .1 mi. SE of intersection with State Rte. 747.

MOUNTAIN GROVE VICINITY   Bath County (9)

Gatewood House, .1 mi. S of intersection of State Rtes. 39 and 600, 1.8 mi. N of intersection with State Rte. 2.

400

MOUTH OF WILSON VICINITY

Grayson County (39)

Cox House, W side of State Rte. 712, .3 mi. S of intersection with State Rte. 710.
Parson House, NW side of State Rte. 767, 1.1 mi. SW of intersection with State Rte. 716.

NACE VICINITY

Botetourt County (12)

Rader, Samuel, House, SE side of U.S. Rte. 11, 1.4 mi. SW of intersection with State Rte. 606.
Stair, Henry, House, NW side of U.S. Rte. 11, .7 mi. NE of intersection with State Rte. 640.
Woodsdale Farm, .2 mi. S of U.S. Rte. 11, .6 mi. SW of intersection with State Rte. 606.

NAOLA VICINITY

Amherst County (5)

Pedlar Farm, .8 mi. SW of State Rte. 635, .2 mi. NW of intersection with State Rte. 642.
Red Hill Farm, .3 mi. NW of State Rte. 647, 2 mi. E of intersection with State Rte. 644.
St. Luke's Church, NW side of State Rte. 635, .3 mi. NE of intersection with State Rte. 647.
Tavern, .1 mi. S of intersection of State Rtes. 643 and 635, .5 mi. NE of intersection with State Rte. 647.
Verdant Vale, 1.6 mi. W of SW end of State Rte. 695, 2.4 mi. SW of intersection with State Rte. 650.

NATHALIE

Halifax County (42)

House, E side of State Rte. 644, .1 mi. SW of intersection with State Rte. 631.

NATHALIE VICINITY

Halifax County (42)

House, SW side of State Rte. 632, 2.8 mi. N of intersection with State Rtes. 634 and 626.

NATURAL BRIDGE VICINITY

Rockbridge County (82)

Barclay's Tavern, W side of State Rte. 609, .1 mi. S of intersection with State Rte. 692.
Gilmore House, W side of State Rte. 743, .2 mi. S of intersection with State Rte. 686.

Greenlee House (Herring Hall), N side of State Rte. 686, .4 mi. E of intersection with State Rte. 690.

Hamilton's School House, SE side of State Rte. 611, 2 mi. NE of intersection with State Rte. 661.

Liberty Hill, 1 mi. N of State Rte. 690, .8 mi. N of intersection with State Rte. 686.

Moranda, W side of intersection of State Rtes. 610 and 692, 1.5 mi. NW of intersection with State Rte. 609.

Oak Lawn, .4 mi. W of intersection of State Rte. 684 and U.S. Rte. 11, 1 mi. NE of intersection with State Rte. 609.

Pine Hill Farm, NW side of State Rte. 610, .6 mi. NE of intersection with State Rte. 691.

Rural Valley, N side of State Rte. 691, 1 mi. NW of intersection with State Rte. 609.

Stone Castle, W side of State Rte. 609, .5 mi. N of intersection with State Rte. 692.

Sunny Knoll, .3 mi. N of intersection of State Rte. 609 and U.S. Rte. 11, 1.3 mi. W of intersection with State Rte. 760.

NAXERA VICINITY

Gloucester County (37)

Level Green, .4 mi. NE of State Rte. 614, 1.6 mi. NW of intersection with State Rte. 629.

Warner Hall, .1 mi. S of State Rte. 629, 1 mi. SE of intersection with State Rte. 614.

NELLYSFORD

Nelson County (63)

Woods House, SE side of State Rte. 151, .1 mi. NE of intersection with State Rte. 634.

NELLYSFORD VICINITY

Nelson County (63)

Elk Hill, W side of State Rte. 151, .9 mi. SW of intersection with State Rte. 627.

Glen Thorn, .4 mi. E of State Rte. 627, .9 mi. S of intersection with State Rte. 151.

Rockfish Church, .1 mi. SE of State Rte. 151, .5 mi. NE of intersection with State Rte. 613.

NEW CANTON

Buckingham County (15)

Trinity Presbyterian Church, N side of State Rte. 670, .6 mi. NE of intersection with U.S. Rte. 15.

NEW CASTLE   Craig County (23)

Central Hotel, N corner of intersection of Court and Main Sts.
Craig County Courthouse, W corner of intersection of Court and Main Sts.
Locust Hill, 510 Main St.
Sheriff's House and Jail, 203 Court St.

NEW CASTLE VICINITY   Craig County (23)

Aken-McCarteney House, N side of State Rte. 611, .6 mi. W of intersection with
    State Rte. 685.
Bellview Farm, N corner of intersection of State Rtes. 625 and 42, 4.4 mi. SW
    of intersection with State Rte. 622.
Sinking Creek Church (Salem Methodist Church), S side of State Rte. 42, 1.6 mi.
    SW of intersection with State Rte. 623.

NEW HOPE VICINITY   Augusta County (9)

Bellemont, SE side of intersection of State Rtes. 778 and 608, 1 mi. N of inter-
    section with State Rte. 616.
Bonny Doon (River Bend Farm), NW end of State Rte. 777, .6 mi. NW of inter-
    section with State Rte. 774.
Brick Kiln, E of S end of State Rte. 614, 1.4 mi. S of intersection with State
    Rte. 5.

NEW KENT   New Kent County (64)

Dandridge House, NW side of State Rte. 33, .2 mi. NE of intersection with State
    Rte. 605.
Lawyer's Office, S side of State Rte. 33, .3 mi. NE of intersection with State
    Rte. 605.
New Kent County Courthouse, SE corner of intersection of State Rtes. 648 and
    33.
Tavern, N side of State Rte. 33, .3 mi. NE of intersection with State Rte. 605.

NEW KENT VICINITY   New Kent County (64)

Aspen Grove, .1 mi. N of State Rte. 628, .3 mi. W of intersection with State
    Rte. 627.
Cedar Lane, .3 mi. N of State Rte. 33, 2 mi. W of intersection with State Rte. 608.
House, N side of State Rte. 33, 1 mi. SE of intersection with State Rte. 623.
New Kent Poor House, .1 mi. S of State Rte. 33, .6 mi. E of intersection with
    State Rte. 608.

NEW LONDON ACADEMY   Bedford County (10)

New London Academy, N side of State Rte. 297, .1 mi. E of intersection with
State Rte. 811.

NEW MARKET   Shenandoah County (86)

Lee-Jackson Hotel, SE corner of intersection of U.S. Rte. 11 and State Rte. 1002.
Log House, W side of U.S. Rte. 11, between State Rte. T1010 and U.S. Rte. 211.
Stone Corner, NW corner of intersection of U.S. Rte. 11 and State Rte. 1002.
Town Pump, NE corner of intersection of U.S. Rte. 11 and State Rte. 1008.

NEW POINT COMFORT   Mathews County (58)

New Point Comfort Lighthouse, southernmost tip of Mathews Co. at the intersection of Mobjack Bay and Chesapeake Bay.

NEWBERN   Pulaski County (78)

Hanes House, S corner of intersection of State Rte. 697 and 611.
Jail, NW side of intersection of State Rtes. 611 and 697.
Newbern Christian Church, NW side of State Rte. 611, .2 mi. SW of intersection
with State Rte. 697.
Reservoir, NW side of State Rte. 611, .1 mi. NE of intersection with State Rte.
697.

NEWBERN VICINITY   Pulaski County (78)

Rock House, .1 mi. E of State Rte. 100, .7 mi. SW of intersection with State
Rte. 644.

NEWPORT   Augusta County (9)

Cedars, The, W side of State Rte. 252, .2 mi. N of intersection with State Rte.
620.

NEWPORT NEWS

End View, .2 mi. E of State Rte. 238, .4 mi. N of intersection with State Rte. 143.
Warwick County Clerk's Office (Virgil L. Grissom Branch Library), W side of
U.S. Rte. 60, .1 mi. NW of intersection with State Rte. 173.

NEWPORT NEWS VICINITY   York County (100)

Lee Hall, .6 mi. NW of intersection of U.S. Rte. 60 and State Rte. 238.

NEWTOWN VICINITY   King and Queen County (49)

Boulware, SE intersection of State Rtes. 721 and 625.
Hill, The, W side of State Rte. 625, .2 mi. S of intersection with State Rte. 721.
House, W side of State Rte. 625, .1 mi. S of intersection with State Rte. 721.
Lot, The, N side of State Rte. 721, .2 mi. W of intersection with State Rte. 625.
Motley, Colonel, House, .2 mi. W of State Rte. 721, .9 mi. N of intersection with
    State Rte. 627.
Motley House, .2 mi. W of State Rte. 721, 1.8 mi. N of intersection with State
    Rte. 627.
Providence, N side of State Rte. 627, .6 mi. W of intersection with State Rte. 721.
Tutor Hall, .1 mi. S of State Rte. 721, 1.2 mi. W of intersection with State Rte.
    625.

NICKELSVILLE VICINITY   Scott County (80)

Killgore Fort House, SE side of State Rte. 71, .8 mi. S of intersection with State
    Rte. 670.

NOMINI GROVE VICINITY   Westmoreland County (97)

Level Grove, .1 mi. NE of State Rte. 3, .1 mi. N of intersection with State Rte.
    612.

NORFOLK

Allmand House, 327 Duke St.
Boush-Tazewell House (Tazewell Hall), 6225 Powhatan Ave.
Camp-Hubard House, 308 W Freemason St.
Christ Church, 421 E. Freemason St.
First Methodist Church, 208-14 Cumberland St.
First Orthodox Synagogue, 432 Cumberland St.
Fort Norfolk, 803 Front St.
Freemason Street Baptist Church, 400 E Freemason St.
Glisson, Oliver, House, 405 Duke St.
House, 407-15 Bank St.
House, 515 Bank St.
House, 403 W Bute St.
House, 327 Cumberland St.
House (Dabney House), 332 Duke St.

House, 803 Main St.
Lamb House, 420 Bute St.
Myers, Moses, House, SW corner E. Freemason and N. Bank Sts.
Norfolk Academy, 420 Bank St.
Norfolk City Hall (MacArthur Memorial), 140 Bank St.
Presbyterian Church, 501 Bank St.
St. John House, 414 Bute St.
St. Mary's Academy, 1000 Holt St.
St. Mary's Church, 232 Chapel St.
St. Paul's Church, 201 St. Paul's Blvd.
School Building, 512 Bank St.
School Building, NE corner of Brambelton Ave. and Bank St.
Seldon, Dr. Wm. Boswell, House, 351 Botetourt St.
Stores, S of intersection of Commercial Pl. and E. Main St.
Talbot Hall, 600 Talbot Hall Rd.
Theatre, 931 Bank St.
U.S. Customs House, 101 E. Main St.
Willoughby-Baylor House, 601 Freemason St.

NORTH VICINITY   Mathews County (58)

Auburn, .6 mi. S of W end of State Rte. 620, 2.2 mi. SW of intersection with
    State Rte. 14.
Green Plains, .8 mi. S of State Rte. 620, 1.7 mi. SW of intersection with State
    Rte. 14.

NORTH GARDEN VICINITY   Albemarle County (2)

Edgemont, .4 mi. W of State Rte. 712, 1.5 mi. SE of intersection with State
    Rte. 631.
House, E side of U.S. Rte. 29, 3.1 mi. NE of intersection with State Rte. 708.
House, .5 mi. SE of State Rte. 20, 2.5 mi. N of intersection with State Rte. 708.
Mooreland, NW side of U.S. Rte. 29, .8 mi. N of intersection with State Rte. 708.
Sunny Bank, .4 mi. W of State Rte. 712, 1.1 mi. S of intersection with State Rte.
    813.
Tudor Grove, .3 mi. W of State Rte. 631, 1.6 mi. NE of intersection with State
    Rte. 706.
Woodlands, E side of U.S. Rte. 20, 4 mi. NE of intersection with State Rte. 708.

NORWOOD   Nelson County (63)

Christ Church, S side of State Rte. 626, .1 mi. E of intersection with State Rte.
    655.

NORWOOD VICINITY   Nelson County (63)

Edgewood, SE side of State Rte. 626, 1.4 mi. NE of intersection with State Rte. 743.

Montezuma, .3 mi. N of State Rte. 626, .6 mi. NE of intersection with State Rte. 655.

Soldier's Joy, .3 mi. N of State Rte. 647, 1.5 mi. E of intersection with State Rte. 626.

Union Hill, .2 mi. N of State Rte. 647, 1.4 mi. E of intersection with State Rte. 626.

NOTTOWAY   Nottoway County (68)

Old Brick Church, W side of intersection of U.S. Rte. 460 and State Rte. 625.

NOTTOWAY VICINITY   Nottoway County (68)

Fancy Hill, W side of State Rte. 611, .2 mi. S of intersection with State Rte. 607.

NUTTSVILLE VICINITY   Lancaster County (52)

Epping Forest, .1 mi. S of State Rte. 622, .6 mi. E of intersection with State Rte. 618.

OILVILLE VICINITY   Goochland County (38)

Monterey, .2 mi. N of State Rte. 637, .4 mi. NW of intersection with State Rte. 635.

Poor House, S side of State Rte. 633, 1 mi. SW of intersection with State Rte. 634.

Woodlawn, NE side of intersection of State Rte. 612 and U.S. Rte. 250, 1.2 mi. SE of intersection with State Rte. 654.

OLDHAM VICINITY   Westmoreland County (97)

Ebenezer Methodist Church, SW side of State Rte. 600, .1 mi. SE of intersection with State Rte. 203.

ONANCOCK   Accomack County (1)

Hopkins and Brother Store, NW side of State Rte. T1023, NW side of intersection with State Rte. 178.

Meadville, .3 mi. E of State Rte. 778, .8 mi. N of intersection with State Rte. 638.

ORANGE   Orange County (69)

Ballard, Garland, House, 158 E. Main St.
Holladay House (Chapman, Reynolds, House), N side of State Rte. 20, .1 mi. W of intersection with State Rte. 615.
Horn Tavern, 109 May-Fray Ave.
Orange County Courthouse, NW corner of Madison Rd. and W. Main St.
Orange Hotel, 164 E. Main St.
Peliso, 205 Morton St.
St. Thomas Episcopal Church, E side of U.S. Rte. 15, .1 mi. S of intersection with State Rte. 20.
Spring Garden, 154 Madison Rd.

ORANGE VICINITY   Orange County (69)

Berry Hill, .3 mi. NE of State Rte. 647, .1 mi. SE of intersection with U.S. Rte. 15.
Bloomsbury, 1 mi. N of State Rte. 20, .5 mi. E of intersection with State Rte. 629.
Clifton, .5 mi. SW of State Rte. 639, .9 mi. NW of intersection with U.S. Rte. 15.
Glenmary, .3 mi. W of U.S. Rte. 15, .2 mi. S of intersection with State Rte. 639.
Greenfields, .4 mi. N of State Rte. 615, .8 mi. E of intersection with State Rte. (Alt.) 20.
Mayhurst, .3 mi. NW of U.S. Rte. 15, .4 mi. SW of intersection with State Rte. 647.
Meadow Farm, .3 mi. NE of State Rte. 612, 1.6 mi. SE of intersection with State Rte. 20.
Middle Hill, .3 mi. N of State Rte. 20, 1.3 mi. E of intersection with State Rte. 612.
Woodley, .3 mi. W of U.S. Rte. 15, 2.6 mi. S of intersection with State Rte. 647.

ORCHID VICINITY   Louisa County (55)

Attonce, .5 mi. SE of State Rte. 698, .2 mi. W of intersection with State Rte. 640.
Bellefast, N side of U.S. Rte. 33, .4 mi. E of intersection with State Rte. 635.
Braehead, .2 mi. NE of State Rte. 629, 2 mi. SW of intersection with State Rte. 640 and U.S. Rte. 522.
Brick House, .1 mi. N of U.S. Rte. 33, .5 mi. E of intersection with State Rte. 601.
Dunlora, N side of State Rte. 698, .6 mi. W of intersection with State Rte. 640.

Farrar House, .1 mi. NE of U.S. Rte. 522, 1.8 mi. SE of intersection with State Rte. 756.

Southanna Baptist Church, .1 mi. NW of U.S. Rte. 522, .5 mi. SW of intersection with State Rte. 648.

ORDINARY VICINITY   Gloucester County (37)

Timberneck Hall, 1.4 mi. S of State Rte. 635, .7 mi. SW of intersection with State Rte. 636.

OWENS VICINITY   Botetourt County (12)

Snider, John, House, N side of State Rte. 655, 1.3 mi. SW of intersection with State Rte. 682.

Stover, Jacob, House, .2 mi. SE of State Rte. 655, .4 mi. E of intersection with U.S. Rte. 220.

OWENS VICINITY   King George County (50)

Caledon, .2 mi. N of State Rte. 218, 1.2 mi. W of intersection with State Rte. 206.

Cedar Grove, 3 mi. NE of State Rte. 218, .5 mi. E of intersection with State Rte. 206.

Liberty, .9 mi. NW of State Rte. 624, 1.4 mi. NE of intersection with State Rte. 635.

Panorama, 1 mi. N of State Rte. 206, .4 mi. W of intersection with State Rte. 624.

OWENTON VICINITY   King and Queen County (49)

Peach Grove, .2 mi. N of State Rte. 721 at intersection with State Rte. 660.

Traveler's Rest, .2 mi. SW of State Rte. 721, .8 mi. SE of intersection with State Rte. 639.

PACES VICINITY   Halifax County (42)

Barksdale Tobacco Factory, .1 mi. N of State Rte. 659, 1 mi. W of intersection with State Rte. 662.

Brooklyn Store, NW side of State Rte. 659, .2 mi. SW of intersection with State Rte. 820.

Carter's Tavern, S side of State Rte. 659, .5 mi. W of intersection with State Rte. 662.

Creekside, NW side of State Rte. 659, 2.6 mi. E of intersection with State Rte. 691.

Elm Hill, .1 mi. NW of State Rte. 659, .9 mi. E of intersection with State Rte. 691.

Grace Episcopal Church, W side of State Rte. 671, .5 mi. S of intersection with State Rte. 659.

Redfield, N side of State Rte. 683, 1.5 mi. NW of intersection with State Rte. 680.

School, N side of State Rte. 659, .1 mi. E of intersection with State Rte. 662.

Springfield, N side of State Rte. 659, .3 mi. E of intersection with State Rte. 683.

PALMER SPRINGS   Mecklenburg County (59)

House, N corner of intersection of State Rtes. 711 and 712.

PALMER SPRINGS VICINITY   Mecklenburg County (59)

House, .4 mi. SE of State Rte. 711, 2 mi. SE of intersection with U.S. Rte. 1.

House, .4 mi. E of U.S. Rte. 1, .5 mi. S of intersection with State Rte. 712.

Logsdale, .4 mi. S of State Rte. 712, .8 mi. NE of intersection with State Rtes. 711 and 713.

PALMYRA   Fluvanna County (33)

Fluvanna County Courthouse, SE side of State Rte. 1005, at intersection with U.S. Rte. 15 and State Rte. 601.

Fluvanna County Jail, SW side of State Rte. 1006, .1 mi. S of intersection with State Rte. 601.

PALMYRA VICINITY   Fluvanna County (33)

Cary's Brook, .4 mi. N of State Rte. 615, .8 mi. NE of intersection with U.S. Rte. 15.

Chatham, E side of State Rte. 609, 2 mi. S of intersection with State Rte. 615.

Cole's Tavern, W side of State Rte. 601, W corner of intersection with State Rte. 608.

Cumber, .4 mi. SW of State Rte. 616, 2.4 mi. NW of intersection with State Rte. 600.

Curren House, NE side of State Rte. 608, E corner of intersection with State Rte. 601.

Fair View (Stacked Arms), .2 mi. N of State Rte. 640, 1.5 mi. W of intersection with State Rte. 647.

Glen Burnie, .3 mi. E of U.S. Rte. 15, immediately S of intersection with State Rte. 661.

Union, The, .2 mi. SW of State Rte. 616, 1.8 mi. NW of intersection with State Rte. 600.

PAMPLIN   Appomattox County (6)

Elon Baptist Church, W side of State Rte. T600, .3 mi. S of intersection with
    State Rte. 678.

PAMPLIN VICINITY   Appomattox County (6)

Piney Ridge Church, W side of State Rte. 628, .5 mi. S of intersection with State
    Rte. 629.
Woodlawn, .2 mi. E of State Rte. 600, 1 mi. NE of intersection with State Rte.
    601.

PARIS VICINITY   Fauquier County (31)

Amandale, 50 yds. S of Loudoun Co. line, .2 mi. E of intersection with State
    Rte. 618.
Belle Grove, .2 mi. W of U.S. Rte. 17, .2 mi. S of intersection with State Rte. 710.
Greystone Farm, S side of U.S. Rte. 50, opposite intersection with State Rte. 618.
Ovoka, .3 mi. W of State Rte. 701, .3 mi. S of intersection with State Rte. 759.
Smith House, .1 mi. S of Loudoun Co. line, .1 mi. W of intersection with State
    Rte. 618.

PARTLOW VICINITY   Spotsylvania County (89)

Pine Forest, 1.4 mi. W of State Rte. 605, 1.5 mi. NE of intersection with State
    Rte. 622.

PEARISBURG   Giles County (36)

Giles County Courthouse, NE corner of U.S. Rte. 460 and State Rte. 100.
House, 300 S. Main St.
Johnson, Dr. Andrew, House, 208 N. Main St.
Johnson, Dr. Harvey, Office, 210 N. Main St.
Price, David, House, 100 block N. Main St.

PEARISBURG VICINITY   Giles County (36)

Prospect, W side of State Rte. 100, 1 mi. S of intersection with State Rte. 665.

PEARY VICINITY   Mathews County (58)

Port Haywood House, .3 mi. S of State Rte. 608, .7 mi. NW of intersection with
    State Rte. 649.

PEMBERTON VICINITY

Goochland County (38)

Bolling Island, .2 mi. SE of State Rte. 616, .2 mi. SW of intersection with State Rte. 618.

Howard's Neck, 1 mi. W of State Rte. 45, 1 mi. N of Pemberton.

Locust Grove, .1 mi. N of State Rte. 625, .6 mi. E of intersection with State Rte. 616.

Mannsville, .7 mi. SW of State Rte. 678, 1.2 mi. S of intersection with State Rte. 616.

Snowden, .3 mi. SE of State Rte. 618, 2 mi. SE of intersection with State Rte. 45.

PEMBROKE VICINITY

Giles County (36)

Maybrook, N side of State Rte. 730, 1 mi. E of intersection with State Rte. 625.

Wheatland, NE side of U.S. Rte. 460, .4 mi. NW of intersection with State Rte. 625.

Willowcroft, W side of U.S. Rte. 460, .4 mi. W of intersection with State Rte. 605.

PENDLETON VICINITY

Louisa County (55)

Cuckoo House, E side of U.S. Rte. 33, .7 mi. S of intersection with U.S. Rte. 522.

Fork Creek, .2 mi. W of State Rte. 640, 1.6 mi. S of intersection with State Rte. 605.

Gilboa Christian Church, SW side of U.S. Rte. 33, .4 mi. SE of intersection with U.S. Rte. 522.

Hickory Forest, W side of U.S. Rte. 522, .2 mi. S of intersection with State Rte. 647.

North Bend, .1 mi. W of State Rte. 646, .5 mi. NW of intersection with State Rte. 697.

Oak Shade, .1 mi. E of U.S. Rte. 522, 2.9 mi. S of intersection with State Rte. 699.

White Walnut, .8 mi. NW of State Rte. 605, 1 mi. S of intersection with U.S. Rte. 33.

Woodberry, 1.4 mi. SE of State Rte. 640, .7 mi. SE of intersection with State Rte. 605.

Yanceyville Mill, N side of State Rte. 697, .1 mi. W of intersection with State Rte. 646.

PENHOOK VICINITY

Franklin County (34)

Clements, Dr. George W., House, NW side of State Rte. 890, 1 mi. SW of intersection with State Rte. 782.

PETERSBURG

Beazley House, 558 High St.
Blandford Church, 319 S. Crater Rd.
Blandford Masonic Lodge No. 3, W. Tabb St., opposite Union St.
Burgess Double House, 132-34 S. Adams St.
Chelsea, SE corner of Jefferson and Franklin Sts.
Dodson House, NE corner of Marshall and Sycamore Sts.
Dodson's Tavern (Bissett House), 311 High St.
Farmer's Bank, NW corner of Bollingbrook St. and Cockade Alley.
Folly Castle, Washington St., opposite Perry St.
Gas Works, SE corner of Bank and Madison Sts.
Gillfield Manor, 26 Perry St.
Grace Episcopal Church, High and Cross Sts.
House, 112 Franklin St.
House, 114 Franklin St.
House, 142 Franklin St.
House, 558A High St.
House, 103 N. Jefferson St.
Jones, Peter, II, Store, Market St., near Old St.
Kevan, Andrew, House, 32 S. Market St.
Ladies' Hospital, 203 Bollingbrook St.
Lyons House, 132 Franklin St.
McCabe House, S. Sycamore St., near College Pl.
McIlwaine House, 106 Market St.
McIlwaine House, S. Market St., near Lawrence St.
McIlwaine House, SW corner of Washington and Perry Sts.
Mountain View, 801 Fort Henry St.
Ragland House, 123 S. Sycamore St.
Ragland House, 129 S. Sycamore St.
St. Paul's Episcopal Church, 110 N. Union St.
Second Presbyterian Church, NE corner of Washington and Lafayette Sts.
Smith, John, House, 126 S. Adam St.
Tabb Street Church Office, NE corner of W. Tabb and Union Sts.
Wallace, Thomes, House, SW corner of Market and Brown Sts.
Water Works, 424 St. Andrew St.

PETERSBURG VICINITY   Dinwiddie County (27)

Burlington, .1 mi. NE of State Rte. 600, NW side of intersection with State Rte. 601.
Mansfield, .2 mi. N of State Rte. 601, .9 mi. W of intersection with State Rte. 600.
Mayfield, S side of U.S. Rte. 1/460, .5 mi. E of intersection with U.S. Rte. 460, on grounds of Central State Hospital.
Mayfield Cottage, S side of U.S. Rte. 1/460, .5 mi. E of intersection with U.S. Rte. 460, on grounds of Central State Hospital.
Sysonby, .2 mi. N of State Rte. 601, .6 mi. W of intersection with State Rte. 600.

PHENIX VICINITY

Gravel Hill, .3 mi. NW of State Rte. 649, 1.7 mi. SW of intersection with State Rte. 746.

Green Level, 1 mi. E of State Rte. 649, .6 mi. NE of intersection with State Rte. 746.

House, SW side of State Rte. 619, .3 mi. NW of intersection with State Rte. 649.

House, .3 mi. E of State Rte. 649, .3 mi. N of intersection with State Rte. 40.

PLAIN VIEW VICINITY
King and Queen County (49)

House (William Anderson House), .2 mi. W of State Rte. 605, .2 mi. S of intersection with State Rte. 14.

Shackelfords Chapel, NE side of State Rte. 14, .4 mi. NW of intersection with State Rte. 605.

PLEASANT VALLEY VICINITY
Buckingham County (15)

Buckingham White Sulphur Springs Hotel, .4 mi. SE of State Rte. 635, .8 mi. SW of intersection with State Rte. 633.

PORT HAYWOOD
Mathews County (58)

Woodstock, .2 mi. SW of State Rte. 14, .2 mi. N of intersection with State Rte. 608.

PORT REPUBLIC
Rockingham County (83)

Boxwood Gardens, NW side of State Rte. 605, .2 mi. SW of intersection with State Rte. 865.

PORT REPUBLIC VICINITY
Rockingham County (83)

Lynnwood, .1 mi. E of State Rte. 659, .1 mi. NW of intersection with U.S. Rte. 340.

PORT RICHMOND VICINITY
King William County (51)

Kentuckey, .8 mi. N of State Rte. 634, .8 mi. NE of intersection with State Rte. 625.

PORT ROYAL

Catlett House, S corner of intersection of State Rtes. 1002 and 1008.
Hipkins-Carr House, S corner of intersection of U.S. Rte. 301 and State Rte. 1004.
Lightfoot House, NE side of end of State Rte. 1005.

PORT ROYAL VICINITY

Emmanuel Episcopal Church, W side of U.S. Rte. 301, 1.1 mi. S of intersection with State Rtes. 660 and 625.

PORTSMOUTH

Bain House, 326 North St.
Brooks House, 415 Crawford St.
Brooks House, 419 Crawford St.
Brooks House, 421 Crawford St.
Butt, Dr. R. B., House, 327 Crawford St.
Crawford House, 450-54 Crawford St.
Day, John, House, 214 Glasgow St.
Grice House, 202 North St.
House, 205 Glasgow St.
House, 220 Glasgow St.
McRae House, 108 London St.
Mast House, Building #33, Norfolk Navy Yard.
Murdaugh House, 222 Crawford St.
Murdaugh House, 228 North St.
Nivison, John, House (Ball House), 417 Middle St.
Norfolk County Courthouse (Portsmouth Courthouse), NE corner of Court and High Sts.
Old Town Market, 215 Glasgow St.
Peters, William, House, 315 Court St.
Quarters "A," Norfolk Navy Yard.
Riddick, Dr. William, House, 201 London St.
Salt Box House, 101 Glasgow St.
Supply Building, Building #17, Norfolk Navy Yard.
Thompson-Hill House, 221 North St.
Thompson House, 201 Middle St.
Trinity Church, SW corner of High and Court Sts.
Trinity Church Rectory, 340 Court St.
U.S. Naval Hospital, on Hospital Point at Washington and Crawford Sts.
Varnish House, Building #6, Norfolk Navy Yard.
Watts, Capt. Dempsey, House, 500 North St.
Work Shop, Building #18, Norfolk Navy Yard.

Bowen House, NE side of State Rte. 609, .3 mi. NW of intersection with State Rte. 91.

POWHATAN   Powhatan County (73)

Bienvenue, .1 mi. E of State Rte. 1004, immediately N of intersection with State Rte. 13.
Homestead (Ligon House), .1 mi. NE of State Rte. 300, E of intersection with State Rte. 13.
Law Office, E side of State Rte. 13, .1 mi. S of intersection with State Rte. 300.
Powhatan County Courthouse, SE corner of intersection of State Rtes. 300 and 13.

POWHATAN VICINITY   Powhatan County (73)

Bassie, .1 mi. N of U.S. Rte. 60, 1.6 mi. SE of intersection with State Rte. 628.
Calais, .5 mi. NE of State Rte. 711, at intersection with State Rte. 614.
Center Hill, .9 mi. N of State Rte. 711, .5 mi. E of intersection with State Rte. 615.
Dispatch, .3 mi. N of State Rte. 628, .5 mi. N of intersection with State Rte. 667.
Elmington, .6 mi. W of U.S. Rte. 522, 3 mi. N of intersection with U.S. Rte. 60.
Emmanuel Church, W side of U.S. Rte. 522, .3 mi. S of intersection with U.S. Rte. 60.
Erin Hill, .1 mi. E of State Rte. 13, .2 mi. S of intersection with State Rte. 1003.
Fighting Creek, 1 mi. W of State Rte. 620, 1 mi. S of intersection with State Rte. 13.
Harris House, N side of State Rte. 661, .2 mi. W of intersection with State Rte. 603.
House, SE corner of intersection of State Rtes. 611 and 628.
Mill Quarter, .8 mi. S of State Rte. 620, 1.3 mi. S of intersection with State Rte. 13.
Millwood, .1 mi. S of State Rte. 711, 1.1 mi. E of intersection with State Rte. 615.
Moorwood, E side of S end of State Rte. 661, 1.1 mi. S of intersection with State Rte. 603.
Musket Factory, .1 mi. W of State Rte. 628, .6 mi. N of intersection with State Rte. 615.
Powhatan County Public Records Office, N side of State Rte. 300 Y, E of intersection with State Rte. 13.
Stratton, .1 mi. N of U.S. Rte. 60, .9 mi. W of intersection with State Rte. 684.

PRINCE GEORGE   Prince George County (75)

Prince George County Courthouse, N side of State Rte. 106, .2 mi. SW of intersection with State Rte. 616.

Ralphis, .1 mi. NE of State Rte. 616, .1 mi. SE of intersection with State Rte. 106.

Belsches House, N side of State Rte. 629, 2.2 mi. W of intersection with State Rte. 630.

Milton, .1 mi. W of U.S. Rte. 301, .4 mi. SE of intersection with State Rte. 632.

Smith House, .1 mi. NE of U.S. Rte. 301, .4 mi. SE of intersection with State Rte. 632.

PROSPECT   Prince Edward County (74)

House (Davis House), N side of State Rte. 655.

PROSPECT VICINITY   Prince Edward County (74)

Cedar Hill, .8 mi. N of State Rte. 627, .9 mi. NW of intersection with State Rte. 609.

Fort Hill, .6 mi. E of State Rte. 650, 1.9 mi. E of intersection with State Rte. 626.

Glenn, Peyton, House, .2 mi. E of State Rte. 652, .2 mi. NE of intersection with State Rte. 626.

PROVIDENCE FORGE VICINITY   New Kent County (64)

Rose Garden, .1 mi. S of State Rte. 617, .5 mi. E of intersection with State Rte. 618.

South Garden, .2 mi. W of U.S. Rte. 60, .1 mi. NW of intersection with State Rte. 615.

PULASKI   Pulaski County (78)

Pulaski County Courthouse, N side of State Rte. 99, .1 mi. W of intersection with U.S. Rte. 11.

PULASKI VICINITY   Pulaski County (78)

Draper House, SE side of U.S. Rte. 11, .8 mi. SW of intersection with State Rte. 100.

Draper's Valley Presbyterian Church, NE side of State Rte. 654, 1 mi. SE of intersection with U.S. Rte. 11.

Hillcrest, NW side of U.S. Rte. 11, 1.4 mi. SW of intersection with State Rte. 100.

Liberty Hall, .5 mi. NW of U.S. Rte. 11, .5 mi. W of intersection with State Rte. 100.

Sunnyside, N side of State Rte. 636, 1.1 mi. NE of intersection with State Rte. 643.

House, .4 mi. S of State Rte. 608, .4 mi. NW of intersection with State Rte. 605.

QUICKSBURG VICINITY   Shenandoah County (86)

Armentrout Mill, .1 mi. W of State Rte. 728, 1.4 mi. SW of intersection with
    State Rte. 42.
Moore House, W side of State Rte. 728, 1.4 mi. SW of intersection with State
    Rte. 42.
Moore's Store, SW corner of intersection of State Rtes. 614 and 728, 1.5 mi. SW
    of intersection with State Rte. 42.

QUINTON VICINITY   New Kent County (64)

Beech Spring Farm, .1 mi. W of State Rte. 612, 1 mi. S of intersection with
    State Rte. 33.

RADCLIFFE VICINITY   Mecklenburg County (59)

Baskerville House, E side of U.S. Rte. 1, .1 mi. S of intersection with U.S. Rte. 58.
Buena Vista, W side of State Rte. 637, 2 mi. S of intersection with State Rte.
    630.
Eureka, SE side of State Rte. 709, .2 mi. NE of intersection with State Rte. 615.
Invermay, .3 mi. E of intersection of State Rtes. 615 and 637, 2.7 mi. S of
    intersection with State Rte. 630.
Sycamore Lodge, .3 mi. NW of State Rte. 637, .1 mi. NE of intersection with
    State Rte. 650.

RADIANT VICINITY   Madison County (57)

Mount Fern, .5 mi. SW of State Rte. 616, 1.8 mi. S of intersection with State
    Rte. 621.

RANDOLPH VICINITY   Charlotte County (20)

Morotock, .4 mi. N of State Rte. 607, 2.3 mi. E of intersection with State
    Rte. 641.
Mulberry Hill, .2 mi. E of State Rte. 641, 1 mi. N of intersection with State
    Rte. 607.
Street, The, S side of State Rte. 607, 1.1 mi. SE of intersection with State Rte.
    641.

418

Oak Spring Farm, W side of State Rte. 706, .1 mi. S of intersection with U.S.
   Rte. 11.
Raphine Hall, .1 mi. W of State Rte. 606, 1 mi. SE of intersection with State
   Rte. 613.
Steeles' Fort, W side of State Rte. 706, 1.6 mi. S of intersection with State Rte.
   606.
Walnut Grove (Shenandoah Valley Research Station), N side of State Rte. 606,
   .7 mi. E of intersection with State Rte. 706.

RAPPAHANNOCK ACADEMY VICINITY   Caroline County (17)

Hayfield, .3 mi. NE of U.S. Rte. 17, .3 mi. NW of intersection with State Rte.
   610.
Moss Neck Manor, .4 mi. SW of State Rte. 607, 1.3 mi. SW of intersection with
   U.S. Rte. 17.
Prospect Hill, 1 mi. S of U.S. Rte. 17, 2.2 mi. W of intersection with State Rte.
   610.
Rock Stop, .7 mi. NE of U.S. Rte. 17, 1 mi. SE of intersection of State Rte. 719.

RAWLINGS VICINITY   Brunswick County (13)

Farmfield, .8 mi. N of State Rte. 629, .2 mi. E of intersection with State Rte.
   630.
House, N side of State Rte. 616, .6 mi. W of intersection with State Rte. 612.
Oaks, The, W side of State Rte. 610, 2 mi. NE of intersection with State Rte.
   629.
Waqua Outbuilding, .1 mi. E of State Rte. 622, .1 mi. S of intersection with
   State Rte. 630.

RECTORTOWN VICINITY   Fauquier County (31)

Gibson House, E side of State Rte. 716, 1.5 mi. S of intersection with State Rte.
   713.
Glenmore, .3 mi. W of State Rte. 624, 1.2 mi. N of intersection with State Rte.
   710.
Kelvedon, W side of State Rte. 713, 1.2 mi. N of intersection with State Rte. 710.
Maidstone Ordinary, NW corner of intersection of State Rtes. 710 and 624.

REDWOOD VICINITY   Franklin County (34)

Store, S side of State Rte. 122, 1.7 mi. NE of intersection with State Rte. 116.

REHOBOTH VICINITY Lunenburg County (56)

Magnolia Grove, .3 mi. SE of State Rte. 49, .5 mi. SW of intersection with State Rte. 630.

Magnolia Grove Slave Quarters, .3 mi. SE of State Rte. 49, .5 mi. SW of intersection with State Rte. 630.

REMLIK VICINITY Middlesex County (60)

Hampstead Farm, NE side of State Rte. 691, .1 mi. NW of intersection with State Rte. 602.

REPUBLICAN GROVE VICINITY Halifax County (42)

Goshen, E side of State Rte. 628, 1.1 mi. S of intersection with State Rte. 647.

House, .2 mi. W of U.S. Rte. 501, 1.2 mi. S of intersection with State Rte. 621.

House, .2 mi. S of State Rte. 832, .1 mi. E of intersection with State Rte. 753.

RHOADESVILLE VICINITY Orange County (69)

Morton Hall (Oakgreen), .6 mi. SE of State Rte. 663, 1 mi. NE of intersection with U.S. Rte. 522.

Verdiersbille, NE side of State Rte. 621, 1 mi. N of intersection with State Rte. 20.

RICE VICINITY Prince Edward County (74)

Pleasant Shade, S side of State Rte. 619, .2 mi. E of intersection with State Rte. 726.

RICHMOND

Adams, Samuel, House, 2705 E. Grace St.
Ahern, John, House, 300 E. Leigh St.
Ainslie, George A., House, 2519 E. Grace St.
Allen-McKildoe Double House, 2309-11 E. Franklin St.
Alvis-Brown House, 2605 E. Franklin St.
Baker, Hilary, House, 2302 E. Grace St.
Beers, William, House, 1228 E. Broad St.
Belgian Building, W side of Lombardy St., at intersection with Brook Rd.
Blair, Samuel Jordan, House, 632 N. Seventh St.
Bray Cottage, 1013 N. Third St.
Brett, Rebecca C., House, 2815 E. Grace St.

Broad St. Railroad Station, Broad and Robinson Sts.
Burton House, 2308 E. Broad St.
Cabell, Henry Coatler, House, 116 S. Third St.
Campbell, Charles, House (Pulliam House), 217 S. Third St.
Carrington, Ann Adams, House, 2306 E. Grace St.
Carrington Row, 2307-11 E. Broad St.
Catlin, William, House, 2300 E. Broad St.
City Hall, E. Broad St., between Tenth and Eleventh Sts.
Clarke, A. B., House, 2517 E. Grace St.
Confederate Memorial Chapel, 2900 Grove Ave.
Craig, Adam, House, 1812 E. Grace St.
Crew, Cornelius, House, 310 N. Nineteenth St.
Crump, Sterling J., Double House, 1813-15 E. Grace St.
Digges-Bullock-Christian House, 204 W. Franklin St.
Dill, Addolph, House, 00 Clay St.
Ebenezer Baptist Church, NE corner of Leigh and Judah Sts.
Egyptian Building, SW corner of College and Marshall Sts.
First African Baptist Church, NE corner of College and E. Broad Sts.
First Baptist Church, NW corner of Twelfth and E. Broad Sts.
Freeland, Archibald, House, 1015 Bainbridge St.
Governor's Mansion, Capitol Square
Grant House (Sheltering Arms Hospital), 1008 E. Clay St.
Grant, William H., Tobacco Factory, 1900 E. Franklin St.
Graves House, 509 N. 27th St.
Hardgrove, Samuel, House, 2300 E. Grace St.
Haxall, Bolling W., House, 211 E. Franklin St.
Haxall, Philip, House (Columbia), 601 N. Lombardy St.
Hill, Robert, House, 611 W. Cary St.
Johnson, George M., House, 2305 E. Broad St.
Lacy, Matthew M., Cottage, 512 N. Monroe St.
Leigh Street Baptist Church, 517 N. 25th St.
Liggon and McMinn Double House, 2204-06 E. Broad St.
Liggon, John L., House, 2601 E. Franklin St.
Liggon, McMinn, and Catlin Double House, 2214-16 E. Broad St.
Lyne, Robert B., House, 2718 E. Broad St.
McMinn, David A., House, 2717 E. Broad St.
Maupin-Maury House, 1105 E. Clay St.
Maymont, Spottswood Rd.
Mayo Memorial Church House (Taylor House), 110 W. Franklin St.
Meredith-Christian House, 2714 E. Franklin St.
Morris, John, Cottage, 207 N. 25th St.
Morson, James, Row, 219-23 Governor St.
Monumental Episcopal Church, 1224 E. Broad St.
Page-Archer-Anderson House, 103 W. Franklin St.
Parkinson, James, House, 501 N. 27th St.
Putney-Ayers House, 1010-12 E. Marshall St.
Rhodes, Holden, House, Forest Hill Park.
Richards, Anson, Houses, 1708-10 E. Franklin St.

Ritchie, William F., Cottage, 616 N. Ninth St.
Royster, James B., House, 2600 E. Franklin St.
St. Paul's Episcopal Church, SW corner of Ninth and Grace Sts.
St. Peter's Roman Catholic Church, 800 E. Grace St.
Second Presbyterian Church, 13 N. Fifth St.
Sinton Double House, 2510-12 E. Grace St.
Sinton, William, Row, 2514-18 E. Grace St.
Skinner-Bodeker House, 2801 E. Grace St.
Slater House, 405 N. 27th St.
Slater, William, House, 2611 E. Franklin St.
Sublett, George W., House, 531 N. Fourth St.
Talavera, 2313 W. Grace St.
Taylor, Thomas, House, 2602 E. Franklin St.
Tinsley, Peter, House, 509 N. Sixth St.
Tredegar Iron Works, U.S. Rtes. 1/301 and the James River.
Tucker, Joel, House, 612 N. Third St.
Turner, Anthony, House, 2520 E. Franklin St.
Turner, George, Double House, 2800-02 E. Grace St.
Turner-Turpin House, 2607 E. Grace St.
Turpin, Miles, House, 2209 E. Broad St.
Turpin-Yarbrough Double House, 2208-10 E. Broad St.
U.S. Post Office and Customs House, 1000 E. Main St.
Van Lew Houses, 2403-07 E. Grace St.
Virginia State Capitol Building, Capitol Square.
Von Groning, Daniel, House, 1901 Pleasant St.
Whitlock, Charles, House, 1523 E. Cary St.
Whitlock, Richard H., House, 316 N. 24th St.
Wickham-Leigh House, 1000 E. Clay St.
Winston, George, House, 2314-16 E. Broad St.
Woodward, John, House, 3017 Williamsburg Ave.
Wortham and McGruder Warehouse, 23 S. Fifteenth St.
Yarbrough, William J., House, 2215 E. Broad St.

RICHMOND VICINITY   Chesterfield County (21)

Bellwood, .1 mi. W of U.S. Rte. 1/301, .6 mi. S of intersection with State Rte.
    638.
British Camp Farm, 5900 Dorset Rd.
Brookbury Farm, .4 mi. SW of State Rte. 10, .2 mi. S of intersection with State
    Rte. 651.
Westover Farm, .2 mi. SW of State Rte. 683, .1 mi. NW of intersection with
    State Rte. 1914.

RICHMOND VICINITY   Henrico County (44)

Crewes House, .1 mi. N of State Rte. 156 at S edge of Richmond National
    Battlefield Park.
Locust Hill, at end of Wallo Rd., .6 mi. S of Kingsland Rd.

RIDGEWAY VICINITY
Halifax County (42)

Town of Meadville, SE side of State Rte. 642, .4 mi. NE of intersection with State Rte. 832.

RIDGEWAY VICINITY
Henry County (45)

Bellevue, S side of State Rte. 641, .3 mi. SE of intersection with State Rte. 687.

RINER VICINITY
Montgomery County (61)

Feathers House, .3 mi. S of State Rte. 669, .1 mi. E of intersection with State Rte. 679.

RIVERVILLE VICINITY
Amherst County (5)

Edgehill, .9 mi. S of State Rte. 622, 1.6 mi. SW of intersection with State Rte. 600.

Islington, W side of State Rte. 622, 1.2 mi. SW of intersection with State Rte. 623.

Rosedale, .3 mi. S of State Rte. 622, 1.6 mi. SW of intersection with State Rte. 600.

RIXEYVILLE
Culpeper County (24)

Auburn, .4 mi. SW of State Rte. 685, 1.1 mi. E of intersection with State Rte. 665.

RIXEYVILLE VICINITY
Culpeper County (24)

Beauregard, .3 mi. NE of State Rte. 663, 1 mi. SE of intersection with State Rte. 679.

Bleak Hill, .5 mi. SW of State Rte. 711, 1.2 mi. E of intersection with State Rte. 630.

Pleasant Hill, 1 mi. SW of State Rte. 640, 1.4 mi. W of intersection with State Rte. 229.

Sans Souci (Farley), .3 mi. N of N end of State Rte. 679, 1.5 mi. NE of intersection with State Rte. 663.

ROANOKE

Buena Vista, Jackson Park, Penmar Ave. and Tenth St., SE.
Elmwood, center of Elmwood Park.

Garst, Jacob, Log House, S side of State Rte. 686, .1 mi. SW of intersection with State Rte. 682.

Grayholme House, 6100 Plantation Rd., NW.

Huntington, 320 Huntington Blvd., NW.

Lone Oak, 324 King George Ave., SW.

Magnolia (Dr. Hart House), 1206-18 Williamson Rd.

Martin-Persinger House, 1606 Persinger Rd., SW.

Moomaw, Elder D. C., House, 3201 Cove Rd., NW.

Thrasher, Rev. Paul, House, 1001 Vinton Rd., NE.

Trout, George, House, 3842 Neely Rd., NW.

ROANOKE VICINITY   Roanoke County (81)

Belle Grove (Johnson House), E side of State Rte. 605, .5 mi. SE of intersection with State Rte. 115.

Belmont, NE side of State Rte. 1512, .1 mi. S of intersection with State Rte. 605.

Belmont (Monterey), .1 mi. N of State Rte. 1512, .5 mi. SE of intersection with State Rte. 605.

Brubaker House, NE side of State Rte. 116, immediately NW of intersection with U.S. Rte. I-81.

Cave Spring Methodist Church, NE side of State Rte. 419, .1 mi. NW of intersection with U.S. Rte. 221.

Gale House, W side of U.S. Rte. 221, .1 mi. S of intersection with State Rte. 687.

Homewood, S side of State Rte. 681, .3 mi. E of intersection with State Rte. 720.

House, NW side of State Rte. 1859, .1 mi. NE of intersection with State Rte. 628.

Huff, Andrew, House, .2 mi. E of State Rte. 601, .1 mi. N of intersection with State Rte. 1891.

Josylvia Farm, W side of U.S. Rte. 460, opposite intersection with State Rte. 653.

Lynbraye Farm, W side of State Rte. 1361, .4 mi. W of intersection with State Rte. 682.

Moomaw House, W side of State Rte. 604, .6 mi. N of intersection with U.S. Rte. 460.

Nestlebrook Farm, 2502 Salem Turnpike.

Peters Creek Church of the Brethren, N side of State Rte. 116, .1 mi. W of intersection with State Rte. 629.

Petty-Gray House, 6100 Plantation Rd., NW.

Richardson, Green, House, E side of State Rte. 659, .5 mi. S of intersection with State Rte. 658.

Richardson, John, House, N side of Hershberger Rd. at intersection with Plantation Rd., at N edge of Roanoke city limits.

Southview, N side of State Rte. 117, SW corner of intersection with State Rte. 626.

Starkey House (Speedwell), S side of State Rte. 613, .4 mi. W of intersection with State Rte. 119.

Stoner, Jacob, Spring House, W side of State Rte. 604, 1.6 mi. N of intersection with U.S. Rte. 460.

Tavern, S side of U.S. Rte. 11/220, .1 mi. NE of intersection with State Rte. 1815.

Waverly, .5 mi. W of State Rte. 118, Roanoke Municipal Airport (Woodrum Field).

Wynmere, 3402 Grandin Rd., extension.

Zion Lutheran Church, S side of U.S. Rte. 11, .3 mi. E of intersection with State Rte. 684.

ROCK CASTLE   Goochland County (38)

Rock Castle, E side of S end of State Rte. 600.

ROCKBRIDGE BATHS VICINITY   Rockbridge County (82)

Bethesda Presbyterian Church, SW side of State Rte. 39, 1 mi. SE of intersection with State Rte. 602.

Porter House, .1 mi. SW of State Rte. 39, 5.6 mi. SE of intersection with State Rte. 601.

Windy Glen, W bank of State Rte. 39, .3 mi. SW of intersection with State Rte. 716.

ROCKFISH VICINITY   Nelson County (63)

Rock Spring, E side of State Rte. 6, .2 mi. SE of intersection with U.S. Rte. 29.

ROCKY MOUNT   Franklin County (34)

Franklin County Courthouse, SE corner of Main and E. Court Sts.

Grove, The, SW corner of Franklin St. and Floyd Ave.

Meade House, E side of intersection of Maple and Church Sts.

Mount Pleasant, 115 Church St.

ROCKY MOUNT VICINITY   Franklin County (34)

Davis House, .3 mi. W of State Rte. 863, 1.5 mi. SE of intersection with State Rte. 754.

Hill, John, House, S corner of intersection of State Rtes. 754 and 863, 1.3 mi. SE of intersection with State Rte. 40.

Locust Hill, SE side of State Rte. 919, .3 mi. NE of intersection with State Rte. 641.

Waid House, W side of U.S. Rte. 220, .8 mi. S of intersection with State Rte. 718.

Washington Iron Furnace, S side of State Rte. 877 (Old Furnace Rd.), .1 mi. W of intersection with U.S. Rte. 220.

ROSEDALE   Russell County (84)

Old Rosedale, .1 mi. NE of U.S. Rte. 19, .3 mi. SW of intersection with State
    Rte. 80.
Rosedale, .2 mi. NE of U.S. Rte. 19, .3 mi. SW of intersection with State Rte. 80.

RUCKERSVILLE VICINITY   Greene County (40)

Dickerson House, .1 mi. N of State Rte. 607, W side of intersection with U.S.
    Rte. 29.

RURAL RETREAT   Wythe County (99)

Buck, Sol, House (Bailey House), W side of Main St., between State Rtes. 615
    and 1101 (Parsonage Ave.).

RURAL RETREAT VICINITY   Smyth County (87)

House, S side of U.S. Rte. 11, .7 mi. W of intersection with State Rte. 682.

RURAL RETREAT VICINITY   Wythe County (99)

Castle, Jacob, House, W side of State Rte. 735, .3 mi. NW of intersection with
    State Rte. 617.
Laurel Glen Farm, E side of State Rte. 025, 1 mi. N of intersection with State
    Rte. 680.
Ripplemead (Stuart, Dr. John, House), .1 mi. NW of intersection of State Rtes.
    681 and 680, 1.2 mi. N of intersection with State Rte. 617.
Snavely House, .3 mi. S of State Rte. 617, .3 mi. SW of intersection with State
    Rte. 680.

RUSHMERE VICINITY   Isle of Wight County (47)

Bay Church Site, W side of intersection of State Rtes. 677 and 10, 1.6 mi. S of
    intersection with State Rte. 621.

RUSTBURG   Campbell County (16)

Campbell County Courthouse, NE corner of intersection of State Rtes. 24 and
    838.
Fountain Hotel (Finch's Tavern), S side of intersection of U.S. Rte. 501 and
    State Rte. 24, .5 mi. W of intersection with State Rte. 615.

426

RUSTBURG VICINITY

Campbell County (16)

First County Clerk's Office, .4 mi. S of State Rte. 24, 1.5 mi. W of intersection with U.S. Rte. 501.
Solitude, .4 mi. SE of State Rte. 687, .2 mi. S of intersection with State Rte. 24.

RUTHER GLEN VICINITY

Caroline County (17)

Concord Baptist Church, E side of State Rte. 602, .3 mi. SE of intersection with State Rte. 653.
Glamorgan, S side of State Rte. 652, 2 mi. SE of intersection with State Rte. 602.
Meadow Farm, .1 mi. N of State Rte. 602, .1 mi. W of intersection with State Rte. 652.

RUTHVILLE VICINITY

Charles City County (19)

House, .8 mi. E of S end of State Rte. 621, 2.8 mi. SE of intersection with State Rte. 623.

ST. BRIDES VICINITY

Glencoe, E side of State Rte. 630, 1 mi. N of intersection with State Rte. 740, near St. Brides, near Chesapeake.
Happer House (Ballyhack), .2 mi. N of State Rte. 740, 1.25 mi. W of intersection with State Rte. 634, near Chesapeake.
Murray House, S end of State Rte. 2801, .3 mi. S of intersection with State Rte. 603, near Chesapeake.

ST. STEPHENS CHURCH

King and Queen County (49)

Saint Stephen's Baptist Church, E side of State Rte. 14, .1 mi. S of intersection with U.S. Rte. 360.

ST. STEPHENS CHURCH VICINITY

King and Queen County (49)

Bewdley, .7 mi. S of SW end of State Rte. 633, .3 mi. S of intersection with State Rte. 675.
Goshen, .4 mi. S of U.S. Rte. 360, 1.5 mi. E of intersection with State Rte. 631.
Greenmount (Pickle Hill), .3 mi. S of State Rte. 628, 1 mi. W of intersection with State Rte. 721.
Melville, .3 mi. N of U.S. Rte. 360, 1.6 mi. E of intersection with State Rte. 631.
Mount, The (Fanny's Mount), 1 mi. NW of State Rte. 628, 1.3 mi. W of intersection with State Rte. 721.

North Bank, W side of State Rte. 633, 1.4 mi. W of intersection with State Rte. 634.

Rosemount, .2 mi. S of State Rte. 633, .7 mi. SE of intersection with State Rte. 634.

Shepherds Methodist Episcopal Church, .1 mi. S of U.S. Rte. 360, .4 mi. E of intersection with State Rte. 631.

Smithfield, .6 mi. NE of State Rte. 721, .3 mi. N of intersection with State Rte. 628.

SALEM

Administration Building, Roanoke College.
Bittle Memorial Chapel and Library, Roanoke College.
Evans, John M., House, 213 Broad St.
Hook-Logan House, 101 W. Main St.
Miller Hall, Roanoke College.
Mount Airy, .3 mi. N of Roanoke River, S side of Roanoke Blvd.
Newcastle, 12 S. Union St.
Newcastle Slave House, 12 S. Union St.
Roanoke County Courthouse, NE corner College Ave. and Main St.
Salem Presbyterian Church, NW corner E. Main and Market Sts.
Trout Hall, Roanoke College.

SALEM VICINITY   Roanoke County (81)

Belle Aire, S side of U.S. Rte. 11, .2 mi. W of intersection with State Rte. 684.
Boxwood Summit, E side of State Rte. 419, .1 mi. N of S intersection with State Rte. 685.
Cedar Bluff, E side of State Rte. 612/639, .2 mi. N of intersection with State Rte. 639.
Intervale, N side of Midland Rd., .2 mi. E of intersection with Easton Rd.
Pleasant Grove, W side of U.S. Rte. 11, .1 mi. NE of intersection with State Rte. 612.

SALUDA   Middlesex County (60)

Middlesex County Courthouse, NE corner of intersection of State Rtes. 618 and 33 and U.S. Rte. 17.

SANDSTON VICINITY   Henrico County (44)

Trent House, .4 mi. SW of State Rte. 156, .3 mi. E of intersection with Washington St.

SANDY LEVEL VICINITY   Henry County (45)

Thornfield, .7 mi. E of State Rte. 610, .5 mi. S of intersection with State Rte. 622.

SAXE VICINITY   Charlotte County (20)

Cottage Valley Farm, .1 mi. W of State Rte. 641, .8 mi. S of intersection with State Rte. 612.
Do Well, W side of State Rte. 637, 2.3 mi. N of intersection with State Rte. 612.
Mildwood, 1 mi. W of State Rte. 746, 1 mi. NE of intersection with State Rte. 612.
Roanoke Plantation Outbuildings, 1.4 mi. SE of State Rte. 746, 1.3 mi. S of intersection with State Rte. 612.

SEAFORD VICINITY   York County (100)

Marl Bank, .1 mi. NE of State Rte. 693, .2 mi. NE of intersection with State Rte. 634.
Water View, NW side of State Rte. 631, .2 mi. N of intersection with State Rte. 707.

SCOTTSBURG VICINITY   Halifax County (42)

Smoke House, .2 mi. E of State Rte. 304, 1.8 mi. SW of intersection with U.S. Rte. 360 and State Rte. 344.

SCOTTSVILLE   Albemarle County (2)

Jefferies House, W side of Harrison St., .2 mi. N of Byrd St.
Old Hall, SW corner of Byrd and Harrison Sts.
Scottsville Presbyterian Church, S side of Byrd St., between Valley and Harrison Sts.

SCOTTSVILLE VICINITY   Albemarle County (2)

Blenheim, .3 mi. SE of State Rte. 727, 1.5 mi. N of intersection with State Rte. 795.
Blenheim, library, .3 mi. SE of State Rte. 727, 1.5 mi. N of intersection with State Rte. 795.
Chester, E side of State Rte. 726, .1 mi. S of intersection with State Rte. 6.
Cliffside, .2 mi. W of State Rte. 1302, .6 mi. SE of intersection with State Rte. 726.

Jefferson Mill, .3 mi. N of State Rte. 618, 1.5 mi. NE of intersection with State Rtes. 712 and 795.

Morrisena, .1 mi. E of State Rte. 626, 2.6 mi. SW of intersection with State Rte. 6.

Tavern, E side of State Rte. 627, .6 mi. S of intersection with State Rte. 726.

SCOTTSVILLE VICINITY   Fluvanna County (33)

Oak Grove, .2 mi. S of State Rte. 646, .4 mi. S of intersection with State Rte. 6.

SEALSTON VICINITY   King George County (50)

Whitehall, W side of State Rte. 664, .5 mi. W of intersection with State Rte. 694.

SELMA VICINITY   Alleghany County (3)

Oakland Presbyterian Church, N side of State Rte. 696, 1 mi. SW of intersection with U.S. Rte. 60/220.

SHACKLEFORDS VICINITY   King and Queen County (49)

Hockley, .8 mi. SW of State Rte. 605, .9 mi. NW of intersection with State Rte. 606.

SHADWELL VICINITY   Albemarle County (2)

Edgehill, .4 mi. N of State Rte. 22, .1 mi. E of intersection with U.S. Rte. 250.

Glenmore, .5 mi. SW of U.S. Rte. 250, .7 mi. SE of intersection with State Rte. 731.

New Shadwell, .6 mi. N of U.S. Rte. 250, 1.2 mi. W of intersection with State Rte. 22.

SHANGHAI VICINITY   King and Queen County (49)

Dixon Hall, 1.6 mi. W of intersection of State Rtes. 657 and 14, 1.2 mi. S of intersection with State Rte. 603.

New Church of Stratton-Major Parish, SW side of State Rte. 14, .3 mi. SE of intersection with State Rte. 611.

SHAWSVILLE VICINITY   Montgomery County (61)

Alleghany Spring House, S side of State Rte. 757, .2 mi. E of intersection with State Rte. 637.

SHILOH VICINITY   King George County (50)

Union Methodist Church, NW side of State Rte. 623, 1 mi. NE of intersection
   with State Rte. 650.

SHILOH VICINITY   Pulaski County (78)

Cecil House, SE side of State Rte. 693, .3 mi. NE of intersection with State Rte.
   672.

SHIPMAN VICINITY   Nelson County (63)

Oak Ridge, .3 mi. SE of State Rte. 650, 1.2 mi. SW of intersection with State
   Rte. 56.
St. Mary's Chapel (Roman Catholic), W side of State Rte. 653, .2 mi. SE of
   intersection with State Rte. 650.
Trinity Church, N side of State Rte. 653, 1.5 mi. W of intersection with State
   Rte. 710.
White Plains, E side of State Rte. 56, 1.6 mi. NW of intersection with State Rte.
   650.

SHUMANSVILLE VICINITY   Caroline County (17)

Green Falls, S corner of intersection of State Rtes. 623 and 627, 1 mi. NW of
   intersection with State Rte. 654.
Spring Grove, .5 mi. SW of State Rte. 627, 2.2 mi. NW of intersection with State
   Rte. 623.
Stanhope, .1 mi. SW of State Rte. 627, .6 mi. NW of intersection with State
   Rte. 647.

SKINQUARTER   Chesterfield County (21)

House, in middle of U.S. Rte. 360 at intersection with State Rte. 603.

SMITHFIELD   Isle of Wight County (47)

Boykin House, 201 S. Church St.
Christ Church, NW side of S. Church St., between U.S. Rte. 258 and Cedar St.
Cocke, W. H., House, 319 Main St.
Drew, Benjamin, Store House, 373 Church St.
Grove, The, 220 W. Grace St.
Hayden Hall, 222 Grace St.
House, 131 Church St.

House (Smithfield Public Library), SE side of S. Church St., between Cedar and Hill Sts.

House, SE side of U.S. Rte. 258, between Cockes Lane and S. Mason St.

House, 22 Main St.

House, 402 Main St.

House, 213 S. Mason St.

House, 214 S. Mason St.

Isle of Wight County Jail, 106 Mason St.

Jackson, Mary, House, 113 S. Mason St.

Lightfoot, Bartholomew, House, 365 Church St.

Oak Grove Academy, 204 Grace St.

Pierceville, NW side of U.S. Rte. 258A, .1 mi. NW of intersection with U.S. Rte. 258.

Smithfield Academy, SE corner of Cedar and S. Mason Sts.

Wentworth-Grinnan House, 123 S. Church St.

Woodley House, 220 S. Church St.

SMITHFIELD VICINITY   Isle of Wight County (47)

Butler House, W side of U.S. Rte. 258, .3 mi. SW of intersection with State Rte. 680.

Four Square, N side of State Rte. 620, 1.5 mi. W of intersection with U.S. Rte. 258.

House, NW side of U.S. Rte. 258, .6 mi. SW of intersection with State Rte. 655.

House, SE side of U.S. Rte. 258, .4 mi. SW of intersection with State Rte. 655.

Oak Wood, .2 mi. SW of State Rte. 655, .3 mi. SE of intersection with State Rte. 656.

Six Oaks (Lightfoot House), N corner of intersection of State Rtes. 620 and 655, 2.3 mi. S of intersection with State Rte. 656.

Windsor Castle, E side of State Rte. 656, .3 mi. SE of intersection with State Rte. 258.

SMITHFIELD VICINITY   Russell County (84)

Elk Garden Mill, S side of State Rte. 656, .3 mi. W of intersection with State Rte. 657.

Hendricks, Aaron, House, .1 mi. S of State Rte. 656, .3 mi. W of intersection with State Rte. 657.

Hendricks-Stuart House, .1 mi. NW of State Rte. 656, .2 mi. W of intersection with State Rte. 657.

Smithfield, NW side of U.S. Rte. 19, .4 mi. NE of intersection with State Rte. 80.

SNELL VICINITY   Spotsylvania County (89)

Green Branch, .8 mi. S of State Rte. 647, .6 mi. SE of intersection with State Rte. 738.

Linden Hall, .4 mi. SE of State Rte. 208, .7 mi. N of intersection with State Rte. 606.

SNOWVILLE   Pulaski County (78)

Cypress Grove Church, SE side of State Rte. 693, .3 mi. SW of intersection with State Rte. 613.

SOMERSET VICINITY   Orange County (69)

Fairview (Hazelhurst), .1 mi. E of State Rte. 231, .5 mi. N of intersection with State Rte. 655.
Frascati, .1 mi. E of State Rte. 231, .4 mi. S of intersection with State Rte. 655.
Somerset House, .3 mi. SE of State Rte. 20, .6 mi. S of intersection with State Rte. 609.

SOUTH BOSTON VICINITY   Halifax County (42)

Belle View, .1 mi. N of State Rte. 729, 1.5 mi. E of intersection with State Rte. 802.
Berry Hill Presbyterian Church, SW side of State Rte. 682 (Berry Hill Rd.), 2 mi. NW of intersection with Edmunds St.
Green's Folly, S side of State Rte. 654, .4 mi. W of intersection with U.S. Rte. 501.
House, E side of State Rte. 659, 1 mi. S of intersection with State Rte. 682.
Seaton, .1 mi. NE of U.S. Rte. 501, .2 mi. N of intersection with State Rte. 654.
Tarover, .1 mi. NW of State Rte. 659, 2 mi. SW of intersection with State Rte. 682.

SOUTH HILL VICINITY   Mecklenburg County (59)

House, N side of intersection of State Rtes. 657 and 655, .9 mi. SW of intersection with State Rte. 47.

SPARTA VICINITY   Caroline County (17)

Auburn Hill, .9 mi. NW of State Rte. 644, 1.7 mi. SW of intersection with State Rte. 721.
Elm Grove, .1 mi. S of State Rte. 627, .2 mi. W of intersection with State Rte. 644.
White Plains, .1 mi. SE of State Rte. 654, .2 mi. SW of intersection with State Rte. 721.

Gannaway, Jack, House, .4 mi. SW of State Rte. 749, 1.3 mi. W of intersection
with State Rte. 672.
Gannaway, John, House, .1 mi. W of State Rte. 684, .2 mi. N of intersection
with State Rte. 619.

SPERRYVILLE VICINITY   Rappahannock County (79)

Montpelier, .2 mi. SE of State Rte. 231, 1.5 mi. S of intersection with State
Rte. 707.
Rosewood, .2 mi. E of Thornton River, .3 mi. E of State Rte. 612, .6 mi. NW of
intersection with U.S. Rte. 211/522.
Thornton Hill, .2 mi. S of State Rte. 620, .5 mi. E of intersection with U.S. Rte.
522.

SPOTSYLVANIA   Spotsylvania County (89)

Christ Episcopal Church, NE side of State Rte. 208, .1 mi. SE of intersection
with State Rte. 613.
Spotswood Inn, SW side of intersection of State Rtes. 208 and 613.
Spotsylvania County Courthouse, SE side of State Rte. 208, .1 mi. NE of intersection with State Rte. 613.

SPOTSYLVANIA VICINITY   Spotsylvania County (89)

Kenmore Woods, .8 mi. NW of State Rte. 208, 1.2 mi. S of intersection with
State Rte. 608.
Millbrook, .8 mi. SW of State Rte. 608, .4 mi. W of intersection with State Rte.
648.
Oakley, .4 mi. W of State Rte. 612, 2 mi. SW of intersection with State Rte. 649.
Rosemount, .3 mi. SE of State Rte. 208, 2.1 mi. NE of intersection with State
Rte. 613.
Stirling, .1 mi. NE of State Rte. 607, .6 mi. SE of intersection with U.S. Rte. 1.

SPOTTSWOOD VICINITY   Augusta County (8)

Old Providence Stone Church, NW side of intersection of State Rtes. 613 and
620, .6 mi. NW of intersection with State Rte. 671.

SPOUT SPRING   Appomattox County (6)

Tavern, .3 mi. SE of State Rte. 647, .1 mi. SW of intersection with U.S. Rte. 460.

SPOUT SPRING VICINITY   Appomattox County (6)

Concord Church, NW side of State Rte. 648, .5 mi. SW of intersection with U.S.
    Rte. 460.
Davidson, Samuel, House, .1 mi. SW of intersection with State Rte. 613, .8 mi.
    NW of intersection with State Rte. 703.
House, N side of State Rte. 613, .8 mi. N of intersection with State Rte. 647.

SPRING GROVE VICINITY   Surry County (91)

Glebe House, NE side of State Rte. 10, 4.4 mi. SE of intersection with State
    Rtes. 40 and 646.

SPRINGWOOD   Botetourt County (12)

Springwood Mill, E side of State Rte. 630.

SPRINGWOOD VICINITY   Botetourt County (12)

Timber Ridge Farm, .1 mi. W of State Rte. 634, .4 mi. S of intersection with
    State Rte. 635.

STAFFORD   Stafford County (90)

Stafford County Courthouse, NW corner of intersection of U.S. Rte. 1 and State
    Rte. 630.

STANARDSVILLE   Greene County (40)

Greene County Courthouse, NW corner of State Rte. 649, .1 mi. S of inter-
    section with State Rte. 33.

STANARDSVILLE VICINITY   Greene County (40)

Mountain View, S side of State Rte. 33, 2.5 mi. NW of intersection with State
    Rte. 810.

STANLEY VICINITY   Page County (70)

Brubaker House (Wall Brook), S side of State Rte. 615, 1 mi. S of intersection
    with U.S. Rte. 211.
Fort (Phillip) Long, 1 mi. NW of State Rte. 616, .8 mi. N of intersection with
    U.S. Rte. 340.

Spitler, Isaac, House, S end of State Rte. 644, .8 mi. S of intersection with State Rte. 616.

White Hall (Abraham, Spitler, House), .3 mi. NW of State Rte. 638, .5 mi. N of intersection with State Rte. 633.

STANLEYTOWN VICINITY   Henry County (45)

Hordsville, .1 mi. E of State Rte. 682, .3 mi. SE of intersection with State Rte. (Alt.) 57.

STAUNTON

Augusta County Courthouse, NE corner of intersection of Johnson and Augusta Sts.

Hill Top, Mary Baldwin College.

Kalorama, NW corner of intersection of Kalorama and Coalter Sts.

Mary Baldwin Chapel, Mary Baldwin College.

Sears House, NE end of Sears Hill Rd.

Stuart House, 120 Church St.

Trinity Episcopal Church, SW corner of intersection of Beverly and Lewis Sts.

Virginia School for Deaf and Blind, SE side of intersection of E. Beverly St. and Pleasant Ter.

Western State Hospital, SE corner of U.S. Rtes. 11 (Greenville Ave.) and 250.

STAUNTON VICINITY   Augusta County (8)

Aspen Hill, .1 mi. W of State Rte. 612, .7 mi. S of intersection with U.S. Rte. 250.

Belefont, S side of State Rte. 254, 1.2 mi. E of intersection with U.S. Rte. 11.

Merrifield, NW side of U.S. Rte. 11, 1 mi. NE of intersection with State Rte. 793.

Old Virginia, N side of State Rte. 793, .6 mi. NE of intersection with U.S. Rte. I-81.

Prospect Hill, .4 mi. S of State Rte. 793, 1 mi. E of intersection with U.S. Rte. 11.

STEPHENS CITY VICINITY   Frederick County (35)

Stonewood, immediately W of Clarke Co. line, .2 mi. W of U.S. Rte. 522, .8 mi. S of intersection with State Rte. 277.

STERLING VICINITY   Loudoun County (54)

Broad Run Bridge and Toll House, at intersection of State Rtes. 7 and 28.

STEVENSBURG VICINITY   Culpeper County (24)

Greenville, .6 mi. SE of State Rte. 647, .4 mi. SW of intersection with State Rte.
    661.
Rose Hill, .1 mi. W of State Rte. 663, .4 mi. S of intersection with State Rte. 3.
Salubria, .3 mi. S of State Rte. 3, .8 mi. E of intersection with State Rte. 663.
Struan, .2 mi. S of State Rte. 647, 1.2 mi. SW of intersection with State Rte. 663.

STEVENSVILLE VICINITY   King and Queen County (49)

Belle Mount, .3 mi. S of State Rte. 633, 1.4 mi. W of intersection with State
    Rte. 14.
Oakland, N side of State Rte. 14, .2 mi. E of intersection with State Rte. 620.
Woodbine, E side of intersection with State Rte. 631.

STONY CREEK VICINITY   Sussex County (92)

Parham-Dillard House, .3 mi. W of State Rte. 649, 1.1 mi. SW of intersection
    with State Rte. 645.

STORMONT VICINITY   Middlesex County (60)

Rosegill, 1.7 mi. NW of N end of State Rte. 639, .8 mi. N of intersection with
    State Rte. 33.

STRASBURG   Shenandoah County (86)

Alton House, E side of S end of S. Holliday St.
Presbyterian Church, E side of S end of S. Holliday St.

STRASBURG VICINITY   Shenandoah County (86)

Huddle, George, House, .4 mi. NW of State Rte. 623, .4 mi. SW of intersection
    with State Rte. 651.
Hupp Distillery, NW side of U.S. Rte. 11, .4 mi. N of intersection with State
    Rte. 55.
Hupp Mansion, SE side of U.S. Rte. 11, .4 mi. NE of intersection with State
    Rte. 55.
Mill, S side of U.S. Rte. 11, .4 mi. W of intersection with State Rtes. 638 and 761.
Snapp House (Charles House), N side of State Rte. 640, .1 mi. W of intersection
    with U.S. Rte. 11.
Spengler Hall (Matin Hill), N side of U.S. Rte. 11, .4 mi. W of intersection with
    State Rtes. 638 and 761.

Stickley House, 1.2 mi. E of U.S. Rte. 11, .4 mi. NE of intersection with State Rte. 660.

Stickley Mill, 1.2 mi. E of U.S. Rte. 11, .4 mi. NE of intersection with State Rte. 660.

STUART   Patrick County (71)

Patrick County Courthouse, SW corner of intersection of Blue Ridge and Main Sts.
Staples House, NE corner of intersection of Main and Blue Ridge Sts.

STUARTS DRAFT VICINITY   Augusta County (8)

Montezuma (Barterbrook Farm), .6 mi. NE of State Rte. 649, .1 mi. S of intersection with State Rte. 608.

Stony Point, .2 mi. NW of intersection of State Rtes. 635 and 643, 1.3 mi. NE of intersection with State Rte. 649.

STUDLEY VICINITY   Hanover County (43)

Buckeye, W side of N end of State Rte. 647, .9 mi. N of intersection with State Rte. 606.

Ditchley, .2 mi. NE of State Rte. 606, .8 mi. SE of intersection with State Rte. 629.

Gould Hill, .4 mi. NE of State Rte. 605, N side of intersection with State Rte. 615.

Ingleside, .1 mi. S of State Rte. 606, 1 mi. E of intersection with State Rte. 628.

Ingleside Overseer's House, .1 mi. S of State Rte. 606, 1 mi. E of intersection with State Rte. 628.

Marlbourne, .3 mi. SE of intersection of State Rte. 628 and U.S. Rte. 360, 1.2 mi. NE of intersection with State Rte. 606.

Pine Slash, .5 mi. E of State Rte. 643, .8 mi. SE of intersection with State Rte. 606.

Pine Slash Honeymoon House, .5 mi. E of State Rte. 643, .8 mi. SE of intersection with State Rte. 606.

Tavern, N side of intersection of State Rtes. 628 and 606.

Totomoi, .7 mi. S of State Rte. 643, 1.3 mi. W of intersection with State Rte. 651.

SUFFOLK

House, 227 Main St.
House, 431 N. Main St.
Kilby House, 504 W. Washington St.
Nansemond County Courthouse, SE corner of intersection of Main St. and Constance Rd.

Richardson House, 356 N. Main St.
Riddick House, 510 Main St.

SUNNYSIDE VICINITY   Frederick County (35)

Rosedale, NW corner of intersection of State Rtes. 678 and 679, .9 mi. W of
    intersection with U.S. Rte. 522.

SURRY   Surry County (91)

Surry County Clerk's Office, Courthouse Sq.
Surry County Courthouse, SW corner of intersection of State Rtes. T1001 and 10.

SURRY VICINITY   Surry County (91)

Chippokes, NE side of State Rte. 658, .4 mi. NW of intersection with State Rte.
    633.
Cross Creek, at E end of State Rte. 640, 1.3 mi. E of intersection with State
    Rte. 618.
Floods, N side of State Rte. 610, 3.4 mi. NW of intersection with State Rte. 618.
Melville, .2 mi. NE of State Rte. 635, .4 mi. NW of intersection with State Rte.
    636.
Mount Pleasant, .8 mi. NE of State Rte. 610, 1.3 mi. NE of intersection with
    State Rte. 618.
New Chippokes, .1 mi. E of intersection of State Rtes. 658 and 633, 1.5 mi. NE
    of intersection with State Rte. 634.
Oak Hill, SE side of State Rte. 31, opposite intersection with State Rte. 641.
Rich Neck, NW side of State Rte. 633, 1.3 mi. NE of intersection with State
    Rte. 616.
Walnut Valley, .2 mi. E of State Rte. 634, .4 mi. S of intersection with State
    Rte. 633.

SUSSEX   Sussex County (92)

Banister, John, House, E side of State Rte. 735, .1 mi. N of intersection with
    State Rte. 634 (east).
Sussex County Courthouse, W side of intersection of State Rtes. 735 and 634.
Sussex County Treasurer's Office (Sussex County Farm Bureau and Early Settlers
    Insurance Company offices), W side of State Rte. 735, .1 mi. N of inter-
    section with State Rte. 634.
Tavern, W side of State Rte. 735, .3 mi. S of intersection with State Rte. 40.

Bonnie Doone, S side of State Rte. 642, 1.2 mi. W of intersection with State Rte. 735.
Cedar Level, .4 mi. W of State Rte. 735, at intersection with State Rte. 642.
Chester, .5 mi. E of State Rte. 625, .1 mi. N of intersection with State Rte. 35.
Coman's Well, S side of State Rte. 642, 1.4 mi. W of intersection with State Rte. 735.
House, S side of State Rte. 642, .8 mi. W of intersection with State Rte. 735.
Hunting Quarter, .2 mi. E of State Rte. 632, .2 mi. S of intersection with State Rte. 608.
Invermay, .2 mi. W of State Rte. 735, 1.2 mi. S of intersection with State Rte. 634.
Oakland, .2 mi. E of State Rte. 641, .2 mi. N of intersection with State Rte. 662.
Princeton, S side of State Rte. 634, .3 mi. SE of intersection with State Rte. 40.

SUTHERLAND VICINITY   Dinwiddie County (27)

Fairfield, .9 mi. N of U.S. Rte. 460, .2 mi. E of intersection with State Rte. 632.
Olive Branch (Laurel Brook), .3 mi. NE of State Rte. 623, 1 mi. N of intersection with State Rte. 708.

SWEET CHALYBEATE   Alleghany County (3)

Sweet Chalybeate Hotel, NW corner of intersection of State Rtes. 673 and 311.

SWEET HALL VICINITY   King William County (51)

Custis Mill, E side of State Rte. 625 (Custis Mill Rd.), .9 mi. N of intersection with State Rte. 634.
Riverview Farm, .2 mi. N of W end of State Rte. 630, 1.4 mi. SW of intersection with State Rte. 632.

SWOOPE VICINITY   Augusta County (8)

Bellevue, W side of State Rte. 703, .6 mi. NW of intersection with State Rte. 706.
Fairmont Farm, S side of State Rte. 703, .6 mi. E of intersection with State Rte. 708.
Gray Gables, .2 mi. W of State Rte. 708, .2 mi. S of intersection with State Rte. 703.
Idle Wilde, .1 mi. NE of State Rte. 254, .3 mi. NW of intersection with State Rte. 876.

Intervale, E side of State Rte. 720, 1 mi. NW of intersection with State Rte. 833.

Walnut Grove, NW side of State Rte. 708, .9 mi. NE of intersection with State Rte. 876.

TALLEYSVILLE VICINITY   New Kent County (64)

Emmaus Baptist Church, NW side of State Rte. 609, .8 mi. NE of intersection with State Rte. 662.

House, .2 mi. E of State Rte. 609, .2 mi. N of intersection with State Rte. 33.

Marl Hill, .4 mi. NE of State Rte. 642, .6 mi. NE of intersection with State Rte. 609.

Meadow Farm, S side of State Rte. 33, .9 mi. E of intersection with State Rte. 618.

Pearson House Site, exact location unknown.

Whitehall, SW side of State Rte. 640, .8 mi. N of intersection with U.S. Rte. 60.

White House Site, .6 mi. E of State Rte. 614, .3 mi. NE of intersection with State Rte. 608.

TAMWORTH   Cumberland County (25)

Muddy Creek Mill, E side of NE end of State Rte. 659, .4 mi. NE of intersection with State Rte. 684.

Muddy Creek Mill Post Office, N side of State Rte. 659, .3 mi. NE of intersection with State Rte. 684.

TAPPAHANNOCK   Essex County (29)

Beale Memorial Baptist Church, 200 S. Church Lane.

Clerk's Office, 307 Prince St.

Coleman-Anderton House, 400 Water Lane, St. Margaret's School.

Essex County Courthouse, 309 Prince St.

House, 123 Prince St.

Little Egypt, 515 Faulconer Cle.

McCall-Brockenbrough House, 500 Water Lane, St. Margaret's School.

Monument Place, 310 Prince St.

Roane, Lawrence D., House, 203 Duke St.

St. John's Episcopal Church, 210 Duke St.

TAPPAHANNOCK VICINITY   Essex County (29)

La Grange, .2 mi. NW of U.S. Rte. 360, .5 mi. W of intersection with U.S. Rte. 17.

Mount Clement, .6 mi. N of U.S. Rte. 360, .4 mi. W of intersection with U.S. Rte. 17.

Poplar Springs, .5 mi. SE of U.S. Rte. 360, .4 mi. W of intersection with U.S. Rte. 17.

TAYLORSTOWN VICINITY   Loudoun County (54)

Hunting Hill, N side of State Rte. 663 at intersection with State Rte. 665.
Taylorstown Mill, S side of State Rte. 663, .1 mi. W of intersection with State
    Rte. 665.

TAZEWELL   Tazewell County (93)

Tazewell County Courthouse, SW corner of intersection of Main and Moore Sts.

TAZEWELL VICINITY   Tazewell County (93)

Chimney Rock Farm, SE side of State Rte. 91, 3 mi. SW of intersection with
    U.S. Rte. 460/19.
Fair Hill, SW side of State Rte. (Alt.) 16, .3 mi. W of intersection with U.S. Rte.
    460/19.
Witten House, .6 mi. N of U.S. Rte. 460/19, 1 mi. W of intersection with State
    Rte. 632.
Witten's Fort, SW side of U.S. Rte. 460/19, 1.5 mi. N of intersection with State
    Rte. 91.

TETOTUM VICINITY   King George County (50)

Spy Hill, .2 mi. N of State Rte. 619, .2 mi. NE of intersection with State Rte.
    218.

THAXTON   Bedford County (10)

Ivy Pillars, E side of State Rte. 684, .1 mi. N of intersection with State Rte. 831.

THAXTON VICINITY   Bedford County (10)

Aspen Grove, .4 mi. W of State Rte. 680, 1.1 mi. S of intersection with State
    Rte. 744.
Hopkins Manor, S side of State Rte. 682, .8 mi. E of intersection with State
    Rte. 683.

THE PLAINS VICINITY   Fauquier County (31)

Avenel, .7 mi. NE of State Rte. 55, 1.6 mi. SE of intersection with State Rte. 626.
Byrnley, .7 mi. W of State Rte. 626, 1.2 mi. N of intersection with State Rte. 55.
Glenville, N side of State Rte. 55, .6 mi. W of intersection with State Rte. 245.
Gordonsdale, .1 mi. SW of State Rte. 750, .6 mi. W of intersection with State
    Rte. 245.

442

Wilna, .1 mi. SW of end of State Rte. 657, .9 mi. SW of intersection with State
Rte. 610.

TRENHOLM VICINITY   Powhatan County (73)

Derwent, 1.4 mi. NW of State Rte. 629, .1 mi. N of intersection with State Rte.
630.
Gibralter, .1 mi. S of State Rte. 630, .8 mi. NE of intersection with U.S. Rte. 60.
Glebe, The, .2 mi. N of U.S. Rte. 60, .6 mi. E of intersection with State Rte. 629.
Lethe (Land of Sleep), .2 mi. E of State Rte. 629, .5 mi. S of intersection with
State Rte. 715.
Laurel Springs, 1.2 mi. SE of State Rte. 715, .5 mi. E of intersection with State
Rte. 629.
Muddy Creek Church, E side of State Rte. 629, 1.3 mi. N of intersection with
State Rte. 630.

TREVILIANS   Louisa County (55)

Trevilian House, .1 mi. N of U.S. Rte. 33, .3 mi. SE of intersection with State
Rte. 613.
Trevilian Station and Freight Room, N side of U.S. Rte. 33, .4 mi. SE of inter-
section with State Rte. 613.

TREVILIANS VICINITY   Louisa County (55)

Ben Lomond, .4 mi. W of State Rte. 749, 1.8 mi. S of intersection with U.S.
Rte. 33.
Berea Church, N side of State Rte. 613, .3 mi. SW of intersection with State
Rte. 637.
Boswell's Tavern, N side of State Rte. 22, .1 mi. SE of intersection with U.S.
Rte. 15.
Boxley, .5 mi. NW of State Rte. 613, .5 mi. SW of intersection with State Rte.
633.
Brackets, NW side of State Rte. 638, 2.1 mi. S of intersection with State Rte. 22.
Company House, .1 mi. N of State Rte. 33, .4 mi. SE of intersection with State
Rte. 613.
Corduroy, .3 mi. N of State Rte. 22, 1.2 mi. W of intersection with State Rte.
636.
Galway, .1 mi. N of State Rte. 22, 1 mi. W of intersection with State Rte. 636.
Glen Burnie, .1 mi. W of State Rte. 613, .6 mi. S of intersection with State Rte.
695.
Gooch House, N side of State Rte. 613, .3 mi. W of intersection with State Rte.
649.

Gordon-Waldrop House, S side of State Rte. 22, .6 mi. W of intersection with U.S. Rte. 15.

Grassdale, .5 mi. W of U.S. Rte. 15, 2 mi. S of intersection with State Rte. 22.

Green Spring, .5 mi. SE of State Rte. 617, .8 mi. SW of intersection with State Rte. 640.

Grey Gables, .4 mi. NW of State Rte. 637, .3 mi. W of intersection with State Rte. 649.

Hawkwood, .5 mi. NE of State Rte. 617, .5 mi. W of intersection with U.S. Rte. 15.

Inglewood, .3 mi. SW of U.S. Rte. 15, 1.4 mi. N of intersection with State Rte. 22.

Ionia, .1 mi. E of State Rte. 640, .8 mi. N of intersection with State Rte. 613.

Kenmuir, .5 mi. SW of State Rte. 613, .9 mi. SW of intersection with State Rte. 607.

Lasley Church, N side of State Rte. 633, .4 mi. SE of intersection with State Rte. 613.

Mechanicsville Baptist Church, .1 mi. S of State Rte. 22, .8 mi. W of intersection with U.S. Rte. 15.

Mount Airy, .4 mi. N of State Rte. 613, .4 mi. SW of intersection with State Rte. 633.

Quaker Hill, .2 mi. E of State Rte. 613, 1.2 mi. S of intersection with State Rte. 695.

St. John's Chapel, NW corner of intersection of State Rtes. 617 and 640, 1.5 mi. NW of intersection with State Rte. 613.

St. John's Episcopal Church, N side of State Rte. 22, .5 mi. W of intersection with U.S. Rte. 15.

Spring Dale, .2 mi. S of State Rte. 22, 2 mi. W of intersection with U.S. Rte. 33.

Sylvania, .3 mi. SE of U.S. Rte. 15, 2.4 mi. S of intersection with State Rte. 22.

Westend, .5 mi. W of State Rte. 638, 1.1 mi. S of intersection with State Rte. 22.

Wood, William, House, .5 mi. E of intersection of State Rtes. 649 and 633.

TRIPLET VICINITY   Brunswick County (13)

House, NE side of State Rte. 690, .7 mi. NW of intersection with State Rte. 672.

House, W side of State Rte. 672, .9 mi. S of intersection with State Rte. 602.

House, N side of State Rte. 611, .2 mi. E of intersection with State Rte. 673.

TROUTDALE VICINITY   Grayson County (39)

Ripshin, N side of State Rte. 732, .1 mi. E of intersection with State Rte. 603.

TROUTVILLE VICINITY   Botetourt County (12)

Maple Grove, W side of U.S. Rte. 11, .5 mi. NE of intersection with State Rte. 670.

444

TUCKAHOE VICINITY   Henrico County (44)

Cheswick, .1 mi. N of Three Chopt Rd., .3 mi. SE of intersection with Michael Rd.
House, W side of Gaskins Rd., 1.1 mi. SW of intersection with River Rd.

TUNSTALL VICINITY   New Kent County (64)

Hampstead, 1.3 mi. NE of State Rte. 619, .7 mi. W of intersection with State
    Rte. 653.
Hampstead, Granary, .2 mi. W of State Rte. 606, .1 mi. N of intersection with
    State Rte. 608.
Hampstead, Icehouse and Office, .2 mi. W of State Rte. 606, .1 mi. N of inter-
    section with State Rte. 608.
House, 1.5 mi. W of State Rte. 606, .3 mi. S of intersection with State Rte. 619.

TURBEVILLE VICINITY   Halifax County (42)

House, .1 mi. NW of U.S. Rte. 58, .8 mi. NE of intersection with State Rte. 747.
House, NW side of U.S. Rte. 58, .3 mi. NE of intersection with State Rte. 747.

UNION HALL VICINITY   Franklin County (34)

Booker T. Washington National Monument, .3 mi. S of State Rte. 122, .8 mi. W
    of intersection with State Rte. 616.
Burwell House, .1 mi. SW of State Rte. 673, .7 mi. SE of intersection with State
    Rte. 40.

UNION LEVEL VICINITY   Mecklenburg County (59)

Lombardy Grove, E side of U.S. Rte. 1/58, .1 mi. NE of intersection with State
    Rte. 664.

UPPERVILLE   Fauquier County (31)

Armstead House, N side of U.S. Rte. 50, .1 mi. W of intersection with State Rte.
    712.
Carr, Caldwell, House, S side of U.S. Rte. 50.
Carr House, S side of U.S. Rte. 50, .2 mi. E of intersection with State Rte. 712.
Gibson, Gilbert, House, N side of U.S. Rte. 50, .1 mi. E of intersection with
    State Rte. 712.
House, N side of U.S. Rte. 50, at intersection with State Rte. 712.
Methodist Church, W side of State Rte. 712, .1 mi. S of intersection with U.S.
    Rte. 50.

Bollingbrook, .5 mi. W of State Rte. 712, 1.3 mi. S of intersection with U.S. Rte. 50.

Brookmeade, .2 mi. N of U.S. Rte. 50, .4 mi. W of intersection with State Rte. 619.

Carr House (Lumpy Valley), .1 mi. N of State Rte. 710, 2 mi. W of intersection with State Rte. 712.

Hill, The, E side of State Rte. 712, .5 mi. S of intersection with U.S. Rte. 50.

Maples, The, .2 mi. N of U.S. Rte. 50, opposite intersection with State Rte. 624.

Montmorency, S side of State Rte. 710, .1 mi. W of intersection with State Rte. 712.

Mount Airy, .2 mi. S of U.S. Rte. 50, 1.8 mi. W of intersection with State Rte. 712.

Oakley, 1.5 mi. S of U.S. Rte. 50, 1.2 mi. E of intersection with State Rte. 712.

Seaton, .4 mi. S of State Rte. 710, .8 mi. W of intersection with State Rte. 712.

Lansdowne, N side of State Rte. T1002, .1 mi. W of intersection with State Rte. T1005.

Old Middlesex County Courthouse (Epiphany Church), S side of State Rte. T1002, SW corner of intersection with State Rte. T1005.

Dromgoole House, .3 mi. NE of State Rte. 46, 1 mi. SE of intersection with State Rte. 600.

Mason's Chapel, exact location unknown.

Pea Hill Plantation, Manager's House, N side of State Rte. 626, .5 mi. W of intersection with State Rte. 669.

Pea Hill Plantation, Slave Quarters, .1 mi. N of State Rte. 626, .5 mi. W of intersection with State Rte. 669.

Dodson House, NW side of U.S. Rte. 360, .3 mi. SW of intersection with State Rte. 635.

Cypress Falls Farm, S side of State Rte. 706, .3 mi. W of intersection with State Rte. 707.

House, W side of State Rte. 608, .4 mi. S of intersection with State Rte. 56.

VICTORIA VICINITY   Lunenburg County (56)

Hungary Hill, SW corner of intersection of State Rtes. 626 and 723, 1.9 mi. N
    of intersection with State Rte. 739.
Woodhill, E side of State Rte. 651, .5 mi. NE of intersection with State Rte. 653.

VIENNA   Fairfax County (30)

Moorefield, 600 Nutley Rd., NW.

VIENNA VICINITY   Fairfax County (30)

Longview Plantation, 2606 Ogden St.
Mount Pleasant, 1713 Virginia Lane.

VIEWTOWN VICINITY   Rappahannock County (79)

Mont Elery, .5 mi. E of State Rte. 618, 1 mi. W of intersection with State Rte.
    729.

VILLAMONT VICINITY   Bedford County (10)

Rieley House, .3 mi. W of U.S. Rte. 460, .1 mi. SE of intersection with State
    Rte. 697.

VINTON   Roanoke County (81)

Vinyard, Christian, House, SW corner of Hardy and Vinyard Rd.
Vinyard, White, House, SW corner of Highland and Washington Sts.

VIRGINIA BEACH

Bayville, .5 mi. SE of State Rte. 650, .4 mi. SW of intersection with U.S. Rte. 60.
Bell House, .2 mi. W of State Rte. 615, .4 mi. S of intersection with State Rte.
    636.
Broad Bay Manor, .5 mi. NE of State Rte. 615, .2 mi. SE of intersection with
    State Rte. 690.
Brown's Tavern, E side of intersection of Oceana Blvd. and London Bridge Rd.
Eastern Shore Chapel, .1 mi. NW of U.S. Rte. 58, .7 mi. NE of intersection with
    State Rte. 632.
Ferry Farm, .9 mi. SE of State Rte. 647, .2 mi. E of intersection with State
    Rte. 648.

First Princess Anne County Jail, .1 mi. N of State Rte. 165, .1 mi. W of intersection with State Rte. 646.

Friendly Oak, N side of State Rte. 165, .2 mi. W of intersection with State Rtes. 190 and 646.

Green Hill, .4 mi. NE of State Rte. 615, .7 mi. SE of intersection with State Rte. 753.

Hermitage, N side of SE end of Hermitage Rd., 1 mi. E of intersection with State Rte. 652.

Murray House, W side of U.S. Rte. 13, 1.7 mi. S of intersection with State Rte. 657.

Murray, Richard, House, .4 mi. NE of State Rte. 603, .4 mi. W of intersection with U.S. Rte. 13.

Murray, Thomas, House, .4 mi. SW of U.S. Rte. 13, .8 mi. S of intersection with State Rte. 657.

Nimmo Methodist Church, E side of intersection of State Rtes. 615 and 149, 1.2 mi. NE of intersection with State Rte. 628.

Old Cape Henry Lighthouse, SW side of Atlantic Ave., .2 mi. NW of intersection of Atlantic Ave. and Hospital Rd.

Old Comfort, 1437 Woodhouse Rd.

Old Donation Church, S side of State Rte. 647, .3 mi. E of intersection with State Rte. 648.

Pembroke, .7 mi. N of U.S. Rte. 58, 1.5 mi. E of intersection with State Rtes. 627 and 647.

Poplar Hall, 1.3 mi. SW of U.S. Rte. 58, .3 mi. W of intersection with U.S. Rte. 13.

Princess Anne County Courthouse, W side of State Rte. 165, at intersection with State Rte. 149.

Princess Anne County Jail, E side of State Rte. 165, SE side of intersection with State Rte. 149.

Rose Hall, S side of U.S. Rte. 58, .1 mi. W of intersection with State Rte. 643.

Shepherd, Capt. John, House, .1 mi. E of Great Neck Rd., .4 mi. N of intersection with Rose Hall Dr.

Upper Wolf Snare, .2 mi. N of State Rte. 635, .7 mi. E of intersection with State Rte. 632.

Weblin House, .4 mi. E of Baker Rd., .8 mi. NW of intersection with Absolom Rd.

Wolf Snare, .2 mi. SE of State Rte. 632, .7 mi. N of intersection with U.S. Rte. 58.

WAIDSBORO VICINITY   Franklin County (34)

Oak Knoll, .1 mi. NW of intersection of State Rtes. 606 and 607, .9 mi. S of intersection with State Rte. 757.

WAKEFIELD VICINITY   Sussex County (92)

Bell Farm, .2 mi. E of State Rte. 628, .6 mi. S of intersection with State Rte. 620.

Shingleton, .5 mi. E of State Rte. 613, at intersection with State Rtes. 40 and 613 (east).

WALKERTON VICINITY   King and Queen County (49)

Canterbury, .4 mi. SW of State Rte. 634, .4 mi. NW of intersection with State Rte. 636.
Locust Grove, .7 mi. SE of State Rte. 629, .2 mi. NE of intersection with State Rte. 634 (north).
White Hall, .4 mi. SW of State Rte. 634, 1.3 mi. NW of intersection with State Rte. 629.
Woodville, W side of State Rte. 633, .6 mi. S of intersection with State Rte. 629.

WALLACE VICINITY   Washington County (96)

Campbell House, .4 mi. S of State Rte. 808, .4 mi. S of intersection with U.S. Rte. I-81.
Preston, Dr. Robert, House, .2 mi. N of U.S. Rte. 11/19, .1 mi. NE of intersection with State Rte. 659.
Preston, Henry Thomas, House, .2 mi. NE of U.S. Rte. 11/19, .7 mi. NE of intersection with State Rte. 659.

WARDTOWN VICINITY   Northampton County (66)

Grapeland, .1 mi. NW of N end of State Rte. 606, .6 mi. N of intersection with State Rte. 183.

WARE NECK VICINITY   Gloucester County (37)

Belleville, E side of NE end of State Rte. 701, 1.4 mi. NE of intersection with State Rte. 623.
Belleville, Kitchen, E side of NE end of State Rte. 701, 1.4 mi. NE of intersection with State Rte. 623.
Burgh Westra, .7 mi. SE of E end of State Rte. 676, 1 mi. SE of intersection with State Rte. 14/3.
Elmington, 1.7 mi. SE of State Rte. 14, .5 mi. NE of intersection with State Rte. 676.
Glenroy Icehouse, .7 mi. S of State Rte. 623, 1.1 mi. NW of intersection with State Rte. 624.
Hockley Icehouse, .6 mi. S of State Rte. 623, .3 mi. NW of intersection with State Rte. 692.
Lowland Cottage, .6 mi. S of State Rte. 623, .5 mi. NW of intersection with State Rte. 692.

Bothwick Hall, .2 mi. S of State Rte. 632, 3 mi. E of intersection with State Rte. 630.

Bothwick Hall, Manager's House, S side of State Rte. 632, 3.1 mi. E of intersection with State Rte. 630.

Ebenezer Academy Site, SE side of U.S. Rte. 1, .1 mi. SW of intersection with State Rte. 643.

Prestwood, .2 mi. S of State Rte. 691, 1.4 mi. SE of intersection with State Rte. 631.

Rome, .2 mi. N of State Rte. 631, 1.2 mi. E of intersection with State Rte. 691.

WARM SPRINGS   Bath County (9)

Bath County Courthouse, N side of State Rte. 619, .1 mi. E of intersection with State Rte. 645.

Warm Springs Bath Houses, W side of U.S. Rte. 220, SW corner of intersection with State Rte. 39.

Warm Springs Episcopal Church, NW side of State Rte. 39, .4 mi. SW of intersection with U.S. Rte. 220.

Warm Springs Presbyterian Church, NW side of State Rte. 39, .4 mi. SW of intersection with U.S. Rte. 220.

WARRENTON   Fauquier County (31)

Fauquier Club, 37 Culpeper St.
Fauquier County Courthouse, SE corner of Main and Ashby Sts.
Governor William Smith's Stables, 345 Culpeper St.
House, 115 Culpeper St.
Jail and Jailor's House, SE corner of intersection of Waterloo and Ashby Sts.
Marr House, 118 Culpeper St.
Moore, Thomas L., House (Keith Place), 127 Culpeper St.
Morris House, 97 Culpeper St.
Neptune Lodge, 343 Culpeper St.
Warren Green Hotel, SW side of Hotel St.

WARRENTON VICINITY   Fauquier County (31)

Bethel Methodist Church, SE side of State Rte. 628, .4 mi. NE of intersection with U.S. Rte. 17.

Bowers Run Baptist Church, W side of State Rte. 802, 1.5 mi. S of intersection with State. Rte. 688.

Clifton, .5 mi. N of State Rte. 628, 1 mi. NE of intersection with U.S. Rte. 17.

Edge Hill, E side of U.S. Rte. 17, 1.5 mi. N of intersection with State Rte. 628.

Loretto, .1 mi. E of U.S. Rte. 17, 2 mi. N of intersection with U.S. Rte. (Byp) 29/211.

Oak Springs, .3 mi. E of U.S. Rte. 17, .2 mi. N of intersection with U.S. Rte. (Byp) 29/211.

WARSAW VICINITY   Richmond County (80)

Belleville, .3 mi. E of State Rte. 1001, .5 mi. S of intersection with State Rte. 3.

Bladensfield, .7 mi. S of State Rte. 203, .6 mi. E of intersection with State Rte. 3.

Grove Mount, .1 mi. W of State Rte. 635, .7 mi. N of intersection with State Rte. 624.

Harlyn, SW intersection of State Rtes. 690 and 621.

Menokin Baptist Church, W side of State Rte. 690, .8 mi. SW of intersection with State Rte. 637.

Wilna, .7 mi. W of State Rte. 640, .2 mi. S of intersection with State Rte. 624.

WASHINGTON   Rappahannock County (79)

Presbyterian Church (now Library), SW corner of Calvert and Gay Sts.

Trinity Episcopal Church, SW corner of Gay and Middle Sts.

Washington Baptist and Washington Lodge Number 78, SE corner of Gay and Porter Sts.

Washington House, NW corner of intersection of State Rte. 628 and U.S. Rte. 211/522.

WASHINGTON VICINITY   Rappahannock County (79)

Avon Hall, .1 mi. S of U.S. Rte. 211/522, .3 mi. SE of intersection with State Rte. 622.

Battle Run Primitive Baptist Church, E side of State Rte. 729, .9 mi. N of intersection with U.S. Rte. 211.

Ben-Venue, E side of State Rte. 729, .3 mi. N of intersection with U.S. Rte. 211.

Greenfield, .3 mi. SE of U.S. Rte. 211/522, 1.3 mi. S of intersection with State Rte. 626.

Horseshoe Farm, W side of State Rte. 628, 2.6 mi. NE of intersection with State Rte. 622.

Jessimine Hill, .5 mi. S of State Rte. 626, .8 mi. SE of intersection with State Rte. 621.

Maples, The, .1 mi. E of U.S. Rte. 211/522, .3 mi. S of intersection with State Rte. 626.

Mountain Green, .4 mi. N of State Rte. 622, .2 mi. NW of intersection with State Rte. 624.

Mount Salem Church, W side of State Rte. 626, .9 mi. S of intersection with State Rte. 627.

Red Hill, .5 mi. E of State Rte. 729, 1.3 mi. S of intersection with U.S. Rte. 211.

Rose Hill, E side of U.S. Rte. 211/522, .3 mi. NE of intersection with State Rte. 627.

Shades, The, 1.4 mi. S of State Rte. 622, .8 mi. SE of intersection with U.S. Rte. 211/522.

Sunnyside, N end of State Rte. 624, 1 mi. N of intersection with State Rte. 622.

WASHINGTON'S BIRTHPLACE VICINITY   Westmoreland County (97)

Ingleside, NW side of State Rte. 638, .5 mi. SW of intersection with State Rte. 636.

Liberty Farm, on State Rte. 696, .8 mi. SW of intersection with State Rte. 638.

Roxbury, N side of State Rte. 638, .1 mi. NE of intersection with State Rte. 636.

Twiford, 1 mi. S of State Rte. 625, 1.2 mi. SE of intersection with State Rte. 638.

Walnut Hill, .6 mi. E of State Rte. 638, 3.7 mi. SW of intersection with State Rte. 3.

Wirtland, .2 mi. NW of State Rte. 638, .1 mi. S of intersection with State Rte. 636.

WATERFORD   Loudoun County (54)

Bond, Asa, Cottage, N side of Bond St., at E end.

Bond, Asa, House, N side of Bond St.

Braden-Roberts House, SW side of Main St. Hill.

Gover-Lytle-Hollingsworth House, SW side of Main St.

Hollingsworth-Scott House, W side of Second St., at intersection with Patrick St.

Hollingsworth-Taylor House, W side of Second St., at intersection with Patrick St.

Ratcliffe House, NE side of Main St.

Shuey, Louis V., House (Moxley Hall), NE side of Water St., at intersection with Butcher's Row.

Smallwood-Graham House, SW side of Main St.

Steer-Schooley House, E side of Clark's Gap Rd., at intersection with Factory St.

Wood-Hollingsworth House (Hillside), NE corner of intersection of Bond St. and John Brown's Rdwy.

WATERFORD VICINITY   Loudoun County (54)

Greystone, E side of Clark's Gap Rd., 1 mi. S of intersection with Factory St.

WATERLICK VICINITY   Warren County (94)

House, S side of State Rte. 55, 2.1 mi. W of intersection with State Rte. 616.

Long Meadows Farm, .1 mi. E of State Rte. 611, .8 mi. S of intersection with State Rte. 635.

WAYNESBORO

House, 332 W. Main St.

WAYNESBORO VICINITY   Nelson County (63)

Swannanoa, .5 mi. W of State Rte. 610, .4 mi. S of intersection with U.S. Rte.
    250.

WESTMORELAND POST OFFICE VICINITY   Westmoreland County (97)

Spence's Point, 1 mi. N of State Rte. 610, .7 mi. NW of intersection with State
    Rte. 604.

WEYERS CAVE VICINITY   Augusta County (8)

House, S side of State Rte. 680, .1 mi. W of intersection with U.S. Rte. 11.
Rankin House, SW side of State Rte. 690, .1 mi. NW of intersection with State
    Rte. 680.

WHALEYVILLE VICINITY   Nansemond County (62)

House, N side of State Rte. 675, .3 mi. E of intersection with State Rte. 673.
House, E side of State Rte. 643, .1 mi. N of intersection with State Rte. 668.
House, E side of intersection of State Rtes. 668 and 643, .3 mi. N of intersection
    with U.S. Rte. 13.
House, NW corner of intersection of State Rtes. 668 and 643, .3 mi. N of inter-
    section with U.S. Rte. 13.
House, SW corner of intersection of State Rtes. 668 and 643, .3 mi. N of inter-
    section with U.S. Rte. 13.
House, N side of State Rte. 668, .6 mi. W of intersection with State Rte. 669.
House, N corner of intersection of State Rtes. 664 and 668, 2.1 mi. W of inter-
    section with State Rte. 669.

WHITE MARSH   Gloucester County (37)

Hickory Fork, SW corner of intersection of State Rte. 614 and U.S. Rte. 17.

WHITE MARSH VICINITY   Gloucester County (37)

Blue Bottle House, .1 mi. NW of State Rte. 616, .2 mi. SW of intersection with
    State Rte. 682.

Concord, 1.1 mi. SW of NW end of State Rte. 708, .7 mi. NW of intersection with State Rte. 616.

Shelly, .1 mi. SW of State Rte. 634, .3 mi. SW of intersection with State Rte. 659.

White Marsh, .7 mi. E of U.S. Rte. 17, 1 mi. N of intersection with State Rte. 614.

White Marsh Icehouse, .8 mi. E of U.S. Rte. 17, 1 mi. N of intersection with State Rte. 614.

WHITE PLAINS VICINITY   Brunswick County (13)

Drummonsburg, S side of State Rte. 611, .2 mi. E of intersection with State Rte. 751.

Hicks, Paschel, House, E side of State Rte. 644, 2 mi. N of intersection with State Rte. 611.

Hicks, Scrapey, House, .1 mi. E of State Rte. 644, 2.4 mi. N of intersection with State Rte. 611.

House, E side of State Rte. 659, 1.8 mi. S of intersection with State Rte. 611.

House, S end of State Rte. 704, .5 mi. S of intersection with State Rte. 611.

House, exact location unknown.

Steed House, exact location unknown.

Thrower House, 2.1 mi. N of State Rte. 611, .5 mi. E of intersection with State Rte. 751.

Woodlands, .2 mi. W of State Rte. 659, .7 mi. NW of intersection with State Rte. 611.

WHITE POST   Clarke County (22)

Bishop Meade Memorial Episcopal Church, W side of U.S. Rte. 340, .1 mi. N of intersection with State Rte. 628.

WHITE POST VICINITY   Clarke County (22)

Farnley, .4 mi. W of State Rte. 658, .3 mi. S of intersection with State Rte. 622.

Federal Hill, .2 mi. N of State Rte. 622, .2 mi. E of intersection with State Rte. 658.

Greenway Court Porter's Office, E side of State Rte. 658, .6 mi. SW of intersection with State Rte. 627.

Greenway Court (Thomas Kennerly House), .3 mi. W of State Rte. 658, .6 mi. SW of intersection with State Rte. 627.

Guilford, .1 mi. S of State Rte. 644, .4 mi. SE of intersection with State Rte. 658.

Hay, William, House, .6 mi. S of State Rte. 658, .2 mi. SE of intersection with State Rte. 644.

Hickory Green, .2 mi. S of State Rte. 628, 1.6 mi. E of intersection with U.S. Rte. 340.

Lucky Hit, .2 mi. E of State Rte. 628, .8 mi. NE of intersection with U.S. Rte. 340.

Mesilla, NW side of State Rte. 658, .2 mi. S of intersection with State Rte. 627.

Mountain View, .3 mi. NE of State Rte. 627, .4 mi. NW of intersection with State Rte. 622.

Mount Airy, W side of U.S. Rte. 340, 1.3 mi. NW of intersection with State Rte. 628.

Providence, .2 mi. N of State Rte. 622, .3 mi. NE of intersection with State Rte. 627.

Stone Fort, .5 mi. S of State Rte. 658, .6 mi. SE of intersection with State Rte. 644.

Walnut Grove, .2 mi. E of U.S. Rte. 340, .4 mi. SW of intersection with U.S. Rte. 50.

WICOMICO CHURCH   Northumberland County (67)

Wicomico Methodist Church, NW intersection of State Rtes. 200 and 609.

WICOMICO CHURCH VICINITY   Northumberland County (67)

Anchorage, .1 mi. N of State Rte. 605, .8 mi. E of intersection with State Rte. 669.

Cloverdale, at end of State Rte. 606, .7 mi. SE of intersection with State Rte. 605.

Magnolia Office, .5 mi. N of State Rte. 605, .3 mi. E of intersection with State Rte. 669.

West End, NE side of State Rte. 679, .5 mi. SE of intersection with State Rte. 200.

Wicomico View, at end of State Rte. 664, .6 mi. E of intersection with State Rte. 665.

WILLIAMSBURG

Armistead House, NE corner of Duke of Gloucester and Nassau Sts.

Bell Farm, 316 Indian Springs Rd.

Bell Mead, 209 Burns Lane.

Custis Kitchen, S of Francis St., between Nassau and S. England Sts.

Geddy, Baker, & Inman Law Office, 137 York St.

Rectory Site, S side of Duke of Gloucester St., between Nassau St. and Palace Green.

Roberts House Site, S side of Duke of Gloucester St., between Botetourt and Blair Sts.

Tazewell Hall Site, 340 S. England St.

Travis House, NE corner of Francis and Henry Sts.

Wheatland, W side of Henry St., between Scotland and Lafayette Sts.

WILLIAMSBURG VICINITY   James City County (48)

Ewell Plantation, .3 mi. W of U.S. Rte. 60, .4 mi. N of intersection with State
    Rte. 658.

WILLIAMSBURG VICINITY   York County (100)

Cherry Hall, .3 mi. NW of State Rte. 646, 1 mi. SW of intersection with State
    Rte. 168.

WILLIAMSVILLE   Bath County (9)

Williamsville Presbyterian Church, SW corner of intersection of State Rtes. 614
    and 678.

WILLIAMSVILLE VICINITY   Bath County (9)

Wallace House, W side of State Rte. 678, 1.3 mi. SW of intersection with State
    Rte. 628.
Wilderness Farm, .2 mi. SE of State Rte. 629, 2.8 mi. NE of intersection with
    State Rte. 640.

WILLIS VICINITY   Floyd County (32)

Goodykoontz House, .1 mi. W of State Rte. 729, .5 mi. N of intersection with
    State Rte. 746.
Matthews' Cabin, E side of Blue Ridge Pkwy., 1 mi. S of intersection with State
    Rte. 778.

WILSONS VICINITY   Dinwiddie County (27)

Oak Forest, W side of State Rte. 625, 2.2 mi. N of intersection with U.S. Rte.
    460.

WINCHESTER

Abram's Delight, NE corner of intersection of Parkview St. and Rouss Spring Rd.
Braddock Street Methodist Church, SW corner of Braddock and Wolf Sts.
Centenary Reformed Church, SE corner of Cork and Cameron Sts.
Christian Church, 20 Cork St.
Christ Protestant Episcopal Church, NE corner of Washington and Boscawen Sts.
Conrad House, 12 N. Cameron St.

Dowdall House, 21 S. Loudoun St.

Frederick County Courthouse, SE corner of Loudoun St. and Rouss Ave.

Handley Library, NW corner of Braddock and Piccadilly Sts.

Jackson's Headquarters, W side of N. Braddock St., SW corner of intersection with Piccadilly St.

Linden Hill, 106 N. Cameron St.

Little, James, House, 137 W. Boscawen St.

Logan, Lloyd, House (Elks Lodge), 135 N. Braddock St.

Mackey House, 215 W. Cork St.

Madison I. O. O. F. Lodge No. 6, SW corner of Cameron and Boscawen Sts.

Market Street Methodist Church, NW corner of Cork and Cameron Sts.

Methodist Episcopal Church, 119 Cork St.

Miller House, 117 S. Loudoun St.

Norton-Morgan House, 226 Amherst St.

Old Stone Presbyterian Church, NE corner of Piccadilly St. and East Lane.

Phillips, Thomas, House, 124 W. Boscawen St.

Plains, The, .1 mi. N of State Rte. 7, 1 mi. E of intersection with U.S. Rte. 11.

Presbyterian Church, 114 S. Loudoun St.

Red Lion Tavern, 204 and 208 S. Loudoun St.

Reed, George, House, 35 Piccadilly St.

Rutherford House, 217 S. Loudoun St.

Seymour, William, House, SE corner of Washington and Boscawen Sts.

Sowers, Daniel, House (Godfrey Miller House), 28 S. Loudoun St.

Taylor-McCormick House, 19 N. Washington St.

Ward House, 521 S. Washington St.

Washington, George, Office, NE corner of Cork and Braddock Sts.

WINCHESTER VICINITY   Frederick County (35)

Brightside, .4 mi. W of U.S. Rte. 11, 1.1 mi. S of intersection with State Rte. 628.

Glen Burnie, .1 mi. S of U.S. Rte. 50, .8 mi. W of intersection with U.S. Rte. 11.

Hawthorne, .1 mi. N of U.S. Rte. 50, .6 mi. W of intersection with U.S. Rte. 11.

Hillwood, S side of State Rte. 7, .4 mi. E of intersection with State Rte. 659.

Opequon Church, .4 mi. SW of U.S. Rte. 11, 1.4 mi. S of intersection with State Rte. 628.

Willow Lawn, W side of U.S. Rte. 11, .9 mi. SW of intersection with U.S. Rte. 17/50.

WINDSOR VICINITY   Isle of Wight County (47)

Darden House, .1 mi. E of State Rte. 637, .8 mi. N of intersection with State Rte. 600.

Eley House (Nelms), .1 mi. N of U.S. Rte. 460, .6 mi. SE of intersection with State Rte. 600.

House, .1 mi. E of State Rte. 607, .8 mi. S of intersection with State Rte. 636.

House, .4 mi. E of State Rte. 637, .4 mi. N of intersection with State Rte. 600.

Adventure Hill, S side of State Rte. 621, 1.3 mi. E of intersection with State Rte. 603.

Clover Hill, S side of E end of State Rte. 748, .4 mi. E of intersection with State Rte. 664.

Emmasville, .1 mi. S of State Rte. 602, .3 mi. E of intersection with State Rte. 621.

Eppington, 1.3 mi. SE of State Rte. 621, 1.6 mi. S of intersection with State Rte. 602.

Field School, .1 mi. S of State Rte. 602, .7 mi. E of intersection with State Rte. 676.

Forkland (Wilkinson's Tavern), W side of intersection of State Rtes. 659 and 602, .8 mi. E of intersection with State Rte. 658.

House, SE side of U.S. Rte. 360, .3 mi. NE of intersection with State Rte. 666.

Laurel Hill, 1 mi. S of State Rte. 602, .6 mi. E of intersection with State Rte. 658.

Mantua, .4 mi. E of State Rte. 646, 2 mi. N of intersection with State Rte. 602.

Montevideo, .3 mi. S of State Rte. 668, 1 mi. W of intersection with State Rte. 667.

WISE   Wise County (98)

Wise County Courthouse, SW side of State Rte. T640, .1 mi. SE of intersection with State Rte. T636.

WOODFORD VICINITY   Caroline County (17)

Blenheim, .2 mi. SE of State Rte. 638, .9 mi. SE of intersection with State Rte. 626.

Braynefield, .1 mi. NW of State Rte. 626, .6 mi. SW of intersection with State Rte. 638.

Edge Hill, .3 mi. SE of State Rte. 632, 2.9 mi. NE of intersection with State Rte. 605.

Woodpecker, .4 mi. N of State Rte. 605, .5 mi. N of intersection with State Rte. 626.

WOODLAWN   Carroll County (18)

Oak Hill, NE corner of intersection of U.S. Rte. 58 and State Rte. 620.

WOODSTOCK   Shenandoah County (86)

Clower House, 302 N. Main St.

Shenandoah County Courthouse, SE corner of intersection of W. Court and S. Main Sts.

WOODSTOCK VICINITY

Shenandoah County (86)

Willow Grove Tavern, S corner of intersection of State Rte. 672 and U.S. Rte. 11, .9 mi. S of intersection with State Rte. 605.

WOODVILLE VICINITY

Rappahannock County (79)

Clover Hill, .3 mi. W of U.S. Rte. 522, .6 mi. N of intersection with State Rte. 621.
Oak Forrest, N side of State Rte. 621, 1 mi. W of intersection with U.S. Rte. 522.
Pleasant Hill, .3 mi. NE of U.S. Rte. 522, .9 mi. S of intersection with State Rte. 618.
Thermopylae, .1 mi. E of U.S. Rte. 522, .9 mi. S of intersection with State Rte. 626.

WOOLWINE VICINITY

Patrick County (71)

Covered Bridge, NE side of State Rte. 615, .1 mi. NW of intersection with State Rte. 8.

WORSHAM

Prince Edward County (74)

Debtors' Prison, W side of U.S. Rte. 15, .1 mi. S of intersection with State Rte. 665.
Dupuy Kitchen, E side of U.S. Rte. 15, .1 mi. S of intersection with State Rte. 665.
Prince Edward County Clerk's Office, E side of U.S. Rte. 15, .2 mi. S of intersection with State Rte. 665.
Venable-Dupuy House, E side of U.S. Rte. 15, .1 mi. S of intersection with State Rte. 665.

WORSHAM VICINITY

Prince Edward County (74)

Briery Church, N side of N end of State Rte. 747, .3 mi. N of intersection with State Rte. 671.
Locust Grove, .3 mi. E of U.S. Rte. 15, 1.1 mi. S of intersection with State Rte. 630.
Providence, .3 mi. W of State Rte. 630, 1.6 mi. S of intersection with State Rte. 665.
Rotherwood, .5 mi. N of State Rte. 637, 1.5 mi. E of intersection with State Rte. 630.
Sharon Baptist Church, SE corner of intersection of State Rtes. 612 and 696, 1.4 mi. S of intersection with State Rte. 636.
Slate Hill, .5 mi. W of U.S. Rte. 15, .9 mi. S of intersection with State Rte. 665.
Travis, NE side of State Rte. 636, 1 mi. SE of intersection with State Rte. 637.

WYLLIESBURG   Charlotte County (20)

Wyllies House, S side of State Rte. 607, .2 mi. W of intersection with U.S. Rte. 15/360.

WYTHEVILLE   Wythe County (99)

Cherry Hill, 325 E. Spring St.
Colwell House (St. John's Rectory), 465 Church St.
Hay, William, Store, 145 E. Main St.
Hotel Wytheville, 219 E. Main St.
House, 280 Church St.
Huffard, William, House, W side of Tazewell St., opposite Umberger St.
Leftwich, John, House, SE corner Fifth and E. Main Sts.
Rock House, NW corner Monroe and Tazewell Sts.
Rudy House, 201 Franklin St.
St. John's Episcopal Church, 226 E. Main St.
Saint Mary's Church (Roman Catholic), in Wytheville Cemetery, S side of State
    Rte. 610, .4 mi. SW of intersection with State Rte. 603.
Sexton, John, House, 287 W. Main St.
Walker Hall, SE corner E. Franklin and S. First Sts.
Wythe County Courthouse, NE corner Fourth and Spring Sts.

WYTHEVILLE VICINITY   Wythe County (99)

Crockett, Allen, House, W side of intersection of State Rtes. 600 and 603,
    3.1 mi. N of intersection with State Rte. 659.
Crockett, Thompson, House, .1 mi. SE of State Rte. 600, 1.3 mi. NE of inter-
    section with State Rte. 603.
Locust Hill Farm, N side of State Rte. 619, 1.1 mi. NE of intersection with
    State Rte. 643.
St. John's Lutheran Church, N side of intersection of State Rte. 657 and U.S.
    Rte. 21, 1.3 mi. NW of intersection with U.S. Rte. 11.

YORKTOWN   York County (100)

Grace Church, SE side of State Rte. 1003, NE side of intersection with Main St.
Pate, Thomas, House (Digges House), N corner of intersection of State Rte.
    1004 and Main St.

ZANONI VICINITY   Gloucester County (37)

Goshen, .6 mi. N of State Rte. 626, .3 mi. NW of intersection with State Rte.
    689.

White Hall, .2 mi. E of State Rte. 668, .8 mi. SE of intersection with State Rte. 627.

ZUNI VICINITY   Isle of Wight County (47)

Beale, Sam, House, SE side of intersection of State Rtes. 646 and 644.